MATH Trailblazers®

A BALANCED MATHEMATICS PROGRAM INTEGRATING SCIENCE AND LANGUAGE ARTS

Teacher Implementation Guide

THIRD EDITION

KENDALL/HUNT PUBLISHING COMPANY
4050 Westmark Drive   Dubuque, Iowa 52002

A TIMS® Curriculum
University of Illinois at Chicago

Teacher Implementation Guide

Math Trailblazers®

A Balanced Mathematics Program Integrating Science and Language Arts

A TIMS® Curriculum from the University of Illinois at Chicago

---

Dedication

This book is dedicated to the children and teachers who let us see the magic in their classrooms and to our families who wholeheartedly supported us while we searched for ways to make it happen.

—The TIMS Project—

 UIC The University of Illinois at Chicago

The original edition was based on work supported by the National Science Foundation under grant No. MDR 9050226 and the University of Illinois at Chicago. Any opinions, findings, and conclusions or recommendations expressed in this publication are those of the authors and do not necessarily reflect the views of the granting agencies.

Acknowledgments

Teaching Integrated Mathematics and Science (TIMS) Project Directors

Philip Wagreich, Principal Investigator

Joan L. Bieler

Howard Goldberg (emeritus)

Catherine Randall Kelso

Director

Third Edition — Joan L. Bieler

Curriculum Developers

Third Edition

Lindy M. Chambers-Boucher	Leona Peters
Janet Simpson Beissinger	Philip Wagreich
Carol Inzerillo	

Contributors

Third Edition

Eileen Wynn Ball	Sandy Niemiera
Jenny Bay-Williams	Christina Nugent
Ava Chatterjee-Belisle	Janet M. Parsons
Elizabeth Colligan	Leona Peters
Marty Gartzman	Catherine Reed
Carol Inzerillo	

Editorial and Production Staff

Third Edition

Kathleen R. Anderson	Christina Clemons
Lindy M. Chambers-Boucher	Anne Roby

TIMS Professional Developers

Barbara Crum	Cheryl Kneubuhler
Catherine Ditto	Lisa Mackey
Pamela Guyton	Linda Miceli

TIMS Director of Media Services

Henrique Cirne-Lima

TIMS Research Staff

Stacy Brown	Catherine Ditto
Reality Canty	Kathleen Pitvorec
Alison Castro	Catherine Randall Kelso

TIMS Administrative Staff

Eve Ali Boles	Enrique Puente
Kathleen R. Anderson	Alice VanSlyke
Nida Khan	

Director

Second Edition Catherine Randall Kelso

Curriculum Developers

Second Edition

Lindy M. Chambers-Boucher
Elizabeth Colligan
Marty Gartzman
Carol Inzerillo
Catherine Randall Kelso

Jennifer Mundt Leimberer
Georganne E. Marsh
Leona Peters
Philip Wagreich

Editorial and Production Staff

Second Edition

Kathleen R. Anderson
Ai-Ai C. Cojuangco
Andrada Costoiu
Erika Larsen

Georganne E. Marsh
Cosmina Menghes
Anne Roby

Principal Investigators

First Edition Philip Wagreich Howard Goldberg

Senior Curriculum Developers

First Edition

Janet Simpson Beissinger
Joan L. Bieler
Astrida Cirulis
Marty Gartzman
Howard Goldberg

Carol Inzerillo
Andy Isaacs
Catherine Randall Kelso
Leona Peters
Philip Wagreich

Curriculum Developers

First Edition

Janice C. Banasiak
Lynne Beauprez
Andy Carter
Lindy M. Chambers-Boucher
Kathryn Chval
Diane Czerwinski

Jenny Knight
Sandy Niemiera
Janice Ozima
Polly Tangora
Paul Trafton

Illustrator

First Edition Kris Dresen

Editorial and Production Staff

First Edition

Glenda L. Genio-Terrado
Mini Joseph
Lynette Morgenthaler

Sarah Nelson
Birute Petrauskas
Anne Roby

Research Consultant

First Edition Andy Isaacs

Mathematics Education Consultant

First Edition Paul Trafton

National Advisory Committee

First Edition

Carl Berger
Tom Berger
Hugh Burkhart
Donald Chambers
Naomi Fisher
Glenda Lappan

Mary Lindquist
Eugene Maier
Lourdes Monteagudo
Elizabeth Phillips
Thomas Post

Preface

This third edition of *Math Trailblazers* is the product of about 20 years of concerted effort by the TIMS (Teaching Integrated Mathematics and Science) Project. The TIMS Project has its roots in the pioneering work of Howard Goldberg, Professor of Physics at the University of Illinois at Chicago (UIC) and a Carnegie Foundation Professor of the Year in 1995. Over the past two decades, the TIMS Project has worked with children, teachers, and administrators to improve the quality of mathematics and science curricula and instruction in the Chicago area and nationwide. In 1990, the TIMS Project was awarded a grant by the National Science Foundation to develop a new elementary mathematics curriculum to meet the needs of children who will be entering the world of work in the 21st century. After years of research and development, including pilot- and field-testing in hundreds of classrooms, the first edition of the curriculum was published as *Math Trailblazers* in 1997 and 1998.

The primary goal of *Math Trailblazers* has been to create an educational experience that results in children who are flexible mathematical thinkers, who see the connections between the mathematics they learn in school and the thinking they do in everyday life, and who enjoy mathematics. The curriculum is based on the premise that children can succeed in mathematics and that if more is expected of them, more will be achieved. The curriculum incorporates the best of traditional mathematics, while widening the horizons of students' mathematical thinking.

Since the initial publication of *Math Trailblazers*, the TIMS Project has continued its research and development work, studying how to implement the curriculum in the most effective ways. We have learned considerably more about the importance of teacher professional development and whole-school change. The dedication and insight of our teacher collaborators constantly encouraged us. Feedback from hundreds of teachers who tested early versions of *Math Trailblazers* and thousands of others who used the program over the past ten years significantly reshaped our view of the curriculum and inspires our continuing efforts to improve it.

The first edition of *Math Trailblazers* was grounded in mathematics education research literature as well as our own research and experience as curriculum and staff developers. It was also inspired by the 1989 publication of the National Council of Teachers of Mathematics *Curriculum and Evaluation Standards for School Mathematics*. In this edition we drew from advances in research over the decade as well as NCTM's updated vision for school mathematics, as embodied in the NCTM's *Principles and Standards for School Mathematics*.

New editions of *Math Trailblazers* have made the curriculum easier for teachers to use. The math facts program was realigned in the 2nd edition and in this edition assessment and review components of the curriculum are more clearly highlighted. This edition also features an improved format for the *Unit Resource Guide* as well as new content in the *Teacher Implementation Guide* aimed at teachers and administrators. This content was suggested and shaped by our experience as professional developers working with schools and districts across the country that implement *Math Trailblazers*. It includes **Building the *Math Trailblazers* Classroom,** strategies and tips gathered from classroom teachers; **Teaching the *Math Trailblazers* Student: Meeting Individual Needs,** integral structures and features of *Math Trailblazers* that make it accessible to all children, including sections on working with English Language Learners, Special Education students and gifted and talented students; **Language in the *Math Trailblazers* Classroom,** strategies to help students learn to effectively communicate in the math classroom; and an **Administrator Handbook,** strategies to successfully guide implementation of the curriculum.

This third edition of *Math Trailblazers* is one more step in the continuing evolution of the curriculum. The Project is now housed within UIC's Learning Sciences Research Institute, providing a permanent home for interdisciplinary collaboration between mathematicians, scientists, mathematics educators, learning scientists, and teachers as we continually work at providing the best possible mathematics curriculum. We hope that teaching *Math Trailblazers* will be an enjoyable and productive experience for you and your students.

Philip Wagreich
Professor, Department of Mathematics, Statistics, and Computer Science
Director Emeritus, TIMS Project
University of Illinois at Chicago

Joan L. Bieler and Catherine R. Kelso
Co-Directors, TIMS Project
University of Illinois at Chicago

GRADE

K

Teacher Implementation Guide
Table of Contents

Kindergarten *Math Trailblazers*
Table of Contents

This Table of Contents includes page numbers for the *Teacher Resource Book.*

Section 2

Kindergarten: Month-by-Month

Month 1

Month 2

Month 3

Thematic Units

Introduction

Introduction

The Introduction outlines this guide's various sections and explains how to best use them.

A teacher and a student explore equivalent fractions.

Introduction

PART 1

What Is the *Teacher Implementation Guide?*

The *Teacher Implementation Guide* is the reference manual for *Math Trailblazers®*. It, combined with the *Unit Resource Guide,* provides a comprehensive set of resources to assist in implementing the curriculum. The *Unit Resource Guide* is the teacher's working guide, providing information and instructions related to the planning and teaching of units and individual lessons—it is intended to be used on a day-to-day basis. The *Teacher Implementation Guide* supplements the *Unit Resource Guide* by addressing larger issues related to the curriculum. Information in the *Teacher Implementation Guide* can be roughly categorized into three groups: general background about *Math Trailblazers;* specific information about the program; and deep background about important math and science concepts. The *Teacher Implementation Guide* is a valuable resource for long-range planning for math instruction, curriculum, related implementation issues, and staff development.

Brief descriptions of sections found in the *Teacher Implementation Guide* follow:

- **Foundations of *Math Trailblazers***
  The underlying philosophy of the program is described.

- **Components and Features Guide**
  Math Trailblazers is a multicomponent program. Kindergarten includes two volumes for teachers (the TRB and the TIG). The Components and Features Guide is a road map for understanding the purposes of the various components and where to find key information. Important features taken from actual student and teacher pages are illustrated.

- **Kindergarten Overview**
  The Overview is an extended table of contents for the kindergarten curriculum. It includes a narrative description and bulleted list of the focus for the Ongoing Content and each Mathematical Strand. The Overview also includes outlines for each month and each thematic unit. This provides a snapshot view of the curriculum for your grade.

- **Connections with the NCTM *Principles and Standards***
  Math Trailblazers was developed to reflect the goals and approaches outlined in the *Principles and Standards for School Mathematics* of the National Council of Teachers of Mathematics (NCTM). This section includes detailed information about how the program aligns with the *Principles and Standards.*

- **Scope and Sequence**
  The curriculum's scope and sequence is presented in the TIG. The Scope and Sequence is organized to correspond with the NCTM *Principles and Standards,* providing additional detailed information about *Math Trailblazers'* alignment with the *Standards.*

need teacher resource guide for K6

- **Summary of Approaches to Math Facts and Whole-Number Operations**

  The *Math Trailblazers* program for presenting the math facts and whole-number operations is summarized in the TIG. Background information about our approach and expectations for the grades are outlined.

- **Homework Guide**

  This section outlines the homework philosophy and types of homework included in *Math Trailblazers* curriculum. The Homework Guide also features a letter in English and Spanish, to family members outlining various math activities that can be done at home.

- **Assessment**

  Math Trailblazers includes a comprehensive program of student assessment. The philosophy and components of this program are described in the TIG. Assessment materials from the curriculum illustrate key ideas. Specific suggestions for implementing the assessment program are included.

- **TIMS Tutors: Background Information for Teachers**

  This section includes a series of documents called TIMS Tutors, which provide extensive information on topics in pedagogy, mathematics, and science. The tutors serve as a source of deep background information. Some tutors, such as the tutor on math facts, supply specific information needed by teachers to plan particular portions of the *Math Trailblazers* program. Other tutors, such as the tutor on mass, focus on math and science content. Still others, such as the tutor on portfolios, address teaching strategies.

- **Building the *Math Trailblazers* Classroom**

  This section contains strategies and tips gathered from classroom teachers. Topics include the organization of materials and classrooms, as well as student groupings to best implement *Math Trailblazers*.

- **Teaching the *Math Trailblazers* Student: Meeting Individual Needs**

  From its earliest days, the authors developed the *Math Trailblazers* curriculum on a foundation of equity. This means that all children in all classrooms have the right to access rigorous mathematics. This section describes the integral structures and features of *Math Trailblazers* that make it accessible to all children. It also contains a section for working with English Language Learners and Special Education students, as well as suggestions for working with gifted and talented students.

- **Language in the *Math Trailblazers* Classroom**

  Language plays an important role in the *Math Trailblazers* Classroom. Language is used to convey mathematical problems. For example, vignettes of everyday situations are often used as contexts for establishing and exploring mathematical content. Both written and spoken language are essential to communicate mathematical ideas, strategies, and solutions. This section describes strategies to help students learn to effectively communicate in the math classroom, including tips on how to help students learn mathematical vocabulary in context.

- **Manipulatives List**
  A listing of the manipulatives required for program implementation is included in this section.

- **Literature List**
  Math Trailblazers uses commercially available trade books in many lessons. A listing of these trade books is included in this section.

- **Games List**
  Games are often used in *Math Trailblazers* to engage students in practicing basic arithmetic skills and other math concepts. Once introduced, these games can be used throughout the year for ongoing practice. A complete listing and description of the games for your grade are provided.

- **Software List**
  Math Trailblazers does not require the use of computers. We do, instead, suggest some software programs that can supplement the curriculum. A listing of these programs and some suggested uses for them are provided.

- **Suggestions for Working with Parents**
  When adopting a math program that is new and different, such as *Math Trailblazers,* it is important to keep parents informed and educated about the program. Some hints for working with parents regarding *Math Trailblazers* are outlined in this section. A brochure about the curriculum and a parent letter describing the math facts program are also provided. The documents are in both English and Spanish.

PART II

How to Use the *Teacher Implementation Guide*

Use of this guide will differ depending upon your purpose. Suggestions for using it for different purposes are described here.

If you are a teacher considering whether to use *Math Trailblazers:*
The *Teacher Implementation Guide* provides useful information for adoption

committees or individual teachers who are considering *Math Trailblazers*. General information about the program that will be most helpful for this group includes the Foundations, alignment with the NCTM *Principles and Standards,* Scope and Sequence, and the Overview. The Components and Features Guide will help reviewers understand the purposes of the different student and teacher books. Other specific information, such as the Math Facts and Whole-Number Operations section and the Assessment section, may also be useful for potential users of the curriculum.

If you are a teacher who is about to use *Math Trailblazers* for the first time:

There is too much information in the *Teacher Implementation Guide* and the *Unit Resource Guide* for any teacher to digest all at once. To make effective use of the *Teacher Implementation Guide,* it is best to select portions to examine at different points in the curriculum implementation. Prior to using *Math Trailblazers,* glance at the Foundations section to get a sense of our overall philosophy. However, you will probably want to spend more time reviewing the sections that provide specific information about using the curriculum. This information will help you get started and plan for the year.

Carefully review the Components and Features Guide to see the big picture of the program's components and features. This information will eventually become second nature as you gain experience with the curriculum, but it will be helpful at first to see what is included in the program. We suggest you review the Overview to get a feel for what is covered over the year and can plan ahead. It will be easier to make instructional decisions if you know what is planned for later lessons. The manipulatives and literature lists are useful tools if you are ordering manipulatives. The sections on homework and working with parents will also be useful to read prior to using the curriculum. Use the rest of the TIG as the need arises.

If you are a teacher who is already using *Math Trailblazers:*

During your first several years of using *Math Trailblazers,* you will likely refer to the TIG on an ongoing basis. You will find the TIMS Tutors particularly valuable in helping you better understand the content and approaches of key parts of the curriculum. There are pointers in the TRB that refer you to individual tutors. The Scope and Sequence supplements the Overview in providing detailed information about when specific concepts are covered. Any background information not found in the TRB is probably in the TIG.

If you are a school administrator in a school using *Math Trailblazers:*

Principals and other school administrators are likely to be queried by parents or even the media about the school's math program. It is therefore useful to have some familiarity with the program's philosophy and a general view of the program's content. The Foundations of *Math Trailblazers* section of the TIG is a good start. The sections that outline the curriculum's alignment with the NCTM *Principles and Standards* provide useful information about the national recommendations that underlie *Math Trailblazers.* We strongly recommend that administrators read the section on working with parents. This section provides suggestions and resources for communicating the curriculum goals to parents. Administrators may also want to review the section that outlines our approaches to teaching math facts and whole-number operations; most potential parental concerns are likely to address that topic.

If you are planning staff development sessions about *Math Trailblazers:*

Implementation of *Math Trailblazers* is most effective when accompanied by a comprehensive professional development program. An orientation to *Math Trailblazers* is made available to schools using *Math Trailblazers* through Kendall/Hunt Publishing. We recommend that schools continue their professional development throughout the lifetime of the implementation. The TIMS Project has developed presenters' guides for a variety of professional development sessions. These guides, called Teacher Enhancement Resource Modules (TERMs), contain a guide for presenters with explanatory text, discussion questions and answers, and blackline masters. Most TERMs include video that demonstrates the *Math Trailblazers* curriculum in action. Used together the 18 TERMs provide approximately 70 hours of staff development in both the content and pedagogy of *Math Trailblazers.* The TERMs are available through Kendall/Hunt Publishing.

For specific suggestions about planning local staff development related to *Math Trailblazers,* contact the Teaching Integrated Mathematics and Science (TIMS) Project at 800-454-TIMS or Kendall/Hunt Publishing Company at 800-542-6657. Information is also available on the *Math Trailblazers* Implementation Center website at *www.math.uic.edu/IMSE* and at *www.mathtrailblazers.com.*

Foundations of *Math Trailblazers*

The Foundations of *Math Trailblazers* describes the principles behind *Math Trailblazers* and discusses the curriculum's key features.

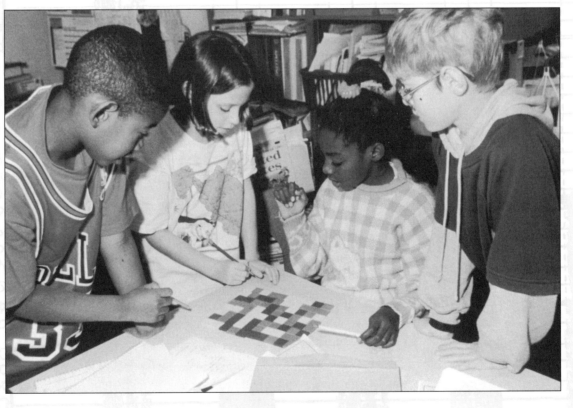

Students work together to solve problems.

Foundations of *Math Trailblazers*

Math Trailblazers is an elementary mathematics curriculum for schools that want their math programs to reflect the goals and ideas of the National Council of Teachers of Mathematics (NCTM) *Principles and Standards for School Mathematics.* With funding from the National Science Foundation (NSF) the TIMS (Teaching Integrated Mathematics and Science) Project at the University of Illinois at Chicago created a comprehensive program that embodies the *Principles and Standards.*

Math Trailblazers is based on the ideas that mathematics is best learned in real-world contexts that make sense to children; that all students deserve a richer and more challenging curriculum; and that a balanced and practical approach to learning mathematics is what students need and teachers want.

Features of *Math Trailblazers*
Alignment with Reform Recommendations

The *Principles and Standards,* which was released in 2000, is an update of three groundbreaking volumes published a decade earlier that collectively became known as the "NCTM *Standards.*" This publication was extended in 2006 with the release of the *Curriculum Focal Points for Prekindergarten through Grade 8 Mathematics: A Quest for Coherence,* which was "offered as a starting point in a dialogue on what is important at particular levels of instruction as an initial step toward a more coherent, focused curriculum in this country." (NCTM 2006, p. vii) However, in describing the relationship between the documents, the NCTM states that the *Principles and Standards* "remains the definitive reference on the development of mathematical content and processes across the grades." (NCTM 2006, p. 1)

The NCTM documents outline a vision for school mathematics that includes: a mathematically challenging curriculum that is coherent and covers a broad range of mathematical content; a strong focus on engaging students in mathematical problem solving; conceptually oriented instruction that stresses thinking, reasoning, and applying; appropriate uses of calculators and computers; and a strong commitment to promoting success in mathematics among all students—not merely those who traditionally have done well. Most states incorporated this vision for mathematics teaching and learning into their mathematics standards.

The first edition of *Math Trailblazers* took more than six years of work that included extensive pilot and field testing of the materials. After publication of the first edition, continued NSF support enabled the TIMS Project to develop implementation models and professional development materials that assisted teachers and schools as they adopted the program.

In developing the second edition of *Math Trailblazers,* we looked carefully at the NCTM *Principles and Standards* and reorganized portions of the *Math Trailblazers,* such as the math facts program, to keep *Math Trailblazers* closely aligned with the new NCTM recommendations. TIMS researchers also studied how the program impacted student achievement. The second edition of *Math Trailblazers* therefore represented more than twelve years of NSF-supported work related to the curriculum.

The third edition provides materials in an easier-to-use format, as well as new content for teachers and administrators. This content was suggested and shaped by other lessons learned from our years of professional development work with schools and districts across the country that implement *Math Trailblazers.*

The importance of a coherent, well-developed curriculum is clear in the *Principles and Standards,* which states:

A curriculum is more than a collection of activities: it must be coherent, focused on important mathematics, and well articulated across the grades. A school mathematics curriculum is a strong determinant of what students have an opportunity to learn and what they do learn. In a coherent curriculum, mathematical ideas are linked to and build on one another so that students' understanding and knowledge deepens and their ability to apply mathematics expands. An effective mathematics curriculum focuses on important mathematics—mathematics that will prepare students for continued study and for solving problems in a variety of school, home, and work settings. A well-articulated curriculum challenges students to learn increasingly more sophisticated mathematical ideas as they continue their studies. (NCTM, 2000, p. 14)

Math Trailblazers was developed with that goal in mind. It is a *Standards*-based curriculum in the truest sense—developed explicitly to reflect national standards for K–5 mathematics, and now revised to maintain close alignment with those standards as they have evolved.

More specific connections between *Math Trailblazers* and the NCTM *Principles and Standards* are discussed in Scope and Sequence & the NCTM *Principles and Standards* (Section 5).

High Expectations and Equity

The first principle in the *Principles and Standards* is the Equity Principle. It challenges a myth prevalent in the United States that only a few students are capable of rigorous mathematics. The Equity Principle states:

> *Excellence in mathematics education requires equity—high expectations and strong support for all students.* (NCTM, 2000, p. 12)

Accordingly, we introduce challenging content in every grade: computation, measurement, data collection, statistics, geometry, ratio, probability, graphing, algebraic concepts, estimation, mental arithmetic, and patterns and relationships.

Contexts for this demanding content begin with students' lives. Lessons are grounded in everyday situations, so abstractions build on experience. By presenting mathematics in rich contexts, the curriculum helps students make connections among real situations, words, pictures, data, graphs, and symbols. The curriculum also validates students' current understandings while new understandings develop. Students can solve problems in ways they understand while being encouraged to connect those ways to more abstract and powerful methods. Within the same lesson, some students may work directly with the manipulatives to solve the problems while other students may solve the same problems using graphs or symbols. The use of varied contexts and diverse representations of concepts allows children of varying abilities to access the mathematics.

Problem Solving

A fundamental principle of *Math Trailblazers* is that mathematics is best learned through actively solving real problems. Questions a student can answer immediately may be worthwhile exercises, but *problems,* by definition, are difficult, but not impossible.

The importance of problem solving is echoed in the NCTM *Principles and Standards,* which states:

> *Problem solving is the cornerstone of school mathematics. . . . The goal of school mathematics should be for all students to become increasingly able and willing to engage with and solve problems.*

> *Problem solving is also important because it can serve as a vehicle for learning new mathematical ideas and skills (Schroeder and Lester). A problem-centered approach to teaching mathematics uses interesting and well-selected problems to launch mathematical lessons and engage students. In this way, new ideas, techniques, and mathematical relationships emerge and become the focus of discussion.* (NCTM, 2000, p. 182)

As recommended by NCTM, problem solving in *Math Trailblazers* is not a distinct topic but permeates the entire program, providing a context for learning concepts and skills. Throughout the curriculum, students apply the mathematics they know and construct new mathematics as needed. Students' skills, procedures, and concepts emerge and develop as they solve complex problems.

Connections to Science and Language Arts

Real-world problems are naturally interdisciplinary, so any problem-solving curriculum should integrate topics that are traditionally separated. Accordingly, we have integrated mathematics with many disciplines, especially science and language arts.

Connections to Science

Math Trailblazers is a full mathematics program that incorporates many important scientific ideas. Traditionally, school science has focused on the results of science. Students learn about plate tectonics, the atomic theory of matter, the solar system, the environment, and so on. Knowing basic facts of science is seen as part of being educated, today more than ever. However, the facts of science, important and interesting as they are, do not alone constitute a comprehensive and balanced science curriculum.

Science has two aspects: results and method. The results of scientific inquiry have enriched human life the world over. More marvelous than the results of science, however, is the method that established those results. Without the method, the results would never have been achieved. *Math Trailblazers* aims to teach students the method of science through scientific investigation of everyday phenomena. During these investigations, students learn both mathematics and science.

The method scientists use is powerful, flexible, and quantitative. The TIMS Project has organized this method in a way that is simple enough for elementary school children to use. Students use the TIMS Laboratory Method in a rich variety of mathematical investigations. In these investigations, students develop and apply important mathematical skills and concepts in meaningful situations. Their understanding of fundamental scientific concepts is also enhanced through the use of quantitative tools.

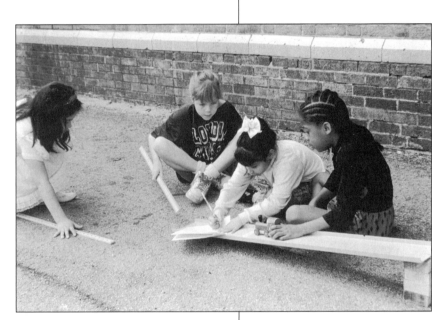

Investigations begin with discussions of experimental situations, variables, and procedures. Then students draw pictures that indicate the experimental procedures and identify key variables. Next students gather and organize data in data tables. Then they graph their data. By analyzing their data or studying their graphs, students are able to see patterns. These patterns show any relationships between the variables. Students can use the relationships to make predictions about future data. The last phase of the experiment is an in-depth analysis of the experimental results, structured as a series of exploratory questions. Some questions ask students to make predictions and then to verify them. Other questions probe students' understanding of underlying concepts and explore the role of controlled variables. As students advance through the curriculum, the questions progress from simple to complex, building eventually to problems that require proportional reasoning, multiple-step logic, and algebra.

The TIMS Laboratory Method initiates children into the authentic practice of science. Identifying variables, drawing pictures, measuring, organizing data in tables, graphing data, and looking for and using patterns are a major part of many scientists' work. This is a major goal of science: to discover and use relationships between variables—usually expressed in some mathematical form—in order to understand and make predictions about the world.

The science content in *Math Trailblazers* focuses on a small set of simple variables that are fundamental to both math and science: length, area, volume, mass, and time. Understanding these basic variables is an essential step to achieving scientific understanding of more complex concepts. Measurement is presented in meaningful, experimental situations.

Emphasizing the scientific method and fundamental science concepts helps students develop an understanding of how scientists and mathematicians think. These habits of mind will be important in all aspects of life in the 21st century. See the TIMS Tutor: *The TIMS Laboratory Method* for more discussion of these ideas.

Connections to Language Arts

Reading, writing, and talking belong in mathematics class, not only because real mathematicians and scientists read, write, and talk mathematics and science constantly, but also because these activities help students learn. The NCTM *Principles and Standards* emphasizes the importance of communication and discourse for students to achieve at higher levels.

In school mathematics, results should be accepted not merely because

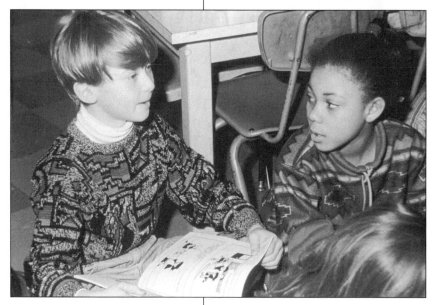

someone in authority says so, but rather because persuasive arguments can be made for them. A result and a reason are often easier to remember than the result alone. By discussing the mathematics they are doing, students increase their understanding. They also extend their abilities to discuss mathematics and so to participate in a community of mathematicians. Talking or writing about mathematics is part of every lesson. Journal and discussion prompts are standard features in the teacher's guide for each lesson.

Reading is also built into this curriculum. Many lessons, especially in the primary grades, use trade books to launch or extend mathematical investigations. The curriculum also includes many original stories, called *Adventure Books,* that show applications of concepts or sketch episodes from the history of mathematics and science. Literature is used to portray mathematics as a human endeavor, so that students come to think of mathematicians and scientists as people like themselves. Mathematics embedded in a narrative structure is also easier to understand, remember, and discuss. And, of course, everyone loves a good story. In addition, students regularly write about their mathematical investigations, even in the early grades.

Collaborative Work

Scientists, mathematicians, and most others who solve complex problems in business and industry have always worked in groups. The reasons for this are simple: Most interesting problems are too difficult for one person. Explaining one's work to another person can help clarify one's thinking. Another person's perspective can suggest a new approach to a problem. Ideas that have been tested through public scrutiny are more trustworthy than private notions.

All these are reasons for collaborating in schools as well. But there are other reasons, too. Students can learn both by receiving and by giving explanations. The communication that goes with group work provides practice in verbal and symbolic communication skills. In group discussion, a basic assumption is that mathematics and science ought to make sense—something, unfortunately, that many students stop believing after only a few years of school. Social skills, especially cooperation and tolerance, increase, and the classroom community becomes more oriented towards learning and academic achievement.

Assessment

There are three major purposes for assessment. First, assessment helps teachers learn about students' thinking and knowledge: information that can then be used to guide instruction. Secondly, it communicates the goals of instruction to students and parents. Finally, it informs students and parents about progress toward these goals and suggests directions for further efforts.

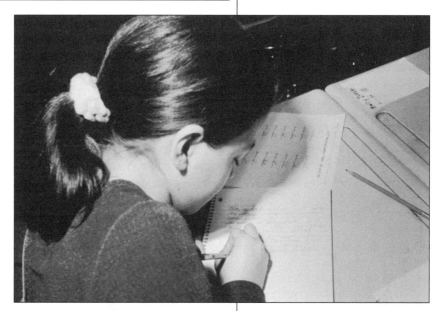

Assessment in *Math Trailblazers* reflects the breadth and balance of the curriculum. Numerous opportunities for both formal and informal assessment of student learning are integrated into the program. Many assessment activities are incorporated into the daily lessons; others are included in formal assessment units. Assessment activities include a mix of short, medium-length, and extended activities. Some are hands-on investigations, others are paper-and-pencil tasks. In all cases, assessment activities further students' learning.

For a detailed discussion of assessment in *Math Trailblazers,* refer to Assessment (Section 8) and the TIMS Tutor: *Portfolios.*

More Time Studying Mathematics

One cannot reasonably expect to cover all the concepts in a traditional program, add many new topics, and utilize an approach that emphasizes problem solving, communication, reasoning, and connections in the same amount of time used to teach a traditional math curriculum. In developing *Math Trailblazers,* we have attempted to achieve some efficiencies, such as building review into new concepts and using effective strategies to teach math facts and procedures. However, there is no magic in *Math Trailblazers.* Implementing a comprehensive, reform mathematics curriculum will require a significant amount of time. **We assume that in Grades 1–5 one hour**

every day will be devoted to teaching mathematics. In Kindergarten, the class make-up and the activity will determine the length of the class.

In some schools, finding an hour per day for math instruction may require a restructuring of the daily school schedule. Please note, however, that because *Math Trailblazers* includes extensive connections with science and language arts, *some* time spent with *Math Trailblazers* can be incorporated within science or language arts time. Thus, it may be possible to allot the one hour per day of mathematics instruction by simply scheduling math and science instruction back to back or including literature connections and journal writing in language arts.

Hard work on the part of students and more time engaged in mathematical problem solving are important ingredients to success in mathematics— no matter what program you are using. Because students using *Math Trailblazers* are actively involved in applying mathematics in meaningful contexts, our experience is that students will be highly motivated to spend extra time studying mathematics.

Staff Development and Broad School Support: Essential Ingredients

Developing the curriculum and working with schools over the last 20 years has taught us that implementing a *Standards*-based mathematics program will progress more smoothly if it is accompanied by a solid support system for teachers. Ideally, this includes a professional development program that includes workshops on content and pedagogy, leadership development, in-school support, and the means to address a variety of concerns as they arise.

Overall implementation of *Math Trailblazers* will be much easier in a school that organizes support for the new program. Necessary tools such as manipulatives, overhead projectors, and transparency masters need to be provided in adequate quantities. Institutional considerations, such as classroom schedules that allot necessary time for instruction and provide time for teachers to meet and plan together, need to be implemented. In-classroom support from resource teachers is extremely helpful. Storage and check-out systems for shared manipulatives need to be in place. Ways to engender parental support for the program, including possible ways to involve some parents in providing classroom assistance to interested teachers during math time, should be developed.

Administrators need to maintain a long-term perspective recognizing that program implementation will take some time—and they need to communicate this clearly to teachers. In short, schools need to examine their current situations and make necessary modifications to develop a school environment that supports the kind of teaching and learning that characterizes *Math Trailblazers*.

A Balanced Approach

A reform mathematics program should take a balanced and moderate approach. *Math Trailblazers* is balanced in many different ways with whole-class instruction, small-group activities, and individual work. New mathematical content is included, but traditional topics are not neglected.

Children construct their own knowledge in rich problem-solving situations, but they are not expected to reinvent 5000 years of mathematics. Concepts, procedures, and facts are important, but are introduced thoughtfully to engender the positive attitudes, beliefs, and self-image that are also important in the long run. Hands-on activities of varied length and depth, as well as paper-and-pencil tasks, all have their place. The program's rich variety of assessment activities reflects this broad balance.

Either-or rhetoric has too often short-circuited real progress in education: problem solving vs. back-to-basics, conceptual understanding vs. procedural skill, paper-and-pencil computation vs. calculators. *Math Trailblazers* is based on the view that these are false dichotomies. Students must solve problems, but of course they need basic skills to do so. Both concepts and procedures are important, and neglecting one will undermine the other. There is a place in the curriculum both for paper-and-pencil algorithms and for calculators, and for mental arithmetic and estimation. The careful balance in *Math Trailblazers* allows teachers and schools to move forward with a reform mathematics curriculum while maintaining the strengths of their current teaching practices.

Research Foundations of *Math Trailblazers*

The first edition of *Math Trailblazers* was completed in 1997. The roots of the curriculum, however, date back to the late 1970s and the work of Howard Goldberg, a particle physicist at the University of Illinois at Chicago (UIC). Building on the work of Robert Karplus and others, Goldberg developed a framework for adapting the scientific method for elementary school children and applied that framework within a series of elementary laboratory investigations (Goldberg & Boulanger, 1981). Goldberg was joined in 1985 by UIC mathematician Philip Wagreich and, together with others, formed the Teaching Integrated Mathematics and Science Project (TIMS).

Thus, the motivation behind TIMS came from two sources, one with roots in science and one with roots in mathematics. The scientific impetus stemmed from the desire to teach science to children in a manner that reflects the practice of scientists. Modern science is fundamentally quantitative; therefore, quantitative investigations should have an important role in children's science education. The mathematical impetus was to find a way to make mathematics meaningful to children. Engaging children in quantitative investigations of common phenomena harnesses their curiosity in a way that builds on their understanding of the natural world, which, in turn, helps promote study of rigorous mathematics (Isaacs, Wagreich, & Gartzman, 1997).

Initially, TIMS focused primarily on the development and implementation of a series of quantitative, hands-on activities, the *TIMS Laboratory Investigations* (Goldberg, 1997). The laboratory investigations continue the tradition of Dewey (1910) and others in focusing on the method of science and on exploring a relatively small set of fundamental scientific concepts in depth. Several studies provided clear evidence that the *TIMS Laboratory Investigations* are effective in promoting students' development of mathematics and science concepts (Goldberg & Wagreich, 1990; Goldberg, 1993).

Based largely on the success with the supplemental *TIMS Laboratory Investigations,* the National Science Foundation (NSF) supported the TIMS Project to develop a comprehensive, elementary mathematics curriculum that would align with the National Council of Teachers of Mathematics (NCTM) *Curriculum and Evaluation Standards for School Mathematics* (NCTM, 1989). The first edition of *Math Trailblazers* is the result of this work. As part of the revision process for the second edition, the authors made changes so that the new edition aligns with the current NCTM recommendations as outlined in the *Principles and Standards for School Mathematics* (NCTM, 2000).

The third edition provides materials in an easier-to-use format, as well as new content for teachers and administrators. This content embodies the lessons learned from our TIMS Project's 20 years of professional development work with schools and districts that implement *Math Trailblazers.*

In developing each edition of *Math Trailblazers,* the authors drew upon research findings from a wide variety of sources, as well as from the broad experiences of the authoring group. In this section we highlight a portion of the research that helped guide the curriculum's development and other current research that validates the approaches used.

A Problem-Solving Curriculum

A distinguishing element of any *Standards*-based mathematics curriculum is that problem solving is used as a context for students to learn new concepts and skills. Throughout *Math Trailblazers,* students apply the mathematics they know and construct new mathematics as needed. Students' skills, procedures, and concepts emerge and develop as they solve problems. Students also practice skills and procedures as they apply them in diverse and increasingly challenging contexts. Problem-solving contexts can emerge from real-life investigations or from more mathematical situations. The problems serve as the motivation for purposeful use of mathematics.

Using problem solving as a cornerstone of the mathematics curriculum has been promoted by educators dating back to Dewey and has received considerable support from current mathematics education researchers. (See Hiebert et al., 1996; Schoenfeld, 1985 and 1994; National Research Council, 2001; and NCTM 1989 and 2000 for a discussion of problem solving in the curriculum.)

A curriculum that emphasizes solving problems can use many different contexts. In developing *Math Trailblazers,* the authors first identified the key mathematical concepts and skills to be developed and then selected problem-solving contexts to support student learning in these areas. Our earlier work and that of others (e.g., Cognition and Technology Group at Vanderbilt, 1997) had confirmed the value of using quantitative laboratory investigations for this purpose. Drawing from this work, eight to ten laboratory investigations were adapted and integrated into *Math Trailblazers* in each grade, beginning with first grade. These investigations are supplemented by many other contexts for problem solving.

Challenging Mathematics in All Grades for All Students

An assumption in the development of *Math Trailblazers* was that students can learn more challenging mathematics than is covered in traditional mathematics curricula. This has been underscored in international comparison studies (Heibert, 1999; McKnight et al., 1987; Stigler & Perry, 1988; Schmidt, McKnight, & Raizen, 1996; Stigler & Hiebert, 1997; Stevenson & Stigler, 1992) and in analyses of U.S. mathematics instruction (Flanders, 1987; Lindquist, 1989). Maintaining high expectations and providing access to rigorous mathematics for all students has proven effective regardless of the socioeconomic status and ethnicity of the students (National Research Council, 2001; Newmann, Bryk, & Nagaoka, 2001; Smith, Lee, & Newmann, 2001). Therefore, mathematical expectations in *Math Trailblazers* are high and grow steadily. Review of concepts and skills is carefully built into new and increasingly challenging problems as the program builds upon itself both within and across grades.

Balancing Concept and Skill Development

The importance of developing a strong conceptual foundation is emphasized in research that guided the development of all content strands in *Math Trailblazers*. Many educators have long recognized the importance of balancing conceptual and skill development. New conceptual understandings are built upon existing skills and concepts; these new understandings in turn support the further development of skills and concepts.

A wide body of research affirms that instructional programs that emphasize conceptual development can facilitate significant mathematics learning without sacrificing skill proficiency (see Hiebert, 1999). Research affirms that well-designed and implemented instructional programs can facilitate both conceptual understanding and procedural skill.

This research had a profound effect on development of *Math Trailblazers*. For example, such research helped define the curriculum's program for developing number sense and estimation skills (Sowder, 1992) and for learning math facts and whole-number operations (Carpenter, Carey, & Kouba, 1990; Carpenter, et al., 1999; Fuson, 1987, 1992; Fuson & Briars, 1990; Fuson et al., 1997; Isaacs & Carroll, 1999; Lampert, 1986a, 1986b; Thornton, 1978, 1990a, 1990b). Work with fractions and decimals was informed by research that stressed the need to develop conceptual understandings of fractions and decimals prior to introducing procedures with the four arithmetic operations (see Behr & Post, 1992; Ball, 1993; Cramer, Post, & del Mas, 2002; Lesh, Post, & Behr, 1987; Mack, 1990; Hoffer & Hoffer, 1992). Similar research findings on student understanding of geometric concepts shaped the development of lessons in geometry (see Burger & Shaughnessy, 1986; Crowley, 1987; Fuys, Geddes, & Tishler, 1988).

In direct response to research such as that cited here, every content strand within *Math Trailblazers* interweaves the promotion of conceptual understanding with distributed practice of skills and procedures.

Field Testing and Research on the Curriculum in Classrooms

NSF funding allowed sequential development of the program to be coupled with extensive field testing in schools. As a result, curriculum development became an iterative process involving considerable interaction between the developers and field-test teachers. Comments and suggestions from teachers were incorporated into revisions that were often retested in classrooms one or more times before final revisions were made. Field-test teachers met regularly with the program's authors, and classrooms were often visited as part of the development process. Teachers using the early versions in their classrooms addressed content, language, format, practical considerations, and other issues related to each lesson.

In addition to assessing feedback from field-test teachers, independent researchers and TIMS Project staff conducted preliminary studies that helped affirm the efficacy of the content placement and approaches in the early versions of the materials (Burghardt, 1994; Perry, Whiteaker, & Waddoups, 1996; Whiteaker, Waddoups, & Perry, 1994). These preliminary studies provided an additional means for the authors to monitor the effectiveness of the developing program.

Early studies of student achievement in *Math Trailblazers* classrooms in both urban and suburban schools have shown that students using the curriculum performed as well, and often better, on mandated standardized tests than students in those schools prior to implementation of *Math Trailblazers*. (Carter, et al., 2003; Putnam, 2003) "[The results] indicate that the balanced problem-solving approach found in *Math Trailblazers* has been successful in improving student learning and achievement in mathematics." (Carter, et al., 2003)

In developing the second edition, we benefited from the suggestions and comments of teachers throughout the country who were using the published *Math Trailblazers* materials. Input from teachers, for example, resulted in the major changes to the second edition's teacher guides. Teachers' feedback also directed us to modify or eliminate some lessons.

In third edition development, changes were made to the format and content for teachers and administrators based on surveys, focus groups, and feedback from teachers and administrators. The format of the third edition materials is easier for teachers to use. New content for teachers and administrators assists with implementation issues in the classroom, school, and district. This content embodies 20 years of professional development work by the TIMS Project with schools and districts that implement *Math Trailblazers*.

Extensive field testing during the program's development, current research and evaluation in schools, and our ongoing conversations with *Math Trailblazers* teachers have helped us develop a challenging, yet grade-level-appropriate program that reflects the needs and realities of teachers and students.

References

The following references are cited in the above document. Additional references to research literature are included in many *Unit Resource Guides* following the Background and in many sections of the *Teacher Implementation Guide* including the Assessment section and the TIMS Tutors.

Ball, D. "Halves, Pieces, and Twoths: Constructing and Using Representational Contexts in Teaching Fractions." In T. P. Carpenter, E. Fennema, and T.A. Romberg (Eds.), *Rational Numbers: An Integration of Research,* pp. 157–195. Lawrence Erlbaum Associates, Hillsdale, NJ, 1993.

Behr, M.J., and T.R. Post. "Teaching Rational Number and Decimal Concepts." In *Teaching Mathematics in Grades K–8: Research Based Methods.* Allyn and Bacon, Boston, 1992.

Burger, W., and J.M. Shaughnessy. "Characterizing the Van Hiele Levels of Development in Geometry." *Journal for Research in Mathematics Education,* 17, pp. 31–48, National Council of Teachers of Mathematics, Reston, VA, 1986.

Burghardt, B. Results of Some Summative Evaluation Studies: 1993–1994 Evaluation Report. (An unpublished report to the National Science Foundation.) 1994.

Carpenter, T.P., D. Carey, and V. Kouba. "A Problem-Solving Approach to the Operations." J.N. Payne, ed., *Mathematics for the Young Child.* National Council of Teachers of Mathematics, Reston, VA, 1990.

Carpenter, T.P., E. Fennema, M.L. Franke, L. Levi, and S.E. Empson. *Children's Mathematics: Cognitively Guided Instruction.* Heinemann, Westport, CT, 1999.

Carter, M.A., J.S. Beissinger, A. Cirulis, M. Gartzman, C.R. Kelso, and P. Wagreich. "Student Learning and Achievement with *Math Trailblazers.*" S.L. Senk and D.R. Thompson, eds., *Standards-Based School Mathematics Curricula: What Does the Research Say about Student Outcomes?* Lawrence Erlbaum Associates, Inc., Hillsdale, NJ, 2003.

Cognition and Technology Group at Vanderbilt. *The Jasper Project: Lessons in Curriculum, Instruction, Assessment, and Professional Development.* Erlbaum, Mahwah, NJ, 1997.

Cramer, K., T. Post, and R. del Mas. "Initial Fraction Learning by Fourth- and Fifth-Grade Students: A Comparison of the Effects of Using Commercial Curricula with the Effects of Using the Rational Number Project Curriculum." *Journal for Research in Mathematics Education,* 33(2), pp. 111–144.

Crowley, M.L. "The Van Hiele Model of Development of Geometric Thought." *Learning and Teaching Geometry, K–12, 1987 Yearbook.* Edited by Mary Montgomery Lindquist. National Council of Teachers of Mathematics, Reston, VA, 1987.

Curriculum and Evaluation Standards for School Mathematics. National Council of Teachers of Mathematics, Reston, VA, 1989.

Dewey, J. "Science as Subject-Matter and as Method." *Science,* 31(787), pp. 121–127, 1910.

Flanders, J. "How Much of the Content in Mathematics Textbooks Is New?" *The Arithmetic Teacher,* 35(1), pp. 18–23, 1987.

Fuson, K.C. "Teaching Addition, Subtraction, and Place-Value Concepts." L. Wirszup and R. Streit (eds.), *Proceedings of the UCSMP International Conference on Mathematics Education: Developments in School Mathematics Education Around the World: Applications-Oriented Curricula and Technology-Supported Learning for All Students.* National Council of Teachers of Mathematics, Reston, VA, 1987.

Fuson, K.C. "Research on Whole Number Addition and Subtraction." *Handbook of Research on Mathematics Teaching and Learning,* pp. 243–275, D.A. Grouws, ed. Macmillan Publishing Company, New York, 1992.

Fuson, K.C., and D.J. Briars. "Using a Base-Ten Blocks Learning/Teaching Approach for First- and Second-Grade Place-Value and Multidigit Addition and Subtraction." *Journal for Research in Mathematics Education,* 21, pp. 180–206, 1990.

Fuson, K.C., D. Wearne, J. Hiebert, H. Murray, P. Human, A. Olivier, T. Carpenter, and E. Fennema. "Children's Conceptual Structures for Multidigit Numbers and Methods of Multidigit Addition and Subtraction." *Journal for Research in Mathematics Education,* 28, pp. 130–162, 1997.

Fuys, D., D. Geddes, and R. Tishler. "The Van Hiele Model of Thinking in Geometry among Adolescents." *Journal for Research in Mathematics Education, Monograph Number 3.* National Council of Teachers of Mathematics, Reston, VA, 1988.

Goldberg, H. *A Four Year Achievement Study: The TIMS Program.* University of Illinois at Chicago Institute for Mathematics and Science Education, Chicago, IL, 1993.

Goldberg, H. *The TIMS Laboratory Investigations.* Kendall/Hunt, Dubuque, IA, 1997.

Goldberg, H.S., and F.D. Boulanger. "Science for Elementary School Teachers: A Quantitative Approach." *American Journal of Physics,* 19(2), pp. 120–124, 1981.

Goldberg, H., and P. Wagreich. "A Model Integrated Mathematics Science Program for the Elementary School." *International Journal of Educational Research,* 14(2), pp. 193–214, 1990.

Goldberg, H., and P. Wagreich. "Teaching Integrated Math and Science: A Curriculum and Staff Development Project for the Elementary School." *Issues in Mathematics Education: Mathematicians and Education Reform.* N. Fisher, H. Keynes, and P. Wagreich, eds., American Mathematical Society, Providence, RI, 1990.

Hiebert, J. "Relationships between Research and the NCTM Standards." *Journal for Research in Mathematics Education,* 30(1), pp. 3–19, 1999.

Hiebert, J., T.P. Carpenter, E. Fennema, K.C. Fuson, P. Human, H. Murray, A. Olivier, D. Wearne. "Problem Solving as a Basis for Reform in Curriculum and Instruction: The Case of Mathematics." *Educational Researcher,* 25(4), pp. 12–21, 1996.

Hoffer, A.R., and S.A.K. Hoffer. "Ratios and Proportional Thinking." In *Teaching Mathematics in Grades K–8: Research Based Methods.* Allyn and Bacon, Boston, 1992.

Isaacs, A.C., and W.M. Carroll. "Strategies for Basic-Facts Instruction." *Teaching Children Mathematics,* 5(9), pp. 508–515, 1999.

Isaacs, A.C., P. Wagreich, and M. Gartzman. The Quest for Integration: School Mathematics and Science. *American Journal of Education,* 106(1), pp. 179–206, 1997.

Lampert, M. "Knowing, Doing, and Teaching Multiplication." *Cognition and Instruction,* 3 (4), pp. 305–342, 1986a.

Lampert, M. "Teaching Multiplication." *Journal of Mathematical Behavior,* 5, pp. 241–280, 1986b.

Lesh, R., T. Post, and M. Behr. "Representations and Translations Among Representations in Mathematics Learning and Problem Solving." C. Janvier, ed., *Problems of Representation in the Teaching and Learning of Mathematics.* Lawrence Erlbaum Associates, Hillsdale, NJ, 1987.

Lindquist, M.M., ed. *Results from the Fourth Mathematics Assessment of the National Assessment of Educational Progress.* National Council of Teachers of Mathematics. Reston, VA, 1989.

Mack, N.K. "Learning Fractions with Understanding: Building on Informal Knowledge." *Journal for Research in Mathematics Education,* 21(1), National Council of Teachers of Mathematics, Reston, VA, January 1990.

McKnight, C.C., F.J. Crosswhite, J.A. Dossey, E. Kifer, J.O. Swafford, K.T. Travers, and T.J. Cooney, *The Underachieving Curriculum: Assessing U.S. School Mathematics from an International Perspective.* Stipes Publishing Company, Champaign, IL, 1987.

National Research Council. *Adding It Up: Helping Children Learn Mathematics.* J. Kilpatrick, J. Swafford, and B. Findell, eds. National Academy Press, Washington, DC, 2001.

Newmann, F.M., A.S. Bryk, and J.K. Nagaoka. *Authentic Intellectual Work and Standardized Tests: Conflict or Coexistence?* Consortium on Chicago School Research, Chicago, 2001.

Perry, M., M. Whiteaker, and G.L. Waddoups. "Students' Participation in a Reform Mathematics Classroom: Learning to Become Mathematicians." In K. Fuson (Chair), *Effects of Reform Mathematics Curricula on Children's Mathematical Understanding.* Symposia conducted at the annual meeting of the American Educational Research Association, New York, 1996.

Principles and Standards for School Mathematics. National Council of Teachers of Mathematics, Reston, VA, 2000.

Putnam, R.T. "Commentary on Four Elementary Mathematics Curricula." S.L. Senk and D.R. Thompson, eds., *Standards-Based School Mathematics Curricula: What Does the Research Say about Student Outcomes?* Lawrence Erlbaum Associates, Inc., Hillsdale, NJ, 2003.

Schmidt, W.H., C.C. McKnight, and S.A. Raizen. *A Splintered Vision: An Investigation of U.S. Science and Mathematics Education.* Kluwer, Norwell, MA, 1996.

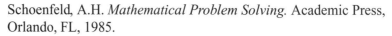

Schoenfeld, A.H. *Mathematical Problem Solving.* Academic Press, Orlando, FL, 1985.

Schoenfeld, A.H. "What Do We Know about Mathematics Curricula?" *Journal of Mathematical Behavior,* 13(1), pp. 55–80, 1994.

Schroeder, T.L., and F.K. Lester, Jr. "Developing Understanding in Mathematics via Problem Solving." In *New Directions for Elementary School Mathematics,* 1989 Yearbook. National Council of Teachers of Mathematics, Reston, VA, 1989.

Smith, J.B., V.E. Lee, and F.M. Newmann. *Instruction and Achievement in Chicago Elementary Schools.* Consortium on Chicago School Research, Chicago, 2001.

Sowder, J. "Estimation and Number Sense." *Handbook of Research on Mathematics Teaching and Learning,* pp. 243–275, D.A. Grouws, ed., Macmillan Publishing Company, New York, 1992.

Stevenson, H.W., and J.W. Stigler. *The Learning Gap.* Simon & Schuster, New York, 1992.

Stigler, J.W., and J. Hiebert. "Understanding and Improving Classroom Mathematics Instruction: An Overview of the TIMSS Study." *Phi Delta Kappan,* 79(1), pp. 14–21.

Stigler, J.W., and M. Perry. "Mathematics Learning in Japanese, Chinese, and American Classrooms." G.B. Saxe and M. Gearhart, eds., *New Directions for Child Development, No. 41: Children's Mathematics.* Jossey Bass, San Francisco, CA, 1988.

Thornton, C.A. "Emphasizing Thinking Strategies in Basic Fact Instruction." *Journal for Research in Mathematics Education,* 9 (3), pp. 214–227, 1978.

Thornton, C.A. "Solution Strategies: Subtraction Number Facts." *Educational Studies in Mathematics,* 21 (1), pp. 241–263, 1990a.

Thornton, C.A. "Strategies for the Basic Facts." *Mathematics for the Young Child,* pp. 133–151, J.N. Payne, ed. National Council of Teachers of Mathematics, Reston, VA, 1990b.

Whiteaker, M., G.L. Waddoups, and M. Perry. "Implementing a New Mathematics Curriculum: Constructing Models for Success." Paper presented at annual meeting of the American Educational Research Association, New Orleans, 1994.

Components and Features Guide

The Components and Features Guide presents reduced-size curriculum pages and descriptive boxes that cover each element of *Math Trailblazers*.

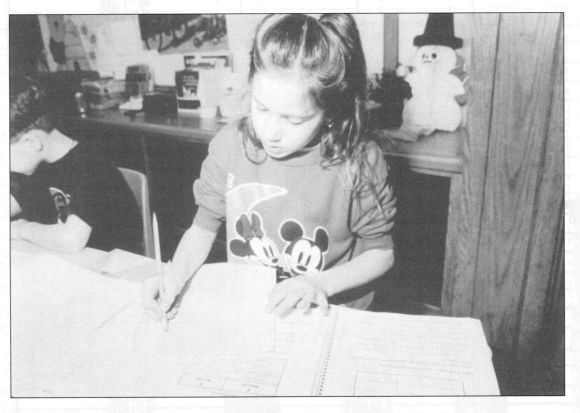

Students use Activity and Game Pages, which are provided within the lessons.

Components of *Math Trailblazers*

The following pages offer a walk-through of the *Teacher Resource Book* and the *Teacher Implementation Guide.*

TEACHER RESOURCE BOOK (TRB)

The *Teacher Resource Book* is a black and white, nonconsumable, comprehensive guide providing essential background information about materials, including lesson guides for day-to-day planning, instruction, and assessment. This book is divided by tabs into the following sections:

- Overview
- Ongoing Content
- Mathematical Strands
- Kindergarten Month-by-Month
- Thematic Units

ONGOING CONTENT

- Calendar Connections
- Problem Solving in the Kindergarten Day
- Data Collection: How Many? How Much? How Far?
- Counting Connections

Each component contains Background information and teaching ideas.

MATHEMATICAL STRANDS

- Patterns
- Number and Operations
- Geometry
- Measurement

Each strand contains a Strand Outline and a Background.

KINDERGARTEN MONTH-BY-MONTH

Each month contains Letters Home, Unit Outlines, Observational Assessment Record, Planner, Lesson Guides, and Blackline Masters.

THEMATIC UNITS (OPTIONAL)

- Buildings
- On the Go
- Crawly Creatures

There is one Background for all three units.

Each unit contains a Letter Home, Unit Outline, Lesson Guides, and Blackline Masters.

TEACHER IMPLEMENTATION GUIDE (TIG)

The *Teacher Implementation Guide* is a black and white, nonconsumable, reference guide for teachers, containing program philosophy, overview, and in-depth reference documents, including an Assessment section.

ADMINISTRATOR HANDBOOK

- Describes important components of a math implementation.
- Strategies for administrators to successfully guide implementation
- Blackline Masters for presentations to staff, parents, or other audiences
- Important sections for administrators from *Teacher Implementation Guides*
- black and white, nonconsumable

Overview

This section outlines the philosophy and components of *Math Trailblazers* kindergarten.

Math Trailblazers
Kindergarten Curriculum

Overview

Philosophy

The *Math Trailblazers*® kindergarten curriculum is built on the tenet that kindergartners are naturally curious and learn best when they can manipulate and interact directly with their environment. Our goals are to combine what is known about good mathematics instruction, particularly as outlined in the *Principles and Standards for School Mathematics* (National Council of Teachers of Mathematics, 2000) with the best instructional practice for young children. We created lessons that are developmentally appropriate and that allow children to build their own understanding of mathematical concepts.

Mathematical concepts are developed through the solving of realistic problems, open-ended activities, children's literature, and a variety of problem-solving strategies and materials. Involvement in the program will help students see mathematics as an important and exciting part of their lives, not just a school subject.

Many disciplines are integrated with the mathematics in *Math Trailblazers*, but the primary ties are to science and language arts. We take advantage of young children's natural curiosity by giving them access to tools for scientific and mathematical investigation. In this way, young children [...] their own learning. In kindergarten, students begin using important tools of s[...] data tables—as part of simple activities where children collect, organize, and [...] texts. The introduction in kindergarten of these tools and the simple explorati[...] foundation for scientific investigations in succeeding grades of *Math Trailbla[...]

The link between mathematics and children's literature is strong within *Math [...] not only in offering children opportunities to discover mathematical connectio[...] contexts, but also to create an environment for posing problems to solve and q[...]

Developing communication skills is an important goal of the *Math Trailblaze[...] encouraged to communicate about their mathematical thinking in a number [...] drawing pictures, and acting out situations using manipulatives. They are enc[...] using pictures, invented spelling, and adult recording. Over the course of the [...] communication skills progresses and we see that teachers modify their practi[...]

The following ideas helped frame the creation of the *Math Trailblazers* kinde[...]

Prior Knowledge. Young children already possess a great deal of mathemat[...] begin their formal school careers. Through play, children often develop some[...] as addition, subtraction, multiplication, and division, as well as problem-solv[...] tering them in formal school instruction. The *Math Trailblazers* program seek[...] edge to formal school knowledge and to provide concrete experiences with s[...] concepts, such as fractions, multiplication, and division. These kindergarten [...] for more extensive work with these topics in later grades. Activities are frequ[...] involve natural student language, and rely on children's innate problem-solvi[...] that students master sophisticated concepts at this point, only that they are in[...] stage in a developmentally appropriate manner.

Children's Natural Language. Critical thinking and problem-solving skills [...] open-ended activities and student discourse. The frequent use of questions in t[...] determine student mastery of a topic, but rather to help students make connecti[...] and new information or concepts. The questions are carefully worded to provid[...] construct new understandings.

Kindergarten • Math Trailblazers Kinderg[...]

Young children learn through verbal interactions as well as play. The kindergarten lessons in *Math Trailblazers* utilize large groups, small groups, and partner work to encourage student discussion. Children tell mathematical stories using their own natural language, which then helps them make connections to more formal mathematical language, vocabulary, and concepts.

Equity. The best way to address the wide range of abilities and cognitive needs found in a typical class of students is through open-ended activities. Similar concepts and skills are presented many times throughout the year, and because of the open-ended nature of the activities in *Math Trailblazers*, children are given an opportunity to grasp the concepts at their developmental level. Students with more sophisticated mathematical knowledge may apply and learn more advanced skills, while at the same time children who are at an earlier stage of development may also use what they know to solve problems successfully.

The *Math Trailblazers* kindergarten curriculum brings challenging mathematics to all children. It was designed with the knowledge that kindergarten classrooms and kindergarten children are quite diverse. There is diversity in the way that each district's kindergarten day is organized. For example, the hours of daily attendance range from two to six hours, and the amount of time assigned to each subject varies. There is diversity in the preschool experiences that children bring to school and, consequently, there are differences in the instructional needs of students. Finally, there is diversity in the educational expectations of teachers, administrators, and parents.

Given this diversity, the *Teacher Resource Book* contains a series of activities that can meet the needs of a wide range of classrooms.

The goal of the kindergarten curriculum is to provide all kindergarten teachers with a way of integrating mathematics into their classrooms. The program is flexible and compatible with a variety of teaching methods. All that is required is a belief that mathematics instruction should be meaningful, multifaceted, and engaging, and a conviction that children should be valued as thinkers and communicators.

How the *Teacher Resource Book* Is Organized

In designing this book the authors of *Math Trailblazers* considered several factors about kindergarten. First, kindergarten classrooms are very diverse. Second, most kindergarten teachers do not ordinarily break their teaching into subject areas. The *Math Trailblazers* kindergarten curriculum introduces challenging mathematics into the school day. To address a wide range of mathematical skills and concepts, the *Teacher Resource Book* is divided into four general sections: Ongoing Content, Mathematical Strands, Kindergarten: Month-by-Month, and Thematic Units.

Ongoing Content. This section deals with mathematical ideas that students explore throughout the curriculum. They are revisited over the course of the year providing all students with opportunities for growth. Components of this ongoing work are:

- Calendar Connections
- Problem Solving in the Kindergarten Day
- Data Collection: How Many? How Much? How Far?
- Counting Connections

Mathematical Strands. This section contains a Background and Outline for the mathematical content of the Month-by-Month activities in the following section. The Background provides an overview of the content and the Outline shows the distribution of the content over the year. The following strands form the basis for the mathematics distributed across the Month-by-Month lessons.

- Patterns
- Number and Operations
- Geometry
- Measurement

2   Kindergarten • Math Trailblazers Kindergarten Curriculum • Overview

Overview — The Overview states the philosophy of the *Math Trailblazers* kindergarten curriculum. This document also explains how the book is organized.

Components & Features

Ongoing Content deals with mathematical ideas that students explore throughout the curriculum.

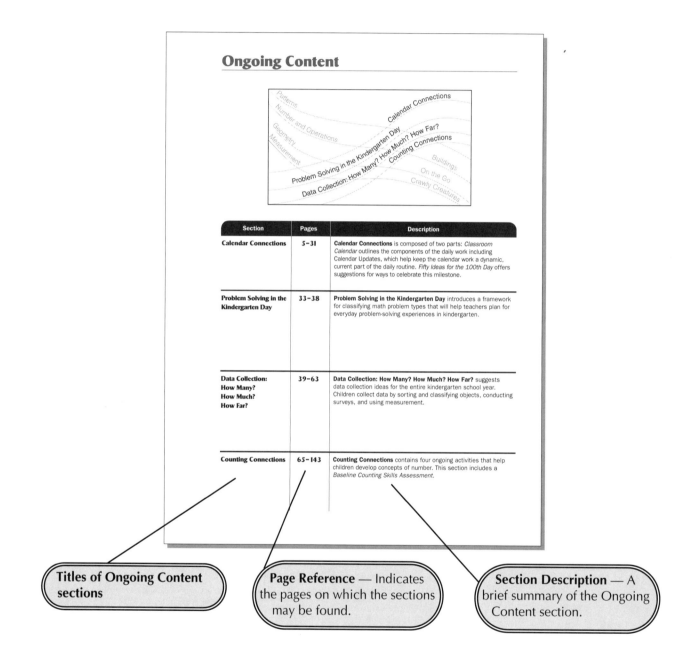

Ongoing Content

Section	Pages	Description
Calendar Connections	5–31	**Calendar Connections** is composed of two parts: *Classroom Calendar* outlines the components of the daily work including Calendar Updates, which help keep the calendar work a dynamic, current part of the daily routine. *Fifty Ideas for the 100th Day* offers suggestions for ways to celebrate this milestone.
Problem Solving in the Kindergarten Day	33–38	**Problem Solving in the Kindergarten Day** introduces a framework for classifying math problem types that will help teachers plan for everyday problem-solving experiences in kindergarten.
Data Collection: How Many? How Much? How Far?	39–63	**Data Collection: How Many? How Much? How Far?** suggests data collection ideas for the entire kindergarten school year. Children collect data by sorting and classifying objects, conducting surveys, and using measurement.
Counting Connections	65–143	**Counting Connections** contains four ongoing activities that help children develop concepts of number. This section includes a *Baseline Counting Skills Assessment*.

Titles of Ongoing Content sections

Page Reference — Indicates the pages on which the sections may be found.

Section Description — A brief summary of the Ongoing Content section.

Calendar Connections

Calendar Connections includes a guide to setting up a calendar center for daily activities and ideas for the 100th day.

Section Tab — Used to separate the main sections of the *Teacher Resource Book.*

Calendar Connections

Calendar work is, to some extent, a fixture in most kindergarten classrooms. The day, the date, the number of days in school, and the weather are the most common components. Mathematical topics that are routinely integrated into calendar work are:

- counting (ones, fives, tens)
- understanding of hundreds, tens, ones
- daily schedule (time and duration)
- visual and number patterns
- graphing

Math Trailblazers extends this traditional calendar work by offering children an opportunity to acquire a feel for the pattern and rhythm of our number system. Children acquire oral language through exposure to words within a meaningful context. Similarly, the calendar provides exposure to numbers in a meaningful context. It is through the naturally occurring repetition of numbers, connected with both the monthly calendar cycle and the accumulation of school days, that all children have an opportunity to participate in the journey to numeracy.

The calendar setting also provides a context for solving problems and for exploring relationships among numbers. The opportunity for making connections among models, words, and symbols is constant. Problems that have multiple solutions, multiple solution paths, [...]dar and connected activities.

The Calendar Connections section has two parts:

Classroom Calendar outlines the daily work compone[...]a weather graph, and a Centipede to Count On. Calen[...]Month section, help keep the calendar work a dynami[...]gresses and students mature, new instructional empha[...]introduce the labeling of days as "Yesterday," "Today,"[...]rather to examine later as an idea, when you can use a[...]explore the idea more meaningfully. Updates are pres[...]out the year, approximately one every two weeks.

Fifty Ideas for the 100th Day offers a range of sugges[...]in anticipation of the event, while others are done on[...]counting the days of school until the end of the year. [...]benchmark number in the kindergarten curriculum.

The Calendar Connections should take 15 to 20 minut[...]ties, as well as the other kinds of knowledge they ad[...]

Classroom Calendar

Key Content

- Measuring time on a calendar.
- Identifying, describing, and extending patterns.
- Representing numbers using ten frames.
- Counting by ones, fives, and tens.
- Developing number sense for hundreds, tens, and ones.
- Collecting, organizing, graphing, and analyzing data.

Materials

Pattern for the Centipede Blackline Master, Page 14
Ten Frames Blackline Master, Page 15
Weather Graph Labels Blackline Master, Page 16

Following is an outline of the classroom calendar components for you to prepare for the beginning of the year. Although there is an initial investment of some time, you will use these pieces for the entire year. Dedicate a section of bulletin board or wall to the display. An example is shown in Figure[...]The individual pieces are labeled "A" through "D" for easy reference.

Materials List — Everything the teacher and students need for the lesson.

Fifty Ideas for the 100th Day

Materials

Note Home Blackline Masters (English/Spanish), Pages 27–28
100 Day Eyeglasses Blackline Master, Page 29
Hubert Hundred Blackline Master, Page 30
100 Chart Blackline Master, Page 31

This section of Calendar Connections contains ideas for helping students celebrate the one hundredth day of school. The suggestions fall into two main categories: those you need to start before the big day and those designed to be implemented on the 100th day. Many of the ideas integrate mathematics into other curricular areas. The Problem Solving icon 🔍 appears periodically when there is a strong opportunity to extend mathematics in the activity. There are, for example, many chances to reinforce the relationship of 10 to 100.

Ideas for Activities Leading Up to the 100th Day

1. **One Hundred Day Week.** Consider making the celebration a week-long event. The opportunity to explore the number 100 in a variety of contexts will help children understand the importance of this benchmark number.

2. **Reading One Hundred Books.** Keep a count of books read to the children. This is a good opportunity for the children to use tallying to keep a running total. Try to reach one hundred close to the hundredth day.

3. **Ways to Say 100.** Have children learn to say one hundred in several different languages. For example:

	100	
		Cien (Spanish)
Hiyaku (he-ah-koo) (Japanese)		Cento
Cent (French)		

Components & Features

Problem Solving in the Kindergarten Day

This section outlines a systematic plan so that students have an opportunity to solve many different types of problems.

Problem Solving in the Kindergarten Day

Recent research shows that kindergarten children are capable of dealing with many different kinds of math problems. In this section we present a conceptual framework to help you bring a variety of problem types into the school day and to help you think about your children's mathematical learning.

"When the teaching and learning of mathematics is approached from a problem-solving perspective, concepts and procedural skills are developed on the basis of problem settings that require those concepts and skills. A problem-solving approach helps young children make sense of the concepts, skills, and relationships that are essential in an early childhood mathematics curriculum." (Worth, 1990)

Most children begin to develop problem-solving abilities before their formal schooling begins. Consider the following vignette:

Sasha is almost three years old. One night she asked her father if she could have a cookie. He told her that she could and asked her to bring one for everyone. There are four family members. Sasha reached into the cookie bag and brought out 3 cookies. She looked at the cookies, thought for a minute, then reached back into the bag for 1 more cookie.

Sasha knew that three cookies were not enough, and that she had to add one more. As students begin their work in school, encourage and cultivate this kind of problem-solving ability. A classroom atmosphere that enthusiastically encourages children to persevere, risk trying new ideas, and share their strategies is critical. Plan problem-solving activities to allow students enough time to explore multiple approaches to a problem and to focus on the process of seeking the answer as well as on the correct solution. Problems are no longer viewed as just a way to apply previously taught skills and procedures but as a way to introduce new mathematical concepts that will allow students to construct meaning within their own internal framework.

The kindergarten day provides a wealth of problem-solving opportunities. They can be found within a thematic unit, in planning for a school event, during shared literature time, or in carrying out everyday classroom experiences.

When creating problems from these varied contexts, it is important that students encounter a range of different kinds of problems. The work of Thomas Carpenter and his colleagues (Carpenter, Fennema, and Peterson, 1987; Carpenter, Carey, and Kouba, 1990) with the Cognitively Guided Instruction Project (CGI) provides insights that can help teachers with this process. They devised a classification scheme for problems most adults would solve by addition, subtraction, multiplication, or division. CGI classifies these mathematical situations as:

- join
- separate
- part-part-whole
- compare
- multiplication
- measurement division
- partitive division

Sample problems illustrating each of the CGI prob-[...] dents should be exposed to problems from each of[...] to include opportunities for weekly problem solvi[...]

When solving problems, your students should hav[...] strategies, which commonly include direct model[...] working from facts they know (reasoning from kn[...] room at all times. You can expect children to use d[...] development.

It is important to observe students as they problem [...] Use the *Individual Assessment Record Sheet* locate[...] *Guide* to record their progress.

Kindergarten • Ongoi[...]

Section Tab — Used to separate the main sections of the *Teacher Resource Book*.

Example — Gives a specific word problem that fits in that problem category.

Workspace — Space for teacher notes or additional examples.

Problem Type — Specifies one of seven different problem types.

BLACKLINE MASTER

Kindergarten • Ongoing Content • Problem Solving in the Kindergarten Day

37

Cognitively Guided Instruction Problem Types Worksheet

Problem Type	Example	Workspace
Join—Result Unknown	Kyle had 8 action figures. His father gave him 3 new ones. How many does he have now?	
Separate—Result Unknown	Luke had 8 cookies. He ate 6. How many cookies does he have?	
Part/Part/Whole— Whole Unknown	Ian has some action figures. He has 8 good guys and 3 bad guys. How many action figures does Ian have?	
Join—Change Unknown	Janice had 9 stickers. Her mother gave her some more. Janice then had 16 stickers. How many stickers did Janice's mother give her?	
Compare—Difference Unknown	Leah had 12 baseball cards. Jim has 5 baseball cards. How many more cards does Leah have than Jim.	
Compare—Compare Quantity (Q2) Unknown	Michael had 4 marbles. Leah has 8 more than Michael. How many marbles does Leah have?	
Compare—Referent (Q1) Unknown	Lamar has some markers. Robin has 17 markers, 7 fewer than Lamar. How many markers does Lamar have?	

ONGOING CONTENT

Data Collection: How Many? How Much? How Far?

This section contains suggestions for data collection experiences to include throughout the year.

Data Collection: How Many? How Much? How Far?

Children become more actively engaged in problem solving when they work with numbers that come from their own experience and are meaningful to them. Whether children are collecting data by sorting and classifying objects, conducting surveys, or using measurement, activities involving student-collected data are a rich source for these kinds of numbers. Data collection has the added benefit of being a natural way to integrate mathematics into multiple curricular areas. The models of algebraic thinking in the context of data collection lay the foundation for future exploration. You should include data collection opportunities one or more times each week.

Key Content

- Sorting and classifying objects.
- Collecting, organizing, graphing, and analyzing data.

Sorting and Comparing

This section outlines many suggestions for sorting and comparing. In Figure 1, children are shown sorting apples by color. Sorting activities can be an important element in developing children's language and reasoning skills. From the beginning of the year, children need to grow accustomed to listening to one another as they explain their thinking. Sorting activities are a good place to start.

Figure 1: Children sorting apples by color

By the second or third month of the school year, it may be appropriate to introduce Venn diagrams in sorting activities. It is best to begin by sorting concrete objects. Apples may be sorted and compared according to their colors. A Venn diagram provides a tool for organizing such a sort. Venn diagrams can be made from large plastic hoops or from string or yarn tied to make two overlapping circles when placed on the floor. See Figure 2.

Section Tab — Used to separate the main sections of the *Teacher Resource Book*.

Monthly Ideas — A list of events and suggestions for related data collection activities for each month.

A Year's Worth of Ideas

Following is a list of ideas for data collection experiences that you can link to the Calendar Connections. Add any date used in the classroom to the class calendar. These are only suggestions. Other ideas will occur as you move through the year. Children often offer great ideas about how to sort a set of objects. Often, a book is suggested to launch the data collection. Check availability in your local library. Find the list of ideas for each month and insert them into the appropriate month in the Kindergarten: Month-by-Month section of this book.

September has:

National Chicken Month
Does your family eat chicken? Yes/No
How do you like chicken prepared?
How do you like your eggs prepared? Ask students to vote on their favorite ways. Use pictures to represent the data on the graph.

Carle, Eric. *Rooster's Off to See the World.* Little Simon, New York, 2002.
Ernst, Lisa Campbell. *Zinnia and Dot.* Viking, New York, 1992.
Galdone, Paul. *The Little Red Hen.* Houghton Mifflin Co., Boston, 1985.
Heller, Ruth. *Chickens Aren't the Only Ones.* Paper Star, Topeka, KS, 1990.
Hutchins, Pat. *Rosie's Walk.* Macmillan, New York, 1968.
Kellogg, Steven. *Chicken Little.* William Morrow, New York, 1987.
Polacco, Patricia. *Chicken Sunday.* Paper Star, Topeka, KS, 1998.

Fall Hat Week
How can we sort a group of hats? (size, color, shape)
Have each child bring in a hat. Brainstorm various ways to sort them. Use the hats as data points on the graph.
Geringer, Laura. *A Three Hat Day.* Harper & Row, New York, 1987.
Morris, Ann. *Hats, Hats, Hats.* Scholastic, New York, 1995.
Slobodkina, Esphyr. *Caps for Sale.* HarperCollins, New York, 1987.

Farm Animals Week (third week in September)
What is your favorite farm

Counting Connections

This section provides ideas for incorporating daily activities into classroom routines.

Counting Connections

The *Baseline Counting Skills Assessment* provides a framework for assessing and recording individual student's counting skills and concepts. This will help you differentiate by building on the knowledge that each child brings to school.

The following activities, along with the Ongoing Calendar work and the Month-by-Month Lessons, provide varied opportunities for children to practice counting skills, to attach meaning to counting, and to develop other number relationships.

These activities help students make connections between ways to represent num[...]luding visual (ten frames and dot patterns) and symbolic (numerals), as well as concrete representations [...] objects).

The following ongoing activities work well in stations and provide multiple [...] opportunities.

Counting Boxes provide ongoing, differentiated counting practice. The a[...] number cards for which the child builds sets of objects.

Counting Bags contain teacher-selected sets of objects for students to [...]

Number Books develop connections between different representation[...] numerals, and student-created pictures.

Baseline Counting Skills Assessment

This performance assessment provides [...] framework for [...] and will facilitate helping [...] ALL children move forward in c[...]structing and applying basic understanding of number.

Key Content

- Orally counting forward to 30.
- Orally counting backward from 10.
- Counting using one-to-one correspondence.
- Demonstrating an understanding of cardinality.
- Demonstrating an understanding of order irrelevance.

Materials

For the Teacher
Baseline Counting Skills Assessment Observational Assessment Record Blackline Masters, Pages 69–70
30 square-inch tiles

Teaching the Activity

Plan to use the *Baseline Counting Skills Assessment* as early in the year as you can manag[...] will help to determine where each child is in his or her attainment of basic counting sk[...] instance, you may find that some children can accurately say the number names [...] developing their conceptual understanding of the meaning of numbers and cou[...]

Many children come to Kindergarten able to count well beyond 30. At the [...] very limited experience with numbers. The irregular patterns of the tee[...] [...]re repeated practice for some children. [...] [...]line assessment informatio[...] [...]addressing a wide vari[...] [...]ills Assess[...] [...]d to help yo[...]

Baseline Counting Skills Assessment
OBSERVATIONAL ASSESSMENT RECORD

- **A1** Can students orally count forward to 30?
- **A2** Can students orally count backward from 10?
- **A3** Can students count 30 objects using one-to-one correspondence?
- **A4** Do students understand that the last number counted indicates the number of objects in the set? (cardinality)
- **A5** Do students understand that a given set of objects can be counted in any order without altering the outcome? (order irrelevance)
- **A6**

Name	A1	A2	A3	A4	A5	A6	Comments
1.							
2.							
3.							
4.							
5.							
6.							

Key Content — Lists important mathematical ideas students will encounter.

Materials List — Everything the teacher and students need for the lesson.

Teaching the Activity — Describes what teacher and students will do in each activity.

Assessment Indicators — This list consists of skills, behavior, and knowledge you should look for as you observe students working on activities in this section.

Assessment Icons — Each of the Assessment Indicators is numbered and labeled with an icon (e.g., **A1** – **A5**).

Counting Connections

This section contains a series of activities that can be used to develop student counting skills throughout the year.

Counting Boxes

The counting box station activity provides differentiated opportunities for students to link numerals (abstract symbols) to sets of objects.

Key Content

• Counting and creating sets of given sizes.

Materials

For the Student
Note Home Blackline Masters (English/Spanish), Pages 75–76
one counting box containing 4 workmats and 30–40 sm... objects
4 teacher-selected number cards

For the Teacher
classroom number card organizer
library pockets or sturdy envelopes, 1 per child
Number Cards 1–20, Blackline Masters, Pages 9...
15 boxes
Workmats A–O, Blackline Masters, Pages 77–9...
15 collections of 30–40 small objects or smal...

Before the Activity

Send the *Note Home* s...
...igure 1.

Counting Bags

Children independently count and record the number of objects in a bag. The number of objects varies from 4 to 30 so each child can work at his or her own skill level to develop a broader conceptual understanding of number. Counting bags provide an opportunity for children to develop the concept of one-to-one correspondence and cardinality.

Key Content
• Counting quantities using one-to-one correspondence.
• Developing the concept of cardinality.
• Connecting symbols (numerals) to quantities.

Materials

For the Student
Note Home Blackline Masters (English/Spanish), Pages 97–98
counting bags

For the Teacher
Link Number Tags Blackline Masters, Pages 99–100
Cube Number Tags Blackline Masters, Pages 101–102
Everyday Object Number Tags Blackline Masters, Pages 103–104
Counting Bag Tracker Blackline Masters, Pages 105–106
connecting links
connecting cubes
collections of 4–30 objects
30 one-gallon size resealable plastic bags
crayons

Before the Activity

Each counting bag contains a number (4–30) of links or cubes or... matches the color. With 10 different colors of connecting cub... objects to develop 14 diff... know which bag was c... *Number Tags* (pp. 99... ...s so yo... ...nd cut a...

Number Books

Children make books for numbers one through 20 connecting number dot patterns, the written symbol, or visual patterns on the ten frame.

Key Content
• Translating between numbers, dot patterns, ten frames, and pictures.

Materials

For the Student
Number Books: Dot Patterns 0–12 Blackline Masters, Pages 109–122
Number Books: Ten Frames 1–20 Blackline Masters, Pages 123–143

Teaching the Activity

We provide you with two sets of blackline masters for students to make number books. Each page in both sets will include three representations: numbers, a visual organizer, and drawings. The *Number Books: Dot Patterns 0–12* (pp. 109–122) use number dot patterns for the visual representation. The *Number Books: Ten Frames 1–20* (pp. 123–143) use ten frames for the visual representation. Chil... the connections between the different representations as they prac... ...ing each number and d... number of objects. Se... Figure 1 for an example... ...k pages... individual decision b... ...d work...

> **Key Content** — Lists important mathematical ideas students will encounter.

> **Materials List** — Everything the teacher and students need for the lesson.

> **Before the Activity** — Covers what teachers need to prepare for the lesson ahead of time.

> **Teaching the Activity** — Describes what students will do in each activity.

Components & Features

MATHEMATICAL STRANDS

Background and Outline

The Background explains what students will learn in the strand or month and places the material in the larger context of the *Math Trailblazers* curriculum. It describes the purpose of each lesson and how lessons accomplish their goals. The Outline describes the lessons in each strand and their locations in the curriculum.

Number of Lessons — Indicates the number of lessons within each strand.

Strand Description — A brief summary of the contents of the strand.

Name of Lesson — Identifies the lesson within the strand.

Strand Icons — These icons indicate which strand is being presented.

Lesson Description — Provides a detailed look at the mathematics that will help support the activities done by students.

Number of Activities — Indicates the number of activities found within each lesson.

Outline

This section organizes both the Ongoing Content and the Mathematical Strands into a comprehensive month-by-month plan for the year.

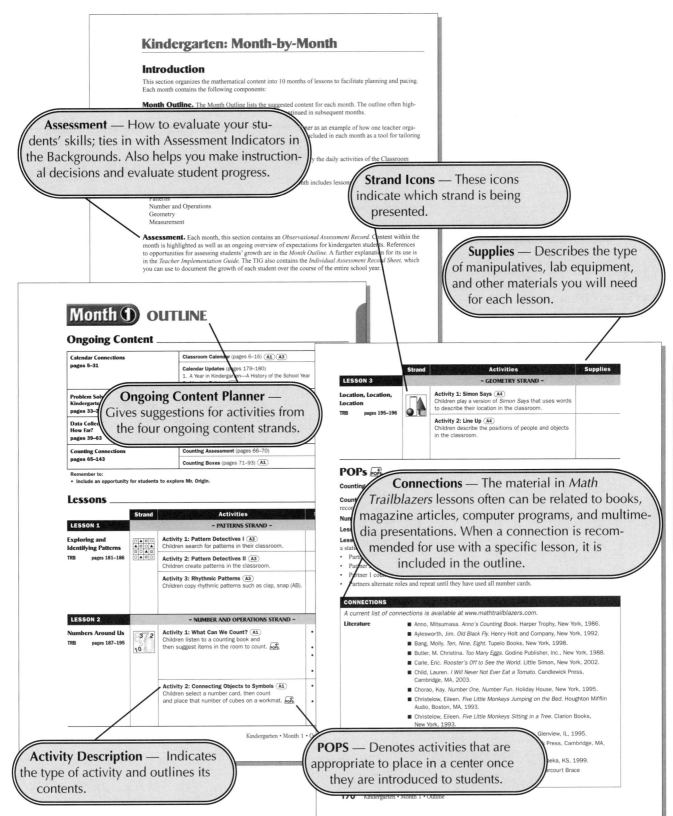

Kindergarten: Month-by-Month

Introduction

This section organizes the mathematical content into 10 months of lessons to facilitate planning and pacing. Each month contains the following components:

Month Outline. The Month Outline lists the suggested content for each month. The outline often high-... ...ntinued in subsequent months.

Assessment — How to evaluate your students' skills; ties in with Assessment Indicators in the Backgrounds. Also helps you make instructional decisions and evaluate student progress.

Strand Icons — These icons indicate which strand is being presented.

Supplies — Describes the type of manipulatives, lab equipment, and other materials you will need for each lesson.

Patterns
Number and Operations
Geometry
Measurement

Assessment. Each month, this section contains an *Observational Assessment Record*. Content within the month is highlighted as well as an ongoing overview of expectations for kindergarten students. References to opportunities for assessing students' growth are in the *Month Outline*. A further explanation for its use is in the *Teacher Implementation Guide*. The TIG also contains the *Individual Assessment Record Sheet*, which you can use to document the growth of each student over the course of the entire school year.

Month ① OUTLINE

Ongoing Content

Calendar Connections pages 5–31	**Classroom Calendar** (pages 6–16) (A1) (A3)
	Calendar Updates (pages 179–180) 1. A Year in Kindergarten—A History of the School Year
Problem Solv... Kindergarte... pages 33–3...	**Ongoing Content Planner** — Gives suggestions for activities from the four ongoing content strands.
Data Colle... How Far? pages 39–63	
Counting Connections pages 65–143	**Counting Assessment** (pages 66–70)
	Counting Boxes (pages 71–93) (A1)

Remember to:
• Include an opportunity for students to explore Mr. Origin.

Lessons

	Strand	Activities	
LESSON 1		– PATTERNS STRAND –	
Exploring and Identifying Patterns TRB pages 181–186		**Activity 1: Pattern Detectives I** (A3) Children search for patterns in their classroom.	
		Activity 2: Pattern Detectives II (A3) Children create patterns in the classroom.	
		Activity 3: Rhythmic Patterns (A3) Children copy rhythmic patterns such as clap, snap (AB).	
LESSON 2		– NUMBER AND OPERATIONS STRAND –	
Numbers Around Us TRB pages 187–195		**Activity 1: What Can We Count?** (A1) Children listen to a counting book and then suggest items in the room to count.	•
			•
			•
		Activity 2: Connecting Objects to Symbols (A1) Children select a number card, then count and place that number of cubes on a workmat.	•

Kindergarten • Month 1 • O...

	Strand	Activities	Supplies
LESSON 3		– GEOMETRY STRAND –	
Location, Location, Location TRB pages 195–196		**Activity 1: Simon Says** (A4) Children play a version of *Simon Says* that uses words to describe their location in the classroom.	
		Activity 2: Line Up (A4) Children describe the positions of people and objects in the classroom.	

POPs

Counting ...
Count... recor...
Num...
Les...
Les... a stati...
• Part...
• Partner...
• Partner 1 cou...
• Partners alternate roles and repeat until they have used all number cards.

Connections — The material in *Math Trailblazers* lessons often can be related to books, magazine articles, computer programs, and multimedia presentations. When a connection is recommended for use with a specific lesson, it is included in the outline.

CONNECTIONS

A current list of connections is available at www.mathtrailblazers.com.

Literature
■ Anno, Mitsumasa. *Anno's Counting Book*. Harper Trophy, New York, 1986.
■ Aylesworth, Jim. *Old Black Fly*. Henry Holt and Company, New York, 1992.
■ Bang, Molly. *Ten, Nine, Eight*. Tupelo Books, New York, 1998.
■ Butler, M. Christina. *Too Many Eggs*. Godine Publisher, Inc., New York, 1988.
■ Carle, Eric. *Rooster's Off to See the World*. Little Simon, New York, 2002.
■ Child, Lauren. *I Will Never Not Ever Eat a Tomato*. Candlewick Press, Cambridge, MA, 2003.
■ Chorao, Kay. *Number One, Number Fun*. Holiday House, New York, 1995.
■ Christelow, Eileen. *Five Little Monkeys Jumping on the Bed*. Houghton Mifflin Audio, Boston, MA, 1993.
■ Christelow, Eileen. *Five Little Monkeys Sitting in a Tree*. Clarion Books, New York, 1993.
... Glenview, IL, 1995.
... Press, Cambridge, MA,
...beka, KS, 1999.
...arcourt Brace

Activity Description — Indicates the type of activity and outlines its contents.

POPS — Denotes activities that are appropriate to place in a center once they are introduced to students.

170 Kindergarten • Month 1 • Outline

Components & Features

Planner

This component is a tool for organizing the content to meet the needs of your class.

Month 1 PLANNER

Ongoing Content

Calendar Connections pp. 5–31

Calendar Update	Dates
1. A Year in Kindergarten—A History of the School Year p. 179	
2. Monthly Tallying p. 180	

Problem Solving in the Kindergarten Day pp. 33–38

Week	Problem Type	Problem
One		
Two		
Three		
Four		
Five		

Data Collection: How Many? How Much? How Far? pp. 39–63

Week	Event	Type of Graph	Question
One			
Two			
Three			
Four			
Five			

Calendar Connections — Space for scheduling new and continuing calendar activities.

Problem Solving — Space for recording problem types and sample problems to be presented during each week as part of ongoing problem-solving activities.

Dates — Space to record scheduling of lessons from the four content strands.

Data Collection — Space for recording data collection events that are part of the ongoing activities.

Counting Connections pp. 65–143

Activity	Dates
Counting Assessment pp. 66–70	
Counting Boxes pp. 71–93	

Remember to include an opportunity for students to explore Mr. Origin.

Lessons

Patterns pp. 181–186

Lesson 1: Exploring and Identifying Patterns pp. 181–186	Dates
Activity 1: Pattern Detectives I p. 181	
Activity 2: Pattern Detectives II p. 182	
Activity 3: Rhythmic Patterns pp. 182–186	

Number and Operations

Lesson 2: Numbers Around Us pp. 187–195	Dates
Activity 1: What Can We Count? pp. 187–188, 191–194	
2: Connecting Objects to Symbols 188–189	

Observational Assessment Record and Calendar Updates

The *Observational Assessment Record* is a form used to record observations of students' progress. The Calendar Updates keep the calendar a dynamic part of the mathematics curriculum by periodically introducing new activities.

Month Tab — Used to separate the Calendar Updates for each month.

Calendar Update 1

A Year in Kindergarten–A History of the School Year

Key Content

- Exploring time and its measurement.
- Developing an awareness of the passage of time.
- Measuring time on a calendar.

When the first month of school draws to a close, have children reflect on all that took place. As a group, brainstorm the month's events and have students ask each other questions about the events. In particular, include the story of the weather graph. Each child can then draw pictures and dictate sentences to illustrate one of the ideas. Bind the individual stories together into one class book for the month. This book will become a treasured history of the school year.

Later, take the monthly class books apart to include individual work in the child's own folder. Some teachers find this to be... journal entries and send t...

Key Content — Highlights the mathematical focus.

Assessment Indicators — They highlight the skills and concepts you should look for as you observe students working on activities in the month.

Dictated Sentences

Figure 1: Examples of student work

Kindergarten • Month

OBSERVATIONAL ASSESSMENT RECORD

Month 1

- **A1** Can students use numbers to describe sets of objects?
- **A2** Do students have a developmentally appropriate strategy for problem solving?
- **A3** Can students identify and describe patterns?
- **A4** Do students use spatial language to describe relationships?
- **A5**

Name	A1	A2	A3	A4	A5	Comments
1.						
2.						
3.						
4.						
5.						
6.						
7.						
8.						
9.						
10.						
11.						
12.						
13.						

Assessment Icons — Each of the Assessment Indicators is numbered and labeled with an icon (e.g., **A1** – **A5**).

Additional lines are provided to help document students' progress with other content.

Kindergarten • Month 1 • Observational Assessment Record **173**

Illustrations — Show samples of student work or help explain the activities.

Components & Features

Lessons

This section has lessons from the four mathematical strands organized on a monthly basis. The months are numbered to accommodate a variety of school scheduling schemes.

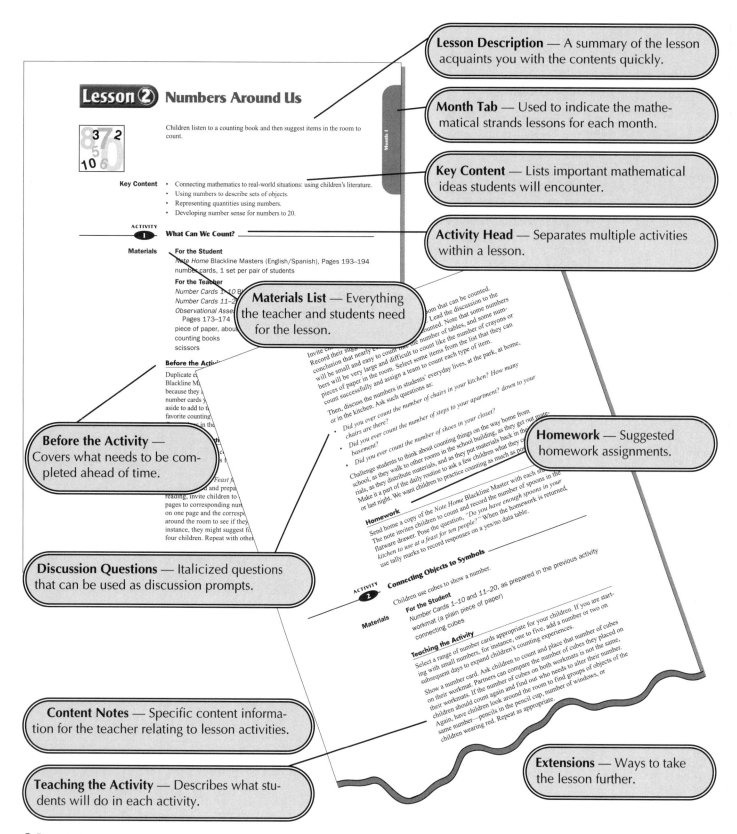

Lesson Description — A summary of the lesson acquaints you with the contents quickly.

Month Tab — Used to indicate the mathematical strands lessons for each month.

Key Content — Lists important mathematical ideas students will encounter.

Activity Head — Separates multiple activities within a lesson.

Materials List — Everything the teacher and students need for the lesson.

Before the Activity — Covers what needs to be completed ahead of time.

Discussion Questions — Italicized questions that can be used as discussion prompts.

Homework — Suggested homework assignments.

Content Notes — Specific content information for the teacher relating to lesson activities.

Teaching the Activity — Describes what students will do in each activity.

Extensions — Ways to take the lesson further.

Lesson ② Numbers Around Us

Children listen to a counting book and then suggest items in the room to count.

Key Content
- Connecting mathematics to real-world situations: using children's literature.
- Using numbers to describe sets of objects.
- Representing quantities using numbers.
- Developing number sense for numbers to 20.

ACTIVITY 1 What Can We Count?

Materials **For the Student**
Note Home Blackline Masters (English/Spanish), Pages 193–194
number cards, 1 set per pair of students

For the Teacher
Number Cards 1–10 B...
Number Cards 11–2...
Observational Asse...
Pages 173–174
piece of paper, abou...
counting books
scissors

Lessons, continued

Note Home

The *Note Home* is designed to go out under the teacher's signature and usually accompanies a homework assignment or request for family involvement. English and Spanish versions of the Note Home are provided.

Note Home

Month 1—Exploring and Identifying Patterns

Date: _____

Dear Family Member:

In class we have been exploring and identifying repeating patterns in the world around us. Please help your child choose clothing with a pattern to wear to school (blue stripe/red stripe; thin line/thick line) on _____. If you have no clothing with a pattern, your child can make a simple pattern on a strip of paper and pin it to a plain shirt. Also, help your child look for and bring in a patterned item from home (game board, pillow case, etc.) on the same day. See the picture below for examples.

Thank you for your support.

Sincerely,

_____

Copyright © Kendall/Hunt Publishing Company

BLACKLINE MASTER   Kindergarte

Carta al hogar

Mes 1—Explorar e identificar patrones

Fecha: _____

Estimado miembro de familia:

En la clase, hemos estado explorando e identificando patrones que se repiten en el mundo que nos rodea. Por favor ayude a su hijo/a a escoger ropa que tenga un patrón (por ejemplo, raya azul/raya roja; raya fina/raya gruesa) para traer a la escuela el día _____. Si no tiene ropa con patrones, su hijo/a puede diseñar un patrón sencillo usando una tira de papel y prenderlo con imperdibles a una camiseta lisa. Además, ayude a su hijo/a a buscar y traer a la escuela el mismo día un objeto de la casa que muestre un patrón (un tablero de un juego, una funda de almohada, etc.). En el dibujo que aparece en esta página verá algunos ejemplos.

Gracias por su apoyo.

Atentamente,

_____

Copyright © Kendall/Hunt Publishing Company

Art — Each *Note Home* includes an illustration relating to the lesson's activities.

186   Kindergarten • Month 1 • Lesson 1   BLACKLINE MASTER

Lessons, continued

Blackline Masters and Transparency Masters

Background

Thematic Units are an optional part of the kindergarten program. They provide three illustrations of how the mathematical and pedagogical ideas of the previous sections can be woven together into thematic units.

Unit Icons — Identify the thematic unit being presented.

Number of Lessons — Indicates the number of lessons in each unit.

Unit Description — Provides a brief summary of the contents of the unit.

Background — Gives an overview of the *Math Trailblazers* approach to thematic units.

Resources — Pointers to additional information on the ideas covered in the unit are sometimes included.

Components & Features

Unit Outline

Buildings
Unit Outline

	Number of Parts	Description	Supplies
LESSON 1 **City at Night**	1	Children cut out silhouettes of sky-scrapers to make a City at Night mural. The buildings are used for measurement and data collection.	• self-adhesive notes • want ad pages • yellow construction paper • index cards • scissors • glue • black crayons • connecting links • dark-colored paper
LESSON 2 **Building with Blocks**	1	Children construct buildings in a center to help them develop comparison, classification, numeration, fraction, and geometric concepts.	• collection of building blocks • construction paper
LESSON 3 **Buildings Around Our School**	2	**PART 1:** Students discuss the kinds of buildings they expect to see around their school. **PART 2:** Students list, count, and compare the buildings found in a series of walks around the school.	• crayons or markers

Lesson Description — Outlines the content of the lesson.

Supplies — Describes the types of manipulatives, materials, and other supplies essential for each lesson.

Number of Parts — Indicates the number of parts in the lesson. A part might correspond to one day's work.

CONNECTIONS
A current list of connections is available at www.mathtrailblazers.com.

Literature
■ Barton, Byron. *Building a House*. Scott Foresman, Glenview, IL, 1999.
■ Dorros, Arthur. *This Is My House*. Holiday House, New York, 1996.
■ Gibbons, Gail. *How a House Is Built*. Scholastic, New York, 1998. (Lesson 4)
■ Gibbons, Gail. *Up Goes the Skyscraper!* McMillan Publishers, New York, 1981. (Lesson 1)
■ Hoberman, Mary Ann. *A House Is a House for Me*. Puffin Books, New York, 1982. (Lesson 4)
■ Jackson, Thomas Campbell. *Hammers, Nails, Planks and Paint*. Cartwheel Books, New York, 1994.
■ Liebman, Dan. *I Want to Be a Builder*. Firefly Book, Inc., Buffalo, NY, 2003.
■ McLerran, Alice. *Roxaboxen*. Lothrop, Lee & Shepard, New York, 1991.
■ Morris, Ann. *Houses and Homes*. HarperCollins Publishers, New York, 1992.
■ Ringgold, Faith. *Tar Beach*. Random House, New York, 1991. (Lesson 4)
■ Seltzer, Isadore. *The House I Live In*. Scholastic, New York, 1992. "New Mexico Magazine. Santa Fe, NM, 1984.
■ Smith, Mary Lou. "Grandmother's Adobe Doll House." New Mexico Magazine. Santa Fe, NM, 1984.
■ Wilcox, Charlotte. *A Skyscraper Story*. Carolrhoda Books, Inc., Minneapolis, MN, 1990. (Lesson 1)
■ Zelinsky, Paul O. *The Maid and the Mouse and the Odd-shaped House*. Puffin Unicorn Books, New York, 1981. (Lesson 5)

Software

Connections — The material in *Math Trailblazers* lessons often can be related to books, magazine articles, and computer programs. When a connection is recommended for use with a specific lesson, it is included in the outline.

The *Teacher Implementation Guide* is the reference manual for *Math Trailblazers.* Information in the *Teacher Implementation Guide* can be roughly categorized into three groups: general background about *Math Trailblazers,* specific information about the program, and deep background about important math and science concepts.

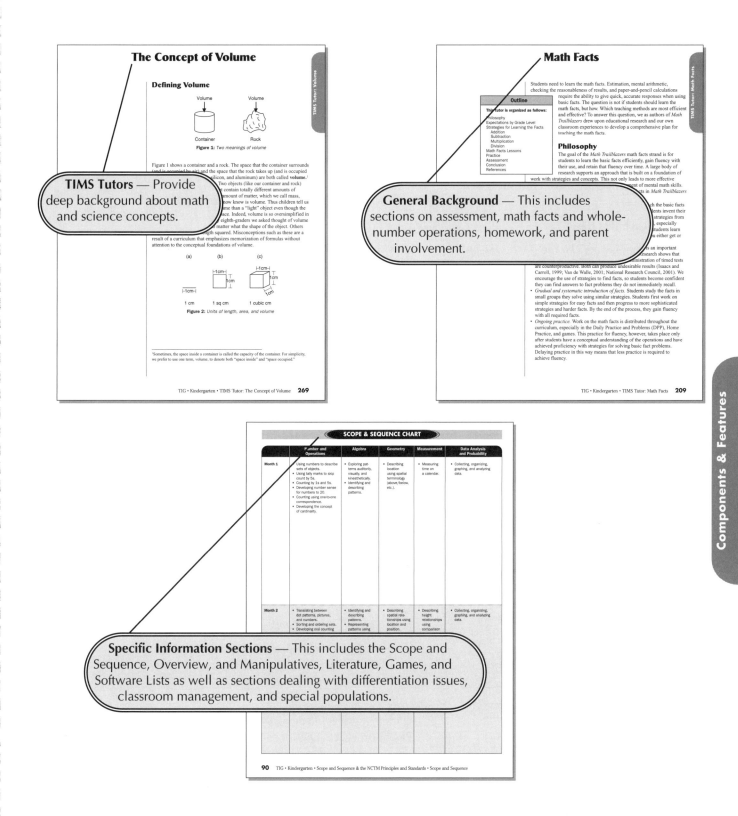

TIMS Tutors — Provide deep background about math and science concepts.

General Background — This includes sections on assessment, math facts and whole-number operations, homework, and parent involvement.

Specific Information Sections — This includes the Scope and Sequence, Overview, and Manipulatives, Literature, Games, and Software Lists as well as sections dealing with differentiation issues, classroom management, and special populations.

Quick Reference Guide

What I Want to Know	Where to Find It
How do I organize the pieces in the curriculum?	*Teacher Resource Book*–Overview
Where are the Lesson Guides?	*Teacher Resource Book*–Month-by-Month and Thematic Units
What does this lesson cover?	*Teacher Resource Book*–Outline *Teacher Resource Book*–Lesson Guide
What are the "big ideas" in this lesson or the entire unit?	*Teacher Resource Book*–Outline *Teacher Resource Book*–Lesson Guide–Key Content
What do I need to prepare for this lesson?	*Teacher Resource Book*–Lesson Guide–Before the Activity *Teacher Resource Book*–Lesson Guide–Materials List
What manipulatives do I need for this lesson?	*Teacher Resource Book*–Outline *Teacher Resource Book*–Lesson Guide–Materials List
How do I teach this lesson?	*Teacher Resource Book*–Lesson Guide
How do I organize my class to do this lesson?	*Teacher Resource Book*–Lesson Guide
Where are the Blackline Masters?	*Teacher Resource Book*–Lesson Guide
What information is available for parents?	*Teacher Resource Book*–Notes Home *Teacher Implementation Guide*–Parent Brochure
What should I assign as homework?	*Teacher Resource Book*–Lesson Guide–Homework *Teacher Implementation Guide*–Homework Guide section
How do I assess students' progress?	*Teacher Resource Book*–Lesson Guide–Assessment *Teacher Implementation Guide*–Assessment section
Where do I find connections to literature and computer software?	*Teacher Resource Book*–Outline *Teacher Implementation Guide*–Literature List *Teacher Implementation Guide*–Software List
How do I find background information about concepts underlying each activity?	*Teacher Resource Book*–Background *Teacher Resource Book*–Lesson Guide–Content Notes *Teacher Implementation Guide*–TIMS Tutors
How does this activity fit into the "big picture" for kindergarten?	*Teacher Resource Book*–Background *Teacher Implementation Guide*–Overview *Teacher Implementation Guide*–Scope and Sequence
What manipulatives do I need for the entire year?	*Teacher Implementation Guide*–Manipulatives List
Where is the scope and sequence?	*Teacher Implementation Guide*–Scope and Sequence
Does this curriculum match my district's objectives?	*Teacher Implementation Guide*–Scope and Sequence & the NCTM *Principles and Standards* *Teacher Implementation Guide*–Overview
What information is available for parents?	*Teacher Resource Book*–Parent Letter *Teacher Implementation Guide*–Parents and *Math Trailblazers*–Parent Brochure (English and Spanish)

Overview

The Overview presents brief descriptions and lists of featured concepts for each unit. It provides a quick reference to locate concepts and activities.

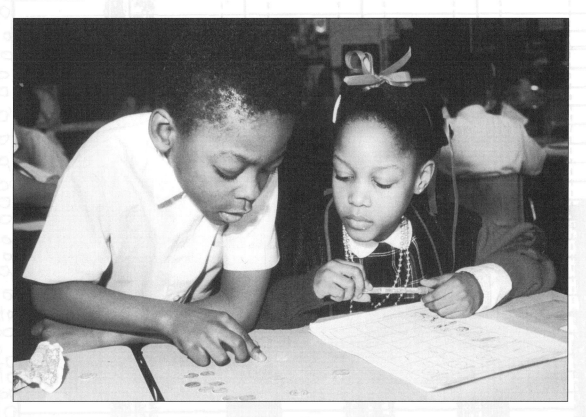

Students solve a problem using money.

Overview

The overview reflects the scope and sequence of the kindergarten curriculum. The fundamental assumption is that math concepts and skills are best acquired through active involvement in counting, measuring, sorting, comparing, graphing, and data analysis. Problem solving and communication are ongoing themes throughout all the activities.

Summaries of the kindergarten Ongoing Content, Mathematical Strands, and Thematic Units are included. Outlines of the kindergarten Month-by-Month activities also follow. The summaries provide a brief description and a list of the major concepts. This list may be used as a quick reference to the skills and concepts included in each section.

Ongoing Content

The four ongoing components in this section contain counting, estimation, data collection, and problem-solving activities to be used on an ongoing basis throughout the year. The components are: Calendar Connections; Problem Solving in the Kindergarten Day; Data Collection: How Many? How Much? How Far?; and Counting Connections.

Calendar Connections

Component Summary

Classroom Calendar offers a plan for a classroom calendar display area, which includes the ten frame, a monthly calendar, weather and attendance graphs, and a growing number line. Working with the calendar on a daily basis provides a meaningful context for solving problems and exploring relationships among numbers. Calendar Updates provide suggestions for new instructional emphases as the year progresses and students mature. The updates are presented in chronological order and are to be introduced throughout the year, approximately one every two weeks.

Fifty Ideas for the 100th Day offers suggestions for activities that focus on the benchmark number 100 prior to and during the celebration of the 100th day of school.

Concept Focus

- counting by ones, fives, and tens
- counting forward and counting back on the calendar
- using a ten frame as a visual organizer
- comparing numbers and quantities
- exploring shape, color, weather, and number patterns
- solving addition, subtraction, multiplication, and division problem types
- sorting and classifying
- recording data using tallies and numbers
- creating and reading graphs
- exploring concepts of measurement
- building an awareness of time and its passage including hours, days, weeks, months, seasons, and years
- developing an understanding of the value of a nickel and a penny

Problem Solving in the Kindergarten Day

Component Summary

This ongoing component presents a conceptual framework for thinking about problem solving involving numbers. Recent research has shown that kindergarten children are capable of dealing with many different kinds of math problems. This component encourages teachers to design instruction that introduces children to a rich variety of problems. The component is broken into four sections: Creating Problem-Solving Situations through Thematic Units, Creating Problem-Solving Situations through School Year Celebrations, Creating Problem-Solving Situations through Children's Literature, and Problem Solving through Everyday Classroom Situations.

Concept Focus

- exploring different addition, subtraction, multiplication, and division problem types
- communicating problem-solving strategies
- solving problems using manipulatives
- solving problems using counting strategies
- exploring the operations of addition, subtraction, multiplication, and division

Data Collection: How Many? How Much? How Far?

Component Summary

Data collection is an integral part of the *Math Trailblazers* kindergarten curriculum. Children become actively engaged in problem solving when they work with numbers that come from their own experience and are meaningful to them. Data collection activities may include sorting and classifying objects, conducting surveys, or using measurement. Data collection has the added benefit of being a natural way to integrate mathematics into multiple curricular areas. Some of the ideas for data collection activities in this component can be linked to the calendar. Additional data collection activities can be developed as they arise naturally in the classroom context. Ideally, an opportunity for data collection should be included each week.

Concept Focus

- counting using one-to-one correspondence
- making number comparisons
- sorting objects using Venn diagrams and real object graphs
- predicting the outcome of a data collection activity
- measuring length and width
- using tallies
- creating data tables and graphs to represent information
- analyzing data

Counting Connections

Component Summary

The ongoing activities and games in this component provide practice in counting, exploring patterns, and estimating. Students make connections between different representations of numbers including ten frames, dot patterns, numerals, sign language, and concrete representations of numbers. The component is broken into four sections: *A Baseline Counting Skills Assessment* provides suggestions on assessing individual students' counting skills. *Counting Boxes* provides a setting for children independently to count out sets to ten. *Counting Bags* provides children with multiple opportunities to count objects and record the number counted. *Number Books* provide an opportunity for children to make connections between multiple representations of numbers.

Concept Focus

- using one-to-one correspondence to count sets of objects
- understanding that the result of counting a set of objects should be the same each time the set is counted, independent of the order in which the objects are counted
- connecting symbols to different representations of numbers including ten frames, number dot patterns, and counted sets
- developing oral and sign language counting skills
- discovering patterns in our number system
- recording used numbers
- developing estimation skills based on comparison to a known referent set
- understanding that estimates of quantities should be approximate rather than specific
- using the language of estimation: more than, less than, about, close to

Mathematical Strands

This section provides core lessons that explore the topics of patterning, numbers and number relationships, geometry, and measurement. This section includes four strands: Patterns; Number and Operations; Geometry; and Measurement.

Patterns

Strand Summary

Repeating, linear patterns are explored visually, kinesthetically (using movement), and auditorily. Students are involved in a series of activities to identify and describe repeating patterns. Core patterns are described, first using object names, then using symbolic AB coding. These activities also introduce children to copying, extending, creating, comparing, and translating patterns using both manipulatives and pictorial representations.

Concept Focus

- describing patterns by object name
- copying a rhythmic pattern modeled by the teacher
- identifying the core of a repeating, linear pattern
- copying a pattern using two- or three-dimensional materials
- extending a given pattern using corresponding materials
- identifying patterns using symbolic (AB) coding
- creating a pattern using two- or three-dimensional materials
- comparing patterns made from different materials
- translating patterns from one material to another

Lessons	Number of Activities	Description	Month
Exploring and Identifying Patterns	3	Children explore and identify patterns in their environment.	1
Copying and Extending Patterns	4	Children copy and extend a given linear pattern. They begin to use symbols to describe patterns.	2
Creating and Comparing Patterns	3	Children create patterns for classmates to compare and translate from one medium to another.	3

Number and Operations

Strand Summary
Early lessons in this strand have students counting, comparing, and ordering sets of objects. They explore number relationships by comparing numbers to the benchmarks of five and ten and by describing numbers as more than, less than, or the same as. Students make model-word-symbol connections by playing matching games involving ten frames, dot patterns, and written numbers. They partition numbers into smaller sets and explore the concept of "half."

Concept Focus
- counting objects accurately to determine the quantity of a set
- comparing and ordering sets of objects
- describing number relationships using the language of more than, less than, and the same as
- developing visual representations of quantities using ten frame and number dot patterns
- exploring number relationships using the benchmark numbers five and ten
- using model-word-symbol connections
- exploring the part-part-whole relationship of numbers to ten
- exploring the relationship of fractional parts to the whole for halves and other fractions as appropriate
- exploring one more, two more, one less, two less

Lessons	Number of Activities	Description	Month
Numbers Around Us	2	Children listen to a counting book and then relate counting to their everyday world.	1
We All Count!	2	Children listen to a counting book and then make their own class number book.	2
Number Dot Patterns	5	In this collection of activities and games, children explore numbers through patterned arrangements of dots.	3
Pennies and Things	2	Children use pennies to partition the benchmark number five.	3
Looking at the Number Five	4	Children use familiar rhymes and a book to explore two-part partitions of the number five.	4

Lessons	Number of Activities	Description	Month
Number Comparisons	8	In this collection of activities and games, children compare and order numbers using a variety of contexts and materials.	5
Estimation Jar	1	Children use the benchmark number 10 to develop estimation language and estimation skills.	5
Dominoes and Number Cubes	5	Children use the number dot patterns on dominoes to explore number relationships.	6
Looking at the Number Ten	1	Children explore two-part partitions of the number ten using an action book and patterns in a data table.	7
Partitioning Seven, Eight, and Nine	1	Children explore three-part partitions of numbers by placing manipulatives in circus cars.	7
Partitioning Ten	1	Children explore three-part partitions of the number ten after reading the book *Mouse Count*.	8
Balloon Stories	2	Children create and solve problems about balloons. Then children create and illustrate stories for a class book.	8
Fractions	1	Children use broken paper cookies to explore the meaning of one half. Then they use a two-pan balance to determine which objects are cut in half.	9
One More, One Less	1	Children use dominoes to explore the one more than, one less than, two more than, two less than relationships of numbers to twelve.	10

Overview

Geometry

Strand Summary

Students develop spatial sense by having many experiences that focus on geometric relationships such as the direction and orientation of objects in space and on maps. Exploration of both two- and three-dimensional shapes starts by sorting and classifying objects according to their properties. The names of the shapes are introduced informally. Students also explore in a variety of ways shapes with a line of symmetry.

Concept Focus

- understanding and using terms to describe spatial relationships
- using spatial terms to describe the location and position of an object
- using spatial terms to describe movement from one place to another
- applying spatial terms to a map
- comparing the length of paths using the terms "longest" and "shortest"
- developing the language to describe shapes
- exploring three-dimensional shapes in the environment
- classifying three-dimensional shapes
- comparing and contrasting three-dimensional shapes
- exploring the properties of two-dimensional shapes
- comparing and contrasting two-dimensional shapes
- investigating the relationship between two- and three-dimensional shapes
- organizing data in a table
- exploring one line of symmetry
- completing and creating symmetrical designs

Lessons	Number of Activities	Description	Month
Location, Location, Location	2	This lesson focuses on the use of terms for spatial relationships to describe locations of children relative to themselves and to other objects.	1
Meet Mr. Origin	2	The plastic figure Mr. Origin is used as a point of reference to help children think of position and location in relation to an object outside themselves.	2
A Moving Experience	1	In this lesson, children focus on terms to describe movements and give directions.	3
Mapmaking	2	Children help make a map of their classroom. They follow a map according to directions given in a story.	4

Lessons	Number of Activities	Description	Month
Trailblazing	1	Children compare the number of steps needed to travel different paths to find the longest and the shortest.	5
Three-Dimensional Shapes	3	Children explore the properties of three-dimensional shapes through the process of comparing and sorting three-dimensional shapes.	6
Exploring Two-Dimensional Shapes	3	Children investigate and describe the properties of two-dimensional shapes.	7
Making a Pattern Block Clown	1	Children use pattern blocks to create a clown. They then count and record the number of each shape they used.	8
Shapes on the Geoboard	1	Children create shapes on the geoboard and explore their properties.	8
Connecting Three-Dimensional and Two-Dimensional Shapes	2	Children focus on the relationship between two- and three-dimensional shapes by looking at individual sides of three-dimensional shapes.	9
Introducing Symmetry	2	Children use pattern blocks and paper folding to explore symmetrical figures.	10

Overview

Measurement

Strand Summary

Students use estimation and develop measurement skills for the variables of length, area, volume, and weight (or mass). They compare and order objects according to measurements that they make using a variety of nonstandard and standard units. In some activities, students measure the same object using different units, which helps them notice what happens when the unit changes. Measurement of time is included in this strand as students record some of the events of their day.

Concept Focus

- estimating and comparing height
- comparing the size of objects
- ordering objects by height, capacity, and weight
- using the language of approximation
- placing units consistently and correctly
- estimating the number of units needed to measure
- revising estimates based on new information
- introducing the notion that the size of the unit will determine the number of units needed
- using nonstandard and standard units to measure
- understanding the meaning of area as the number of units needed to cover a shape
- exploring and estimating the capacity of various containers
- using a two-pan balance to compare the weights of objects
- recording events according to the hour of the day to promote an awareness of the passage of time
- placing numbers in intervals
- representing and interpreting data in a data table and a graph

Lessons	Number of Activities	Description	Month
As Tall as a _____ **?**	1	Students predict whether their height is greater than, less than, or about the same as the height of a giant pencil. This lesson is offered as a model for similar lessons that can be incorporated into other thematic units.	2
Height Comparisons	1	Children put a collection of objects in order by comparing their heights.	3
Length Comparisons	1	Children investigate the relative length of objects compared to a train of 6 connecting cubes.	4
If the Shoe Fits	1	Pairs of students use shoes in a variety of sizes as units to measure a path. Measurement results are recorded in a data table, and the differences in the data are explored.	4

Lessons	Number of Activities	Description	Month
Teddy Bear Lineup	1	Students use links to measure the heights of their favorite stuffed animals. The links and stuffed animals are then placed in order from shortest to tallest.	5
Jumpers!	1	Students use links to measure distances jumped, then record the results on a graph and analyze the data.	5
Measuring Area	1	Students use their bodies to measure the area of a magic carpet in nonstandard units.	6
A Garden's Area	1	Children use two different sizes of nonstandard units to find the area of a garden. They learn that area is the number of units needed to cover a region.	7
Measuring Area with a Standard Unit	1	Children predict and count the number of square-inch tiles that fit in different-shaped areas.	7
Exploring Capacity	2	Students explore volume by ordering containers according to their capacities.	8
Container Comparisons	2	Children predict the size of container needed to hold a quantity of beans, rice, or pasta. Children refine estimates as they gain new information.	8
Weighing In	1	Students explore weight by sorting and ordering objects. The use of a two-pan balance is introduced.	9
Balancing Numbers	1	Students use a number cube, a balance, and blocks to explore the concept of equal and unequal.	9
The Time of Our Lives	1	Students record the events of their day, focusing on a clock's hour hand.	10

Kindergarten Month-by-Month
Month 1 Outline

Ongoing Content

Calendar Connections pages 5–31	Classroom Calendar (pages 6–16) (A1) (A3)
	Calendar Updates (pages 179–180) 1. A Year in Kindergarten—A History of the School Year 2. Monthly Tallying (A1)
Problem Solving in the Kindergarten Day pages 33–38	Include one problem-solving session per week. (pages 37–38) (A1) (A2)
Data Collection: How Many? How Much? How Far? pages 39–63	Include one data collection per week. (pages 43–63) (A1) (A2)
Counting Connections pages 65–143	Counting Assessment (pages 66–70)
	Counting Boxes (pages 71–93) (A1)

Remember to:
• Include an opportunity for students to explore Mr. Origin.

Lessons

	Strand	Activities	Supplies
LESSON 1		**– PATTERNS STRAND –**	
Exploring and Identifying Patterns TRB pages 181–186		**Activity 1: Pattern Detectives I** (A3) Children search for patterns in their classroom.	
		Activity 2: Pattern Detectives II (A3) Children create patterns in the classroom.	
		Activity 3: Rhythmic Patterns (A3) Children copy rhythmic patterns such as clap, snap (AB).	
LESSON 2		**– NUMBER AND OPERATIONS STRAND –**	
Numbers Around Us TRB pages 187–195		**Activity 1: What Can We Count?** (A1) Children listen to a counting book and then suggest items in the room to count. /POPS/	• number cards • paper • counting books • scissors
		Activity 2: Connecting Objects to Symbols (A1) Children select a number card, then count and place that number of cubes on a workmat. /POPS/	• connecting cubes • paper

	Strand	Activities	Supplies
LESSON 3		*– GEOMETRY STRAND –*	
Location, Location, Location **TRB**　　pages 195–196		**Activity 1: Simon Says** (A4) Children play a version of *Simon Says* that uses words to describe their location in the classroom.	
		Activity 2: Line Up (A4) Children describe the positions of people and objects in the classroom.	

Ongoing Content

Calendar Connections pages 5–31	**Classroom Calendar** (pages 6–16) (A1)
	Calendar Updates (pages 205–206) 3. Daily Schedule 4. Monthly Count Down (A1)
Problem Solving in the Kindergarten Day pages 33–38	**Include one problem-solving session each week.** (pages 37–38) (A1) (A2)
Data Collection: How Many? How Much? How Far? pages 39–63	**Include one data collection each week.** (pages 43–63) (A1) (A2)
Counting Connections pages 65–143	**Counting Boxes** (pages 71–93) (A1)
	Counting Bags (pages 95–106) (A1)

Remember to:
• Include time for students to explore pattern blocks.

Lessons

	Strand	Activities	Supplies
LESSON 1		**– PATTERNS STRAND –**	
Copying and Extending Patterns TRB pages 207–209	[pattern grid]	**Activity 1: Copying Patterns** (A3) Children copy a linear pattern unit using color, shape, size, position, or rhythm. [POPS]	• strips of tagboard • collectibles such as shells, pasta, or buttons • self-sealing plastic bags • clothespins or large paper clips • classroom manipulatives such as connecting cubes, tiles, or links • cutout figures • glue or tape
		Activity 2: Extending Patterns (A3) Children extend a linear pattern unit using color, shape, size, position, or rhythm. [POPS]	• pattern strips • bags of collectibles

	Strand	Activities	Supplies

LESSON 1

Copying and Extending Patterns *(continued)*

TRB   pages 207–209

– PATTERNS STRAND (continued) –

Activity 3: Movement Patterns (A3)
Children copy a pattern unit using rhythmic actions.

Activity 4: Using Symbols (A3)
Children use language to describe the sequence elements in a pattern unit, such as ABB, ABB.

LESSON 2

We All Count!

TRB   pages 210–213

– NUMBER AND OPERATIONS STRAND –

Activity 1: Our Number Book (A1)
Ten Black Dots by Donald Crews provides a setting for children to create a class counting book. (POPS)

Supplies:
- self-adhesive dots
- construction paper
- Book—*Ten Black Dots* by Donald Crews

Activity 2: Oral Counting—Buzz!
Children play a circle game to practice listening skills and a wide variety of counting skills. Use the game on a weekly basis throughout the year.

LESSON 3

Meet Mr. Origin

TRB   pages 214–218

– GEOMETRY STRAND –

Activity 1: Meeting Mr. Origin (A4)
Students describe the location of objects in the classroom using Mr. Origin as a reference.

Supplies:
- plastic Mr. Origin figure
- large paper plates
- stapler or tape

Activity 2: Visiting the Origin Family Garden (A4)
Children describe position and location in relation to an object outside themselves. (POPS)

Supplies:
- scissors
- Mr. or Ms. Origin figures

LESSON 4

As Tall as a _____ ?

TRB   pages 219–226

– MEASUREMENT STRAND –

Activity 1: Shorter? Taller? Or What? (A5)
Children compare their height to a cutout of an object or character. A class graph is made of the results.

Supplies:
- cutout of an object (3.5 to 4 ft tall)
- marker
- paper
- crayons
- construction paper

Overview

Ongoing Content

Calendar Connections pages 5–31	Classroom Calendar (pages 6–16) (A1)
	Calendar Updates (pages 235–236) 5. Changing the Calendar Pattern (A3) 6. Planning for Day 100
Problem Solving in the Kindergarten Day pages 33–38	Include one problem-solving session each week. (pages 37–38) (A1) (A2)
Data Collection: How Many? How Much? How Far? pages 39–63	Include one data collection each week. (pages 43–63) (A1) (A2)
Counting Connections pages 65–143	Counting Boxes (pages 71–93) (A1)
	Counting Bags (pages 95–106) (A1)

Remember to:
• Include one game of *Buzz!* each week.

Lessons

	Strand	Activities	Supplies
LESSON 1		– PATTERNS STRAND –	
Creating and Comparing Patterns TRB pages 237–239	[pattern grid icon]	**Activity 1: Creating Patterns** (A3) Children create patterns for their classmates to compare. [POPS]	• connecting cubes, pattern blocks, tiles, or links • rubber stamps, stencils, sponges, or potato halves • ink pads, paints, markers, crayons
		Activity 2: Comparing Patterns (A3) Children compare patterns constructed with different materials. [POPS]	• pattern strips
		Activity 3: Translating Patterns (A3) Children copy rhythmic patterns such as clap, snap (AB).	• pattern blocks, connecting cubes, tiles, or links • rubber stamps, stencils, sponges, or potato halves • ink pads, paints, markers, crayons • pattern strips • Book—*The Very Busy Spider* by Eric Carle

	Strand	Activities	Supplies
LESSON 2		**– NUMBER AND OPERATIONS STRAND –**	
Number Dot Patterns TRB pages 240–251	3 7 2 8 5 0 10 6	**Activity 1: Build My Number** (A1) Children show numbers on their ten frame workmat.	• connecting cubes
		Activity 2: Show That You Know (A1) After seeing a number card, children count and place that number of cubes on their workmat.	• connecting cubes
		Activity 3: No Ones! Game (A1) Children use a number cube to determine the next number to land on. _POPS_	• number cubes • game markers
		Activity 4: Apple Baskets Game (A1) Children match sets of apples to number dot patterns. _POPS_	
		Activity 5: Cereal Boxes Game (A1) Children match numerals on cereal boxes to number dot patterns. _POPS_	
LESSON 3		**– NUMBER AND OPERATIONS STRAND –**	
Pennies and Things TRB pages 252–259	3 7 2 8 5 0 10 6	**Activity 1: Benny's Pennies** (A1) Children listen to a story and then use the action in the story to create a play that features Benny spending his pennies, one by one. _POPS_	• Book—*Benny's Pennies* by Pat Brisson • pennies
		Activity 2: Number Race 1 (A1) Children write a numeral to record each roll of the number cube. _POPS_	• number cube
LESSON 4		**– GEOMETRY STRAND –**	
A Moving Experience TRB page 260		**Activity 1: Simon Says** (A4) Children use spatial sense to describe movement from place to place.	
LESSON 5		**– MEASUREMENT STRAND –**	
Height Comparisons TRB pages 261–262	1 2	**Activity 1: How Tall Is That Box?** (A5) Children use comparison language to describe the differences between the heights of boxes. _POPS_	• a collection of food boxes or bottles

Overview

Ongoing Content

Calendar Connections pages 5–31	Classroom Calendar (pages 6–16) (A1)
	Calendar Updates (pages 271–272) 7. Ordinal Numbers (A1) 8. Changing the Pattern on the Calendar (A3)
Problem Solving in the Kindergarten Day pages 33–38	Include one problem-solving session each week. (pages 37–38) (A2)
Data Collection: How Many? How Much? How Far? pages 39–63	Include one data collection each week. (pages 43–63) (A2)
Counting Connections pages 65–143	Counting Boxes (pages 71–93) and Counting Bags (pages 95–106)
	Number Books (pages 107–143)

Remember to:
• Include one game of *Buzz!* each week.

Lessons

	Strand	Activities	Supplies
LESSON 1		**– NUMBER AND OPERATIONS STRAND –**	
Looking at the Number Five TRB pages 273–282	8 3 7 2 5 10 0 6	**Activity 1: Five Is a Handy Number** (A6) Children use comparison language for number of rings and fingers.	• pennies or other counters • paint • white construction paper
		Activity 2: Rings on My Fingers (A6) Children use their handprints to explore partitions of the number five. (POPS)	• pennies • handprint work-mat
		Activity 3: Five Little Monkeys (A6) (A7) Children use a literature connection and a finger play to explore partitions of the number five. (POPS)	• Book—*Five Little Monkeys Jumping on the Bed* by Eileen Cristelow • connecting cubes
		Activity 4: Five on the Mat (A6) Children describe partitions of five.	• workmat • pennies or connecting cubes

	Strand	Activities	Supplies
LESSON 2		**– GEOMETRY STRAND –**	
Mapmaking TRB pages 283–288		**Activity 1: Introducing Maps** (A4) Children make a map of their classroom.	• road map • newsprint • markers or crayons
		Activity 2: Mapping a Book (A4) Children map the path of a character in a story. POPS	• Book—*Rosie's Walk* by Pat Hutchins • crayon
LESSON 3		**– MEASUREMENT STRAND –**	
Length Comparisons TRB pages 289–292	1 2	**Activity 1: Longer, Shorter, or Close To?** (A5) Children compare classroom objects to a 6-cube train. POPS	• connecting cubes
LESSON 4		**– MEASUREMENT STRAND –**	
If the Shoe Fits TRB pages 293–294	1 2	**Activity 1: Measuring with Shoes** (A5) Children explore the results of measuring a path with pairs of shoes of different sizes.	• a collection of shoes of various sizes • chart paper • masking tape • markers

Overview

Ongoing Content

Calendar Connections pages 5–31	Classroom Calendar (pages 6–16) (A1) (A3)
	Calendar Updates (pages 303–305) 9. Writing Numbers on the Calendar [POPS] 10. Number Sentences and the Ten Frame (A1)
Problem Solving in the Kindergarten Day pages 33–38	Include one problem-solving session each week. (pages 37–38) (A1) (A2)
Data Collection: How Many? How Much? How Far? pages 39–63	Include one data collection each week. (pages 43–63) (A1) (A2)
Counting Connections pages 65–143	Counting Boxes (pages 71–93) and Counting Bags (pages 95–106)
	Number Books (pages 107–143)

Remember to:
- Include a game of *Buzz!* and *Number Race 1* each week.
- Give students the opportunity to explore dominoes.

Lessons

	Strand	Activities	Supplies
LESSON 1		**– NUMBER AND OPERATIONS STRAND –**	
Number Comparisons TRB pages 306–312	8 3 7 2 5 10 6	**Activity 1: Thumbs Up! Thumbs Down!** (A1) Children compare sets of objects to a number.	• small objects
		Activity 2: Getting the Range of It (A1) Children use benchmark numbers and the language of about, more than, less than, and between to describe their estimates.	• small objects
		Activity 3: More Than, Less Than, The Same As Flash (A1) Children build sets of objects on a workmat to show more than or less than a number.	• counters • paper
		Activity 4: Cube Towers (A1) Children build, compare, and order cube towers.	• connecting cubes
		Activity 5: How Many Links? (A1) Children compare the number of links in a chain to benchmark lengths of 10, 20, and 30 links.	• connecting links
		Activity 6: Collect Six Game (A1) Children compare sets that are more, less, or the same. [POPS]	• spinners • number cubes • counters

	Strand	Activities	Supplies

LESSON 1

LESSON 1 — NUMBER AND OPERATIONS STRAND (continued) —

Number Comparisons (continued)

TRB   pages 306–312

Activity 7: Penny Banks (A1)
Children count out and place the correct number of pennies in labeled banks. [POPS]

- pennies
- coin purse
- small plastic jars
- box

Activity 8: Penny Store Sort (A1)
Children use target numbers to compare and sort priced objects. [POPS]

- collections of small objects
- construction paper
- price cards
- box

LESSON 2 — NUMBER AND OPERATIONS STRAND —

Estimation Jar

TRB   pages 313–320

Activity 1: Let the Estimation Begin! (A1) (A6)
Children use the benchmark number 10 to develop estimation language and estimation skills. [POPS]

- 32-ounce clear plastic jars
- a variety of objects like marshmallows or candies
- ten frame
- same-sized bowls
- shoe box
- connecting links
- cubes

LESSON 3 — GEOMETRY STRAND —

Trailblazing

TRB   pages 321–322

Activity 1: Following a Path (A1) (A4) (A5)
Children count the number of steps taken as they use stepping stones to cross a "river."

- scissors
- construction paper or cardboard

LESSON 4 — MEASUREMENT STRAND —

Teddy Bear Lineup

TRB   pages 323–326

Activity 1: Measuring Stuffed Animals (A1) (A4) (A5)
Children use chains of connecting links to measure the height of their animal, then order the links and the animals from shortest to tallest.

- stuffed animals
- connecting links

LESSON 5 — MEASUREMENT STRAND —

Jumpers!

TRB   pages 327–328

Activity 1: Measuring the Length of a Jump (A1) (A5)
Children use chains of connecting links to measure, record, and compare the length of the jumps of two students of different ages. [POPS]

- masking tape
- self-adhesive notes
- metersticks
- connecting links
- markers
- chart paper

Ongoing Content

Calendar Connections pages 5–31	**Classroom Calendar** (pages 6–16) **(A3)**
	Calendar Updates (pages 337–338) 11. A Change in the Weather **(A6)** 12. Calendar Cover-Up **(A3)**
Problem Solving in the Kindergarten Day pages 33–38	**Include one problem-solving session each week.** (pages 37–38) **(A2)**
Data Collection: How Many? How Much? How Far? pages 39–63	**Include one data collection each week.** (pages 43–63) **(A2) (A6)**
Counting Connections pages 65–143	**Counting Boxes** (pages 71–93) and **Counting Bags** (pages 95–106)
	Number Books (pages 107–143)

Remember to:
- Include one game of *Buzz!* and *Number Race 1* each week.
- Repeat the *Estimation Jar* activity weekly.
- Have students continue to record the date on their individual calendars.
- Allow time for students to explore square-inch tiles.

Lessons

	Strand	Activities	Supplies
LESSON 1		**– NUMBER AND OPERATIONS STRAND –**	
Dominoes and Number Cubes TRB pages 339–353	8 7 2 5 10 6	**Activity 1: Domino Sort (A1)** Children explore domino number dot patterns and use the part-part-whole relationship to place dominoes on a number line. POPS	• dominoes
		Activity 2: Domino Path Game (A1) Children use domino number dot patterns and the part-part-whole relationship to move dominoes on a game board. POPS	• dominoes • game marker
		Activity 3: Boat Dock (A1) (A6) Children use the part-part-whole relationship to park dominoes at designated docks. POPS	• dominoes
		Activity 4: Dot Wars Game (A1) Children compare domino number dot patterns as they play a game. POPS	• dominoes
		Activity 5: Number Race 2 (A1) Children add the total number of dots and record a number for each roll of the number cube. POPS	• number cubes

	Strand	Activities	Supplies
LESSON 2		- GEOMETRY STRAND -	
Three-Dimensional Shapes TRB pages 354–358		**Activity 1: Sorting Boxes and Bottles** (A4) (A6) Children explore and describe the properties of three-dimensional shapes, then sort the shapes using a Venn diagram. /POPS/	• boxes and containers • index cards • marker
		Activity 2: Boxes, Bottles, and Geometric Solids (A4) (A6) Children explore and describe the properties of three-dimensional objects and relate them to the shapes of geometric solids. /POPS/	• boxes and containers • set of geometric solids
		Activity 3: Same and Different (A4) (A6) Children discuss the similarities and differences between two shapes as they search for a hidden shape.	• paper bag • set of geometric solids
LESSON 3		- MEASUREMENT STRAND -	
Measuring Area TRB pages 359–360		**Activity 1: A Magic Carpet Ride** (A5) Children estimate and test the number of students who will fit on the carpet when the children stand, sit, and lie down.	• masking tape • chart paper • marker

Overview

Ongoing Content

Calendar Connections pages 5–31	**Classroom Calendar** (pages 6–16) (A1) (A3)
	Calendar Updates (pages 369–370) 13. Skip Counting on the Calendar 14. Yesterday, Today, and Tomorrow
Problem Solving in the Kindergarten Day pages 33–38	Include one problem-solving session each week. (pages 37–38) (A2)
Data Collection: How Many? How Much? How Far? pages 39–63	Include one data collection each week. (pages 43–63) (A7)
Counting Connections pages 65–143	**Counting Boxes** (pages 71–93) and **Counting Bags** (pages 95–106)
	Number Books (pages 107–143)

Remember to:
- Include one game of *Buzz!* and *Number Race 1* or *Number Race 2* each week.
- Repeat the *Estimation Jar* activity weekly.
- Have students continue to record the date on their individual calendars.
- Allow time for students to explore measuring cups and geoboards.

Lessons

	Strand	Activities	Supplies
LESSON 1		**– NUMBER AND OPERATIONS STRAND –**	
Looking at the Number Ten TRB pages 371–378	8 7 2 5 10 0 6	**Activity 1: 10 in the Bed** (A1) (A3) (A6) Children use manipulatives and a data table to explore part-part-whole relationships of the number 10 through the action of a story. /POPS	• connecting cubes
LESSON 2		**– NUMBER AND OPERATIONS STRAND –**	
Partitioning Seven, Eight, and Nine TRB pages 379–380	8 7 2 5 10 0 6	**Activity 1: Circus Train** (A1) (A3) Children explore the ways that sets of 7 to 9 lima beans can be placed in three wagons and record the partitions on a data table. /POPS	• small lima beans • shallow cups or boxes

	Strand	Activities	Supplies
LESSON 3		**– GEOMETRY STRAND –**	
Exploring Two-Dimensional Shapes TRB pages 381–383		**Activity 1: Looking for Shapes** (A4) (A7) Children look for shapes in a book and their classroom.	• book about shapes
		Activity 2: Exploring Pattern Block Shapes (A4) (A7) Children observe, sort, and describe the two-dimensional shapes in the pattern block set.	• pattern blocks • index cards • markers
		Activity 3: Mystery Shape (A4) (A7) Children feel and describe the shapes in a bag. POPS	• pattern blocks • paper bag
LESSON 4		**– MEASUREMENT STRAND –**	
A Garden's Area TRB pages 384–386		**Activity 1: Measuring Area** (A2) (A5) (A8) Children use nonstandard units to cover a region.	• connecting links • scissors • colored paper • book—*How Many Snails?* by Paul Giganti
LESSON 5		**– MEASUREMENT STRAND –**	
Measuring Area with a Standard Unit TRB pages 387–394		**Activity 1: Using Square-Inch Tiles** (A5) (A8) Children use square-inch tiles to find the area of regions. POPS	• square-inch tiles • overhead square-inch tiles

Overview

Ongoing Content

Calendar Connections pages 5–31	**Classroom Calendar** (pages 6–16) (A1) (A6)
	Calendar Updates (pages 403–404) 15. Extending Patterns 16. Penny Count (A4)
Problem Solving in the Kindergarten Day pages 33–38	**Include one problem-solving session each week.** (pages 37–38) (A2)
Data Collection: How Many? How Much? How Far? pages 39–63	**Include one data collection each week.** (pages 43–63) (A6)
Counting Connections pages 65–143	**Counting Boxes** (pages 71–93) and **Counting Bags** (pages 95–106)
	Number Books (pages 107–143)

Remember to:
- Include one game of *Buzz!, Number Race 1,* or *Number Race 2,* each week.
- Repeat the *Estimation Jar* activity weekly.
- Have students continue to record the date on their individual calendars.
- Allow time for students to explore the balances.

Lessons

	Strand	Activities	Supplies
LESSON 1		**– NUMBER AND OPERATIONS STRAND –**	
Partitioning Ten TRB pages 405–409	8 7 2 5 10 6	**Activity 1: Our Mouse Count** (A1) (A4) Children use counters to explore three-part partitions of the number 10. POPS	• glue stick • scissors • connecting cubes • clear plastic jar
LESSON 2		**– NUMBER AND OPERATIONS STRAND –**	
Balloon Stories TRB pages 410–412	8 7 2 5 10 6	**Activity 1: Balloon Man** (A1) (A4) Children use pennies to show the action in the story and to solve problems.	• pennies
		Activity 2: Our Own Balloon Man Stories (A1) (A4) Children create their own stories and record number sentences that show the action in the story. POPS	• pennies
LESSON 3		**– GEOMETRY STRAND –**	
Making a Pattern Block Clown TRB pages 413–415		**Activity 1: Making the Clown** (A5) Children create a clown out of pattern blocks. They record the number of each pattern block shape on a data table. POPS	• pattern blocks

	Strand	Activities	Supplies
LESSON 4		**– GEOMETRY STRAND –**	
Shapes on the Geoboard TRB pages 416–417		**Activity 1: Geoboard Shapes** (A5) Children construct two-dimensional shapes on geoboards and discuss their properties. POPS	• geoboards • geobands or rubber bands
LESSON 5		**– MEASUREMENT STRAND –**	
Exploring Capacity TRB pages 418–419	1 2	**Activity 1: Ordering Containers** (A7) Children order filled containers from least to most.	• identical containers • measuring cup • water or uncooked rice
		Activity 2: Fill It Fast (A3) (A7) Children predict and test water levels as you add water in half- and quarter-cup increments. POPS	• empty container with straight sides • water or rice • measuring cups • crayon or marker
LESSON 6		**– MEASUREMENT STRAND –**	
Container Comparisons TRB pages 420–421	1 2	**Activity 1: Put It Away** (A3) (A7) Children predict the size of containers needed to hold leftover beans, rice, and pasta.	• different-sized containers • uncooked beans, rice, and pasta • small skillet or pan
		Activity 2: Filling Station (A3) (A7) Children explore and describe the capacity of a variety of sizes of containers. POPS	• plastic basin • sand, rice, or beans • containers

Ongoing Content

Calendar Connections pages 5–31	**Classroom Calendar** (pages 6–16) (A1)
	Calendar Updates (pages 429–430) 17. Guess My Number *POPS* 18. The Clock
Problem Solving in the Kindergarten Day pages 33–38	Include one problem-solving session each week. (pages 37–38) (A1) (A2)
Data Collection: How Many? How Much? How Far? pages 39–63	Include one data collection each week. (pages 43–63) (A1) (A7)
Counting Connections pages 65–143	**Counting Boxes** (pages 71–93) and **Counting Bags** (pages 95–106)
	Number Books (pages 107–143)

Remember to:
- Include one game of *Buzz!, Number Race 1,* or *Number Race 2* each week.
- Repeat the *Estimation Jar* activity weekly.
- Have students continue to record the date on their individual calendars.

Lessons

	Strand	Activities	Supplies
LESSON 1		**– NUMBER AND OPERATIONS STRAND –**	
Fractions TRB pages 431–432		**Activity 1: Broken Cookies** (A3) Children use paper cookie pieces to explore the idea that two halves of a cookie must be equal in size. *POPS*	• construction paper • scissors
LESSON 2		**– GEOMETRY STRAND –**	
Connecting Three-Dimensional and Two-Dimensional Shapes TRB pages 433–434		**Activity 1: Shadows** (A4) Children match two-dimensional shapes with shadows made by three-dimensional shapes.	• set of geometric solids
		Activity 2: Imprints (A4) Children make imprints of shapes in sand or salt and make prints of shapes using paints. *POPS*	• paper

	Strand	Activities	Supplies
LESSON 3		**– MEASUREMENT STRAND –**	
Weighing In TRB pages 435–436	1 2	**Activity 1: A Weight Sort** (A5) Children sort and order objects according to weight. POPS	• two-pan balance • objects • index cards • markers
LESSON 4		**– MEASUREMENT STRAND –**	
Balancing Numbers TRB pages 437–439	1 2	**Activity 1: Using a Balance** (A6) Children roll a number cube to determine the number of blocks to place on each side of the balance, then decide the action to take to balance the pans. POPS	• wooden cubes • number cubes • two-pan balance • chart paper • marker

Overview

Ongoing Content

Calendar Connections pages 5–31	**Classroom Calendar** (pages 6–16)
	Calendar Updates (pages 447–448) 19. Calendar Problems 20. Comparing Monthly Tallies
Problem Solving in the Kindergarten Day pages 33–38	**Include one problem-solving session each week.** (pages 37–38)
Data Collection: How Many? How Much? How Far? pages 39–63	**Include one data collection each week.** (pages 43–63)
Counting Connections pages 65–143	**Counting Boxes** (pages 71–93) and **Counting Bags** (pages 95–106)
	Number Books (pages 107–143)

Remember to:
- Include one game of *Buzz!, Number Race 1,* or *Number Race 2* each week.
- Repeat the *Estimation Jar* activity weekly.
- Have students continue to record the date on their individual calendars.

Lessons

	Strand	Activities	Supplies
LESSON 1		**– NUMBER AND OPERATIONS STRAND –**	
One More, One Less TRB pages 449–450		**Activity 1: One More, One Less Game** Children pull dominoes to show either one more, one less, two more, or two less than a target number.	• dominoes • paper • digit cards
LESSON 2		**– GEOMETRY STRAND –**	
Introducing Symmetry TRB pages 451–460		**Activity 1: Alphabet Symmetry** Children explore the symmetry of letters of the alphabet.	
		Activity 2: Three Ways to Explore Symmetry Children use pattern block shapes, paint and a paper fold, and a mirror to explore symmetry.	• pattern blocks • paint • paintbrush • mirror
LESSON 3		**– MEASUREMENT STRAND –**	
The Time of Our Lives TRB pages 461–465		**Activity 1: Recording Time on the Hour** Children record the events of their day.	• crayons • classroom demonstration clock

Thematic Units

The three units in this section are optional; you can present them as written, modify them, or use them as models to develop your own thematic units. The units are: Buildings; On the Go; and Crawly Creatures.

Buildings

Unit Summary

The mathematics in this unit emerges from activities that explore many types of buildings, with a focus on the school building and students' homes. Children collect data by counting doors and windows, and they conduct surveys about types of homes. Students create and solve problems using an apartment building setting. The skills needed to complete this unit make it appropriate for use any time in the first semester.

Concept Focus

- comparing and classifying data
- collecting, graphing, and discussing data
- developing concepts of length, area, and volume
- developing measuring skills
- developing concepts of geometry, such as shape recognition, symmetry, mapping, and an intuitive sense of spatial relations
- developing number sense using comparison
- creating and solving addition and subtraction problems

Lessons	Number of Parts	Description	Supplies
LESSON 1 **City at Night**	1	Children cut out silhouettes of skyscrapers to make a City at Night mural. They use the buildings for measurement and data collection.	• self-adhesive notes • want ad pages • yellow construction paper • index cards • scissors • glue • black crayons • connecting links • dark-colored paper
LESSON 2 **Building with Blocks**	1	Children construct buildings in a center to help them develop comparison, classification, numeration, fraction, and geometric concepts.	• collection of building blocks • construction paper
LESSON 3 **Buildings Around Our School**	2	**Part 1:** Students discuss the kinds of buildings they expect to see around their school. **Part 2:** Students list, count, and compare the buildings found in a series of walks around the school.	• crayons or markers

Lessons	Number of Parts	Description	Supplies
LESSON 4 **Our Homes**	2	**Part 1:** Students create a "people" graph to represent the different types of homes they live in. **Part 2:** Students create a class bar graph. They analyze the graphs and discuss the information.	• markers • self-adhesive notes • crayons or pencils • chart paper or sentence strip • tape • construction paper
LESSON 5 **Build Sasha's House**	1	Children play this game in groups of 2–4. They complete a house as they draw shapes determined by rolling a number cube.	• number cubes • scrap paper
LESSON 6 **Doors**	1	Students count and record the number of doors in their homes. At school the data are used to make a group bar graph, and the information on the graph is discussed.	• self-adhesive notes • laminated wall graph
LESSON 7 **Windows**	1	Pairs of students count windows in the rooms around the school. Students then sort the class data for analysis.	• index cards • crayons or pencils
LESSON 8 **Class Apartment Building**	1	Students use self-adhesive notes to create and solve addition and subtraction problems about students who move in or out of an imaginary building.	• self-adhesive notes • crayons • chart paper or newsprint • marker

Unit Summary

The mathematics in this thematic unit emerges from exploring different modes of transportation. Surveys are conducted for the color of cars seen by students and the type of transportation used; toy cars are measured for their length and weight; and vehicles are sorted by attributes. The skills needed to complete this unit make it appropriate for the beginning of the second semester of school.

Concept Focus

- sorting and classifying objects
- labeling and explaining sorted groups
- comparing the number of objects in different groups
- constructing picture graphs of data collected
- analyzing data on graphs
- using the language of more than, less than, and the same as
- placing ten numbered objects in sequential order
- grouping specified numbers of objects
- matching two items with identical numbers
- identifying geometric shapes
- estimating the space (area) an object takes
- comparing the use of different units for measuring length
- estimating weight using nonstandard units
- exploring the relationship between weight and size
- investigating the value of pennies, nickels, and dimes
- solving problems using coins
- experiencing time intervals

Lessons	Number of Parts	Description	Supplies
LESSON 1 **Getting to School**	2	**Part 1:** Students listen to a story, then discuss ways to travel. **Part 2:** Students construct a picture graph based on the mode of transportation they take to school. They use the graph to answer questions.	• self-adhesive notes • chart paper • crayons or markers • tape
LESSON 2 **Cube Trains**	2	**Part 1:** A yes/no graph introduces train travel. **Part 2:** Children assemble cube trains that match the number of cars on pictures of trains. They then compare the number of cubes in the trains.	• connecting cubes • string • self-adhesive notes
LESSON 3 **The People on the Bus**	1	Students are given buses, each labeled with a number. They put that number of people on each bus and then put the bus in a garage with the same number.	• toy buses, milk cartons, or pictures of buses • toy people, cubes, or pictures of people • shoe boxes or other boxes

Overview

Lessons	Number of Parts	Description	Supplies
LESSON 4 **Designing Shapes Vehicles**	1	Children design and construct "shapes vehicles" using pattern blocks and circles. Students count and record the number of each shape used.	• pattern blocks • circular disks
LESSON 5 **Car Colors Survey**	2	**Part 1:** Students discuss how to organize a data collection. **Part 2:** Students collect data about the colors of cars they see. After collecting the data, the class creates a class graph. Students analyze the graph's information and tell the story of the graph.	• self-adhesive notes • markers • crayons
LESSON 6 **Fitting a Car in Our Classroom**	1	Students work in groups to find the length and width of a car, then reconstruct the space the car would take up inside the classroom. They estimate how many children can fit in the area of the car and how many cars could fit into the classroom.	• ball of string • tape • scissors or connecting links
LESSON 7 **Measuring Our Car's Length**	2	**Part 1:** Students discuss and determine appropriate units to use. **Part 2:** Children measure the length of one side of a car's outline (from Lesson 6), using units of several different sizes.	• markers or chalk • rulers • connecting links • metersticks
LESSON 8 **Vehicle Sort**	1	Children decide how to sort pictures of vehicles into categories based on shared attributes (variables). Then students label their groups.	• toy vehicles • self-adhesive notes • easel pad • markers • crayons or pencils
LESSON 9 **Comparing Weights of Toy Vehicles**	2	**Part 1:** Students compare the weight of toy cars using other toy cars and a balance. **Part 2:** They use connecting cubes to measure the weight of the cars.	• toy vehicles of different sizes and weights • two-pan balances • connecting cubes • index cards
LESSON 10 **Travel Money**	3	**Part 1:** Students learn about the value of the penny, nickel, and dime. **Part 2:** Students use these coins to "purchase" bus tickets. **Part 3:** Students purchase toy vehicles in a classroom store.	• coins: pennies, dimes, nickels (real or plastic) • toy vehicles • index cards • chart paper or poster board • construction paper

Unit Summary

Crawly Creatures develops mathematical ideas as students investigate the world of insects and spiders. They explore symmetry, shapes, partitions of numbers, and measurement. The skills needed to complete this unit make it appropriate for late in the second semester. You can use this unit earlier in the year if it is modified to suit the developmental level of your students.

Concept Focus

- classifying and sorting according to various characteristics
- tallying
- constructing, reading, and interpreting graphs
- counting and grouping objects
- exploring even and odd numbers informally
- counting by twos
- partitioning numbers
- doubling numbers
- solving problems involving joining and separating groups
- exploring the concepts of multiplication and division
- exploring ideas of symmetry
- developing geometric visualization skills
- sequencing the days of the week
- exploring positions of the hour hand during a 12-hour time period
- measuring area using two different sizes of units

Lessons

	Number of Parts	Description	Supplies
LESSON 1 **Bugs Come to Class**	1	Children bring bugs to class to observe and describe their characteristics. They make drawings of their bugs and use their pictures to sort, collect data, and make graphs. Then children convert a picture graph into a data table with tallies.	• bugs brought from home in jars • 3-inch-square self-adhesive notes or construction paper • centimeter cube • connecting cubes • chart paper
LESSON 2 **Insect Problem Solving**	1	Children build bugs from egg cartons to use as manipulatives for problem solving.	• egg cartons • chenille sticks • paint
LESSON 3 **Time for Bugs**	1	During the reading of *The Grouchy Ladybug* by Eric Carle, children follow the ladybug's activities as the hands on a clock are moved in 1-hour increments. Then children draw in the hour hand on a series of blank clocks. Finally, children draw pictures of their bugs' activities.	• classroom demonstration clock • brads • crayons

Overview

Lessons	Number of Parts	Description	Supplies
LESSON 4 **Ant Number Stories**	1	Children tell number stories and make thumbprint ants to illustrate their number stories.	• paint • paper strips
LESSON 5 **Butterfly Symmetry**	1	Children explore symmetry by painting one half of a butterfly and folding to make a print for the other half.	• paint
LESSON 6 **Designing Bugs**	1	Children construct pattern-block bugs and discuss whether their designs are symmetrical.	• pattern blocks
LESSON 7 **Ladybug Doubles**	1	Children use symmetry to make ladybugs who have the same number of dots on each wing, thereby exploring the doubling of numbers 1 through 7.	• small paper plates • large paper plates • brads • connecting cubes • crayons • chart paper • markers
LESSON 8 **Hungry Bugs**	1	Children identify a skip-counting pattern and then skip count by twos to 14 while listening to a story about hungry bugs and what they eat on successive days.	• paper • counters or connecting cubes • markers • stapler • chart paper
LESSON 9 **Bug Race Game**	1	Children move "bugs" along a race course by adding together the roll of two number cubes.	• number cubes • beans or small plastic bugs • tape
LESSON 10 **Spider Legs**	1	Children explore partitions of the number 8, using spider "legs" as the manipulative.	• paper clips or chenille sticks
LESSON 11 **Big Bug, Little Bug**	1	Children measure the area of the top of a tree stump using two sizes of beans that represent two sizes of bugs.	• small containers • pinto beans • lima beans • markers or colored chalk

Scope and Sequence
& the NCTM *Principles and Standards*

This section provides descriptions and tables that show how *Math Trailblazers* relates to the National Council of Teachers of Mathematics *Principles and Standards for School Mathematics*. It includes a comprehensive scope and sequence for Kindergarten.

Students share their data by recording it on a class data table.

Math Trailblazers and the Principles and Standards

The National Council of Teachers of Mathematics (NCTM) *Principles and Standards for School Mathematics* and *Math Trailblazers* complement each other: The *Principles and Standards* is a vision of what school mathematics should be. *Math Trailblazers* is the curricular structure so teachers can turn that vision into reality. This section starts with an outline of how *Math Trailblazers* complements the five content and five process standards in the *Principles and Standards*. It concludes with a scope and sequence that specifies how the Kindergarten curriculum develops through the year. For information on the scope and sequence across the grades, see the *Math Trailblazers Scope and Sequence Chart* available from Kendall/Hunt Publishing Company.

Content Standards

Principles and Standards for School Mathematics outlines an articulated vision of how learning and teaching in each of five content areas should develop across the grades. These content areas are number and operations, algebra, geometry, measurement, and data analysis and probability. In *Math Trailblazers* the standards for all five content areas are addressed appropriately at every grade level, from Kindergarten through Grade 5. Five process standards prescribe a curriculum where problem solving, communication, reasoning, connections, and representation are integral, not ancillary, issues. By looking at the Scope and Sequence Chart in this section, one can see how mathematical ideas develop throughout the grade.

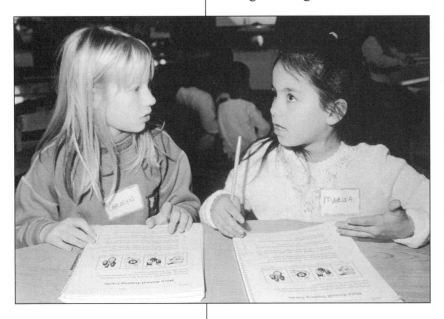

Many activities in *Math Trailblazers* address more than one of the content standards. Consider, for example, *Bouncing Ball,* a fourth-grade laboratory experiment in which students investigate the relationship between the drop height and the bounce height of a tennis ball. The investigation begins with a question: "What is the relationship between how far a tennis ball drops and how high it bounces?" Through class discussion, the variables are identified and named (D, the drop height and B, the bounce height) and experimental procedures are devised. A picture records this information. Next, the students drop the tennis balls repeatedly, measure drop height and bounce height each time, and record the data in a table. As students gather the data, they monitor the measurements for consistency and sense. Then when the data is complete, they examine the data table to see if they can discern a pattern. Next, students graph their data. As they work, they are asked how the data table and the graph relate to the physical system, what the relationship between drop height and bounce height is, and how that relationship is evident in the table and graph. Then students make and verify predictions. Finally, students generalize: "What would the graph look like for a Super ball?" "What would happen if the experiment were repeated on a carpeted floor?"

This single experiment involves measurement, data analysis, number sense, estimation, graphing, multiplication, patterns and functions (algebra), and mathematical reasoning. All these topics, moreover, relate to a single context that unites them. By weaving so many themes into one complex whole, that whole becomes more meaningful and the mathematics more powerful.

Lessons such as *Bouncing Ball* are embedded in a careful sequence of lessons and units that address all the standards. Other lessons develop single skills or concepts that students can then practice in the Daily Practice and Problems. These skills and concepts are extended and applied in more complex lessons and investigations. *Math Trailblazers* is therefore a comprehensive and balanced curriculum that includes geometry, statistics and probability, measurement, algebra, estimation, fractions, numeration, and computation—just what the *Principles and Standards* requires.

For more information on the *Math Trailblazers* approach to selected content areas, see the TIMS Tutors in Section 9 of this *Teacher Implementation Guide.*

Process Standards

The process standards highlight ways to acquire and use content knowledge. Each process standard is connected to the others. Moreover, the learning of mathematical processes is deeply embedded in the learning of content.

Problem Solving. A strong emphasis on problem solving is evident in the NCTM recommendations. Throughout *Math Trailblazers,* students are immersed in complex problem situations in which they both apply the mathematics they know and learn new mathematics. Students develop skills, procedures, and concepts as they work on the problems. For example, in the third-grade laboratory experiment, *The Better "Picker Upper,"* students explore the absorbency of various brands of paper towels by dropping water on each type of towel and comparing the areas of the spots. As students work through this complex problem, they learn about area (by tracing the spots on grid paper and counting square centimeters to find the areas), fractions (as they piece parts of square centimeters together to make whole square centimeters), averaging (as they aggregate the results of several trials), graphing (as they display and interpret their data in graphs), and computation (as they calculate the number of drops of water a whole paper towel absorbs). All this mathematics grows out of one problem: "Which is the more absorbent towel?"

Putting problems first is a different and difficult way to organize a mathematics curriculum. Having the focus on problems requires careful design, meticulous planning, and continual assessment to ensure the timely development of skills and concepts. Despite the difficulties, the benefits are clear: students not only master skills and concepts, they can apply them flexibly to solve problems.

Reasoning and Proof. This standard requires that reasoning permeate the curriculum. Students constantly explain their thinking and justify their solutions, first in small groups and then to the class as a whole. Sometimes they explain their thoughts orally and other times in writing or by using pictures and other tools. Students are always encouraged to find solutions in more than one way and to compare and contrast various solution methods. Thus, meaning and understanding are emphasized, and students find that mathematics makes sense.

"Mathematical reasoning develops in classrooms where students are encouraged to put forth their own ideas for examination. Teachers and students should be open to questions, reactions, and elaborations from others in the classroom. Students need to explain and justify their thinking and learn how to detect fallacies and critique others' thinking. They need to have ample opportunity to apply their reasoning skills and justify their thinking in mathematical discussion." (NCTM 2000, p. 188)

One example of an important area of mathematical reasoning that receives particular attention in *Math Trailblazers,* especially in Grades 3 through 5, is pre-proportional and proportional reasoning. This kind of reasoning is carefully developed over time through a sequence of real-life problems that students can solve with manipulatives, patterns, graphs, or symbols. Students choose the strategies and tools that make sense to them. Using these tools helps students create visual images of this important mathematical concept, which historically has largely been taught symbolically or procedurally and has been difficult for many students to grasp.

Communication. Students need frequent opportunities to communicate their mathematics. "Communication is an essential part of mathematics and mathematics education… Students gain insight into their thinking when they present their methods for solving problems, when they justify their reasoning to a classmate or teacher, or when they formulate a question about something that is puzzling to them." (NCTM 2000, p. 60) Communication is integral to *Math Trailblazers*. In many activities, students handle manipulatives, draw pictures, make graphs, and grapple with mathematical ideas. Many activities are collaborative exercises involving groups of students who work together to obtain, analyze, and generalize their results.

Just as people explain how they solve problems on the job, students who use the labs and activities talk about their mathematics. Students discuss, compare, contrast, and write about their problem-solving methods in both small-group and whole-class settings. This "publication" of students' mathematical thinking gives students access to a broader range of solution strategies and helps them become more reflective about mathematics.

Connections. This standard calls for connections within mathematics, between mathematics and other parts of the school curriculum, and between mathematics and their own interests. Integration of subject matter is a major focus of *Math Trailblazers*. Mathematics arises naturally in science, language, history, and daily life. *Math Trailblazers* does not artificially merge disparate ideas from distinct disciplines, but rather builds up the underlying unity between disciplines that we see in the real world. For example, the basic measurement variables that the curriculum covers extensively —length, area, volume, mass, and time—are fundamental not only to mathematics but also to science and daily life. The TIMS Laboratory Method effectively incorporates the method of science into the mathematics curriculum as a problem-solving tool.

The *Adventure Books* and Literature Connections integrate language arts and social studies with the mathematics curriculum. Some *Adventure Books* recount the history of science and mathematics; others show how the concepts and procedures students are learning apply to the work of real scientists or to everyday life. Students are continually required to communicate their mathematical thinking orally and in writing. *Math Trailblazers* is committed to the ideal of "writing across the curriculum."

Connections within mathematics are equally important. Like most real-world problems, activities in *Math Trailblazers* generally involve a combination of mathematical topics. A single laboratory experiment, for example, might involve arithmetic, data collection, estimation, geometry, probability, and algebraic concepts—each covered at an appropriate level for students.

Representation. "Representing ideas and connecting their representations to mathematics lies at the heart of understanding mathematics." (NCTM 2000, p. 136) *Math Trailblazers* is rich in the many opportunities it gives students to represent mathematical ideas. For example, whole numbers are represented as collections of objects (using manipulatives or drawings), as measurements, as points on a number line, or as items on a *100 Chart.* When children collect data they may organize it in a data table or represent it graphically. If there are patterns in the data, they can describe them numerically or graphically. Ultimately, they describe some relations symbolically.

Throughout *Math Trailblazers* students are encouraged to draw pictures and diagrams to illustrate their ideas and support their thinking. This communicates their reasoning, and as students create these representations, they clarify and build their thinking.

Developing a *Standards*-Based Classroom

The *Professional Standards for Teaching Mathematics* (NCTM, 1991) and the Teaching Principle in the *Principles and Standards* specify what classroom teachers, supervisors, teacher educators, and policy makers should do to improve mathematics instruction. Much of this discussion concerns four key areas: tasks, discourse, environment, and analysis. Teachers decide what tasks to set for students, foster discourse about mathematics, establish a classroom environment conducive to high achievement and positive attitudes, and engage in analysis of students' thinking and their own teaching. While accomplishing these things depends more on teachers' expertise than on curricula, materials that embody the *Principles and Standards* can make the work easier.

Tasks. *Math Trailblazers* provides a logical sequence of well-conceived tasks. Professional mathematicians and scientists helped develop the curriculum so lessons focus on significant concepts and skills. Teachers and mathematics educators also helped write the curriculum, so tasks are engaging, practical, and developmentally appropriate. Lessons develop both skills and concepts, so they make connections within mathematics and between mathematics and other subjects, portray mathematics as a human endeavor, and promote communication and problem solving.

Discourse. Many features of *Math Trailblazers* support discourse. Tasks in the curriculum have enough depth for significant discussion to be possible. An emphasis on multiple solutions to problems encourages students to talk about their own thinking. The *Student Guide* often displays and discusses multiple solutions to problems. Journal and discussion prompts in the teacher materials stimulate and focus classroom discussions. *Adventure Books* and children's literature help students understand that people really do talk about mathematics and science. The wide range of tools and technology in *Math Trailblazers*—manipulatives, calculators, pictures, tables, graphs, and symbols—enhance discourse by broadening the means of communication beyond what is traditional.

Environment. Creating a classroom environment conducive to the development of each student's mathematical power is necessary for the *Principles and Standards* to come alive. This involves arranging space, time, and materials in ways that maximize student learning. *Math Trailblazers'* diverse range of lessons—activities of varied length, activities for groups and individuals, hands-on and paper-and-pencil investigations, and activities that encourage multiple solution paths—all help teachers develop a classroom that builds mathematical understandings and skills for a wide range of students.

Analysis. The curriculum's activities and assessment program provide teachers with many opportunities to analyze students' learning. Teachers using the curriculum will know more about their students' mathematical abilities than they ever have before. The extensive background information in the unit guides and in the *Teacher Implementation Guide* provides accessible ways for teachers to gain additional insight into how students learn mathematics. This enhanced knowledge motivates the teaching of subsequent lessons. *Math Trailblazers* will help you become more attuned both to your students and to your teaching.

For additional discussion on these and related topics, see the following sections in the *Teacher Implemention Guide:*

- Building the *Math Trailblazers* Classroom
- Teaching the *Math Trailblazers* Student: Meeting Individual Needs
- Language in the *Math Trailblazers* Classroom
- Working with *Math Trailblazers* Parents and Families

Math Trailblazers: **A Standards-Based Curriculum**

In summary, NCTM calls for curricula to be coherent within and across the grades, to be conceptually oriented, to involve students actively, to emphasize development of students' mathematical thinking and reasoning abilities, to emphasize applications, to include a broad range of content, and to make appropriate use of calculators and computers.

These are admirable goals and high expectations. No curriculum can finally and fully attain such goals and fulfill such expectations—not only will there always be improvements to be made, but in the end much depends upon individual teachers and students. Yet a curriculum that has been developed specifically to be aligned with the *Principles and Standards* will provide the foundation. The goals and characteristics described above are all hallmarks of *Math Trailblazers.*

The best test of alignment with the *Principles and Standards,* however, is to observe students using the curriculum. Are they actively involved? Do they grapple with significant concepts while learning and applying basic skills? Are they thinking and reasoning? Do they use a broad range of tools to solve realistic problems? We think you will find that *Math Trailblazers* more than meets this test.

References

An Agenda for Action: Recommendations for School Mathematics of the 1980s. National Council of Teachers of Mathematics, Reston, VA, 1980.

Assessment Standards for School Mathematics. National Council of Teachers of Mathematics, Reston, VA, 1995.

Curriculum and Evaluation Standards for School Mathematics. National Council of Teachers of Mathematics, Reston, VA, 1989.

Essential Mathematics for the 21st Century: The Position of the National Council of Supervisors of Mathematics. National Council of Supervisors of Mathematics, Minneapolis, MN, 1988.

National Research Council. "Conclusions and Recommendations." In *Adding It Up: Helping Children Learn Mathematics.* J. Kilpatrick, J. Swafford, and B. Findell (Eds.). National Academy Press, Washington, DC, 2001.

Principles and Standards for School Mathematics. National Council of Teachers of Mathematics, Reston, VA, 2000.

Professional Standards for Teaching Mathematics. National Council of Teachers of Mathematics, Reston, VA, 1991.

Scope and Sequence

Math Trailblazers was developed to meet the NCTM *Principles and Standards for School Mathematics.* The scope and sequence in white type on the following pages indicates how each month and thematic unit aligns with the *Principles and Standards.* By reading the chart horizontally, you will see the integration of the various standards within a given month or unit. By reading the chart vertically, you can track the development of a specific standard throughout the kindergarten curriculum.

	Number and Operations	Algebra	Geometry	Measurement	Data Analysis and Probability
Month 1	• Using numbers to describe sets of objects. • Using tally marks to skip count by 5s. • Counting by 1s and 5s. • Developing number sense for numbers to 20. • Counting using one-to-one correspondence. • Developing the concept of cardinality.	• Exploring patterns auditorily, visually, and kinesthetically. • Identifying and describing patterns.	• Describing location using spatial terminology (above/below, etc.).	• Measuring time on a calendar.	• Collecting, organizing, graphing, and analyzing data.
Month 2	• Translating between dot patterns, pictures, and numbers. • Sorting and ordering sets. • Developing oral counting skills. • Investigating patterns in a number sequence. • Using problem-solving strategies to figure out the number of days until an event. • Developing number sense to 100. • Counting using one-to-one correspondence. • Developing the concept of cardinality. • Exploring different types of addition and subtraction problems.	• Identifying and describing patterns. • Representing patterns using symbols (AB).	• Describing spatial relationships using location and position.	• Describing height relationships using comparison language. • Measuring time on a calendar.	• Collecting, organizing, graphing, and analyzing data.

Problem Solving	Reasoning and Proof	Communication	Connections	Representation
• Exploring different types of addition and subtraction problems. • Creating and testing problem-solving strategies.	• Creating and testing problem-solving strategies.	• Identifying and describing patterns. • Describing spatial relationships. • Explaining solutions verbally and in pictures.	• Connecting mathematics to real-world situations: using children's literature. • Describing the world using spatial terminology.	• Using tally marks to represent numbers in groups of 5s and 1s. • Representing linear patterns auditorily, visually, and kinesthetically. • Representing quantities using numbers.
• Using problem-solving strategies to find the number of days until an event. • Exploring different types of addition and subtraction problems. • Creating and testing problem-solving strategies. • Generalizing problem-solving strategies to other situations.	• Creating and testing problem-solving strategies. • Generalizing problem-solving strategies to other situations.	• Identifying and describing patterns. • Connecting mathematics to real-world situations: using children's literature. • Developing oral counting skills. • Describing spatial relationships using location and position. • Describing height relationships using comparison language. • Explaining solutions verbally and in pictures.	• Translating between dot patterns, pictures, and numbers.	• Representing patterns using symbols (AB). • Translating between dot patterns, pictures, and numbers. • Collecting, organizing, graphing, and analyzing data.

		Number and Operations	Algebra	Geometry	Measurement	Data Analysis and Probability
Month 3		• Developing meaning for addition and subtraction. • Representing numbers using ten frames and number dot patterns. • Translating between different representations of numbers: dot patterns, ten frames, and numerals. • Exploring part-part-whole relationships of the number 5. • Using patterns in data to investigate number relationships. • Translating between dot patterns, pictures, and numbers. • Counting by 1s, 5s, and 10s. • Developing number sense for 100s, 10s, and 1s. • Counting using one-to-one correspondence. • Developing the concept of cardinality. • Ordering objects by their heights.	• Identifying and extending patterns with two elements. • Creating, copying, and extending patterns. • Comparing patterns using multiple representations. • Using patterns in data to investigate number relationships.	• Using spatial terms to describe movement from one place to another.	• Measuring time on a calendar. • Describing height relationships using comparison language: taller than, shorter than, and close to.	• Exploring the likelihood of an event based on collected data. • Collecting, organizing, graphing, and analyzing data.
Month 4		• Understanding cardinal and ordinal numbers. • Using ordinal numbers on the calendar. • Describing number relationships using comparison language: more than, less than, close to, same as. • Exploring part-part-whole relationships of the number five. • Describing the part-part-whole relationships of the number five verbally and pictorially. • Developing meaning for addition and subtraction. • Using patterns in data to investigate number relationships. • Counting by 1s, 5s, and 10s. • Developing number sense for 100s, 10s, and 1s. • Counting using one-to-one correspondence. • Developing the concept of cardinality.	• Exploring patterns with two elements. • Describing similarities between calendar patterns and kinesthetic patterns. • Identifying and extending patterns. • Using patterns in data to investigate number relationships.	• Using spatial terms to create a map. • Translating between locations in the real world and on a map.	• Describing length relationships using comparison language: longer than, shorter than, or close to. • Estimating length. • Exploring the relationship between the size of the unit and the number of units needed to measure an object. • Measuring length with nonstandard units. • Measuring time on a calendar.	• Collecting, organizing, graphing, and analyzing data.

Problem Solving	Reasoning and Proof	Communication	Connections	Representation
• Solving different types of addition and subtraction problems. • Creating and testing problem-solving strategies. • Generalizing problem-solving strategies to other situations.	• Creating and testing problem-solving strategies. • Generalizing problem-solving strategies to other situations.	• Explaining solutions verbally and in pictures. • Using spatial terms to describe movement from one place to another.	• Connecting mathematics to real-world situations: using children's literature.	• Representing patterns in multiple ways. • Comparing patterns using multiple representations. • Translating between dot patterns, pictures, and numerals.
• Developing meaning for addition and subtraction. • Exploring different types of addition and subtraction problems. • Creating and testing problem-solving strategies. • Generalizing problem-solving strategies to other situations.	• Exploring the relationship between the size of the unit and the number of units needed to measure. • Creating and testing problem-solving strategies. • Generalizing problem-solving strategies to other situations.	• Describing number relationships using comparison language: more than, less than, close to, same as. • Connecting the part-part-whole relationships of the number five verbally and pictorially. • Explaining solutions verbally and in pictures.	• Describing similarities between calendar patterns and kinesthetic patterns. • Translating between locations in the real world and on a map. • Connecting mathematics to real-world situations: using children's literature.	• Describing similarities between calendar patterns and kinesthetic patterns. • Describing the part-part-whole relationships of the number five verbally and pictorially. • Using spatial terms to create a map.

	Number and Operations	Algebra	Geometry	Measurement	Data Analysis and Probability
Month 5	• Identifying number patterns on a calendar. • Writing number sentences to describe patterns on a ten frame. • Comparing and ordering groups of objects. • Using comparison language: more than, less than, close to, same as. • Exploring number relationships using the benchmark numbers 5 and 10. • Developing estimation skills using a referent set. • Understanding that estimates should be approximate rather than a specific number. • Developing estimation language: more than, less than, about, and close to. • Counting using number patterns. • Placing numbers in intervals. • Counting by 1s, 5s, and 10s. • Developing number sense for 100s, 10s, and 1s. • Counting using one-to-one correspondence. • Developing meaning for addition.	• Writing number sentences to describe patterns on a ten frame. • Identifying and extending patterns. • Identifying and using number patterns on a calendar.	• Finding the shortest path between two points.	• Estimating length. • Describing height relationships using comparison language. • Measuring length using nonstandard units. • Measuring time on a calendar.	• Connecting real-world measurements to graphical representations. • Collecting, organizing, graphing, and analyzing data.
Month 6	• Exploring part-part-whole relationships of numbers to 12. • Describing number relationships using comparison language: more than, less than, close to, same as. • Translating between dot patterns, pictures, and numbers. • Developing meaning for addition and subtraction. • Estimating area. • Counting using one-to-one correspondence. • Developing number sense for 100s, 10s, and 1s. • Counting by 1s, 5s, and 10s.	• Identifying and using number patterns on the calendar. • Identifying and using pattern units on the calendar to determine missing pattern elements. • Identifying and extending patterns. • Collecting, organizing, graphing, and analyzing data.	• Describing and sorting 3-dimensional shapes using their properties. • Identifying and classifying three-dimensional shapes. • Comparing and contrasting the attributes of three-dimensional objects using descriptive language.	• Exploring area and its measurement. • Measuring area using nonstandard units. • Estimating area. • Exploring the relationship between the size of the unit and the number of units needed to measure. • Measuring time on a calendar.	• Exploring the likelihood of an event based on collected data. • Collecting, organizing, graphing, and analyzing data.

Problem Solving	Reasoning and Proof	Communication	Connections	Representation
• Exploring different types of addition and subtraction problems. • Creating and testing problem-solving strategies. • Generalizing problem-solving strategies to other situations.	• Developing estimation skills using a referent set. • Placing numbers in intervals. • Creating and testing problem-solving strategies. • Generalizing problem-solving strategies to other situations.	• Describing number relationships using comparison language: more than, less than, close to, same as. • Developing estimation language: more than, less than, about, and close to. • Describing spatial relationships using position. • Explaining solutions verbally and in pictures.	• Relating the magnitude of numbers to the magnitude of measurements. • Connecting number sentences to ten frame arrangements.	• Interpreting a graph. • Connecting number sentences to ten frame arrangements. • Translating between different representations of numbers: concrete, pictorial, symbolic.
• Developing meaning for addition and subtraction. • Exploring different types of addition and subtraction problems. • Creating and testing problem-solving strategies. • Generalizing problem-solving strategies to other situations.	• Classifying three-dimensional shapes. • Comparing and contrasting three-dimensional objects using descriptive language. • Exploring the relationship between the size of the unit and the number of units needed to measure. • Creating and testing problem-solving strategies. • Generalizing problem-solving strategies to other situations.	• Comparing and contrasting three-dimensional shapes using descriptive language. • Explaining solutions verbally and in pictures.	• Translating between dot patterns, pictures, and numbers.	• Translating between dot patterns, pictures, and numbers. • Interpreting graphs.

	Number and Operations	Algebra	Geometry	Measurement	Data Analysis and Probability
Month 7	• Using calendar patterns to skip count. • Exploring part-part-whole relationships of the number ten. • Using patterns in data to investigate number relationships. • Counting back from ten. • Developing meaning for addition and subtraction. • Exploring three-part partitions of the numbers 7, 8, and 9. • Translating between different representations of numbers. • Solving problems involving addition and subtraction using objects. • Counting using one-to-one correspondence. • Developing number sense for 100s, 10s, and 1s. • Counting by 1s, 5s, and 10s.	• Recognizing and extending patterns. • Using patterns in data to investigate number relationships.	• Identifying and describing two-dimensional shapes. • Comparing and contrasting two-dimensional shapes using descriptive language. • Sorting two-dimensional shapes according to their attributes.	• Exploring area and its measurement. • Estimating area using two different nonstandard units. • Exploring the relationship between the size of the unit and the number of units needed to measure. • Measuring time on a calendar. • Measuring area using square-inch tiles.	• Collecting, organizing, graphing, and analyzing data.
Month 8	• Solving problems involving pennies and nickels. • Exploring three-part partitions of the number 10. • Developing meaning for addition and subtraction. • Representing addition and subtraction situations using manipulatives and drawings. • Developing number sense for 100s, 10s, and 1s. • Counting using one-to-one correspondence. • Counting by 1s, 5s, and 10s.	• Exploring patterns with more than two elements on the calendar. • Identifying and extending patterns. • Collecting, organizing, graphing, and analyzing data.	• Developing spatial sense. • Identifying and describing two-dimensional shapes. • Investigating the attributes of shapes. • Investigating the effect of rotation on a shape.	• Ordering containers by capacity. • Exploring volume and its measurement. • Estimating volume. • Measuring time on a calendar.	• Collecting, organizing, graphing, and analyzing data.

Problem Solving	Reasoning and Proof	Communication	Connections	Representation
• Exploring different types of addition and subtraction problems. • Creating and testing problem-solving strategies. • Generalizing problem-solving strategies to other situations.	• Using patterns in data to investigate number relationships. • Identifying and describing two-dimensional shapes. • Comparing and contrasting two-dimensional shapes using descriptive language. • Sorting two-dimensional shapes according to their attributes. • Estimating area using two different nonstandard units. • Exploring the relationship between the size of the unit and the number of units needed to measure. • Creating and testing problem-solving strategies. • Generalizing problem-solving strategies to other situations.	• Comparing and contrasting two-dimensional shapes using descriptive language. • Explaining solutions verbally and in pictures.	• Using calendar patterns to skip count. • Understanding the concepts of yesterday, today, and tomorrow. • Connecting mathematics to real-world situations: using children's literature.	• Translating between different representations of numbers: concrete, pictorial, and symbolic. • Collecting, organizing, graphing, and analyzing data.
• Solving problems involving pennies and nickels. • Developing meaning for addition and subtraction. • Creating and solving word problems. • Exploring different types of addition and subtraction problems. • Creating and testing problem-solving strategies. • Generalizing problem-solving strategies to other situations.	• Solving problems involving pennies and nickels. • Developing meaning for addition and subtraction. • Creating and solving word problems. • Investigating the attributes of shapes. • Investigating rotations on a shape. • Creating and testing problem-solving strategies. • Generalizing problem-solving strategies to other situations.	• Identifying and describing two-dimensional shapes. • Explaining solutions verbally and in pictures.	• Connecting mathematics to real-world situations: using children's literature. • Solving problems involving pennies and nickels.	• Identifying and describing two-dimensional shapes. • Representing addition and subtraction situations using manipulatives and drawings. • Collecting, organizing, graphing, and analyzing data.

	Number and Operations	Algebra	Geometry	Measurement	Data Analysis and Probability
Month 9	• Comparing and ordering numbers. • Using problem-solving strategies to locate a number on the calendar. • Building awareness of time and its passage using the hour hand of a clock. • Solving problems involving addition and subtraction. • Developing number sense for 100s, 10s, and 1s. • Counting using one-to-one correspondence. • Counting by 1s, 5s, and 10s. • Recognizing that halves of an object must be "equal."	• Exploring patterns with more than two elements on the calendar. • Identifying and extending patterns.	• Identifying and describing the relationship between three-dimensional shapes and their two-dimensional shadows.	• Ordering objects according to weight. • Exploring mass and its measurement. • Working with a balance. • Measuring time on a calendar. • Developing an awareness of the passage of time using the hour hand of a clock.	• Collecting, organizing, graphing, and analyzing data.
Month 10	• Developing strategies to solve problems related to the calendar. • Comparing and ordering numbers using relations such as one more than, two less than. • Translating between representations of numbers. • Developing meaning for addition and subtraction. • Developing number sense for 100s, 10s, and 1s. • Counting using one-to-one correspondence. • Counting by 1s, 5s, and 10s. • Comparing and ordering numbers using symbols ($<$, $>$, $=$).	• Exploring patterns with more than two elements on the calendar. • Identifying and extending patterns. • Collecting, organizing, graphing, and analyzing data.	• Developing the concept of line symmetry. • Completing and creating symmetrical designs.	• Exploring time and its measurement. • Recording events according to the hour of the day. • Measuring time on a calendar. • Developing an awareness of the passage of time using the hour hand of a clock.	• Collecting, organizing, graphing, and analyzing data.

Problem Solving	Reasoning and Proof	Communication	Connections	Representation
• Using problem-solving strategies to locate a number on the calendar. • Solving problems involving addition and subtraction. • Exploring different types of addition and subtraction problems. • Creating and testing problem-solving strategies. • Generalizing problem-solving strategies to other situations.	• Solving number riddles and puzzles on a calendar. • Identifying and describing the relationship between three-dimensional shapes and their two-dimensional shadows. • Creating and testing problem-solving strategies. • Generalizing problem-solving strategies to other situations.	• Identifying and describing the relationship between three-dimensional shapes and their two-dimensional shadows. • Explaining solutions verbally and in pictures.	• Using problem-solving strategies to locate a number on the calendar.	• Exploring equality using fractional representations. • Collecting, organizing, graphing, and analyzing data.
• Developing strategies to solve problems related to the calendar. • Developing meaning for addition and subtraction. • Exploring different types of addition and subtraction problems. • Creating and testing problem-solving strategies. • Generalizing problem-solving strategies to other situations.	• Developing the concept of line symmetry. • Creating and testing problem-solving strategies. • Generalizing problem-solving strategies to other situations.	• Using comparison language to describe number relationships. • Explaining solutions verbally and in pictures.	• Connecting mathematics to real-world situations: using children's literature. • Finding examples of symmetry in pictures and the real world.	• Translating between dot patterns and number sentences. • Collecting, organizing, graphing, and analyzing data. • Using tally marks to count by 5s.

	Number and Operations	Algebra	Geometry	Measurement	Data Analysis and Probability
Buildings	• Using tally marks. • Interpreting graphs. • Identifying and using number dot patterns. • Developing number sense by comparing quantities. • Using counting to solve problems. • Creating addition and subtraction problems. • Solving addition and subtraction problems. • Comparing and ordering numbers.	• Recognizing and using number dot patterns.	• Developing spatial sense. • Developing concepts of geometry, such as shape recognition, position, symmetry, and mapping. • Comparing and classifying buildings. • Drawing pictures using geometric shapes. • Identifying and using number dot patterns.	• Developing measuring skills. • Developing concepts of length and area. • Measuring length with nonstandard units.	• Collecting, organizing, graphing, and analyzing data. • Using tally marks. • Comparing two types of graphs.
On the Go	• Comparing the number of objects in different groups. • Using comparison language: more than, less than, and same as. • Ordering up to 10 numbers. • Matching two items that have identical numbered labels. • Collecting and recording data. • Solving problems using coins.		• Developing spatial sense. • Identifying geometric shapes.	• Representing lengths with string. • Exploring area. • Estimating volume. • Exploring the relationship between the size of the unit and the number of units needed to measure an object. • Estimating weight. • Exploring the relationship between weight and size. • Using comparison language to compare weights.	• Collecting, organizing, graphing, and analyzing data. • Making a picture graph. • Analyzing data to tell the story of the graph. • Sorting and classifying objects. • Explaining sorting methods.

Problem Solving	Reasoning and Proof	Communication	Connections	Representation
• Using counting to solve problems. • Creating addition and subtraction problems. • Solving addition and subtraction problems. • Representing and solving part-part-whole problems.	• Comparing and classifying buildings. • Interpreting graphs. • Creating addition and subtraction problems.	• Explaining solutions verbally and in pictures.	• Comparing and classifying buildings. • Connecting mathematics to real-world situations: solving problems about buildings.	• Collecting, organizing, graphing, and analyzing data. • Comparing two types of graphs. • Using tally marks. • Recognizing and using number dot patterns.
• Solving problems involving comparisons. • Solving problems using coins.	• Estimating. • Testing a prediction. • Comparing the use of different units for measuring length. • Sorting and classifying objects.	• Analyzing data to tell the story of the graph. • Explaining sorting methods. • Using comparison language to compare weights: more than, less than, and about the same. • Explaining solutions verbally and in pictures.	• Connecting mathematics to real-world situations: solving problems about vehicles.	• Making a picture graph. • Collecting and recording data. • Comparing the use of different units for measuring length. • Collecting, organizing, graphing, and analyzing data. • Using tally marks.

	Number and Operations	Algebra	Geometry	Measurement	Data Analysis and Probability
Crawly Creatures	• Using tally marks grouped in 5s to organize data in a table. • Grouping and counting objects. • Problem solving involving joining or separating groups. • Creating, acting out, drawing, or telling stories that involve addition, subtraction, multiplication, and division. • Using manipulatives to double the numbers 1 through 7. • Exploring odd and even numbers. • Identifying a skip-counting pattern. • Skip-counting by 2s to 14. • Translating between dot patterns and numbers. • Exploring partitions of the number 8.	• Identifying skip-counting patterns. • Making and interpreting picture graphs.	• Exploring line symmetry. • Using shapes (pattern blocks) to construct designs. • Identifying symmetry. • Developing geometric visualization skills. • Relating doubling of numbers to symmetry.	• Measuring area with two different units. • Exploring the relationship between the size of the unit and the number of units needed to measure. • Exploring positions of the hour hand.	• Classifying and sorting. • Using tally marks grouped in fives to organize data in a table. • Making and interpreting picture graphs.

Problem Solving	Reasoning and Proof	Communication	Connections	Representation
• Classifying and sorting. • Problem solving involving joining or separating groups. • Creating, acting out, drawing, or telling stories that involve addition, subtraction, multiplication, and division. • Exploring odd and even numbers.	• Classifying and sorting. • Problem solving involving joining or separating groups. • Creating, acting out, drawing, or telling stories involving addition, subtraction, multiplication, and division. • Exploring the relationship between the size of the unit and the number of units needed to measure.	• Creating, acting out, drawing, or telling stories that involve addition, subtraction, multiplication, and division.	• Constructing and interpreting picture graphs. • Connecting mathematics to real-world situations: solving problems about insects.	• Making and interpreting picture graphs. • Creating, acting out, drawing, or telling stories that involve addition, subtraction, multiplication, and division. • Relating doubling to symmetry. • Translating between dot patterns and numbers.

Math Facts and Whole-Number Operations

The Math Facts and Whole-Number Operations section outlines the *Math Trailblazers* approach to developing fluency with the math facts and whole-number operations.

Calculators are used as a tool for solving problems.

Math Facts and Whole-Number Operations

Work with whole numbers pervades the elementary mathematics curriculum. A major goal of *Math Trailblazers* is to prepare students to compute accurately, flexibly, and appropriately in all situations. Standard topics in arithmetic—acquisition of basic math facts and fluency with whole-number operations—are covered extensively.

In this section, we briefly describe our approach to developing fluency with the math facts and whole-number operations. Table 1 outlines the development of these two topics in Grades K–5. We also summarize below the fundamental characteristics of our work with whole numbers. You can obtain more detailed information from the following sources:

- Two TIMS Tutors *Arithmetic* and *Math Facts;* and
- Background sections and lesson guides from individual *Math Trailblazers* units.

Introduction to the Math Facts in *Math Trailblazers*

In developing our program for the math facts, we sought a careful balance between strategies and drill. This approach is based on a large body of research and is advocated by the NCTM *Principles and Standards for School Mathematics*. The research indicates that the methods used in the *Math Trailblazers* math facts program lead to more effective learning and better retention of the math facts and also helps develop essential math skills.

The *Math Trailblazers* program for teaching the math facts is characterized by these elements:

- *Early emphasis on problem solving.* Students first approach the basic facts as problems to solve rather than as facts to memorize. Students invent their own strategies to solve these problems or learn appropriate strategies from others through class discussion. Students' natural strategies, especially for counting, are explicitly encouraged. In this way, students learn that math is more than memorizing facts and rules that "you either get or you don't."
- *De-emphasis of rote work.* Fluency with the math facts is an important component of any student's mathematical learning. Research shows, however, that overemphasizing memorization and frequent timed tests are counterproductive. We encourage the use of strategies to find facts, so students become confident they can find answers to fact problems that they do not immediately recall.
- *Gradual and systematic introduction of facts.* Students study the facts in small groups of problems that can be solved using similar strategies. Students first work on simple strategies for easy facts and then progress to more sophisticated strategies and harder facts. By the end of the process, they gain fluency with all the required facts.

- *Ongoing practice.* Work on the math facts is distributed throughout the curriculum, especially in the Daily Practice and Problems (Grades 1–5), Home Practice (Grades 3–5), and games. This practice for fluency, however, takes place only after students have a conceptual understanding of the operations and have achieved proficiency with strategies for solving basic fact problems. Delaying practice in this way means that less practice is required to achieve fluency.

- *Appropriate assessment.* Teachers assess students' knowledge of the facts through observations as they work on activities, labs, and games as well as through the appropriate use of written tests and quizzes. Beginning in first grade, periodic, short quizzes in the Daily Practice and Problems naturally follow the study of small groups of facts organized around specific strategies. As self-assessment in Grades 3–5, each student records his or her progress on *Facts I Know* charts and determines which facts he or she needs to study. Inventory tests of all facts for each operation are used sparingly in Grades 2–5 (no more than twice per year) to assess students' progress with fact fluency. The goal of the math facts assessment program is to determine whether students can find answers to fact problems quickly and accurately and retain this skill over time.

- *Multiyear approach.* In Grades 1 and 2, *Math Trailblazers* emphasizes strategies that lead to fluency with the addition and subtraction facts. In Grade 3, students gain fluency with the multiplication facts while reviewing the addition and subtraction facts. In Grade 4, students achieve fluency with the division facts and verify fluency with the multiplication facts. In Grade 5, the multiplication and division facts are systematically reviewed and assessed. This is outlined in Table 1.

- *Facts are not gatekeepers.* Students are not prevented from learning more complex mathematics because they do not perform well on fact tests. Use of strategies, calculators, and other math tools (e.g., manipulatives, hundreds charts, printed multiplication tables) allows students to continue to work on interesting problems and important mathematical concepts while still learning the facts.

While developing fluency with math facts is not a goal of the kindergarten curriculum, exploring number relationships helps develop flexible thinking about numbers that will assist with the eventual acquisition of fluency. The following ideas that are stressed in kindergarten tie directly with strategies that are used in later grades to learn math facts:

- the idea of "one more" or "one less" than a given number;
- partitioning numbers; and
- thinking about numbers in relation to a benchmark number.

Whole-Number Operations in *Math Trailblazers*

Math Trailblazers helps students develop efficient and accurate methods for computation with the four basic operations. The treatment of whole-number computation proceeds in several stages. The grade levels for the stages vary with the operation—full development of division, for example, comes long after addition—but the general pattern is similar for all the operations. Roughly speaking, the stages are:

- developing meaning for the operation,
- inventing procedures for solving problems, and
- becoming more efficient at carrying out procedures, all leading to
- developing mathematical power.

Developing mathematical power with an operation means that students understand *when* to apply the operation and *how* to use varied computational methods to solve problems, even complex or nonroutine problems.

With each operation, we seek a balance between conceptual understanding and procedural skill. Standard methods for solving problems are not introduced until students develop good conceptual and procedural understandings. Research has shown that introducing such procedures too early may short-circuit students' common sense, encouraging mechanical and uncritical behavior. As a result, formal instruction in some standard procedures is delayed slightly beyond the traditional time, but problems that would normally be solved by standard procedures are often introduced sooner than is customary. This forces students to use their prior knowledge to devise their own methods to solve the problems.

Students practice using the operations in activities, games, and laboratory investigations. More practice is provided in the Daily Practice and Problems in Grades 1–5 and in the Home Practice in Grades 3–5. Even after analyzing and practicing standard methods, students are still encouraged to solve problems in more than one way. Flexible thinking and mathematical power are our goals, not rote fluency with a handful of standard algorithms.

The *Math Trailblazers* approach to all mathematics topics promotes the coordinated development of both procedural skill and conceptual understanding. This is particularly apparent in our approach to computation.

The following table describes the development of math facts and whole-number operations in *Math Trailblazers*. The shaded portions of the table highlight development of the math facts program in each grade. Expectations for fluency with math facts are indicated in bold. The white portions of the table highlight development of the whole-number operations.

Grade	Addition	Subtraction	Multiplication	Division
K	Introduce concepts through problem solving and use of manipulatives.			
1	Develop strategies for addition facts. Solve addition problems in context.	Develop strategies for subtraction facts. Solve subtraction problems in context.	Develop concepts through problem solving and use of manipulatives.	
2	Continue use of addition facts in problems. Continue use of strategies for addition facts. **Assess for fluency with addition facts.** Continue solving addition problems in context. Introduce procedures for multidigit addition using manipulatives and paper and pencil.	Continue use of subtraction facts in problems. Continue use of strategies for subtraction facts. **Assess for fluency with subtraction facts.** Continue solving subtraction problems in context. Introduce procedures for multidigit subtraction using manipulatives and paper and pencil.	Continue concept development through problem solving and use of manipulatives.	
3	Diagnose and remediate with addition facts as needed. Develop procedures for multidigit addition using manipulatives and paper and pencil. Practice and apply multidigit addition in varied contexts.	Maintain fluency with subtraction facts through review and assessment. Develop procedures for multidigit subtraction using manipulatives and paper and pencil. Practice and apply multidigit subtraction in varied contexts.	Continue use of multiplication facts in problems. Develop strategies for multiplication facts. **Assess for fluency with multiplication facts.** Solve multiplication problems in context. Introduce paper-and-pencil multiplication (1-digit × 2-digits).	Continue use of division facts in problems. Develop strategies for division facts. Continue concept development. Solve division problems in context.
4	Diagnose and remediate with addition facts as needed. Practice and apply multidigit addition in varied contexts. Review paper-and-pencil procedures for multidigit addition.	Diagnose and remediate with subtraction facts as needed. Practice and apply multidigit subtraction in varied contexts. Review paper-and-pencil procedures for multidigit subtraction.	Maintain fluency with multiplication facts through review and assessment. Develop procedures for multiplication using manipulatives and paper and pencil (1-digit and 2-digit multipliers). Practice and apply multiplication in varied contexts.	Continue use of division facts in problems. Continue development of strategies for division facts. **Assess for fluency with division facts.** Solve division problems in context. Develop procedures for division using manipulatives and paper and pencil (1-digit divisors).
5	Diagnose and remediate with addition facts as needed. Practice and apply multidigit addition in varied contexts.	Diagnose and remediate with subtraction facts as needed. Practice and apply multidigit subtraction in varied contexts.	Maintain fluency with multiplication facts through review and assessment. Review paper-and-pencil procedures. Practice and apply multiplication in varied contexts.	Maintain fluency with division facts through review and assessment. Develop paper-and-pencil procedures (1-digit and 2-digit divisors). Practice and apply division in varied contexts.

Table 1: *Math Facts and Whole-Number Operations Overview*

Homework Guide

The Homework Guide explains the importance of home study.

Parents of kindergarten children have a shared responsibility in helping their children become lifelong learners.

Homework Guide

As children begin their formal schooling, it is important to connect mathematics with the world outside the classroom. This will help them develop confidence in their abilities to use mathematics to make sense of everyday situations and help them understand that doing mathematics is a common human activity. Achieving this should not be the sole responsibility of the classroom teacher. Parents of kindergarten children have a shared responsibility in helping children become lifelong learners. To assist in this process, we suggest several ways to facilitate an early and strong partnership between the kindergarten teacher and parents.

Homework is one way to involve parents with mathematics. Homework assignments are suggested in some but not all kindergarten lessons. Each homework assignment includes a Note Home that explains the assignment. However, we consider assigned homework only one part of the active learning that families must provide in order for their children to be successful in mathematics in school.

More significantly, we want to encourage parents to engage their children in the everyday use of mathematics. We would like parents to involve the children in math-related activities as they arise, such as counting objects, filling containers, or using clocks and calendars. We also want to encourage parents to look for situations that can help reinforce and develop math skills, such as comparing sizes of containers, looking for shapes in the environment, playing math games, or using everyday situations to create simple arithmetic problems. Parents welcome such involvement when encouraged and when provided with some hints about how to do it.

On the following pages, we include reproducible letters (English and Spanish) to parents that introduce family members to the role of homework in the *Math Trailblazers* curriculum and outline suggestions for home study activities to be done on a continuing basis throughout the school year. These home activities help children develop the number sense that is the foundation for later number work while reinforcing the goals of the kindergarten program.

Later in this section, we briefly describe the Note Home feature of the kindergarten program that is designed to enhance home-school communication. Further suggestions for working with parents are outlined in Section 14, Parents and *Math Trailblazers*.

Note Home

Date: _____

Dear Family Member:

This year in kindergarten, your child is using a mathematics curriculum called *Math Trailblazers*. As your child begins his or her formal schooling, you may be wondering about the role of math homework and the part you play in helping your child become a good math student in school.

From time to time, you can expect your child to bring home math homework, which is outlined in a *Note Home*. Each *Note Home* will provide instructions for you to help your child complete the assignment.

However, for kindergarten children, assigned homework is a small part of the active learning that families must provide in order for their child to be successful in mathematics in school. Each day, you can help your child discover that math is an important part of everyday life by looking for opportunities to involve your child in math-related activities. For example, your child can help you:

- count objects to see if there are enough
- fill or empty all sorts of containers
- use a clock or calendar
- compare sizes of objects
- describe positions—above, below, between
- use numbers to describe distances
- look for shapes in the everyday environment
- sort objects according to color, size, shape, or texture
- measure and record the growth of a plant by marking daily or weekly growth on a stick

Look for opportunities for your child to count objects in picture books as you read to him or her on a daily basis.

You can also help your child develop math skills and concepts by setting aside time to play games that involve numbers in a variety of ways. Following are a few suggestions.

- Logic games can help children think about number relationships. For instance, you can play games such as Mystery Number. Say, *"I'm thinking of a number that is smaller than 8 and larger than 2. What's the mystery number?"* If your child does not guess the number, give another clue by saying that the mystery number is larger or smaller than the number that the child guessed. Continue until the secret number is guessed. Take turns.
- Card games can help children develop number relationship concepts as they make decisions about which card shows a larger or smaller number.
- Commercial board games can help children with counting and number comparisons as they recognize and count dots on the cube and move their game pieces along a path.

Your early encouragement can help make home math time a regular and enjoyable time for both you and your child.

Sincerely,

_____

Carta al hogar

Fecha: _____

Estimado miembro de la familia:

Este año en kinder, su hijo está usando un curriculo de matemáticas llamado *Math Trailblazers.* Mientras su hijo comienza sus estudios formales, tal vez usted desea saber del papel de la tarea de matemáticas y la parte que usted tomará para ayudar su hijo llegar a ser un buen estudiante de matematicas en la escuela.

De vez en cuando, puede esperar que su hijo traiga tarea de matemáticas a la casa, la cual estará explicada en una Nota al Hogar. Cada Nota al Hogar proveerá las instrucciones para que usted ayude a su hijo terminar la tarea.

Sin embargo, para los niños en kinder, la tarea es una chiquita parte del estudio activa que las familias deben de proveer para que su hijo avance en matemáticas en la escuela. Cada día puede ayudar a su hijo descubrir que las matemáticas forman una parte importante de la vida cotodiana buscando oportunidades para envolver a su hijo en actividades relacionadas a las matemáticas. Por ejemplo, su hijo le puede ayudar:

- contar objetos para ver si hay lo suficiente
- llenar o vaciar todos tipos de recipientes
- usar un reloj o calendario
- comparar tamaños de objetos
- describir posiciones - encima, abajo, entre
- usar números para describir distancia
- buscar figuras en el ambiente de cada día
- surtir objetos según el color, el tamaño, la figura, o la textura
- medir y apuntar el crecimiento de una planta, marcando diariamente o cada semana el aumento en un palo

Busca oportunidades de contar objetos para su hijo en libros con dibujos cuando le lee.

También le puede ayudar a su hijo desarrollar sus habilidades y conceptos de matemáticas tomando tiempo para jugar juegos de números en varias maneras. Los siguientes son algunas sugerencias.

- Juegos de lógica pueden ayudar que los niños piensen de las relaciones numéricas. Por ejemplo, pueden jugar juegos tal como El Numero Misterioso. Diga, *"Estoy pensando de un número que es más pequeño que 8 y más grande que 2. ¿Cuál es el número misterioso?"* Si su hijo no adivina el número, trate otra indicación, diciendole que el número misterioso es más grande o más pequeño que el número que adivinó el niño. Continue hasta que adivine el número secreto.
- Juegos de barajas pueden ayudar los niños desarrollar los conceptos de las relaciones entre números mientras hacen decisiones sobre cual baraja tiene el número más grande o más pequeño.
- Juegos comerciales pueden ayudar a los niños contar y comparar números mientras reconozcan y cuenten los puntitos en el cubo y mueven sus piezas por un camino.

Su aprobación desde el principio puede ayudar hacer el tiempo de matemáticas en casa un tiempo consistente y agradable para usted y su hijo.

Sinceramente,

_____

Notes Home

In the lessons, periodically you will find a Note Home to family members. Generally, these notes fall into three categories: asking a family member to help the child bring a particular item from home, enlisting a family member's help with an assignment, and providing suggestions for activities that can be done on an ongoing basis at home.

This is an example of a Note Home which asks family members to help their child locate something to bring to school for use in a math activity. (See Figure 1.)

Note Home
Month 1—Exploring and Identifying Patterns

Date: _____

Dear Family Member:

In class we have been exploring and identifying repeating patterns in the world around us. Please help your child choose clothing with a pattern to wear to school (blue stripe/red stripe; thin line/thick line) on _____.
If you have no clothing with a pattern, your child can make a simple pattern on a strip of paper and pin it to a plain shirt. Also, help your child look for and bring in a patterned item from home (game board, pillow case, etc.) on the same day. See the picture below for examples.

Thank you for your support.

Sincerely,

_____

BLACKLINE MASTER   Kindergarten • Month 1 • Lesson 1   **185**

Figure 1: *Note Home from Month 1, Lesson 1*

Occasionally family members are asked to help their child complete an assignment at home as shown in this Note Home. (See Figure 2.)

Note Home
Month 7—Measuring Area with a Standard Unit

Date: _____

Dear Family Member:

We are studying the measurement of area. Your child is bringing home three identical pieces of paper. Please help your child find an object that can be covered with about one piece of paper, another object that needs about two pieces of paper to cover it, and a third object that needs about three pieces of paper to cover it. Please help your child put the information in the table below.

Thank you for your help.

Area	Object
About 1 paper	
About 2 papers	
About 3 papers	

Sincerely,

BLACKLINE MASTER   Kindergarten • Month 7 • Lesson 5   **391**

Figure 2: *Note Home from Month 7, Lesson 5*

This Note Home explains a third type of home study task— a long term project to be carried out at home. (See Figure 3.)

Note Home

**Calendar Connections—
Fifty Ideas for the 100th Day**

Date: _____

Dear Family Member:

Our kindergarten class will soon celebrate the one hundredth day of the school year. We have been working since the beginning of the year on building an understanding of numbers, and 100 serves as an important milestone.

One aspect of our celebration will be having as many representations of the number 100 in the classroom as possible. For this we need your help. Please work with your child to make a collection of 100 small objects to bring to school. They can be put into a clear plastic self-sealing bag, displayed on poster board, or in another creative manner. Some suggested objects for collection are popcorn kernels, pennies, twist ties, toothpicks, milk bottle caps. Use your imaginations!

Please see that the collections are brought to school on _____.

Thank you very much for your help.

Sincerely,

_____

BLACKLINE MASTER Kindergarten • Ongoing Content • Calendar Connections • Fifty Ideas for 100th Day **27**

Figure 3: *Note Home from Ongoing Content, Calendar Connections, Fifty Ideas for the 100th Day*

Sometimes, the Note Home offers ideas for activities which can be done at home several times. The note shown shares ideas for exploring geometry in the child's home environment. (See Figure 4.)

Note Home

Month 4—Mapmaking

Date: _____

Dear Family Member:

Periodically this year, your child will be involved in activities designed to build a solid foundation in geometry. The lessons are divided into three parts:

1. Exploring words which describe position, location, or movement. For example:
   - above/below
   - between/next to/behind
   - shortest way/longest way
   - from here to there.
2. Exploring two-dimensional and three-dimensional shapes.
3. Exploring symmetry.

"What shape is making this shadow?"

You can help at home by sharing some of the following activities with your child.

- **I Spy.** Take turns describing objects by their locations and shapes, then guessing the object being described. For example, *"I spy something on top of the refrigerator. It is square on two sides. It holds food. What is it?"*
- **Maps.** Have your child describe a trip to the grocery store or another place you frequently go together. For example, *"We go to the corner, turn right at the gas station, go past the school, and turn left at the post office."* You can also ask your child which way to turn along a familiar route.

Thank you for your continued support.

Sincerely,

_____

BLACKLINE MASTER   Kindergarten • Month 4 • Lesson 2   **287**

Figure 4: *Note Home from Month 4, Lesson 2*

Assessment

The Assessment section details the philosophy, goals, and components of assessment in the curriculum.

A teacher and her students assess their work on a problem.

Assessment

Assessment

 PART I | **Philosophy of the Assessment Program in *Math Trailblazers***

Assessment in *Math Trailblazers* is ongoing and reflects the program's content and goals. Throughout the program, assessment serves several purposes:

- It helps teachers learn about students' thinking and knowledge. This information is then used to guide instruction.
- It communicates the instruction goals to students, parents, and others.
- It informs students, parents, and others about progress toward these goals.

The assessment program is built around two main principles: assessment should reflect the breadth and balance of the curriculum; and assessment activities should be valuable educational experiences.

Alignment with Goals

The National Council of Teachers of Mathematics (NCTM) *Principles and Standards for School Mathematics* describes the understanding, concepts, and skills students need to acquire. These principles and standards call for a mathematically rich curriculum for all students. The curriculum must teach a broad range of content and develop mathematical processes including problem solving, reasoning, and communication.

Math Trailblazers is designed to meet recommendations in the *Principles and Standards*. As such, the program requires significant shifts in emphases relative to a traditional program—changes in content, learning, teaching, evaluation, and expectations. The implications with regard to student assessment are also significant. We can no longer focus narrowly on the assessment of only isolated skills and procedures, using single sources of information at the end of a learning cycle. Instead, assessment needs to shift toward collecting information over the course of the year from a variety of sources, covering a wide range of mathematical content, and incorporating the rich problem-solving situations that are characteristic of the curriculum. The NCTM *Principles and Standards for School Mathematics* describes this as follows:

> *Many assessment techniques can be used by mathematics teachers, including open-ended questions, constructed-response tasks, selected-response items, performance tasks, observations, conversations, journals, and portfolios.* (NCTM, 2000, p. 23)

Integral with Instruction

Assessment is an integral part of instruction. All assessment activities are valuable educational experiences that have their own merit. By making assessment both integral to instruction and reflective of the overall mathematical content of the curriculum, we communicate what we value in mathematics. Again, the NCTM *Principles and Standards* addresses this idea:

> *To ensure deep, high-quality learning for all students, assessment and instruction must be integrated so that assessment becomes a routine part of ongoing classroom activity rather than an interruption.* (NCTM, 2000, p. 23)

Our assessment program gives teachers frequent opportunities to assess student progress. It assesses concepts and skills in many different ways but especially within the context of solving problems. Assessments are designed to elicit more than just an answer. In solving problems, students show their thinking and give a picture of their understanding of mathematical concepts, strategies, tools, and procedures.

Integrating assessment with instruction has significant implications for the structure of the assessment program. There is no separate assessment book; assessment activities and other components of the assessment program are fully integrated into units. Furthermore, because much of the curriculum's content is revisited many times in varying contexts, students are assessed many times on many concepts. This flavors both instruction and assessment. Teachers can focus on student progress since they know there will be other opportunities to review and assess and thus do not expect mastery at every juncture. At the same time, students' mathematical progress is not put on hold until they pass any particular assessment.

Balanced Assessment

The assessment program reflects the curriculum's instruction in another important way: it is varied and balanced. The *Math Trailblazers* curriculum is balanced across several dimensions:

- **Math Content.** The program incorporates a broad range of mathematical content and procedures, and connections between different topics abound.
- **Communication.** Students are expected to communicate their mathematical work and represent mathematical ideas in many different ways, such as written and oral explanations, number sentences, tables, graphs, pictures, and models.

- **Student Groupings.** Students work individually, in pairs, and in small groups.
- **Length of Activities.** There are short activities (5–15 minutes), tasks that take a full class period, and longer investigations that take several days.
- **Amount of Teacher Direction.** Some activities involve considerable teacher direction; others are more student-directed.
- **Varied Contexts.** Mathematics is presented in a variety of contexts, such as laboratory experiments, real-life settings, word problems, and numerical problems.

Our assessment program is balanced in similar ways. A balanced assessment program gives each student an opportunity to demonstrate what he or she knows by allowing multiple approaches. It covers a wide range of content, allows access to tools when appropriate, varies the difficulty and pedagogy, and assesses within different kinds of contexts.

Using multiple sources of evidence improves the validity of judgments made about students' learning. With more than one source of information about students' progress, strengths in one source can compensate for weaknesses in others. It also helps teachers judge the consistency of students' mathematical work. (NCTM, 2000, p. 24)

Promoting Student Reflection

Assessment activities in *Math Trailblazers* do more than provide momentary snapshots of a student's progress. Students are often asked to revise work based on commonly understood criteria for excellence. In Grades K–2, these criteria are communicated largely by the teachers. Beginning in Grade 3, the Student Rubrics provide an additional source of information to students about what is expected of them. As students become more involved in the assessment process, they become more reflective and can make constructive, critical judgments about their work and the work of others.

Components in Grades 1–5

Watching students grow intellectually throughout the school year is one of
the great satisfactions of teaching. The components of the assessment
program provide teachers with the tools necessary to document students'
progress over time as they acquire skills and concepts, develop their abilities
to solve problems, and learn to communicate their thinking. While most
components are included at all grade levels, the assessment program does
vary from grade to grade based on the students' needs.

All materials provided to assess student learning are located in the units,
either in the student materials or the *Unit Resource Guide.* Each unit contains
assessment ideas and activities appropriate for the unit's content and goals.
Many components are also available in electronic form on the *Teacher
Resource CD.* This section describes the following components:

Observational Assessment
Assessment Indicators
Observational Assessment Record
Individual Assessment Record Sheet

Written Assessments
Assessment Pages
Math Journals
Assessment Section in
   the Lesson Guide
Assessment Lessons
   Assessment Labs
   Open-Response Problems
   Tests
Assessment Units
Portfolios
Facts Assessment

Observational Assessment

Teachers have always assessed
student learning through informal
classroom observations, thus
integrating instruction and
assessment. The NCTM *Principles
and Standards* confirms the
importance of these observations.

*Observations and conversations in the classroom can provide insights
into students' thinking, and teachers can monitor changes in students'
thinking and reasoning over time with reflective journals and portfolios.*
(NCTM, 2000, p. 24)

Teachers use the information gathered from classroom observations to guide
instruction. While watching, questioning, and listening to students, they
make moment-to-moment instructional decisions that change the direction

and emphasis of the lesson. Teacher evaluation of student responses during a lesson will also affect the content of succeeding lessons.

Teachers can also use classroom observations to evaluate student achievement and monitor student progress. Skills such as using a graduated cylinder to measure volume, habits such as estimating regularly to check results, and behaviors such as working effectively within a group are best assessed through observing students at work. Assessing students through observation is especially important in the primary grades, because students at this age can often communicate their thinking very well in a discussion, but not always in writing. Also, what we assess becomes what we value. If we only assess written work, we may neglect other important behaviors such as verbal communication. Finding a manageable way to organize and record these observations is critical to an effective assessment program.

Each unit includes two tools to help teachers organize and document informal assessments: Assessment Indicators and the *Observational Assessment Record.*

Assessment Indicators

The Background for each unit in Grades 1–5 lists several Assessment Indicators that orient teachers to important skills, behavior, and knowledge they should assess in the unit. See Figure 1.

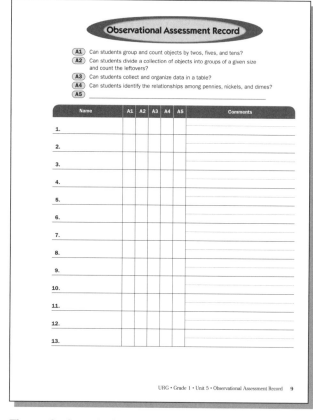

Figure 2: *Sample* Observational Assessment Record *from Grade 1 Unit 5*

Assessment Indicators

- Can students group and count objects by twos, fives, and tens?

- Can students divide a collection of objects into groups of a given size and count the leftovers?

- Can students collect, organize, graph, and analyze data?

- Can students identify the relationships among pennies, nickels, and dimes?

Figure 1: *Assessment Indicators from Grade 1 Unit 5*

Observational Assessment Record

An *Observational Assessment Record* similar to the one shown for Grade 1 Unit 5 in Figure 2 follows the Background in each unit. The Assessment Indicators for that unit are listed at the top of each sheet. Each indicator is identified with an icon. An additional line is provided for teachers to include their own ideas. Each sheet has 32 rows for student names with columns for recording observations and extra space for comments. It is not necessary to record an observation about each child in each column.

The grid provides a snapshot of the class's understanding of the unit's main concepts, procedures, and skills.

In first and second grade, the icons are also placed in the At a Glance sections of the Lesson Guides. These indicate which skills and concepts described in the Assessment Indicators teachers might assess during that particular lesson. Figure 3 is a sample At a Glance section from Grade 1 Unit 5 Lesson 2. The use of the icon (A1) shows that during this lesson teachers can assess students on their abilities to count objects by twos, fives, and tens.

Individual Assessment Record Sheets

Information from the *Observational Assessment Record* can be transferred to *Individual Assessment Record Sheets*. The *Individual Assessment Record Sheet* is located at the end of Part VI of this section and provides an organizational tool for compiling a year-long, anecdotal record for each child. Assessment Indicators for the entire year are listed by unit along with a line for comments as shown in Figure 4.

Figure 3: *Sample At a Glance from Grade 1 Unit 5 Lesson 2*

Figure 4: Observational Assessment Record *from Grade 5 Unit 1 and* Individual Assessment Record Sheet *from Grade 5*

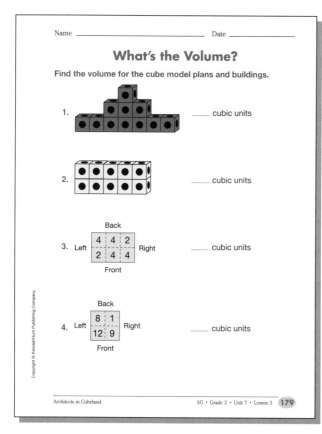

Name _____ Date _____

What's the Volume?

Find the volume for the cube model plans and buildings.

1. _____ cubic units

2. _____ cubic units

3. Left $\begin{array}{|c|c|c|} \hline 4 & 4 & 2 \\ \hline 2 & 4 & 4 \\ \hline \end{array}$ Right _____ cubic units
   Back (top), Front (bottom)

4. Left $\begin{array}{|c|c|} \hline 8 & 1 \\ \hline 12 & 9 \\ \hline \end{array}$ Right _____ cubic units
   Back (top), Front (bottom)

Architects in Cubeland   SG • Grade 2 • Unit 7 • Lesson 3 **179**

Figure 5: *Assessment Page from Grade 2 Unit 7*

Written Assessments

Assessment Pages

Many lessons in *Math Trailblazers* include short paper-and-pencil assessments that teachers can use to check skills or concepts developed in a unit. While teachers can use some assessment pages to assess students as they work in groups, they can often use these pages as quizzes to assess students individually. Checking student work gives both the teacher and the students feedback on their current abilities. The *What's the Volume?* Assessment Page from Grade 2 Unit 7 is shown in Figure 5. Students must combine their arithmetic skills with their measurement skills to complete the page correctly.

Math Journals

Students' entries in their math journals are a rich source of assessment information. Journal Prompts, a regular feature in the lesson guides, elicit information about students' understanding of specific concepts. Figure 6 shows an example of a Journal Prompt in Grade 5 Unit 1 Lesson 3.

Journal Prompt

A stream has an average depth of 1 meter. Can you wade across?

Figure 6: *A Journal Prompt from Grade 5 Unit 1 Lesson 3*

Figure 7: *A second-grade journal entry*

Regular journal writing provides teachers and parents with a means of documenting a student's growth in mathematical thinking, attitudes, and communication skills. (For information on math journals, see the TIMS Tutor: *Journals.*) Young children often begin by drawing pictures in their journals or combining pictures with a few words. The journal entry in Figure 7 is an early effort by Jayne, a second grader, at communicating her thoughts about a math lesson on doubling. Jayne used six circles and six squares to show two examples of doubling three. She also wrote a short paragraph about the class:

> *Today my class did some math. and we did some writ (write) some math too! I like it!*

Assessment Section

The Assessment section at the end of most lesson guides lists ideas for assessing the lesson's content. The following components are often recommended as assessment: Assessment Pages, Journal Prompts, classroom observations corresponding to the Assessment Indicators, and appropriate questions from the student pages and Homework sections. The teacher can also record the level of a student's response to these questions on the *Observational Assessment Record* or in a grade book. Figure 8 shows assessment for Grade 1 Unit 6 Lesson 2.

Assessment Lessons

Some units include specially designed assessment lessons. These lessons are generally one of three types: assessment labs, open-response problems, or written tests composed of short items. Each type provides different kinds of information to teachers so that they can develop and document a complete picture of their students' progress toward the curriculum's goals.

Assessment Labs

Two or three laboratory experiments in each grade are designated as assessment labs. Teachers can use them to assess students' abilities to work with a group on an investigation that takes several days. Teachers can also observe students to see if they are confident enough to tackle new ideas and to use previously learned mathematics in new contexts. Working on projects such as these—problems requiring integration and application of many concepts and skills over a period of time—more closely resembles the work of mathematicians and scientists (as well as working adults in many occupations) than any other kind of work students do in school. Suggestions for evaluating labs are included in Part III.

Open-Response Problems

In these lessons, students are given a task that requires them to demonstrate their problem-solving skills individually or while working in a group. Students are also assessed on their understanding of the mathematical content and their abilities to communicate their strategies. They must produce a product that allows teachers to examine their processes as well as their final answers. More than a few minutes are required to solve such a problem and students will often need a whole class period to find solutions and describe their strategies. To encourage students to give full explanations and improve their writing skills, teachers can comment on students' initial responses and ask them to make revisions. Part III includes rubrics for scoring student responses to these problems.

Math Facts Strategies

DPP item D provides practice with addition math facts.

Homework and Practice

- The *Two Car Roll-off* Homework Page shows a diagram of two cars that rolled down different ramps. Students count the links and compare the distances.
- DPP item C practices addition in a measurement context. For DPP item E, students estimate lengths of objects. Item F reviews even and odd numbers. Item G practices partitioning numbers. Students divide groups of cookies among 4 people and count leftovers. Item H asks students to solve problems using skip counting.

Assessment

- The *Brian's Class* Assessment Page asks students to examine the data for a fictional class. *Questions 1–4* are similar to questions found in the class discussion while *Question 5 is* a challenge.
- Use children's journal entries to assess whether students understand the connection between "fairness" and controlled variables.
- Use the *Observational Assessment Record* to record students' abilities to make and interpret bar graphs and also to solve problems using data involving length.

Extension

Provide additional measurement practice by leaving the ramp in an activity center for student use.

Figure 8: *Grade 1 Unit 6 Lesson 2—Math Facts Strategies, Homework and Practice, Assessment, and Extension*

Name _____ Date _____

Class Party

Suppose there are 25 students in your class and you have $10 for a class party. Use the prices in the table to plan a party.

Tell how you would spend the money, and explain why you would spend it that way. Use as much of the $10 as you can, but do not plan to spend more than $10. (There is no tax.) Be sure your plan works for a class of 25.

Write your plan on another piece of paper. Be sure to explain how you solved the problem and how you made your decisions.

Item	Cost
pitcher of lemonade (10 servings)	$2.50
paper cups (package of 24)	69¢
ice cream bars	30¢
oatmeal cookies (package of 16)	99¢
bag of popcorn (30 servings)	$1.09
napkins (package of 50)	49¢

Assessment Blackline Master   URG • Grade 3 • Unit 10 • Lesson 3   **73**

Figure 9 shows Jayne's response to an open-response problem written at midyear of third grade. Jayne is the same student who wrote the journal entry shown in Figure 7. Compare her writing here with her paragraph from second grade and also with her work at the end of third grade on the Earning Money problem shown in Figure 19 in Part III. Comparing these three responses shows how she has developed her communication skills.

Tests

Tests that assess students' conceptual understanding and procedural skills are short items that teachers can easily grade. There is a test in the final unit of both first and second grade. In third grade, there is a midyear and an end-of-year test. In fourth and fifth grades, there is a midterm test in both the fall and spring semesters in addition to a midyear and end-of-year test.

Jayne

Steps
1. Lemonade $7.50
   $2.50 \times 3 = \$7.50$

2. Paper Cups $1.38
   $69 \times 2 = \$1.38$

3. Popcorn
   1.09
   $1.09 \times 1 = 1.09$

4.
   $\begin{array}{r} \overset{1}{7}.50 \\ 1.38 \\ + 1.09 \\ \hline \$\,9.97 \end{array}$ Lemonade Paper Cups Popcorn

4. 3 ¢ left over

I solved the problems the way I did because number sentences help you get the awnser

My way works because it helped me get the awnser.

The math is the same as other math because they both have driffrent ways of solving their problems and awnsering them.

Figure 9: *Jayne's work for an open-response problem*

126   TIG • Kindergarten • Assessment • Components in Grades 1–5

Assessment Units

In each grade, specific units are designated as assessment units. They include lessons that emphasize assessment at the same time that content is reviewed and new material is introduced. Teachers can assess students' abilities to apply previously studied concepts in new contexts and their willingness to approach new mathematics.

Assessment units at the beginning of each grade provide opportunities to observe students and collect baseline data on students' mathematical knowledge. Teachers can use this information to plan instruction that meets students' needs and to begin documenting students' mathematical growth over the course of the year. See the Assessment Overview in Part VI for specific information on the assessment units.

Portfolios

Portfolios are important tools for documenting students' growth throughout the year. They are collections of students' written work and teachers' anecdotal records. To provide a complete picture of a student's learning, a portfolio should include assessments that demonstrate the range of the child's abilities. Samples of student work on labs, open-response problems, assessment activity pages, and tests can be included along with samples of students' daily work. Work from the year's beginning to end will show students' growth over time. Certain lessons in the assessment units are especially appropriate for inclusion in portfolios. Refer to the TIMS Tutor: *Portfolios* for more information.

Facts Assessment

In *Math Trailblazers,* teachers assess students' knowledge of the facts by observing them as they work on activities, labs, and games and through the appropriate use of quizzes and tests. Periodic, short quizzes in the Daily Practice and Problems naturally follow the study of small groups of facts organized around specific strategies. As self-assessment in third, fourth, and fifth grades, each student can record his or her progress on *Facts I Know* charts and determine which facts he or she needs to study. The goal of the math facts assessment program is to determine the degree to which students can find answers to fact problems quickly and accurately and whether they can retain this skill over time. For more information on teaching and assessing the math facts, see the TIMS Tutor: *Math Facts.*

Assessment

PART III | # Implementing the Assessment Program

Evaluating and reporting on a broad range of student achievement throughout the school year is a complex task. It is only practical if the assessment process is built into day-to-day instruction. Components of the assessment program are designed so teachers can gather information about students as they are learning. This section outlines a plan for gradually introducing the various components of the assessment program during the first weeks of instruction and provides information on evaluating and scoring written work.

Getting Started

An assessment program that emphasizes the documentation of students' growth over time establishes a climate in which each child is valued for the knowledge and skills he or she brings to the classroom and in which each student is expected to make significant gains in mathematics. These are high expectations that also reflect reality. Students begin and end the school year with varying abilities, backgrounds, and accomplishments. Therefore, it is important to record what each student can do initially, as well as during the learning process, so that the teacher, student, and parents can fully appreciate progress throughout the year.

Begin Observational Assessments

Activities in the first two or three units of each grade provide many opportunities to observe students as they use mathematics. These observations provide a rich source of baseline information about students. For example, in Units 1–3 of first grade, students count objects in many contexts. By routinely observing four or five students during appropriate lessons, the teacher can note those students who can count and those who may need additional help. At the same time, all students are working on their counting skills as well as on related concepts such as comparing numbers and organizing data.

Unit 2 of third grade is also designated as an assessment unit. In this unit, students review strategies to maintain fluency with the subtraction facts. Students discuss strategies, play games, work with flash cards, assess themselves using *Facts I Know* charts, and use subtraction facts as part of a data collection activity. Observing students participating in these activities gives teachers information about students' knowledge of the facts and, more importantly, about students' abilities to use the facts to solve problems. Since students will continually use the facts in many activities as well as in the Daily Practice and Problems, the teacher need only record observations for a small number of students at a time. (For more information on assessment of the math facts, see the TIMS Tutor: *Math Facts*.)

Using the *Observational Assessment Record.* Before beginning
assessment observations, teachers need a system for recording short, anecdotal records. Such a system should allow recording of a broad range of evidence of students' behavior, attitudes, and understanding of mathematics and should make recording and retrieving information easy and convenient. The *Observational Assessment Record* and the Assessment Indicators help organize data from observations. Teachers can develop their own shorthand to denote satisfactory progress toward a goal or proficiency with a skill or concept.

In Grades 1–5, information from the *Observational Assessment Record* can be transferred to *Individual Assessment Record Sheets* to create a year-long anecdotal record of growth for each child. The *Individual Assessment Record Sheet* is located at the end of Part VI of this section. Teachers can copy and place it in each student's portfolio. It is also available on the *Teacher Resource CD*. Teachers can use it to maintain records of each student's progress electronically.

As part of lesson planning, the teacher can choose one or two behaviors, concepts, or skills to check during class. The Assessment Indicators for each unit and the Assessment section in the lesson guides can facilitate this process. The teacher should choose no more than four or five students to observe in a day. Additional students can be observed in succeeding lessons or units to provide further information about individual students' progress and the improvement of the class as a whole.

Figure 10 is an example of an *Observational Assessment Record* for Grade 1 Unit 1 that shows one possible scheme for recording classroom observations. Note that the teacher chose to observe students' abilities to work together as well as counting skills.

Other suggestions from teachers for organizing anecdotal records follow:

Student Grid. A teacher can make a grid that allows note-taking about all students on one piece of paper as shown in Figure 11. The grids include as many cells as there are students in the class, labeling each cell with a student's name. Observations are written in the cells. Like the *Observational Assessment Record,* this provides a view of the entire class's progress.

Figure 10: *Sample* Observational Assessment Record *for Grade 1 Unit 1*

Figure 11: *Student grid*

Flip Chart. A flip chart can be made by lining up index cards and taping them to a clipboard or a piece of heavy cardboard so they overlap by all but a strip of about $\frac{1}{2}$ inch as shown in Figure 12. Students' names are written on the uncovered area of each card, so the teacher can easily flip to a student's card and write a quick, dated note about the observation. As a card is filled, it can be removed to a card file or a student's portfolio and replaced with a new card.

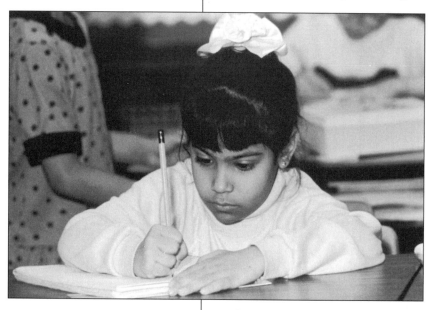

Figure 12: *Flip chart*

Flip Cards. A variation of the flip chart can be made by fastening together a set of index cards—one card labeled for each student in the class. A binder ring is placed through a hole in a corner of each card.

Self-Adhesive Notes. Some teachers prefer to write their observations about individual students on self-adhesive notes, which are then attached to a sheet of paper in the student's portfolio. These notes have the advantage of being easily transferable, so they can be grouped and regrouped by student, subject, day, etc.

Begin Math Journals

At the beginning of the year, math journals provide a safe place for students to start communicating their insights. By writing regularly in their journals, they gain the experience necessary to write more and learn to express themselves clearly. Students can write in response to journal prompts or record answers to questions from the *Student Guide* or Daily Practice and Problems. See the TIMS Tutor: *Journals* for more information on using journals to assess students.

Begin Portfolios

The TIMS Tutor: *Portfolios* recommends establishing portfolios by starting small with modest goals. This implies using portfolios to document progress in one or two specific areas such as communicating mathematically or collecting and analyzing data. One way to begin is to assign each student a collection folder in which early examples of student work are saved. Later in the process, teachers can designate or students can select a smaller number of pieces that show growth in these areas.

It is important to choose examples of work from the beginning of the year so a student's first efforts can be compared to later work. The earliest entries in the portfolio will most likely show much less sophisticated results than those that are added toward the end of the year. For example, to compare students' use of the TIMS Laboratory Method at the beginning of the year to their abilities to conduct an experiment at the end of the year, include a data table and a graph from an early lab in each student's portfolio. Good choices of initial labs to collect in portfolios include the following: In Grade 1, save students' weather graphs from Unit 2; in Grade 2, use the Button Sizer Graph from Unit 3; and in Grade 3, choose student work from the lab *Kind of Bean* in Unit 1 or the graph and write-up from *Spinning Differences* in Unit 2. At the beginning of Grade 4, include *Arm Span vs. Height* from Unit 1 and *Perimeter vs. Length* from Unit 2. In Grade 5, begin portfolios with the labs *Searching the Forest* from Unit 1 and *Distance vs. Time* from Unit 3.

Scoring Open-Response Problems

In *Math Trailblazers,* most lessons involve multiple mathematical topics, skills, and processes. Assessing student progress requires tools that allow students to respond using multiple approaches and that let teachers evaluate student communication and problem-solving strategies as well as mathematical knowledge.

TIMS Multidimensional Rubric

To assist teachers in evaluating student performance and in communicating progress to students and parents, we have developed a rubric—a scoring guide—for evaluating student work on open-response problems. The *TIMS Multidimensional Rubric* addresses three dimensions of mathematical learning: (i) knowing, (ii) solving, and (iii) telling. Using these three dimensions broadens the assessment focus from the traditional emphasis on rote procedures to a more complete view of mathematics learning. The rubric outlines our criteria for excellence and provides an explicit indication of what we value in mathematics. Examples of using the rubric to score student work are included in lesson guides beginning in Grade 3. The ideas embodied in the rubric are generally applicable to younger children and can be modified for use in earlier grades. The rubric is displayed in Part V.

The three dimensions of mathematical understanding emphasized in the *TIMS Multidimensional Rubric* are described here briefly.

- *Solving.* This section focuses on students' understanding of a problem and their abilities to devise a plan for solving it, organize information, analyze results, and reflect on its mathematical implications.
- *Knowing.* This portion of the rubric examines students' comprehension of mathematical concepts and their abilities to apply procedures, rules, and facts to a given mathematical situation. This includes effective use of representations, such as written numbers, words, graphs, tables, or pictures, and the ability to make connections among different mathematical ideas.
- *Telling.* This part stresses students' abilities to explain their problem-solving strategies, justify their solutions, use symbols and terminology correctly, and discuss connections among mathematical topics.

Student Rubric: Knowing

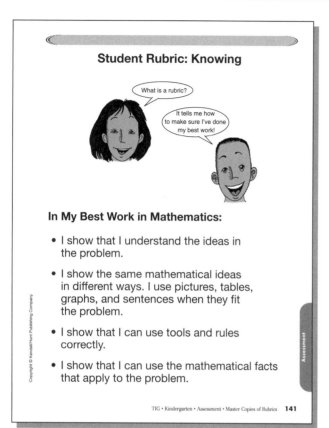

What is a rubric?

It tells me how to make sure I've done my best work!

In My Best Work in Mathematics:

- I show that I understand the ideas in the problem.

- I show the same mathematical ideas in different ways. I use pictures, tables, graphs, and sentences when they fit the problem.

- I show that I can use tools and rules correctly.

- I show that I can use the mathematical facts that apply to the problem.

TIG • Kindergarten • Assessment • Master Copies of Rubrics **141**

The *TIMS Multidimensional Rubric* specifies criteria for assigning scores on each dimension to one piece of student work. Level 4 is the highest and is intended to represent excellence in that particular dimension. A paper might earn, for example, a 3 in *Solving*, a 4 in *Knowing*, and a 3 in *Telling*. It is not necessary to assign a score for all three dimensions for every task. For many tasks, it may be more appropriate to give scores for only one or two dimensions.

Student Rubrics

Corresponding Student Rubrics for each dimension make the expectations of student performance clear. These rubrics provide students with goals as they solve problems, communicate their solutions, and revise their work. Students also use these rubrics as guides when assessing their own work. The student rubrics are introduced gradually in the *Student Guide* throughout the first semester of third, fourth, and fifth grades. They are included in lessons with open-response problems.

The Student Rubrics are shown in Figure 13.

The Student Rubrics are located in Appendices A, B, and C and on the inside backcover of the *Student Guides* for Grades 3–5. Blackline Masters of the Student Rubrics are included in Part V so teachers can make transparencies or use a copier to enlarge the rubrics to make classroom posters.

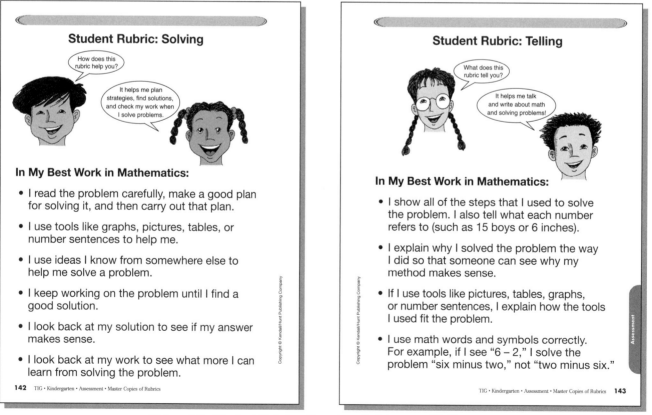

Student Rubric: Solving

How does this rubric help you?

It helps me plan strategies, find solutions, and check my work when I solve problems.

In My Best Work in Mathematics:

- I read the problem carefully, make a good plan for solving it, and then carry out that plan.

- I use tools like graphs, pictures, tables, or number sentences to help me.

- I use ideas I know from somewhere else to help me solve a problem.

- I keep working on the problem until I find a good solution.

- I look back at my solution to see if my answer makes sense.

- I look back at my work to see what more I can learn from solving the problem.

142 TIG • Kindergarten • Assessment • Master Copies of Rubrics

Student Rubric: Telling

What does this rubric tell you?

It helps me talk and write about math and solving problems!

In My Best Work in Mathematics:

- I show all of the steps that I used to solve the problem. I also tell what each number refers to (such as 15 boys or 6 inches).

- I explain why I solved the problem the way I did so that someone can see why my method makes sense.

- If I use tools like pictures, tables, graphs, or number sentences, I explain how the tools I used fit the problem.

- I use math words and symbols correctly. For example, if I see "6 − 2," I solve the problem "six minus two," not "two minus six."

TIG • Kindergarten • Assessment • Master Copies of Rubrics **143**

Figure 13: *Student Rubrics:* Knowing, Solving, *and* Telling

Using the Rubrics: An Early Example

Using the student rubrics to inform students of your expectations as well as using the *TIMS Multidimensional Rubric* to score student work is a process that evolves throughout the year. For example, Grade 3 Unit 2 includes the first assessment lesson with an open-response problem. This is the students' first exposure to the student rubrics. The problem is shown in Figure 14.

To begin the lesson the class reads and discusses the problem. It is similar to the problem in an earlier lesson (Unit 2 Lesson 2 *Spinning Sums*), so students should be familiar with the procedures. They also read and discuss the Student Rubric: *Knowing.* The teacher may ask students what tools, rules, and mathematical facts apply to the problem. She explains that she will grade their work based on the rubric.

After students understand the problem, they work in groups to plan a strategy for solving the problem and to carry out their plans. Then students write paragraphs describing their problem-solving processes and their results. The teacher directs students either to write the paragraph with their groups or to write the paragraph individually. When students have completed their paragraphs, the teacher reviews their work and makes suggestions for improvement.

It is a good idea to make transparencies of exemplary work from previous years or the lesson guide. The teacher discusses the exemplary work with the class, comparing the work to the rubric's standards. Finally, students revise their work based on the teacher's comments. A student response with teacher comments is shown in Figure 15.

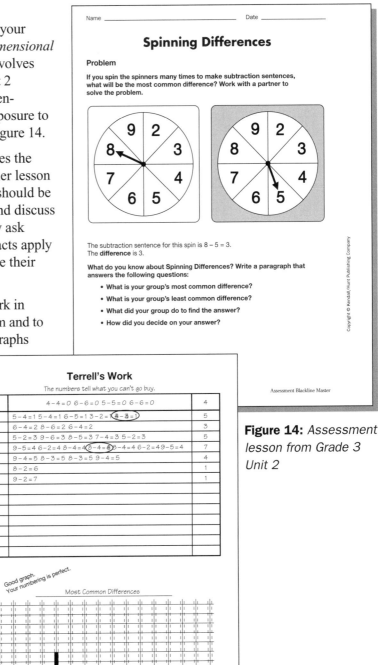

Figure 14: *Assessment lesson from Grade 3 Unit 2*

Figure 15: *A student response to a teacher's comments*

The teacher used the Knowing dimension of the *TIMS Multidimensional Rubric* to score students' work. The Lesson Guide provides questions specific to this problem to guide the teacher's scoring. The questions provided for this problem are given below:

- Were the data table and graph appropriately labeled?
- Was the graph scaled properly?
- Were the bars correctly drawn?
- Were the subtraction sentences correct?
- Were the most common differences identified?

Many of the criteria in the rubric overlap. In addition, the student's data table, graph, and written paragraphs tell us about more than one component of the problem. Consequently, the score for a dimension will result from the compilation of all the evidence, not necessarily from an arithmetic average of scores in each cell of the rubric. Figure 16 shows the Knowing dimension of the *TIMS Multidimensional Rubric* with the teacher's notations after she scored Terrell's paper.

How would you score Terrell's work? Terrell's teacher decided that he earned a 3. He worked with his group using tools to spin the spinners 30 times, record the results in a table, and display the data in a graph. The bars are drawn correctly on the graph and the axes are scaled correctly. However, the incorrect labels on both the data table ("The numbers that tell what you can't go buy") and graph ("Most Common Differences" and "N = of Letters") indicate that he was not clear on his goal for collecting data and therefore did not completely understand the problem's concepts and applications. The incorrect labels also show major errors translating between tables, graphs, and real situations, although he did correctly identify the most common and least common differences. The correct number sentences are evidence that he knows the subtraction facts. (See the Lesson Guide for *Spinning Differences* in Grade 3 Unit 2 for other examples of student work scored using the rubric.)

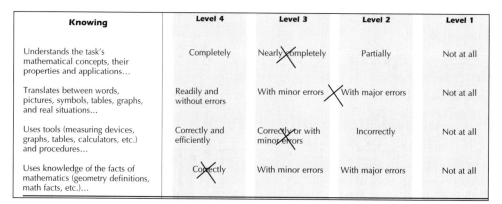

Knowing	Level 4	Level 3	Level 2	Level 1
Understands the task's mathematical concepts, their properties and applications…	Completely	Nearly completely	Partially	Not at all
Translates between words, pictures, symbols, tables, graphs, and real situations…	Readily and without errors	With minor errors	With major errors	Not at all
Uses tools (measuring devices, graphs, tables, calculators, etc.) and procedures…	Correctly and efficiently	Correctly or with minor errors	Incorrectly	Not at all
Uses knowledge of the facts of mathematics (geometry definitions, math facts, etc.)…	Correctly	With minor errors	With major errors	Not at all

Figure 16: *Scoring an open-response problem using one dimension of the* TIMS Multidimensional Rubric

Using the Rubrics: A Second Example

During the school year, students become familiar with all three student rubrics and use them as they solve problems. Depending on the problem, they may use one or more of the rubrics. The results of these assessments are often saved in portfolios to show students and parents progress over time. The problem in Figure 17 is posed to students in the final assessment unit of third grade.

Before students begin solving the problem, the class reads and discusses the problem. Students should understand that play money will be available to help solve the problem and that they will be asked how they can use calculators to solve the problem. The teacher also reviews all three student rubrics and advises students that their work for this problem will be scored using all three dimensions.

Students use the tools available to them to find solutions and write about their strategies. The teacher may use samples of students' work to provide good examples for students to emulate. The teacher also comments on students' first drafts and students revise their work accordingly.

Earning Money

Daniel, Maria, and Cora earned five dollars baby-sitting for the Farleys. Mrs. Farley gave the three sitters one five-dollar bill.

1. If they share the money equally, how much should each baby-sitter get? Explain how you solved the problem.

2. What happens if you try to solve the problem on a calculator? Explain.

Write your solutions to Questions 1 and 2. Be sure to tell about all the ways you solved the problem.

Assessment Blackline Master   URG • Grade 3 • Unit 20 • Lesson 4   59

Figure 17: *An open-response problem from Grade 3 Unit 20*

Samples of two students' work are shown in Figures 18 and 19. Scores for both students for all three dimensions of the *TIMS Multidimensional Rubric* are discussed below. The teacher was guided by additional questions in the Lesson Guide that are specific to this problem and that point out elements to consider while scoring.

The teacher gave Marco a 2 on Solving. Marco chose a legitimate problem-solving strategy—guess and check—but did not use it systematically or efficiently, nor did he organize his work. His work does show evidence that he persisted in the problem-solving process, but does not show that he

Marco's Work

Marco's response the first day:

$3.65
× 3 kids

three dollars and sixey five cenes times three kids, and five dollers minus one doller and foty five cenes egels fore dollers.

$5.00
− $1.45
$4.00   ← not good

Teacher comments:

I'm still not clear from your explanation what you tried. Maybe you should try to explain to me. Did you use the money or the calculator? Try to finish today.

Ms. Ho

Marco's response the second day:

I didn't use the money, But I used a calculator.

75¢
75
75
225

$4.50
3 ×
$1.50

165
×3
4.95

$1.70
× 3
$5.10

3.13
× 3
3.39

1.67
× 3
5.01

1.69
× 3
5.07

3
$1.10
$1.10
+ $1.10
$3.30

1.66
× 3
4.98

Figure 18: *Marco's work*

Assessment

identified all the elements of the problem since he does not indicate that he knows that there will be money left over. He makes no connections to previously studied mathematics or previously solved problems.

On the Knowing dimension, the teacher gave Marco a 3 since he correctly used his knowledge of mathematics and he used appropriate tools (a calculator) and procedures (repeated addition and multiplication) to solve the problem. He did not demonstrate that he completely understood the nature of the task or show that he can translate between symbols and real situations since he did not calculate the amount of money that would be left over.

Marco received a 1 on the Telling dimension. His explanation was very short and totally unclear, with no supporting arguments. Since he did not identify which trial was successful, we are not even sure of his final answer. He used symbols to show his trials, but made no attempt to organize them. Appropriate terminology is not present.

A second sample of student work on the Earning Money problem is shown below:

Jayne's Work

Jayne's response the first day:

1.) Each person should get $1.66 and .2 left over. We got five dollars in change and we divided the money up between them. We got $1.66 for each person, and two cents left over.

2.) If you try on the calculator (5 ÷ 3) you would get 1.6666667. So I think it's much better to use play money or your head. The reason why you can't do it on the calculator is because the calculator will cut the coin up in half.

Teacher comments:

This is an excellent explanation! How can this problem help you solve other problems? Can you think of a way to find the remainder using your calculator?

Mrs. Vasquez

Jayne's response the second day:

1. You can check your answer by the calculator you can put $1.66 + $1.66 + $1.66 + $0.02 = $5.00.

2. This problem can help me solve other problems because it will help me divide money (if it involves money.)

3. A way to find how much is left $5.00 − $1.66 − $1.66 − $1.66 = $0.02.

Figure 19: *Jayne's work*

Jayne's teacher gave her a score of 4 for Solving. She fully met the criteria in the rubric. She clearly identified the elements of the problem when she described the problem first as dividing the play money "up between them." She then found the amount left over and used a calculator to divide (5 ÷ 3) resulting in a repeating decimal. With prompting from the teacher, she looked for other strategies and found she could use repeated addition and subtraction to find the remainder. All her strategies are effective and they are presented in an organized fashion. Jayne's first conclusion that "you can't do it (find the remainder) on the calculator is because the calculator will cut the coin up in half" is insightful, although not quite correct mathematically. Using both repeated addition and subtraction on the calculator to find the remainder shows that she made meaningful connections between the operations and that she was willing to persist in the problem-solving process.

Jayne also received a 4 in Knowing since she clearly understood the problem's mathematical concepts. She readily translated the real situation into words when she described the process of dividing up the money and then translated words into symbols using correct addition, subtraction, and division sentences. The use of play money and a calculator is evidence that she can use tools correctly and efficiently and her calculations show that she can use the facts of mathematics correctly as well.

The teacher gave Jayne a score of 3 for the Telling dimension. Her explanations and responses were fairly complete and clear. However, we are not entirely sure how the group shared the money. Did they trade the dollars for quarters and then the quarters for dimes, etc., or were they able to make the process more efficient in some way? Her supporting arguments are sound, but they contain a few minor gaps. Did she use repeated subtraction or repeated addition first to find the remainder? Why did she choose these operations? She used many symbols and terms correctly. However, she reported that two cents were left over and wrote it first as ".2."

Like any new tool, using the rubric efficiently will require practice. As you begin to work with the rubric, we suggest that you work closely with other teachers. For example, you might score a half-dozen papers and ask one or more colleagues to score the same set; then compare and discuss the results, negotiating any differences. Repeating this process over the course of the year will help establish school-wide norms for applying the rubrics.

Using Assessment Observations, Math Journals, and Portfolios

The rubrics can be combined with other components of the assessment program to provide a more complete picture of students' skills at solving open-response problems. For example, to assess students' willingness to tackle new problems or work cooperatively in a group, teachers can observe students as they work on the problem or ask them to write in their journals about the process. For example, the Journal Prompt for the Earning Money problem concerns students' feelings about working in groups in math class. (See Figure 20.)

How did your group share the work on this problem? How do you feel about working with a group in math class?

Figure 20: *Journal Prompt for Earning Money (Grade 3 Unit 20)*

Considerable growth in mathematical power is often evident when several write-ups of open-response problems from different times of the year are included in a student's portfolio. We can see growth in Jayne's problem-solving and communication skills when we look at her work on both the Class Party and Earning Money problems. (See Figure 9 in Part II and Figure 19.)

Evaluating Labs

Teachers have used the following ideas to evaluate student performance on labs:

Group Work

Students work in their groups to polish a lab write-up and turn in one completed lab or to prepare an oral report to be presented to the class. Their reports may include how the work was distributed among the group members. Students can also write a paragraph in their journals describing how each member functioned in the group and how to improve the process.

Using the Multidimensional Rubric

Choose one or two important questions to score using one or more dimensions of the *TIMS Multidimensional Rubric*. Often suitable questions are suggested in the Assessment section of the Suggestions for Teaching the Lesson in the Lesson Guide. These are usually open-response questions that ask students to make predictions or solve a problem using the data collected during the experiment.

Self-Assessment

Students can grade their own labs in class. This provides a forum for discussing the most important aspects of the lab.

Using a Point System

To grade a lab, teachers can assign a given number of points to each part of the lab and grade each part based on the criteria below. Teachers can also choose to grade only a portion of the lab such as the picture or the graph.

1. Drawing the Picture
   - Are the procedures and the materials clearly illustrated?
   - Are the variables labeled?
2. Collecting and Recording the Data
   - Are the data organized in a table?
   - Are the columns in the data table labeled correctly?
   - Are the data reasonable?
   - Are the correct units of measure included in the data table?
   - If applicable, did students average the data (find the median or mean) correctly?
3. Graphing the Data
   - Does the graph have a title?
   - Are the axes scaled correctly and labeled clearly? Labeling should be consistent with the picture and the data table and should include appropriate units of measure.
   - If it is a bar graph, are the bars drawn correctly?
   - If it is a point graph, are the points plotted correctly?
   - If the points suggest a straight line or a curve, did the student draw a best-fit line or fit a curve to the points?
   - Did the students show any interpolation or extrapolation on the graph?

4. Solving the Problems
  - Are the answers correct based on the data?
  - Did students use appropriate tools (calculators, rulers, graphs, etc.) correctly?
  - Are the answers, including the explanations, clear and complete?

References

Elementary Grades Assessment. *Balanced Assessment for the Mathematics Curriculum.* University of California. Dale Seymour Publications, White Plains, NY, 1999.

Lane, Suzanne. "The Conceptual Framework for the Development of a Mathematics Performance Assessment Instrument" in *Educational Measurement: Issues and Practice.* Vol. 12, Number 2. National Council on Measurement in Education, Washington, DC, 1993.

Mathematics Resource Guide for Fourth- and Eighth-Grade Teachers. Vermont Department of Education, Montpelier, VT, 1996.

Middle Grades Assessment. *Balanced Assessment for the Mathematics Curriculum.* University of California. Dale Seymour Publications, White Plains, NY, 2000.

Pellegrino, J.W., N. Chadowsky, and R. Glaser (Eds.) *Knowing What Students Know: The Science and Design of Educational Assessment.* National Research Council. National Academy Press, Washington, DC, 2001.

Performance Assessment in Mathematics: Approaches to Open-Ended Problems. Illinois State Board of Education, Springfield, IL, 1994.

Principles and Standards for School Mathematics. National Council of Teachers of Mathematics, Reston, VA, 2000.

Stenmark, J.K. (Ed.) *Mathematics Assessment: Myths, Models, Good Questions, and Practical Suggestions.* National Council of Teachers of Mathematics, Reston, VA, 1991.

Master Copies of Rubrics

This section contains the blackline masters of the *TIMS Multidimensional Rubric* and the three Student Rubrics: *Knowing, Solving,* and *Telling.* The Scoring Open-Response Problems section in Part III describes the rubrics and provides examples of their use in the curriculum. The *TIMS Multidimensional Rubric* is provided here so that teachers can use it to score student work. The copies of the three student rubrics in this section can be used to make transparencies for the overhead projector or enlarged to make posters for the classroom.

TIMS Multidimensional Rubric

Solving	Level 4	Level 3	Level 2	Level 1
Identifies the elements of the problem and their relationships to one another.	All major elements identified	Most elements identified	Some, but shows little understanding of relationships	Few or none
Uses problem-solving strategies which are . . .	Systematic, complete, efficient, and possibly elegant	Systematic and nearly complete, but not efficient	Incomplete or unsystematic	Not evident or inappropriate
Organizes relevant information . . .	Systematically and efficiently	Systematically, with minor errors	Unsystematically	Not at all
Relates the problem and solution to previously encountered mathematics and makes connections that are . . .	At length, elegant, and meaningful	Evident	Brief or logically unsound	Not evident
Persists in the problem solving process . . .	At length	Until a solution is reached	Briefly	Not at all
Looks back to examine the reasonableness of the solution and draws conclusions that are . . .	Insightful and comprehensive	Correct	Incorrect or logically unsound	Not present

Knowing	Level 4	Level 3	Level 2	Level 1
Understands the task's mathematical concepts, their properties and applications . . .	Completely	Nearly completely	Partially	Not at all
Translates between words, pictures, symbols, tables, graphs, and real situations . . .	Readily and without errors	With minor errors	With major errors	Not at all
Uses tools (measuring devices, graphs, tables, calculators, etc.) and procedures . . .	Correctly and efficiently	Correctly or with minor errors	Incorrectly	Not at all
Uses knowledge of the facts of mathematics (geometry definitions, math facts, etc.) . . .	Correctly	With minor errors	With major errors	Not at all

Telling	Level 4	Level 3	Level 2	Level 1
Includes response with an explanation and/or description which is . . .	Complete and clear	Fairly complete and clear	Perhaps ambiguous or unclear	Totally unclear or irrelevant
Presents supporting arguments that are . . .	Strong and sound	Logically sound, but may contain minor gaps	Incomplete or logically unsound	Not present
Uses pictures, symbols, tables, and graphs that are . . .	Correct and clearly relevant	Present with minor errors or somewhat irrelevant	Present with errors and/or irrelevant	Not present or completely inappropriate
Uses terminology . . .	Clearly and precisely	With minor errors	With major errors	Not at all

Student Rubric: Knowing

In My Best Work in Mathematics:

- I show that I understand the ideas in the problem.

- I show the same mathematical ideas in different ways. I use pictures, tables, graphs, and sentences when they fit the problem.

- I show that I can use tools and rules correctly.

- I show that I can use the mathematical facts that apply to the problem.

Assessment

Student Rubric: Solving

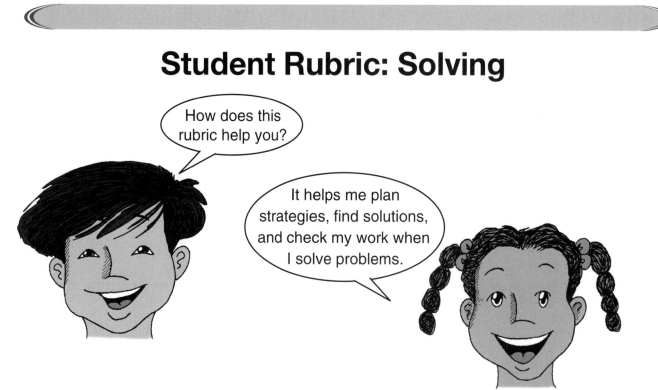

In My Best Work in Mathematics:

I read the problem carefully, make a good plan for solving it, and then carry out that plan.

I use tools like graphs, pictures, tables, or number sentences to help me.

I use ideas I know from somewhere else to help me solve a problem.

I keep working on the problem until I find a good solution.

I look back at my solution to see if my answer makes sense.

I look back at my work to see what more I can learn from solving the problem.

Student Rubric: Telling

What does this rubric tell you?

It helps me talk and write about math and solving problems!

In My Best Work in Mathematics:

- I show all of the steps that I used to solve the problem. I also tell what each number refers to (such as 15 boys or 6 inches).

- I explain why I solved the problem the way I did so that someone can see why my method makes sense.

- If I use tools like pictures, tables, graphs, or number sentences, I explain how the tools I used fit the problem.

- I use math words and symbols correctly. For example, if I see "6 − 2," I solve the problem "six minus two," not "two minus six."

Assessment

PART VI | Assessment Overview for Kindergarten

Children enter kindergarten with a wide range of developmental levels and pre-kindergarten experiences. The *Math Trailblazers* kindergarten curriculum provides opportunities for all children to learn mathematics at their level. All children are expected to show growth in their understanding of mathematics over the span of the school year. As you observe and document the progress of individual students, you will:

- be empowered to make instructional decisions that promote maximum learning of mathematical skills and concepts,
- accumulate data to inform parents about their child's progress, and
- note learning patterns and possible learning challenges of individual students.

Kindergarten assessment is most often a part of the everyday observation of individual students as they participate in teacher-led lesson discussions and more independent station work.

Kindergarten lesson guides often include such prompts as, "Observe children as they . . . ." These are pointers toward opportunities to make an observational assessment.

Key to building an effective assessment program in kindergarten is developing a manageable way to organize and record your classroom observations. Several suggestions for organizing classroom observations are included in the Getting Started portion of Part III in the Assessment section. Each offers a slightly different way to keep track of daily observations.

Whatever system you use for documenting your classroom observations, it is not necessary to comment on every child's performance every day. In addition, care should be taken so that assessment in mathematics is not confounded by tasks, such as cutting and pasting, that may have more to do with a child's motor skill development than with his or her development of mathematical skills and concepts.

Following are descriptions of tools and components in the *Math Trailblazers* kindergarten program that are designed to help you assess student progress in mathematics.

Baseline Counting (Skills and Concepts) Assessment

This performance assessment is part of the ongoing Counting Connections section in the *Teacher Resource Book.* It helps teachers assess student progress with counting and diagnose specific deficiencies with key counting concepts. It can be used as a baseline assessment for all students and to assess and monitor the progress of individual children who are not developing counting skills at their expected rate.

We suggest using the Baseline Counting (Skills and Concepts) Assessment several times over the course of the school year. One way to record student progress is shown in Figure 21. The designations of "S" for Secure, "P" for Progressing, and "E" for Emerging are descriptive of the stages of student development.

Figure 21: *Sample* Observational Assessment Record

Observational Assessment Record

An *Observational Assessment Record* is included in every month of the Month-by-Month section of the *Teacher Resource Book.* It highlights the content of each month and provides an on-going opportunity to record student progress. Figure 21 shows the *Observational Assessment Record* for Month 3. Once again, "S," "P," and "E" are used to denote student progress.

Student Grid. A teacher can make a grid that allows note-taking about all students on one piece of paper as shown in Figure 22. The grids include as many cells as there are students in the class, each cell labeled with a student's name. Observations are written in the cells. Like the *Observational Assessment Record,* this provides a view of the entire class's progress.

Sally Adamji	Feliz Arnez	John Boyd	Barb Crown
Willie Darno	Sarah Frank	Lee Guzman	etc.

Figure 22: *Student grid*

Flip Chart. A flip chart can be made by lining up index cards and taping them to a clipboard or a piece of heavy cardboard so that they overlap by all but a strip of about $\frac{1}{2}$ inch as shown in Figure 23. Students' names are written on the uncovered area of each card, so that the teacher can easily flip to a student's card and write a quick, dated note about the observation. As a card is filled, it can be removed to a card file or a student's portfolio and replaced with a new card.

Figure 23: *Flip chart*

Flip Cards. A variation of the flip chart can be made by fastening together a set of index cards—one index card labeled for each student in the class. A binder ring is placed through a hole in a corner of each card.

Self-Adhesive Notes. Some teachers prefer to write their observations about individual students on self-adhesive notes, which are then attached to a sheet of paper in the student's portfolio. These notes have the advantage of being easily transferable, so that they can be grouped and regrouped by student, subject, day, etc.

Portfolios

Kindergarten teachers have long used portfolios as a means to document individual student progress over time. Portfolios should include a collection of teachers' anecdotal records and students' written work. Refer to the TIMS Tutor: *Portfolios* for suggestions about setting up and using portfolios.

Transfer entries from the class *Observational Assessment Record* for each month to students' *Individual Assessment Record Sheets.* Place them in students' portfolios to provide a year-long look at mathematical growth.

Assessment

Individual Assessment Record Sheet

Name _____

Month 1   ✔   **Date and Comments:**

A1.   Can students use numbers to describe sets of objects?   _____   _____

A2.   Do students have a developmentally appropriate
      strategy for problem solving?   _____   _____

A3.   Can students identify and describe patterns?   _____   _____

A4.   Do students use spatial language to describe relationships?   _____   _____

A5.   _____   _____   _____

Month 2   ✔   **Date and Comments:**

A1.   Can students use numbers to describe sets of objects?   _____   _____

A2.   Do students have a developmentally appropriate
      strategy for problem solving?   _____   _____

A3.   Can students copy and extend patterns?   _____   _____

A4.   Do students use spatial language to describe relationships?   _____   _____

A5.   Do students use comparison language in the context
      of height (length)?   _____   _____

A6.   _____   _____   _____

Month 3   ✔   **Date and Comments:**

A1.   Can students use numbers to describe sets of objects?   _____   _____

A2.   Do students have a developmentally appropriate
      strategy for problem solving?   _____   _____

A3.   Can students create and compare patterns?   _____   _____

A4.   Do students use spatial language to describe relationships?   _____   _____

A5.   Do students use comparison language in the context of
      height (length)?   _____   _____

A6.   _____   _____   _____

Month 4   ✔   **Date and Comments:**

A1.   Can students use ordinal numbers in classroom situations?   _____   _____

A2.   Do students have a developmentally appropriate
      strategy for problem solving?   _____   _____

A3.   Can students identify and extend numeric and symbolic
      patterns on the classroom calendar?   _____   _____

A4.   Can students use spatial sense to create a map?   _____   _____

A5.   Can students measure length using nonstandard units?   _____   _____

A6.   Can students develop meaning for the part-part-whole
      relationships of the benchmark number 5?   _____   _____

A7.   Can students count backward from the number 5?   _____   _____

A8.   _____   _____   _____

Name _____

Month 5

		✔	**Date and Comments:**

A1. Can students use comparison language to describe number relationships? _____   _____

A2. Do students have a developmentally appropriate strategy for problem solving? _____   _____

A3. Can students identify and extend numeric and symbolic patterns on the classroom calendar? _____   _____

A4. Can students use comparison language to order objects according to length? _____   _____

A5. Can students measure length using nonstandard units? _____   _____

A6. Can students estimate a quantity of objects when given a referent amount of the same object? _____   _____

A7. _____   _____   _____

Month 6

		✔	**Date and Comments:**

A1. Can students show understanding of the operations of addition and subtraction? _____   _____

A2. Do students have a developmentally appropriate strategy for problem solving? _____   _____

A3. Can students identify and extend numeric and symbolic patterns on the calendar? _____   _____

A4. Can students sort and compare 3-Dimensional shapes? _____   _____

A5. Can students measure area using nonstandard units? _____   _____

A6. Can students sort objects according to given criteria? _____   _____

A7. Can students estimate a quantity of objects when given a referent amount of the same object? _____   _____

A8. _____   _____   _____

Month 7

		✔	**Date and Comments:**

A1. Can students show understanding of the operations of addition and subtraction? _____   _____

A2. Do students have a developmentally appropriate strategy for problem solving? _____   _____

A3. Can students develop meaning for the part-part-whole relationships of the benchmark number 10? _____   _____

A4. Can students sort and compare 2-Dimensional shapes? _____   _____

A5. Can students measure area using nonstandard and standard units? _____   _____

A6. Can students count backward from the benchmark numbers of 5 and 10? _____   _____

A7. Can students sort and compare objects according to given criteria? _____   _____

A8. _____   _____   _____

Assessment

Name _____

Month 8   ✔   Date and Comments:

A1. Can students show understanding of the operations of addition and subtraction? _____ _____

A2. Do students have a developmentally appropriate strategy for problem solving? _____ _____

A3. Can students estimate a quantity of objects when given a referent amount of the same object? _____ _____

A4. Can students develop meaning for the part-part-whole relationships of the benchmark number 10? _____ _____

A5. Can students identify and describe 2-Dimensional shapes? _____ _____

A6. Can students collect and represent data? _____ _____

A7. Can students order containers by capacity (volume)? _____ _____

A8. _____ _____ _____

Month 9   ✔   Date and Comments:

A1. Can students show understanding of the operations of addition and subtraction? _____ _____

A2. Do students have a developmentally appropriate strategy for problem solving? _____ _____

A3. Can students understand equality using fractional representations? _____ _____

A4. Can students compare 2-Dimensional and 3-Dimensional shapes? _____ _____

A5. Can students sort objects according to weight? _____ _____

A6. Do students understand the meaning of "equal"? _____ _____

A7. Can students formulate questions about collected data? _____ _____

A8. _____ _____ _____

Month 10   ✔   Date and Comments:

A1. Can students use comparison language to describe number relationships? _____ _____

A2. Do students have a developmentally appropriate strategy for problem solving? _____ _____

A3. Do students understand one line of symmetry? _____ _____

A4. Do students understand the passage of time as measured by the classroom calendar, the weekly/daily schedule, and the clock? _____ _____

A5. _____ _____ _____

TIMS Tutors

The TIMS Tutors section provides an in-depth exploration of the mathematical concepts and ideas behind *Math Trailblazers*.

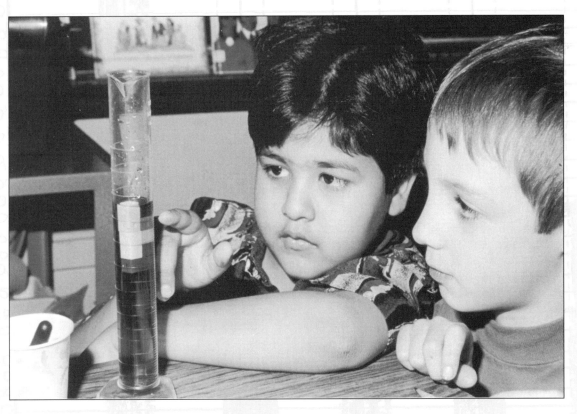

Students use a graduated cylinder to find the volume of small objects.

Introduction

Arithmetic

Introduction

The last half-century has seen many changes in elementary school mathematics. For many people, "mathematics" is synonymous with "arithmetic." But today, while reasonable people can still debate the proper content of an elementary mathematics curriculum, nearly all agree that a curriculum focused largely on rote arithmetic will not meet the needs of students in the twenty-first century.

Outline
This tutor is organized as follows: Introduction   Numeration and Place Value   Basic Number Facts   Concepts of Whole-Number Operations   Whole-Number Computation in *Math Trailblazers*   Fractions and Decimals   Conclusion   References

Much more than just arithmetic is now expected—geometry, probability, statistics, measurement, graphing, even algebra. Technology is dramatically changing the world, making it hard to imagine what our children will need to know in 20 or 40 more years, but also ensuring that many skills critical 50 years ago are less essential. Despite recent advances in psychology, educational research, and curriculum design, we are far from resolving all the uncertainties of the elementary school mathematics curriculum. A few things, however, do seem clear:

- The school mathematics curriculum can and must be more rigorous.
- Arithmetic is only one piece, albeit an important one, of a broad mathematics curriculum.
- We need to do better at helping children connect marks on paper to the real world. Too many children and adults fail to use common sense when dealing with mathematical symbolism. Discussing mathematics and integrating subject matter may help students make these connections.
- As we correct for the overemphasis on skills in the traditional mathematics curriculum, we should avoid over-correcting. Problem solving requires both procedural skill and conceptual understanding. As William Brownell (1956) noted during a previous period of reform, "In objecting to the emphasis on drill prevalent not so long ago, we may have failed to point out that practice for proficiency in skills has its place too." In *Math Trailblazers,* we consistently seek a balance between conceptual understanding and procedural skill.

The National Council of Teachers of Mathematics' (NCTM) *Principles and Standards for School Mathematics* advocates learning mathematics with understanding. "In recent decades, psychological and educational research on the learning of complex subjects such as mathematics has solidly established the important role of conceptual understanding in the knowledge and activity of persons who are proficient. Being proficient in a complex domain such as mathematics entails the ability to use knowledge flexibly, applying what is learned in one setting appropriately in another. One of the most robust findings of research is that conceptual understanding is an important component of proficiency, along with factual knowledge and procedural facility" (Bransford, Brown, and Cocking, 1999). The alliance of factual knowledge, procedural proficiency, and conceptual understanding makes all three components usable in powerful ways. Students who memorize facts or procedures without understanding often are not sure when or how to use what they know, and such learning is often quite fragile (Bransford, Brown, and Cocking, 1999; NCTM, 2000).

Several arguments support the NCTM position. One is that the computational proficiency of American students comes at too high a cost. The hundreds of hours devoted to arithmetic computation in elementary school leave too little time for other important topics. The traditional rote approach to computation undermines higher-level thinking: children learn that mathematics is blindly following rules, not thinking.

Another argument for shifting away from the traditional arithmetic curriculum is that technology has altered the role of paper-and-pencil calculation. As noted in the NCTM *Principles and Standards,* ". . . most of the arithmetic and algebraic procedures long viewed as the heart of the school mathematics curriculum can now be performed with handheld calculators. Thus more attention can now be given to understanding the number concepts and the modeling procedures used in solving problems." (NCTM, 2000) More practical topics—probability and statistics, geometry, measurement, mental computation and estimation—deserve more attention.

A final and most important argument in favor of the changes NCTM recommends is that new approaches to arithmetic instruction are more effective in helping students learn both appropriate calculation skills and how to apply those skills in solving problems. These new approaches build on students' own knowledge and intuitive methods and engage their common sense. This more meaningful approach helps students to be efficient and flexible in their computation and can reduce, though not eliminate, the amount of practice required. Thus a greater emphasis on conceptual understanding can lead to better procedural skills and problem-solving abilities (Brown & Burton, 1978; Skemp, 1978; Hiebert, 1984; Van Lehn, 1986; Carpenter, 1986; Baroody and Ginsburg, 1986; Good, Mulryan, and McCaslin, 1992; Hiebert, 1999; National Research Council, 2001).

> *A final and most important argument in favor of the changes NCTM recommends is that new approaches to arithmetic instruction are more effective in helping students learn both appropriate calculation skills and how to apply those skills in solving problems.*

Numeration and Place Value

Numeration in kindergarten emphasizes developing oral counting skills, making one-to-one correspondence between objects and numbers, developing the concept of cardinality, discovering patterns in our number system, and writing numbers. Students in Grade 1 continue to develop these skills and concepts. They take part in activities that help them become familiar with the structure of the number system.

In kindergarten and Grade 1, students practice their counting skills. They learn to count past 100 by ones, twos, fives, and tens. They count forward and backward from any given number. They group objects for counting.

Students use counting to solve addition and subtraction problems. They learn to write numbers up to and beyond 100. Beginning in kindergarten, a ten frame is frequently used as a visual organizer. See Figure 1. The *100 Chart* is introduced and used for a variety of purposes, including solving problems and studying patterns. Students partition, or break apart, numbers in several ways (25 = 20 + 5, 25 = 10 + 10 + 5, and so on). These activities help children develop number sense that allows them to use numbers flexibly.

Figure 1: *Sample ten frame*

While formal study of place value is not a focus in kindergarten or Grade 1, the multiple grouping and counting experiences described above provide children with a foundation for building an intuitive sense for the meaning of place value.

Work with counting continues in Grade 2, especially skip counting and counting backwards. Place value is explored in the context of counting and grouping by tens. Children continue to count and group everyday objects such as buttons or beans. They use connecting cubes to represent these objects and often group the cubes by tens. Later, base-ten pieces represent these same objects, thus linking the base-ten representations with quantities of actual objects.

Students explore numbers well into the hundreds. Counting is still used for problem solving, but more elaborate procedures may be employed. For example, a student may solve 885 − 255 by counting up, first by hundreds (355, 455, 555, 655, 755, 855) and then by tens (865, 875, 885), yielding 630 as the answer.

More elaborate partitions of numbers are investigated in Grade 2. Particularly important are partitions in which every part is a single digit times 1, 10, 100, or 1000: 359 = 300 + 50 + 9 and so on. Attention is also given to partitioning numbers in more than one way:

$$359 = 300 + 50 + 9$$
$$= 200 + 150 + 9$$
$$= 100 + 250 + 9$$

This work with multiple partitioning is closely related to multidigit addition and subtraction. One way to think about addition and subtraction—indeed, one way to think about much of elementary mathematics—is as procedures for renaming numbers in more convenient forms. For example, 563 + 13 is a number we usually rename as 576. Another number, 875 ÷ 25, is renamable as 35 when it suits our purposes.

In Grade 3, more formal study of place value takes place. Students work in varied contexts involving numbers through the thousands. For example, students draw an outline of a coat and determine how many square centimeters of material are required to make the coat. Using contexts such as this encourages students to associate quantities of actual objects with representations of the quantities using base-ten pieces and with the numerals that represent them. Most of this work is closely connected with addition and subtraction of multidigit numbers. Indeed, a good reason for studying computational algorithms is that they provide a context for learning about place value.

In Grade 4, large numbers up to the millions are studied and used in various contexts. Continued efforts are made to connect the numbers with actual quantities. For example, the class creates its own base-ten pieces for large numbers—pieces we call super skinnies (10,000), super flats (100,000), and megabits (1,000,000). See Figure 2.

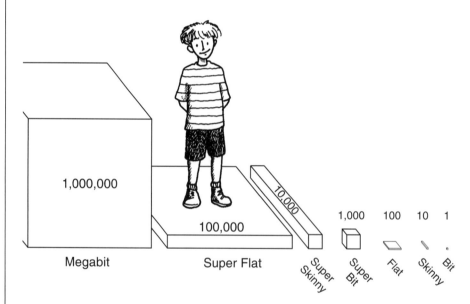

Figure 2: *Base-ten pieces for small and large numbers*

After reviewing and establishing the basics of the base-ten place value system for whole numbers, the system is extended to include decimals beginning in third grade. In Grade 4, the ten-for-one trading rules and other aspects of our number system are extended to the right of the decimal point for the first time.

In Grade 5, we extend the number system to even larger numbers. The story of Archimedes' attempt to calculate the number of grains of sand that would fill the observed universe introduces students to numbers far beyond what we encounter in everyday life. With the use of scientific calculators in Grade 5, scientific notation for large numbers is needed and introduced.

Basic Number Facts

In developing the math facts program, we sought a careful balance between strategies and drill. This approach is based on a large body of research and advocated by the NCTM *Principles and Standards for School Mathematics*. The research indicates that the methods used in the *Math Trailblazers* math facts program lead to more effective learning and better retention of the math facts and also helps develop essential math skills.

The *Math Trailblazers* program for teaching the math facts is characterized by these elements:

- *Early emphasis on problem solving.* Students first approach the basic facts as problems to solve rather than facts to memorize. Students invent their own strategies to solve these problems or learn appropriate strategies from others through class discussion. Students' natural strategies, especially counting strategies, are explicitly encouraged. In this way, students learn that math is more than memorizing facts and rules that "you either get or you don't."

- *De-emphasis of rote work.* Fluency with the math facts is an important component of any student's mathematical learning. Research has shown that an overemphasis on memorization and the frequent administration of timed tests are counterproductive. (National Research Council, 2001) We encourage the use of strategies to find facts, so students become confident they can find answers to fact problems they do not immediately recall.

- *Gradual and systematic introduction of facts.* Students study the facts in small groups that can be solved using similar strategies. Students first work on simple strategies for easy facts and then progress to more sophisticated strategies and harder facts. By the end of the process, they gain fluency with all the required facts.

- *Ongoing practice.* Work on the math facts is distributed throughout the curriculum, especially in the Daily Practice and Problems, Home Practice, and games. This practice for fluency, however, takes place only after students conceptually understand the operations and are proficient with strategies for solving basic fact problems. Delaying practice in this way means students need less practice to achieve fluency.

- *Appropriate assessment.* Teachers assess students' knowledge of the facts through observations as they work on activities, labs, and games as well as through the appropriate use of written tests and quizzes. Beginning in first grade, periodic, short quizzes in the Daily Practice and Problems naturally follow the study of small groups of facts organized around specific strategies. As self-assessment in Grades 2–5, students record their progress on *Facts I Know* charts and determine which facts they need to study. Inventory tests of all facts for each operation are used sparingly in Grades 2–5 (no more than twice per year) to assess students' progress with fact fluency. The goal of the math facts assessment program is to determine the degree to which students can find answers to fact problems quickly and accurately and whether they can retain this skill over time.

- *Multiyear approach.* In Grades 1 and 2, *Math Trailblazers* emphasizes strategies that lead to fluency with the addition and subtraction facts. In Grade 3, students gain fluency with the multiplication facts while reviewing the addition and subtraction facts. In Grade 4, students achieve fluency with the division facts and verify fluency with the multiplication facts. In Grade 5, the multiplication and division facts are systematically reviewed and assessed. This is outlined in Table 1.
- *Facts are not gatekeepers.* Students are not prevented from learning more complex mathematics because they do not perform well on fact tests. Use of strategies, calculators, and other math tools (e.g., manipulatives, hundreds charts, printed multiplication tables) allows students to continue to work on interesting problems and important mathematical concepts while they are still learning the facts.

The *Math Trailblazers* approach to the math facts is discussed more fully in the TIMS Tutor: *Math Facts.*

Concepts of Whole-Number Operations
Concepts and Skills

Throughout the past 150 years, there were numerous attempts to teach mathematics meaningfully rather than by rote. Unfortunately, as Lauren Resnick points out in *Syntax and Semantics in Learning to Subtract,* ". . . the conceptual teaching methods of the past were inadequate to the extent that they taught concepts instead of procedures and left it entirely to students to discover how computational procedures could be derived from the basic structure of the number and numeration system." (1987, p. 136)

Many educators have long recognized, however, that there is no real conflict between skills and concepts. (Whitehead, 1929; Dewey, 1938; Brownell, 1956; May, 1995; National Research Council, 2001) New conceptual understandings are built on existing skills and concepts; these new understandings in turn support the further development of skills and concepts. Thomas Carpenter describes the relationship in this way: ". . . It is an iterative process. Procedures are taught that can be supported by existing conceptual knowledge, and the conceptual knowledge base is extended to provide a basis for developing more advanced concepts. At every point during instruction, procedures are taught that can be connected to existing conceptual knowledge." (1986, p. 130) This integration of concepts and skills underlies our work with arithmetic in *Math Trailblazers.*

Subtraction in Grades K to 5
To illustrate how concepts and skills are balanced in *Math Trailblazers,* we outline in this section how one operation—subtraction—is developed with whole numbers in Grades K–4. Though the details may differ for the other operations, the same general approach described here with subtraction applies to all four arithmetic operations.

In kindergarten and Grade 1 of *Math Trailblazers,* students solve a variety of problems involving subtraction of numbers up to and even beyond 100. These problems are based on hands-on classroom activities and realistic situations from children's experiences. Different subtraction problem types are represented, including take-away, comparison, part-whole, and missing addend problems. (See the TIMS Tutor: *Word Problems* for a discussion of these and other problem types.)

Students in even the earliest grades are thus faced with problems for which they have no ready solution methods, problems that in the traditional view are beyond their ability. They do, however, have much prior knowledge that is relevant. They have their common sense—their conceptual knowledge of the problem situations. They know, for example, that if Grace begins with 50 marbles and loses 17, then she must end with fewer than 50 marbles. Young students also have considerable procedural knowledge, including various kinds of counting skills: ordinary counting, counting on, counting back, and skip counting by twos, fives, and tens. Students have tools to solve the problems. These include connecting cubes, links, *100 Charts,* ten frames, other manipulatives, paper and pencil, calculators, and number lines. Researchers note that initial work with any operation should involve classroom activities that use real-world or imaginary contexts, manipulatives, or drawings that highlight the attributes of the numbers and operations. (Carpenter et al., 1998; Fuson and Briars, 1990, Hiebert et al., 1997) This research further emphasizes the importance of long-term use of the manipulatives and of linking the manipulatives with written notation.

On one side, then, are hard problems involving many types of subtraction. On the other side are the kindergartners and first-graders, with their common sense, their counting skills, and tools. Traditionally, word problems and other applications involving subtraction (and other operations) were introduced only after students had extensive practice with a subtraction algorithm. Research on students' learning of addition and subtraction (Carpenter et al., 1998) strongly suggests that it is more effective to have students solve and pose word problems and other context-based problems (such as problems in the laboratory investigations in *Math Trailblazers*) before they learn formal, paper-and-pencil procedures for subtraction. As students apply their resources to solve the problems, they build their conceptual and procedural understanding of subtraction. They devise methods to solve the problems, make records of their work, and discuss their methods with their teacher and classmates. Their new knowledge about subtraction is closely linked to their prior knowledge, especially their out-of-school knowledge and their counting skills. (Baroody and Ginsburg, 1986)

You comment on students' methods and may show students how to use conventional symbols to describe their work, but you make no attempt to standardize students' methods. Any method that yields a correct result is acceptable—as long as it makes sense. The goal is to encourage students to apply their prior knowledge to problems they encounter and to let students know that their intuitive methods are valid.

> *As students apply their resources to solve the problems, they build their conceptual and procedural understanding of subtraction. They devise methods to solve the problems, make records of their work, and discuss their methods with their teacher and classmates.*

First grade focuses on various strategies students can use to solve single-digit subtraction problems. For example, they can solve a problem like 9 − 3 by counting back 3 from 9: 8, 7, 6. This work aims not at achieving fluency with the subtraction facts, but rather at building conceptual understanding of subtraction and procedural skill with various strategies. (See the TIMS Tutor: *Math Facts.*)

At the beginning of Grade 2, the problem-solving approach to subtraction continues. Problems with numbers up to 1000 are introduced, but again no standard solution method is taught at this point. Students devise their own ways to solve the problems, drawing on their prior knowledge of the problem situations and the number system, and share their thinking with the class.

The strategies approach to the subtraction facts continues in Grade 2. As students' fluency with the addition facts and simple subtraction facts increases, more sophisticated strategies become feasible. For example, a child may solve 14 − 6 by reasoning that "to take away 6 from 14, I first can take away 4, which leaves 10. Then I take away 2 more, which equals 8." These new strategies, sometimes called derived fact strategies or reasoning from known facts, illustrate how new knowledge builds on prior skills.

Giving children only multidigit problems that do not involve borrowing encourages the development of a rote and faulty algorithm that may not carry over into problems that require borrowing.

Later in Grade 2, systematic work begins on paper-and-pencil methods for subtracting two-digit numbers. Students solve two-digit subtraction problems using their own methods and record their solutions on paper. The class examines and discusses the various procedures that students devise. At this time, if no student introduces a standard subtraction algorithm, then the teacher does so, explaining that it is a subtraction method that many people use. The standard method is examined and discussed, just as the invented methods were. Students who do not have an effective method of their own are urged to adopt the standard method.

Problems that require borrowing are included from the beginning. Though this differs markedly from traditional approaches, we view it as important in developing a sound conception of subtraction algorithms. Giving children only multidigit problems that do not involve borrowing encourages the development of a rote and faulty algorithm that may not carry over into problems that require borrowing.

By the beginning of Grade 3, students have a strong conceptual understanding of subtraction and significant experience devising procedures to solve subtraction problems with numbers up to 1000. They also have some experience with standard and invented paper-and-pencil algorithms for solving two-digit subtraction problems. In Grade 3, this prior knowledge is extended in a systematic examination of paper-and-pencil methods for multidigit subtraction.

This work begins with a series of multidigit subtraction problems that students solve in various ways. Many of these problems are set in a whimsical context, the TIMS Candy Company, a business that uses base-ten pieces to keep track of its production and sales. Other problems are based on student-collected data, such as a reading survey.

As in Grade 2, the class discusses and compares the several methods students use to solve these problems. Again, any method that yields correct results is acceptable, but now a greater emphasis is given to methods that are efficient and compact. This work leads to a close examination of one particular subtraction algorithm. See Figure 3. Students solve several problems with base-ten pieces and with this standard algorithm, making connections between actions with the manipulatives and steps in the algorithm. After a thorough analysis of the algorithm, including a comparison of the standard algorithm and other methods, students are given opportunities to practice the algorithm or other methods of their choice.

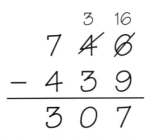

Figure 3: *A standard subtraction algorithm*

Practice in paper-and-pencil methods for multidigit subtraction is distributed throughout Grades 3 and 4. Students encounter sets of problems that encourage them to look at each problem and choose an efficient method to solve it. For many of these problems, a standard algorithm will be the most efficient choice. For others, students can use mental math or counting strategies. For example, students should identify the problem $4001 - 3998$ as a problem they can easily solve by counting up three from 3998 to 4001.

By the beginning of Grade 4, basic work with whole number subtraction is complete. Students have a firm conceptual understanding of subtraction and a diverse repertoire of methods they can use to solve subtraction problems. Work in Grade 4 is designed to maintain and extend these skills and understandings. Fluency with the subtraction facts is verified and remediation is provided for students who need it. In the laboratory experiments and other work, students solve a wide variety of subtraction problems using methods of their own choosing. The Daily Practice and Problems and Home Practice include distributed practice in paper-and-pencil subtraction so that those skills do not deteriorate.

In Grade 5 students continue to use subtraction in activities and labs. As in earlier grades, they are encouraged to decide when it is appropriate to use paper and pencil, calculators, or estimation. A review of subtraction modeled with base-ten pieces is included for students who have not used *Math Trailblazers* in previous grades. Distributed practice is provided in the Daily Practice and Problems and the Home Practice. Fluency with the subtraction facts is assessed in the first unit, and remediation is provided in the Addition and Subtraction Math Facts Review section in the *Facts Resource Guide.*

Whole-Number Computation in *Math Trailblazers*

Many other topics in *Math Trailblazers*—addition, multiplication, division, fractions, and decimals—are treated in ways similar to that sketched for subtraction above. In all these areas, we seek a balance between conceptual understanding and procedural skill. For all operations, standard methods for solving problems are not introduced until students have developed good conceptual and procedural understandings—the too-early introduction of such procedures may short-circuit students' common sense, encouraging mechanical and uncritical behavior. (Brownell & Chazall, 1935; Resnick & Omanson, 1987; Rathmell & Huinker, 1989; Perry, 1991; Hiebert, 1999)

> *We seek a balance between conceptual understanding and procedural skill. For all operations, standard methods for solving problems are not introduced until students have developed good conceptual and procedural understandings—the too-early introduction of such procedures may short-circuit students' common sense, encouraging mechanical and uncritical behavior.*

Grade	Addition	Subtraction	Multiplication	Division
K	• concepts of the operation	• concepts of the operation	• concepts of the operation	• concepts of the operation
1	• concepts of the operation • informal methods	• concepts of the operation • informal methods	• concepts of the operation	• concepts of the operation
2	• concepts of the operation • invented algorithms • standard methods for small numbers	• concepts of the operation • invented algorithms • standard methods for small numbers	• concepts of the operation • informal methods	• concepts of the operation • informal methods
3	• invented algorithms • standard methods for larger numbers	• invented algorithms • standard methods for larger numbers	• concepts of the operation • invented algorithms • standard methods for small numbers	• concepts of the operation
4	• review, practice, apply, and extend	• review, practice, apply, and extend	• invented algorithms • standard methods for larger numbers	• invented algorithms • standard methods for larger numbers
5	• review, practice, apply, and extend	• review, practice, apply, and extend	• review, practice, apply, and extend	• standard methods for larger numbers

Table 1: *Whole-number operations scope and sequence*

Even after analyzing and practicing standard methods students are still encouraged to solve problems in more than one way. Flexible thinking and mathematical power are our goals, not rote fluency with a handful of standard algorithms.

Varieties of Computation

There is much more to computation than the standard paper-and-pencil algorithms for adding, subtracting, multiplying, and dividing. These algorithms are good for obtaining exact answers with simple technology, but, depending on the resources available and the result desired, there are many other kinds of computation. For example, if you are in a supermarket check-out line with several items and you find only $10 in your wallet, then a quick judgment whether you have sufficient funds is desirable. In this case, a rough mental estimate of the total cost of your purchases is what you want. If you are planning an addition to your house, however, different computational demands must be met. The situation is more complex than the supermarket checkout, and the penalty for making a mistake is more severe, so greater care must be taken. You will want more resources—paper and pencil, a calculator, time to work, perhaps a computer spreadsheet—and you will probably want rather precise estimates for the cost of various alternative designs for the addition.

A well-rounded mathematics program should prepare students to compute accurately, flexibly, and appropriately in all situations. Figure 4 shows a classification of computational situations using two criteria, the result desired and the resources available. Although you may want to move some of the questions to other cells or insert your own examples, these six categories of computation indicate the scope required of a complete mathematics curriculum (Coburn, 1989).

Resources Available

		Paper & Pencil	Machine	Mental
Result Desired	Exact	How many students are in the three third grades at my school?	How much will my monthly payment be on my car loan?	How much baking soda do I need if I am tripling a recipe that calls for 2 teaspoons?
	Approximate	What is my share of the national debt?	House remodeling: Which design(s) can I afford?	Supermarket checkout: Do I have enough money for these items?

Figure 4: *Six varieties of computation*

The TIMS Philosophy: Meaning, Invention, Efficiency, Power

The treatment of computation in *Math Trailblazers* proceeds in several stages. The grade levels for the stages vary with the operation—ideas of division, for example, develop long after addition—but the general pattern is similar for all the operations. Roughly speaking, the stages are

- developing meaning for the operation,
- inventing procedures for solving problems, and
- becoming more efficient at carrying out procedures, all leading to
- developing mathematical power.

Developing mathematical power with an operation means that students understand *when* to apply the operation and *how* to use varied computational methods to solve problems, even complex or nonroutine problems.

The goal of the first stage is to help students understand the meaning of the operation. Most of the work involves solving problems, writing or telling "stories" that involve operations, and sharing solution strategies. These methods typically involve a great deal of mental arithmetic and creative thinking. The use of manipulatives, pictures, and counting is encouraged at this stage. Discussing these informal methods helps develop students' understanding of the operation.

In the next stage, the focus shifts from developing the concept of the operation to devising and analyzing procedures to carry out the operation. At this stage, students "invent" methods for carrying out the operation, explaining, discussing, and comparing their procedures. Multiple solution strategies—mental, paper and pencil, manipulative, calculator—are encouraged, and parallels between various methods are explored. There is evidence that this "invented algorithms" approach enhances students' number and operation sense and problem-solving abilities (Madell, 1985; Sawada, 1985; Kamii, Lewis & Jones, 1991; Burns, 1992; Kamii, Lewis & Livingston, 1993; Porter & Carroll, 1995; Carroll & Porter, 1997). Inventing their own methods helps make mathematics meaningful for children by connecting school mathematics to their own ways of thinking. The expectation that mathematics should make sense is reinforced.

In the third stage, a standard algorithm for the operation is introduced. This algorithm is not presented as the one, true, and official way to solve problems, but rather as yet another procedure to examine. The algorithms used in *Math Trailblazers* are not all identical to the traditional ones taught in school. The addition and subtraction algorithms are only a little different, but the procedures for multiplication and division are considerably different. (See Figures 5 and 6.)

$$
\begin{array}{r}
5\ 8 \\
\times\ 3\ 6 \\
\hline
4\ 8 \\
3\ 0\ 0 \\
2\ 4\ 0 \\
1\ 5\ 0\ 0 \\
\hline
2\ 0\ 8\ 8 \\
\end{array}
$$

Figure 5: *All-partials multiplication*

Figure 6: *A division algorithm*

We chose these alternative algorithms for multiplication and division for several reasons. First, they are easier to learn than the traditional methods. Second, they are more transparent, revealing what is actually happening. Third, they provide practice in multiplying by numbers ending in zero, an important skill for estimation. Finally, even though they are less efficient than the traditional algorithms, they are good enough for most purposes—any problem that is awkward to solve by these methods should probably be done by machine anyway.

Students who have no reliable method of their own are urged to adopt the standard algorithm. However, even after introducing and analyzing a standard algorithm for an operation, alternative methods are still accepted, even encouraged, for students who are comfortable with them. In particular, the standard algorithm is very inefficient with some problems. For example, students using *Math Trailblazers* should be able to compute 40×30 mentally to get 1200. Using the standard algorithm here would be inefficient. Or consider $16,000 - 5$. Using a standard algorithm to solve this problem is tedious and often results in errors.

In the last stage, students achieve mathematical power through the mastery of procedures that solve entire classes of problems: efficient and reliable computational algorithms. This procedural fluency, moreover, is based on solid conceptual understandings so that it can be applied flexibly to solve problems. These procedures become part of the students' base of prior knowledge—on which they can build more advanced conceptual and procedural understandings.

Fractions and Decimals

The approach to fractions and decimals in *Math Trailblazers* parallels that for whole numbers. At first, the focus is on developing concepts and meanings for fractions and decimals. Next comes a period in which students invent procedures for solving problems, connecting school mathematics to their own informal methods and common sense. Finally, formal procedures are investigated, not as substitutes for common sense, but as more efficient methods for achieving desired results.

Fraction Meanings

One of the problems with fractions is that they are so useful. Consider some of the meanings for $\frac{1}{2}$:

- half of a cookie (a part-whole fraction)
- $1 \div 2$ (division)
- one cup water to two cups flour (a ratio, sometimes written 1:2)
- $\frac{1}{2}$ mile (a measurement)
- the point midway between 0 and 1 (the name of a point on a number line)
- the square root of $\frac{1}{4}$ (a pure number)
- the chance a fair coin will land heads up (a probability)

Because the same notation can mean so many different things, children and even adults sometimes become confused and may manipulate fraction symbols haphazardly, often with unfortunate results. A better approach develops sound meanings for the symbols before focusing on how to manipulate them (Mack, 1990).

Part-Whole Fractions

Early fraction work focuses on part-whole fractions. Many fractions in daily life are part-whole fractions, so even young children are familiar with terms like one-half and three-fourths in part-whole contexts. Also, many key ideas about fractions are well illustrated in part-whole situations.

There are two concepts that are fundamental in understanding part-whole fractions: knowing what the whole is and understanding what a part is in relation to the whole. For example, to understand the statement, "Last night I ate three-fourths of a carton of ice cream," requires knowing what the whole is. Just how big a carton of ice cream was it? One must also understand that the parts into which the whole is divided must be equal—they should have the same area or mass or number, etc. A way to make this clear to children is to talk about "fair shares."

The whole in a part-whole fraction can be either a single thing (e.g., a pizza) or a collection (e.g., a class of students). When the whole is a collection, then counting is generally used to make fair shares; when the unit is a single thing, the fairness of the shares depends on some measurable quantity. Half of one pizza is different from half of three pizzas. Often, area is the variable that must be equally allocated among the parts; such a situation may be called an area model for fractions.

Symbols and Referents

A key idea in the *Math Trailblazers* approach to fractions is that fractions should be represented in several ways and that students should be able to make connections between those representations. The fraction two-thirds, for example, can be expressed in words, symbols, pictures, or real objects (Figure 7).

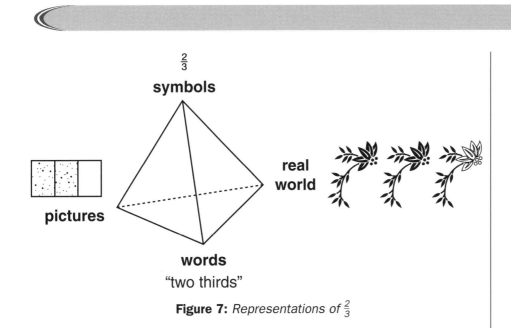

Figure 7: *Representations of $\frac{2}{3}$*

The ability to move freely between these several representations is an essential component of the mathematical understanding of fractions (Lesh, Post & Behr, 1987). Especially important are connections between fraction symbols and the real-world situations to which those fractions refer. Given symbols for a fraction, can students draw an illustrative picture or tell a story? Can students explain the relationship between a group of five girls and two boys and the fraction $\frac{5}{7}$?

Math Trailblazers makes extensive use of manipulatives in teaching fractions in all grades. Pictures, pattern blocks, geoboards, paper folding, and number lines are among many tools used to promote students' conceptual understanding of fractions. When paper-and-pencil procedures for adding, subtracting, multiplying, and dividing fractions are introduced in Grades 4 and 5, they are always linked closely with other representations of fractions, such as manipulatives or pictures.

Decimals

Decimals are treated in two ways in *Math Trailblazers:* first, as another way to write certain common fractions—those with denominators that are powers of ten—and second, as an extension of the whole number place value system. Similar to the coverage of other topics in *Math Trailblazers,* considerable attention is placed upon developing a solid conceptual foundation about decimals before formal, paper-and-pencil operations are introduced. Students with strong conceptual understandings of decimals learn procedures more easily and can apply those procedures to problem situations more effectively

> *The ability to move freely between these several representations is an essential component of the mathematical understanding of fractions. Especially important are connections between fraction symbols and the real-world situations to which these fractions refer.*

(Ball, 1993; Behr & Post, 1992; Hiebert, Wearne & Taber, 1991; Lesh, Post & Behr, 1987). Connections between fractions (common fractions) and decimals (decimal fractions) are stressed throughout.

As with work with whole numbers and fractions, work with decimal fractions includes extensive work with manipulatives. Often these models are used to make strong connections between fractions, decimals, and percents. Figures 8 and 9 show two examples of tools used in Grade 5 lessons on decimals. These representations create visual images of the decimal fractions and link those images with students' previous work with fractions and percent.

Figure 8: *Interlocking centiwheel disks model $\frac{1}{4}$, 0.25, and 25%.*

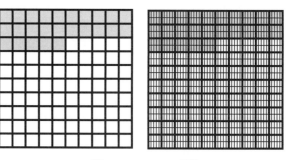

Figure 9: $\frac{25}{100} = 0.25$ and $\frac{250}{1000} = 0.250$

A Developmental Approach

Kindergarten fraction work emphasizes the idea that the fractional parts of a whole must be the same size. Work with symbols is not emphasized.

Fraction work in Grades 1–3 of *Math Trailblazers* focuses primarily on establishing links between symbols and referents for part-whole fractions. Children learn to make connections between marks on paper and the real world. Concepts of the unit—identifying the unit, knowing how the size of the unit affects the value of the fraction, appreciating the importance of fair shares—are also explored (Figure 10). Decimals are treated primarily as an alternative notation for certain fractions, and some attention is given to the interpretation of decimals that appear on calculators. Real-world situations, especially fair sharing, and area models predominate.

If ⬚⬚ is $\frac{1}{3}$,

then what is one whole?

Figure 10: *A concept-of-unit exercise*

In Grade 3, students continue to develop concepts of the unit, but they begin to use more varied models. Children explore the relative size of fractions, especially with respect to the benchmark numbers 0, $\frac{1}{2}$, and 1. They also study equivalent fractions in Grade 3. Fractions are represented with a variety of manipulatives—paper folding, pattern blocks, geoboards. Collections of objects are divided to represent fractions.

Decimals are investigated more extensively in Grade 3, again being treated as a kind of fraction. Decimals in metric length measurement and on number lines are investigated. Base-ten pieces are used to create concrete and visual representations of decimal fractions. Translating between common fractions and decimals is again stressed.

In Grade 4, work on operations with fractions and decimals begins, but standard procedures are not taught. As discussed above, modeling concepts and procedures with manipulatives is intended to establish a basis for more algorithmic work in Grade 5. In fourth grade, students solve problems involving addition and subtraction, largely with the aid of manipulatives and other fraction models.

Operations with fractions and decimals include more than simply the four arithmetic operations. Putting fractions and decimals in order by size, renaming the same number in several equivalent forms, and estimating sums, differences, and so on, are all operations that can be carried out with fractions and decimals. Again, manipulatives, such as pattern blocks and base-ten pieces, are used to develop conceptual understanding and provide a concrete representation of the symbols.

In Grade 5, paper-and-pencil procedures for addition, subtraction, and multiplication of fractions and decimals are explored, including use of common denominators and reducing. Repeating decimals are introduced. Students also use calculators to rename fractions as decimals for comparing and ordering common fractions.

Many contexts are used to reinforce students' understanding of fraction and decimal concepts. For example, in a Grade 5 laboratory investigation, *Comparing Lives of Animals and Soap Bubbles,* students collect data about the "life spans" of soap bubbles. As they analyze the data, they convert the data first to a fractional quantity, then to the equivalent decimal fraction. Making these connections between mathematical concepts and real-world situations helps students make sense of the mathematics they are learning.

Conclusion

Our goal in developing *Math Trailblazers* is to create a balanced program that promotes the coordinated development of both procedural skill and conceptual understanding. Students will connect school mathematics with intuitive knowledge and informal procedures. They will use a variety of techniques and manipulatives for modeling the mathematical ideas. In doing so, students will not only develop skills and concepts, but will be able to use those skills and concepts to solve problems.

References

Ball, D. "Halves, Pieces, and Twoths: Constructing and Using Representational Contexts in Teaching Fractions." In T.P. Carpenter, E. Fennema, and T.A. Romberg (Eds.), *Rational Numbers: An Integration of Research.* pp. 157–195. Lawrence Erlbaum Associates, Hillsdale, NJ, 1993.

Baroody, A.J., and H.P. Ginsburg. "The Relationship between Initial Meaning and Mechanical Knowledge of Arithmetic." In J. Hiebert (ed.), *Conceptual and Procedural Knowledge: The Case of Mathematics.* Lawrence Erlbaum Associates, Hillsdale, NJ, 1986.

Behr, M.J., and T.R. Post. "Teaching Rational Number and Decimal Concepts." In *Teaching Mathematics in Grades K–8: Research Based Methods.* Allyn and Bacon, Boston, MA, 1992.

Bransford, J.D., A.L. Brown, and R.R. Cocking, eds. *How People Learn: Brain, Mind, Experience, and School.* National Academy Press, Washington, DC, 1999.

Brown, J.S., and R.R. Burton. "Diagnostic Models for Procedural Bugs in Basic Mathematical Skills." *Cognitive Science,* 2, pp. 155–192, 1978.

Brownell, W.A., and C.B. Chazal. "The Effects of Premature Drill in Third-Grade Arithmetic." *Journal of Educational Research,* 29 (1), 1935.

Brownell, W.A. "Meaning and Skill—Maintaining the Balance." *Arithmetic Teacher,* 34 (8), pp. 18–25 (Original work published in 1956), 1987.

Carpenter, T.P. "Conceptual Knowledge as a Foundation for Procedural Knowledge." In J. Hiebert (ed.), *Conceptual and Procedural Knowledge: The Case of Mathematics.* Lawrence Erlbaum Associates, Hillsdale, NJ, 1986.

Carpenter, T.P., E. Fennema, and M.L. Franke. *Cognitively Guided Instruction: Building the Primary Mathematics Curriculum on Children's Informal Mathematical Knowledge.* A paper presented at the annual meeting of the American Educational Research Association, San Francisco, CA, April 1992.

Carpenter, T.P., M.L. Franke, V.R. Jacobs, E. Fennema, and S.B. Empson. "A Longitudinal Study of Invention and Understanding in Children's Multidigit Addition and Subtraction." *Journal for Research in Mathematics Education,* 29, pp. 3–20, 1998.

Carroll, W., and D. Porter. "Invented Algorithms: Helping Students to Develop and Use Meaningful Mathematical Procedures." *Teaching Children Mathematics,* pp. 370–374, March 1997.

Coburn, T.G. "The Role of Computation in the Changing Mathematics Curriculum." In P.R. Trafton (ed.), *New Directions for Elementary School Mathematics.* National Council of Teachers of Mathematics, Reston, VA, 1989.

Dewey, J. *Experience and Education.* Macmillan, New York, 1938.

Finn, C.E., Jr. "What If Those Math Standards Are Wrong?" *Education Week,* 20 January 1993.

Fuson, K.C., and D.J. Briars. "Using a Base-Ten Blocks Learning/Teaching Approach for First- and Second-Grade Place-Value and Multidigit Addition and Subtraction." *Journal for Research in Mathematics Education,* 21, pp. 180–206, 1990.

Good, T.L., C. Mulryan, and M. McCaslin. "Grouping for Instruction in Mathematics: A Call for Programmatic Research on Small-Group Processes." In D.A. Grouws (ed.), *Handbook of Research on Mathematics Teaching and Learning: A Project of the National Council of Teachers of Mathematics* (Chapter 9). Macmillan, New York, 1992.

Greenes, C., M. Cavanagh, L. Dacey, C. Findell, and M. Small. *Navigating through Algebra in Pre-kindergarten–Grade 2.* National Council of Teachers of Mathematics, Reston, VA, 2001.

Hiebert, J. "Children's Mathematical Learning: The Struggle to Link Form and Understanding." *Elementary School Journal,* 84 (5), pp. 497–513, 1984.

Hiebert, J. "A Theory of Developing Competence with Written Mathematical Symbols." *Educational Studies in Mathematics,* 19, pp. 333–355, 1988.

Hiebert, J. "Relationships between Research and the NCTM Standards." *Journal for Research in Mathematics Education,* 30 (1), pp. 3–19, 1999.

Hiebert, J. and D. Wearne. "Procedures over Concepts: The Acquisition of Decimal Number Knowledge." In J. Hiebert (Ed.), *Conceptual and Procedural Knowledge: The Case of Mathematics.* Lawrence Erlbaum Associates, Hillsdale, NJ, 1986.

Hiebert, J., D. Wearne, and S. Taber. "Fourth Graders' Gradual Construction of Decimal Fractions during Instruction Using Different Physical Representations." *Elementary School Journal,* 91 (4), pp. 321–341, 1991.

Hiebert, J., T. Carpenter, E. Fennema, K.C. Fuson, D. Wearne, H. Murray, A. Oliver, and H. Piet. *Making Sense: Teaching and Learning Mathematics with Understanding.* Heinemann, Portsmouth, NH, 1997.

Kamii, C., B.A. Lewis, and S. Jones. "Reform in Primary Mathematics Education: A Constructivist View." *Educational Horizons,* 70 (1), pp. 19–26, 1991.

Kamii, C., B.A. Lewis, and S.J. Livingston, "Primary Arithmetic: Children Inventing Their Own Procedures." *Arithmetic Teacher,* 41 (4), pp. 200–203, 1993.

Lesh, R., T. Post, and M. Behr. "Representations and Translations among Representations in Mathematics Learning and Problem Solving." C. Janvier, ed., *Problems of Representation in the Teaching and Learning of Mathematics.* Lawrence Erlbaum Associates, Hillsdale, NJ, 1987.

McKnight, C.C., F.J. Crosswhite, J.A. Dossey, E. Kifer, J.O. Swafford, K.J. Travers, and T.J. Cooney. *The Underachieving Curriculum: Assessing U.S. School Mathematics from an International Perspective.* Stipes, Champaign, IL, 1987.

Mack, N.K. "Learning Fractions with Understanding: Building on Informal Knowledge." *Journal for Research in Mathematics Education,* 21 (1), pp. 16–32, 1990.

Madell, R. "Children's Natural Processes." *Arithmetic Teacher,* 32 (7), pp. 20–22, 1985.

Mathews, J. "Psst, Kid, Wanna Buy a Used Math Book? They're Old-Fashioned and a Bit Tedious, but John Saxon's Books are Hot Stuff in the Education Underground." *Newsweek,* 121, pp. 62–63, 1993.

May, L. "Reflections on Teaching Mathematics Today." *Illinois Mathematics Teacher,* 46 (3), pp. 5–8, 1995.

National Council of Teachers of Mathematics. *Curriculum Focal Points for Pre-kindergarten through Grade 8 Mathematics: A Quest for Coherence.* Reston, VA, 2006.

National Research Council. *Adding It Up: Helping Children Learn Mathematics.* National Academy Press, Washington, DC, 2001.

National Research Council. "The Strands of Mathematical Proficiency." *Adding It Up: Helping Children Learn Mathematics.* pp. 115–156, J. Kilpatrick, J. Swafford, and B. Findell, eds. National Academy Press, Washington, DC, 2001.

Perry, M. "Learning and Transfer: Instructional Conditions and Conceptual Change." *Cognitive Development,* 6, pp. 449–468, 1991.

Porter, D., and W. Carroll. "Invented Algorithms: Some Examples from Primary Classrooms." *Illinois Mathematics Teacher,* pp. 6–12, April 1995.

Press, M. "Drill and Practice Add Up." *San Jose Mercury News,* 27 February 1995.

Principles and Standards for School Mathematics. National Council of Teachers of Mathematics, Reston, VA, 2000.

Rathmell, E.C., and D.M. Huinker. "Using 'Part-Whole' Language to Help Children Represent and Solve Word Problems." In P.R. Trafton (ed.), *New Directions for Elementary School Mathematics,* pp. 99–110. National Council of Teachers of Mathematics, Reston, VA, 1989.

Resnick, L.B. "Syntax and Semantics in Learning to Subtract." In R. Glaser (ed.), *Advances in Instructional Psychology* (Vol. 3). Lawrence Erlbaum Associates, Hillsdale, NJ, 1987.

Resnick, L.B., and S.F. Omanson. "Learning to Understand Arithmetic." In *Advances in Instructional Psychology* (Vol. 3). Lawrence Erlbaum Associates, Hillsdale, NJ, 1987.

Resnick, L.B., S. Lesgold, and V. Bill. *From Protoquantities to Number Sense.* A paper prepared for the Psychology of Mathematics Education Conference, Oaxtapec, Mexico, 1990.

Sawada, D. "Mathematical Symbols: Insight through Invention." *Arithmetic Teacher,* 32 (6), pp. 20–22, 1985.

Shuard, H. "CAN: Calculator Use in the Primary Grades in England and Wales." In J. T. Fey (ed.), *Calculators in Mathematics Education,* Reston, VA, 1992.

Skemp, R.R. "Relational Understanding and Instrumental Understanding." *Arithmetic Teacher,* 26 (3), pp. 9–15, 1978.

Swart, W.L. "Some Findings on Conceptual Development of Computational Skills." *Arithmetic Teacher* 32 (5), pp. 36–38, 1985.

Usiskin, Z. "Paper-and-Pencil Skills in a Calculator/Computer Age." *UCSMP Newsletter,* 16, pp. 7–14, 1994.

Van Lehn, K. "Arithmetic Procedures Are Induced from Examples." In J. Hiebert (ed.), *Conceptual and Procedural Knowledge: The Case of Mathematics.* Lawrence Erlbaum Associates, Hillsdale, NJ, 1986.

Whitehead, A.N. "The Rhythmic Claims of Freedom and Discipline." In *The Aims of Education and Other Essays.* Macmillan, New York, 1929.

Averages

Introduction

"Average" is one of those words that mean different things to different people. Baseball players talk about their batting averages. A teacher might confide to a colleague that "Jim is just an average student." At the university, students always want to know what the class average is on an exam. Sometimes you hear the statement that the temperature will be about average for this time of year. When someone asks you how you feel, you may reply, "Just average." In everyday usage, "average" is a word that can be anything from a synonym for "typical," "normal," or "usual," to a number derived according to some formula or rule. This TIMS Tutor lays out some of the different numerical meanings of "average" and explains some of the importance of averages in mathematics and science.

The Mean—A Wage Dispute

In his wonderful little book, *How to Lie with Statistics,* Darrell Huff gives the example of a factory owner and his workers who are arguing over wages. There are 25 workers including the owner. The owner pays himself $45,000. The others make $15,000, $10,000, $10,000, $5700, $5000, $5000, $5000, $3700, $3700, $3700, $3700, $3000, $2000, $2000, $2000, $2000, $2000, $2000, $2000, $2000, $2000, $2000, and $2000. The owner says the average wage is $5700 but the workers claim the average wage is only $3000. Even though prices have gone way up since Huff wrote his book 50 years ago, the discrepancy is clear: there is a big disagreement over what people are being paid, let alone what they should be paid.

So, what's going on here? Who's right, the owner or the workers? Both! The factory owner's average is the (arithmetic) mean; the workers' average is the median. There are other averages too, such as the **mode** (the number or value that occurs most often in a data set). However, in *Math Trailblazers,* we primarily use the mean and/or the median when finding average values. These two averages will be the focus of our discussion in this tutor.

Usually when people use the term "average," they are referring to the **mean.** This is the familiar add-up-all-the-numbers-and-divide average you learned in school. The mean has many useful properties that make it beloved by schoolteachers, statisticians, and scientists alike. Consider finding the average height of all the children in a class. Data for 23 children from a third-grade class is shown in Figure 1.

The mean height of these 23 children is

$$\langle H \rangle = \frac{\text{sum of heights}}{\text{number of children}}$$

$$= \frac{(133 + 136 + \ldots + 129 + 134) \text{ cm}}{23}$$

$$= \frac{3064 \text{ cm}}{23}$$

$$= 133.2 \text{ cm}$$

Name	H Height (in cm)
Karina	133
Federico	136
Ramon	135
Kiela	127
Aesha	126
Bravlia	128
Zuzia	133
Anthony	139
Iorta	146
Cordeli	135
Mary	137
Gennice	124

Name	H Height (in cm)
Curtis	139
Brian C	125
David	135
Anna	141
Brian M	131
Adriana	137
Boberto	134
Lucas	131
Gennifer	129
Amber	129
Nathan	134

Figure 1: *Data from a third-grade class*

For scientists, the mean is often the first number they calculate when looking at a data sample.

Although no child may have this mean height, it gives everyone a point for making comparisons. For scientists, the mean is often the first number they calculate when looking at a data sample.

There is another way to interpret the mean height of this class. This may seem strange, but consider the following situation. Suppose you walk into another class and find 23 students all exactly the same height. The mean is clearly that height. If the mean height of this new class and the mean in our class are the same, then the sum of the heights of the children is the same. That is, imagine making two stacks of the children, one for our class and one for the new class. Stack the children one on top of another. Then the two stacks would be the same height. So, if two class means are the same and the number of children in each class is the same, then the sums of the heights in the classes are the same, even if the individual heights that make the sums are vastly different.

Statisticians like the mean because it is often the "best" estimate of an unknown quantity like a length, an area, or a mass. For example, suppose you are trying to measure the mass of a large steel sphere. You have an unbiased balance, and you know you need to take repeated readings to get an accurate measurement. So, suppose you make eleven measurements and find the sphere's mass to be 129 gm, 133 gm, 132 gm, 130 gm, 128 gm, 129 gm, 130 gm, 131 gm, 130 gm, 129 gm, and 131 gm. Then

$$\frac{(129 + 133 + \ldots + 130 + 129 + 131) \text{ gm}}{11}$$

$$= \frac{1432 \text{ gm}}{11}$$

$$= 130 \text{ gm}$$

This is the best estimate of the "true" mass of the sphere, given these measurements. (Notice that the quotient above is actually equal to 130.18181818 . . . gm. However, since our original measurements are to the nearest gram, it makes sense to give the average only to the nearest gram.)

Similar situations arise all the time in everyday life. Our factory owner is using the mean. He computes the average wage by adding up everyone's salary (including his big fat one) and dividing by the total number of workers:

$$\frac{\$142,500}{25} = \$5,700$$

As one final example, suppose Marty scores 85, 84, 86, 87, 84, 87, 85, 85, 83, and 85 on 10 rounds of golf and Ellen scores 83, 83, 95, 97, 81, 83, 82, 84, 96, and 84. Then Marty's mean score is

$$= \frac{85 + 84 + 86 + 87 + 84 + 87 + 85 + 85 + 83 + 85}{10}$$

$$= 85.1$$

and Ellen's mean score is

$$= \frac{83 + 83 + 95 + 97 + 81 + 83 + 82 + 84 + 96 + 84}{10}$$

$$= 86.8$$

So, it would appear that Marty is a better golfer than Ellen. (In golf, a lower score is a better score.)

But anyone who plays golf and bets will notice that if Marty and Ellen played 10 rounds against each other and scored as above, then Marty would win three times and Ellen would win seven times. And the factory workers still feel underpaid, despite that nice mean salary. So to get some perspective on what is happening here, let's look at another average, the median.

The Median

The **median** is the number in the middle. That is, roughly speaking, the median splits a set of numbers into two halves: one half is less than the median; the other half is more than the median. So to find the median, rank the numbers from smallest to largest and take the one in the middle.

Suppose you want to find the median selling price of homes in your town. At the town office you find that 15 homes sold in the last six months. The selling prices, in rank order, were $134,000, $156,000, $164,000, $170,000, $184,000, $194,000, $224,000, $236,000, $250,000, $264,000, $266,000, $278,000, $334,000, $350,000, and $372,000. The median price was $236,000: seven houses sold for less than $236,000 and seven houses sold for more than $236,000.

When there is an even number of values, then the median can be a little harder to find. Say only 14 of the homes above have sold. Suppose that the highest-priced house, the one costing $372,000, went unsold. What is the new median? Counting up seven from the $134,000 house, we end up at the $224,000. Counting down seven from the $350,000 house, we end up at $236,000. The seventh house from the bottom is not the seventh house from the top! What to do? Easy. Go halfway between the two numbers closest to the middle. Halfway between $224,000 and $236,000. That comes out to be $230,000. So the median price of the 14 homes that sold would be $230,000.

Going back to our factory workers' example, there were 25 employees including the owner. The thirteenth salary (from the top or from the bottom) is $3000: there are 12 employees who make less than $3000, and 12 who make more than $3000. So, the median salary is $3000.

Sometimes the median is a better average to use than the mean. One common situation where the median may be preferred is when there are extreme values. In such cases, the mean can give a distorted picture of the "average" because the extreme values tend to "pull" the mean away from the typical values. Statisticians say the median is more "robust" than the mean; that is, the median is less affected by extreme values than the mean. This is why the factory workers prefer the median: it gives a truer picture of what a typical worker earns than the mean, which is pulled up by the owner's big salary.

The median offers some insight into our golfing example, too. Marty's (ranked) golf scores were 83, 84, 84, 85, 85, 85, 85, 86, 87, and 87. The two numbers in the middle are 85 and 85, so Marty's median score is 85. Ellen's scores were 81, 82, 83, 83, 83, 84, 84, 95, 96, and 97. The two numbers in the middle are 83 and 84, so Ellen's median score is 83.5. Thus, using medians, Ellen is a slightly better golfer, on average. Every few rounds she has a high score, but her typical score is better than Marty's typical score, so she usually wins.

Obviously, the median has several advantages with respect to the mean: it is less affected by extreme values; it requires little computation; it can be a better indicator of what is typical. You will want to be flexible, sometimes using the mean, sometimes using the median.

The Mode

The **mode** of a data set is the number that appears most often. For example, in Ellen's golf scores, the number that appears most often is 83. In our first example from *How to Lie with Statistics,* we considered the factory owner and his 25 workers who are arguing over wages. The owner pays himself $45,000. The others make $15,000, $10,000, $10,000, $5700, $5000, $5000, $5000, $3700, $3700, $3700, $3700, $3000, $2000, $2000, $2000, $2000, $2000, $2000, $2000, $2000, $2000, $2000, $2000, and $2000. To present their best argument, the workers could have argued that the modal salary was $2,000, since 12 workers had that salary.

> The **mode** of a data set is the number that appears most often.

Making Sense of Measures of Central Tendency

The median, mean, and mode are all "measures of central tendency." They each tell us something about the way the information in the data set clusters. Of course, when we replace a whole data set with one number, we lose a lot of information. Depending on the nature of the data set, the mean, median, or mode may or may not provide us with useful information. These measures of central tendency are most useful when the data clusters around some value.

Averaging in the *Math Trailblazers* Classroom

So how are averages used in *Math Trailblazers?* Suppose your second-grade students collected the data shown in Figure 2 for the TIMS Laboratory Investigation, *Rolling Along in Centimeters.* There are three experimental values for each car, and students need some measure of the middle that fairly represents their data for each car. In this case, the median is a perfectly respectable average.

T Type of Car	D Distance (in cm / unit)			
	Trial 1	Trial 2	Trial 3	Median
Red	83	93	86	
Blue	44	44	43	
Orange	39	53	46	
Black	194	199	189	

Figure 2: *Data from* Rolling Along in Centimeters

One way to get a median from data like this is illustrated in Figure 3. The students cross out the largest and smallest numbers in each row and use the one that is left as their average value. Finding the median value of the three trials does not require young children to do any arithmetic and conceptually illustrates quite nicely the idea of an average representing a middle value.

T Type of Car	D Distance (in $\frac{cm}{unit}$)			
	Trial 1	Trial 2	Trial 3	Median
Red	~~88~~	~~58~~	(86)	86
Blue	~~44~~	(44)	~~45~~	44
Orange	~~30~~	~~55~~	(46)	46
Black	(194)	~~189~~	~~189~~	194

Figure 3: *Finding the median*

42
45
47

Figure 4: *Finding the median in* Rolling Along with Links

You can illustrate finding the median more concretely by using links (or string, adding machine tape, etc.) to create "lengths" that match the actual distance the cars roll each time. At the end of three rolls, students will have three lengths of links each representing the distance a car rolled in a trial.

This is illustrated in Figure 4. The median value can then be found by comparing the lengths and discarding the shortest and longest; the remaining length represents the median. A similar process is used in the first-grade experiment *Rolling Along with Links.*

In fourth grade, students begin finding the mean as well as the median. Again the concepts are introduced concretely. For example, students find the median value for several towers of cubes by lining them up from shortest to tallest and selecting the tower in the middle. This is illustrated in Figures 5a and 5b. Figure 6 illustrates an even number of trials. To find the median here, students have to find the halfway point between the two middle towers.

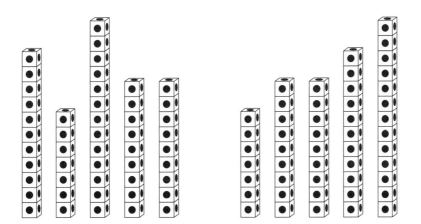

Figures 5a and 5b: *Finding the median with cubes*

Figure 6: *The median number of cubes is $7\frac{1}{2}$.*

You can also use cubes to introduce the mean. For example, suppose students begin with the same five towers illustrated in Figure 5a. They first estimate the mean by figuring out a way to "even out the towers," as illustrated in Figure 7. The mean, to the nearest whole cube, is ten cubes. In this manner, the concept of the mean as a representative measure is stressed rather than focusing purely on the arithmetic procedure. Students then learn to calculate the mean using numerical values.

Figure 7: *Estimating the mean by "evening out" towers of cubes*

Students will often use calculators to calculate the mean of a data set. For example, the mean distance for the red car in Figure 2, when found by calculator, is:

$$\frac{(83 + 93 + 86) \text{ cm}}{3} = 87.333333 \text{ cm}$$

This is an example of too much of a good thing. In this case, the calculator gives many more digits than are meaningful. Students have to determine an appropriate level of significance. Keep in mind that our goal is to get a reasonable number to use as an average. Here, the original measurements were made to the nearest cm, so it makes sense to also report the mean value also to the nearest cm.

Why Average?

Finding the average is critical in a *Math Trailblazers* experiment. It is an important step from raw data to understanding. Errors are inevitable when making measurements, and averaging is one way to detect and control them. If a group of students makes the same measurement three times and gets 67 cm, 64 cm, and 84 cm, they should notice that the 84 cm is way off. They can detect their error and redo that measurement.

When we take a measurement, many factors prevent us from getting an exact answer. First is the precision of our measuring tools. A meterstick can measure only to the nearest tenth of a centimeter. When we measure the area of an irregular figure by counting square centimeters, we have to estimate the area of the fraction pieces of square centimeters, and so on. In addition, when we perform an experiment, we might get somewhat different measurements each time. If we drop a ball from a height of 100 centimeters and try to measure how high it bounces, we will get different answers each time. This is due to the difficulty in controlling variables (can we be sure we dropped the ball exactly the same way each time?) and the difficulty in measuring how high a moving object bounces. Nevertheless, if students are careful and practice measuring, they should get answers that are reasonably close. Even when all the measurements are close, the average minimizes error. If the measurements are 67 cm, 64 cm, and 67 cm, then the mean, 66 cm, is a more accurate prediction of future measurements than any of the actual measurements.

Another function of averaging is to aggregate raw data. Unlike computers, people cannot handle too many numbers at once. If I tell you the height of every child in a school, then you will be overwhelmed by numbers. If I tell you the median height of children in the school, you know less but probably understand more. The situation in a typical *Math Trailblazers* experiment is similar. From 12 actual measurements in *Rolling Along in Centimeters,* we cut down to four medians that are then used to display the data in a graph.

References

Huff, Darrell. *How to Lie with Statistics.* W.W. Norton & Co., New York, 1954.

Johnson, Robert. *Elementary Statistics,* 3rd ed., Wadsworth, Inc., Belmont, CA, 1980.

Estimation, Accuracy, and Error

[handwritten margin notes, illegible]

For many people, one of the most attractive aspects of mathematics is that it is exact. The story problems that we worked on in our youth were reassuring (or terrifying) in the certainty of their answers. If one potato weighs 2 pounds, then 100 potatoes weigh 200 pounds. The only problem is that the real world is not so exact. One potato does not weigh exactly 2 pounds and 100 potatoes probably do not weigh 200 pounds. In this tutor, we discuss ways we deal mathematically with situations where exactness is not called for (when we estimate) or impossible (when we measure within a certain degree of accuracy).

Virtually all mathematics educators agree that estimation should be an important part of any elementary curriculum. Unlike content areas such as number and operation and geometry, there is very little traditional curriculum on estimation as well as some disagreement about exactly what is meant by estimation. Some mathematicians and educators make a distinction between estimation and approximation, but there is no generally agreed definition of these terms. This tutor provides a general overview of the concept of estimation and discusses some of the more common strategies and applications. For a more exhaustive treatment of estimation, we recommend the NCTM yearbook (1986).

What Is Estimation?

According to *Webster's Eleventh New Collegiate Dictionary,* **to estimate** means to judge tentatively or approximately the value, worth, or significance of something. Alternatively, it means to calculate approximately. **An estimate** is a general calculation of size, value, and so on, especially an *approximate* computation of the probable cost of a piece of work. This leads one to ask for the definition of **approximate.** The dictionary states that approximate means located close together, or nearly correct or exact. Moreover, **an approximation** is an *estimate,* guess, or mathematical result that is close in value but not the same as a desired quantity.

Although these definitions appear to be circular (an estimate is an approximation and an approximation is an estimate), the dictionary does give us a general idea of what these words mean. As with most words, these words have several meanings and their exact meaning is determined by the particular context in which they are used. In particular, these words are used in a variety of ways in mathematics. You should first note that unlike most mathematical concepts, estimate and approximate do not have precise definitions. What does it mean for two numbers to be "near in position, close together?" Is 5 close to 10? Is 1250 close to 1300? Is 1000 close to 3000? It's hard to say. In spite of our inability to precisely define closeness, we shall see that the varied uses of estimation are an important ingredient in mathematical problem solving.

Pedagogical Aspects of Estimation

In her survey article, "Estimation and Number Sense," Judith Threadgill-Sowder (1992) points out that

> *Good estimators are flexible in their thinking, and they use a variety of strategies. They demonstrate a deep understanding of number and operations, and they continually draw upon that understanding. Poor estimators seem to be bound, with only slight variations, to one strategy—that of applying algorithms more suitable for finding an exact answer. Poor estimators have only a vague notion of the nature and purpose of estimation; they believe it to be inferior to exact calculation (Morgan, 1988) and equate it with guessing.*

It follows from this view that teaching estimation is a complex task. Rather than being a simple skill that follows a few basic rules, estimation requires a variety of strategies. Rather than being a separate subject, estimation is a habit of mind that is carried out in many mathematical activities. Thus, there are few lessons in the *Math Trailblazers* curriculum devoted solely to estimation, while many lessons offer opportunities for estimation. While estimation is not a simple skill, a number of simple skills, such as rounding and mental multiplication, are extremely useful when doing estimation.

Students often have difficulty with estimation because they are uncomfortable about having more than one correct answer. They want to know "the right answer" and dislike being told "that's a good estimate." So it is your task to keep reminding students of the purpose of estimation and that different strategies can result in different correct answers. The laboratory experiments in *Math Trailblazers* help students develop an appreciation of the approximate nature of measurement and the fact that some problems can have more than one solution.

To help organize our thoughts about estimation, we will break the uses of estimation in the elementary mathematics curriculum into four major categories:

1. Estimating the result of a calculation (in particular, addition, subtraction, multiplication, and division) to see if the answer is reasonable.
2. Measurement error, experimental error, and predictions.
3. Estimating the magnitude of a measurement; for example, the height of a building, the area of a wall, the volume of a jar, or the weight of a person.
4. Estimating how many; for example, the number of peanuts in a jar, the number of students in a school, the number of people at a concert.

Good estimators are flexible in their thinking, and they use a variety of strategies. They demonstrate a deep understanding of number and operations, and they continually draw upon that understanding.

It is your task to keep reminding students of the purpose of estimation and that different strategies can result in different correct answers.

Estimating the Results of a Calculation

Two primary reasons for estimating calculation results are:

1. To check that the exact answer is (possibly) correct. The estimation can be done either before or after the calculation. Getting an answer that is far from your estimate indicates that the calculation is incorrect. On the other hand, an estimate close to the calculation does not guarantee that it is correct.

2. As a substitute for the exact answer. In many situations an exact answer is not needed and may not even make sense.

We will discuss a few of the more common strategies used to estimate the results of a calculation. Undoubtedly, you and your students will find other good strategies.

Addition and Subtraction

For estimation purposes, the most important digits in a number are the ones to the left, i.e., the leading digits. When estimating a sum or difference, one strategy you can usually carry out mentally is to look at the first one or two *place-value columns.* For example, here are some statistics on the New England states from a 1987 almanac:

	Population (1984)	Area (sq mi)
Maine	1,164,000	33,215
New Hampshire	998,000	9304
Vermont	535,000	9609
Massachusetts	5,822,000	8257
Rhode Island	968,000	1214
Connecticut	3,174,000	5009

If we wanted to estimate the total population of New Hampshire and Vermont in 1984 using "front end estimation," we could look at the first column on the left. In this case, it is the hundred thousands column. Adding the 9 and the 5 we get 14, which tells us that the sum is approximately 14 hundred thousands; in other words, one million, four hundred thousand. In fact, the first two digits of the sum must be either 14 or 15 (depending on whether or not there is any carrying when we do the addition algorithm). Your estimate can be 1,400,000 or you can look at the next digits to see if there is likely to be any carrying. In this case, the digits in the ten thousands column are 9 and 3, so there will be carrying. Thus, 1,500,000 is an even better estimate. Of course, the whole point of estimation is to get a quick, approximate answer. If you start looking at too many digits, you might as well find the exact answer.

A second quick method for this estimate is to think that the population of New Hampshire was approximately 1 million and that of Vermont was about $\frac{1}{2}$ million, so the total is about 1.5 million. Since the "exact" answer is 1,533,000, an estimate of 1.5 million is only off by about 2 percent. A more rule-bound approach that says, "round off the nearest million" would give us 1 million plus 1 million which is 2 million. This is not a very close estimate (it's about 30 percent off). In fact, there is no simple rule that gives a good estimate in all situations. A rule that often gives good results is "round each

When estimating a sum or difference, one strategy you can usually carry out mentally is to look at the first one or two place-value columns.

number to one significant digit and then add." (A whole number has one significant digit if all digits after the first one equal zero.) That's what we did in this case, rounding 1,164,000 to 1,000,000 and 535,000 to 500,000.

You can apply the same strategies to estimate the results of subtraction calculations. For example, if we wanted to know how much larger the population of New Hampshire was than the population of Vermont, we could round each population to one significant digit, and subtract 500,000 from 1 million to get 500,000. Rounding to the nearest million definitely doesn't work in this problem, since both populations round to 1 million, and we would get the nonsensical estimate that there were no more people in New Hampshire than there were in Vermont! It should be noted that looking at the difference between two numbers is not always the best way of comparing them. If we wanted to compare the populations of New Hampshire and Vermont, it might be better to look at the ratio of their populations and say that New Hampshire had twice the population of Vermont.

The fact that the population figures are rounded off to the nearest thousand in the table is an acknowledgment that census figures themselves are estimates. In this case, there are two reasons that the data is not exact. Population data for the United States is based on census data. Since the U.S. population is so large and not everyone cooperates with the census takers, it is impossible to count everyone in the country. The population is also a moving target. Every day, tens of thousands of people are born or die. Finally, the figures for 1984 population are obtained by starting with the 1980 figures and extrapolating based on assumptions about the rate of population growth. Since many factors affecting population growth change, it is highly unlikely that predictions for population would be very accurate.

Rounding is also one effective strategy for mentally estimating the sum of a series of numbers. For example, to find the total population of New England from the individual state populations above, you might round the numbers in the population column to the nearest half million, namely 1, 1, $\frac{1}{2}$, 6, 1, and 3 million. Adding these mentally gives $12\frac{1}{2}$ million, which is pretty close to the actual total of 14,238,888 people. Try to estimate the total area of New England, mentally. The exact answer is 62,810 square miles.

Note that these are not the only strategies for estimating the sum or difference of several numbers. For example, if you want to purchase items that cost $3.79, $4.19, $2.23, and $6.49, you might add the dollars mentally $(3 + 4 + 2 + 6 = 15)$ and then round the cents to the nearest quarter, i.e., 79 cents is about 75 cents, etc. This way, you see you need about $1.75 more (or 7 quarters). So, the total is pretty close to $16.75.

Multiplication: Rounding and Mental Math

The most basic technique for estimating the result of a multiplication problem is to replace (if necessary) the original numbers in the problem with other numbers that permit us to do the calculation mentally, or rapidly with paper and pencil. For example, if you want to know the number of minutes in a day, you would multiply 24 hours by 60 minutes per hour. Finding 24×60 is too hard for most people to do mentally, but 25×60 can be done by many fourth- and fifth-graders. Now, 25×60 is the same as $25 \times 6 \times 10$, and 25×6 is 150. (Think of 6 quarters as a dollar-fifty. Most of us are pretty good at calculating

The most basic technique for estimating the result of a multiplication problem is to replace (if necessary) the original numbers in the problem with other numbers that permit us to do the calculation mentally . . .

with multiples of 5, 10, and 25, since we have had a lot of practice doing mental arithmetic with money.) Finally, if 6 × 25 is 150, then 6 × 25 × 10 is 1500. This is a pretty good estimate for 24 × 60. Note that we repeatedly used the commutative property of multiplication—i.e., the order in which we multiply several numbers does not affect the result. An alternative estimate for 24 × 60 can be obtained by rounding off 24 to 20 and multiplying 20 by 60 to get approximately 1200 minutes in a day. This estimate is not as close, but it may suffice for many purposes.

A basic skill fundamental to being able to estimate in multiplication and division situations is the ability to multiply and divide by ten and powers of ten (100, 1000, etc.). Thus, as early as third grade in *Math Trailblazers,* we observe the pattern that multiplying a whole number by 10 amounts to adding the digit 0 to the right of the number, i.e., 10 × 57 = 570, 10 × 365 = 3650, and so on. Similarly, multiplying by 100 amounts to adding two 0 digits to the right, and so on. When we start to work with decimals, we observe that multiplying a decimal by 10 amounts to moving the decimal point to the right one place. For example, 10 × 45.76 = 457.6. This is really the same pattern we see with whole numbers, since 10 × 57.0 = 570, etc.

Another fundamental process in the examples above was finding convenient numbers that were close to the numbers we started with. Here, convenient means numbers with which we can calculate mentally. For example, we rounded 24 to 25, since multiples of 25 are easy to figure out. Often, the convenient numbers are what we call round numbers. For example, when we used our second strategy to estimate 24 × 60, we rounded 24 to the nearest 10, which gave us 20. All this means is that 20 is the multiple of 10 that is nearest to 24 (since 24 is between 20 and 30 but is closer to 20).

Rounding

Traditionally, students were taught a lot of rules about rounding, but they often are not able to apply them successfully since they did not understand the purpose of rounding, nor did they have a good understanding of place value. When we are doing mental estimation, we frequently want to round a number in the hundreds to the nearest hundred, a number in the thousands to the nearest thousand, and so on. For example, 457 rounded to the nearest hundred is 500, while 447 rounded to the nearest hundred is 400. That's because both numbers are between 400 and 500, and 457 is closer to 500 and 447 is closer to 400. Now 450 is exactly halfway between 400 and 500, so it is not obvious how to round 450 to the nearest hundred. Strictly speaking, it does not make sense to talk about **the** nearest hundred in this situation, since 450 is 50 away from 400 and 50 away from 500. In the context of estimation, this means that you can use either 400 or 500 as an estimate for 450. For example, if we wanted to estimate 450 × 321, we could say 400 × 300 = 120,000 is an estimate for the answer. This estimate is certainly smaller than the actual answer, since 400 is less than 450 and 300 is less than 321. On the other hand, 500 × 300 = 150,000, which is probably bigger than the actual answer. So the answer is probably between 120,000 and 150,000 (it's actually 144,450).

It used to be taught that numbers halfway between should always be rounded up, but there is really no reason for doing so. In general, the choice is determined by the context in which the rounding takes place and the reason you are rounding. For example, if you want to make sure you have enough money to purchase the items in your grocery cart, it is probably best to make a conservative estimate and round items that cost $12.50 up to $13.

Division

It may be surprising to realize that the operation we need to estimate most frequently in daily life is division. This is because many decisions we have to make are based on proportional reasoning.

It may be surprising to realize that the operation we need to estimate most frequently in daily life is division. This is because many decisions we have to make are based on proportional reasoning. How many miles per gallon is your car getting? Which brand of cereal is the least expensive? (One costs $2.65 for 14 oz and the other costs $3.55 for 24 oz.) A calculator can answer all these easily, but we often do not have a calculator handy. More significantly, students often perform the wrong calculations on the calculator. Letting students first solve their problem using convenient numbers allows them to focus on the essential parts of the problem, without being distracted by a lot of digits and a lot of mechanical manipulations. Once they have found a reasonable solution strategy, they can return to solve the original messy problem.

The easiest problems are ones that we can turn into a problem that requires dividing by a power of 10. Dividing by 10 is the inverse of multiplying by 10. Thus we can divide by 10 mentally by moving the decimal point one place to the left. For example, $\frac{279}{10} = 27.9$, $\frac{456.2}{10} = 45.62$, and so on. Similarly, we can divide by 100 by moving the decimal point two places to the left. When dividing a whole number by 10, we get a fairly good estimate for the result by just dropping the ones digit. For example, $\frac{279}{10}$ is approximately 27. Note that the estimate we get this way is always smaller than the exact answer.

One method for estimating the results of a division problem is to replace each number by a suitable nearby convenient number and then carry out the first step in the division algorithm. The rounding is chosen to make the division easy. For example, suppose we wanted to estimate the population density of Maine in 1984. The data in Table 1 tells us that the density is 1,164,000 people ÷ 33,215 square miles. We can round off the divisor to 30,000 square miles and round off the dividend to 1,000,000 people. To estimate 1,000,000 ÷ 30,000, we can ask what times 30,000 gives 1,000,000. Multiplying 30,000 by 10 gives 300,000 and multiplying this by 3.3 gets us near 1,000,000. So, our estimate is about 33. Another method is to replace the divisor and dividend with nearby convenient numbers. For example, 33,215 is near 30,000 and 1,164,000 is close to 1,200,000. We chose this pair of numbers because 12 is divisible by 3. So, our estimate now amounts to 1,200,000 people ÷ 30,000 square miles. Again, we see we need to multiply 30,000 by 40 to get 1,200,000. So 40 people per square mile is a reasonable estimate for the population density of Maine. Putting the numbers back into the context of the problem is important for checking any result.

A powerful technique for estimating the result of a division problem is to consider the division as a ratio. For example, suppose you traveled 637 miles and used 22 gallons of gas. To find miles per gallon, divide 22 into 637. Write the ratio 637 miles/22 gallons. Rounding 637 to 600 and 22 to 20 we get

A powerful technique for estimating the result of a division problem is to consider the division as a ratio.

$$\frac{637 \text{ mi}}{22 \text{ gal}} \approx \frac{600 \text{ mi}}{20 \text{ gal}}$$

Note that we used the symbol $\approx$ instead of the equal sign. This symbol means "approximately equal." Now, we can simplify the ratio $\frac{600}{20}$ by dividing both numerator and denominator by 10. So

$$\frac{600 \text{ mi}}{20 \text{ gal}} = \frac{60 \text{ mi}}{2 \text{ gal}}$$

and dividing numerator and denominator by 2 gives us

$$\frac{60 \text{ mi}}{2 \text{ gal}} = \frac{30 \text{ mi}}{1 \text{ gal}}$$

Putting this all together, we get 637 mi/22 gal $\approx$ 30 mi/1 gal; in other words, our estimate is 30 miles per gallon.

A note on canceling. Many people learned to simplify ratios by "canceling" the same thing in the numerator and the denominator. You might be tempted to say that when we wrote 600 mi/20 gal $\approx$ 60 mi/2 gal, we "canceled a 0" in the numerator and the denominator. Unfortunately, this can lead to some bad habits. For example, can you cancel the fives in $\frac{875}{25}$ to get $\frac{87}{2}$, or cancel the fives in $(X + 5)/(Y + 5)$ to get X/Y? You better not, since this amounts to subtracting the 5 from the numerator and denominator and results in a fraction that is not equal to the one we started with.

$$\frac{875}{25} \neq \frac{87}{2}$$

$$\frac{X + 5}{Y + 5} \neq \frac{X}{Y}$$

So canceling does not always result in an equal ratio. For this reason, we always say exactly what we are doing, dividing numerator and denominator by the same number, rather than using the word "cancel."

Here are some examples of estimation in a division context:

Example 1: Estimate the quotient $\frac{80,000}{30}$. This is approximately $\frac{8000}{3}$, which is between $\frac{7500}{3}$ and $\frac{9000}{3}$, i.e., between 2500 and 3000. Note that if we estimated $\frac{80,000}{30}$ by replacing 30 with 40 (since 40 goes into 80,000 evenly) we get $\frac{80,000}{40} = \frac{8000}{4} = 2000$, which is not as good as our previous estimate. This might be a little surprising, since we only made a change of 10 in replacing 30 by 40. But what is important here is not the size of the change (10), but the relative size of the change (10 out of 30 is 33%).

Here are some additional examples of estimation in a division context. See if you can follow the reasoning in these estimates. Can you make an estimate in a different way?

$$\frac{6206}{8271} \approx \frac{6000}{8000} = \frac{6}{8} = \frac{3}{4} = 0.75$$

$$\frac{78{,}221}{987} \approx \frac{80{,}000}{1000} = 80$$

$$\frac{77{,}921}{289} \approx \frac{75{,}000}{250} = \frac{7500}{25} = 300$$

$$\frac{828}{38{,}765} \approx \frac{800}{40{,}000} = \frac{8}{400} = \frac{2}{100} = .02$$

Measurement Error, Experimental Error, and Predictions

The theme of this tutor is the way to deal with "inexactness" in real-world mathematics. One class of situations that involve inexactness is measurement error or experimental error.

Measurement error is the unavoidable error that occurs due to the limitations inherent to any measurement instrument. Any measurement in the real world is an approximation. It is not really possible to guarantee that an object is exactly 1 meter long since any measuring instrument has a limit to its accuracy. For example, our centimeter ruler can only measure to the nearest tenth of a centimeter and the two-pan balance usually used in *Math Trailblazers* can only measure mass to the nearest gram.

Experimental error is the variation in measurement that results from the inability to control extraneous variables in an experiment.

These two types of error are closely related. Let's consider three examples of measurement in real-world contexts to get some idea of the meaning of measurement and experimental error:

Example 1: A volunteer is selected from the class and every student measures the circumference of her head to the nearest tenth of a centimeter. Most students get between 47 and 49 centimeters. One student gets 37.4 centimeters.

Example 2: Students drop a ball from a height of 80 centimeters three times to see how high it bounces. They get 41 centimeters, 45 centimeters, and 44 centimeters.

Example 3: Students measure the volume of a marble using a graduated cylinder. Most students get either 7 or 8 cubic centimeters. Two students get 67 cubic centimeters.

Example 4: A student finds that the mass of one blue pattern block is 11 grams. She predicts that 2 blue pattern blocks will have a mass of 22 grams and 4 blue pattern blocks will have a mass of 44 grams. When she checks her results, she finds that 2 pattern blocks do have a mass of 22 grams, but 4 pattern blocks have a mass of 42 grams.

> *Measurement error is the unavoidable error that occurs due to the limitations inherent to any measurement instrument. . . .*
>
> *Experimental error is the variation in measurement that results from the inability to control extraneous variables in an experiment.*

Errors vs. Mistakes

In Examples 1, 2, and 3, there were repeated measurements of the same thing that produced seemingly different answers. The fact that most students obtained slightly different answers in Example 1 is due to slight variations in how they performed the measurement—where they placed the tape measure, how tight they held it, etc. All these measurements are "close" to each other (see below for a discussion of "what's close?").

However, the student whose measurement was 37.4 centimeters probably made a *mistake* such as reading the tape measure incorrectly or placing the tape measure in the wrong position. In mathematics, we try to distinguish between the words "error" and "mistake." Of course, "mistake" is one of the common meanings of "error." *Webster's New World Dictionary of the American Language* gives as its first definition of the word "error," "the state of believing what is untrue, incorrect, or wrong."

In the current context, however, "error" has a different meaning. This is the fifth definition given for "error" in that dictionary, namely "the difference between a computed or estimated result and the actual value as in mathematics." The dictionary goes on to explain that "error implies deviation from truth, accuracy, correctness, right, [while] mistake suggests an error resulting from carelessness, inattention, misunderstanding, etc."

Most of the measurements in Example 1 involved some measurement error, but those measurements were correct. However, the student who measured 37.4 centimeters must have made a mistake. In this case, the teacher would help the student find the reason for the mistake and then repeat the measurement correctly.

In Example 2, it is not surprising that repeating the activity, that is, dropping the ball from 80 centimeters, results in a different measurement. It's pretty hard to measure how high the ball bounces, since the ball does not stop at the height of its bounce and wait for you to measure its distance from the floor. Also, there can be slight variations because different parts of the ball or different spots on the floor are "bouncier." This is a typical example of the experimental error that results from the inability to control all the fixed variables in an experiment. (See the TIMS Tutor: *The TIMS Laboratory Method,* Fixed Variables in Controlled Experiments.)

In Example 3, students used a graduated cylinder to measure the volume by displacement. Two students forgot to subtract the volume of the water in the cylinder, so they obtained measurements that were very different from the others. This is a clear example of a mistake. The actual volume of the marble was between 7 and 8 cubic centimeters.

Reducing Experimental Error

In Examples 1 through 3, we saw that repeating a measurement does not always give the same answer. To get more reliable and accurate results, scientists often repeat a measurement several times and then take the average of all the measurements. The "average" that we use in this situation can be

In mathematics, we try to distinguish between the words "error" and "mistake."

To get more reliable and accurate results, scientists often repeat a measurement several times and then take the average of all the measurements.

either the mean or the median. (See the TIMS Tutor: *Averages.*) In Example 2, we can take the median of the three measurements and say that dropping the ball from 80 centimeters results in a bounce height of 44 centimeters. We could also use the mean, in which case the bounce height would be nearly the same—approximately 43 centimeters.

In many experiments, we have another way of minimizing experimental error. If the data points plotted on a graph appear close to a straight line, we find a best-fit line that is close to all the data points. (See the TIMS Tutor: *The TIMS Laboratory Method.*) Using the best-fit line is a way of averaging out the experimental error. In *Math Trailblazers,* we draw a best-fit line "by eye," using a transparent ruler. In addition to averaging out the error, these lines help scientists and mathematicians make predictions based upon the patterns in the data. Scientists, mathematicians, and statisticians use a variety of sophisticated methods to find best-fit lines for data, but the "eyeball" method is pretty good for making approximate predictions.

One example of an activity that uses both averaging and best-fit lines to minimize experimental error is the *Math Trailblazers* fourth-grade lab, *The Bouncing Ball.* In this lab, students drop a ball from heights of 40, 80, and 120 cm and record their data in a data table. See Figure 1. Note that the ball was dropped three times from each height. When the data is graphed, we can see that the data points lie close to a straight line. In Figure 2, we see an estimated best-fit line drawn by a student. For further information, see the TIMS Tutor: *The TIMS Laboratory Method,* Point Graphs: Fitting Lines and Curves.

> *Scientists, mathematicians, and statisticians use a variety of sophisticated methods to find best-fit lines for data, but the "eyeball" method is pretty good for making approximate predictions.*

Tennis Ball

D Drop Height in cm	B Bounce Height in cm			
	Trial 1	Trial 2	Trial 3	Average
40	27	22	21	22
80	50	40	43	43
120	72	62	68	68

Figure 1: The Bouncing Ball *data table*

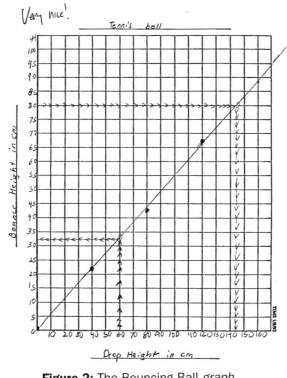

Very nice!

Tennis ball

Bounce Height in cm

Drop Height in cm

Figure 2: The Bouncing Ball *graph*

What's Close?

Recall that the notions of approximation and estimation involve the notion of finding a number that is close to a desired number. But how do we decide what is close? The most fundamental idea about closeness is that it is a **relative** idea. For example, suppose two merchants are selling the same item and the prices differ by $1. Are the prices close? If the merchants were selling cars that cost around $30,000, you would not make your decision based on a $1 difference in price. On the other hand, if you could buy a cup of coffee in one restaurant for $1 and it cost $2 at another restaurant, you might go out of your way for the $1 coffee (provided the quality was not vastly different). Why are these two choices for coffee significantly different? Because one brand costs twice as much as the other! This leads us to the fundamental idea for discussing closeness: when comparing closeness of numbers or measurements, we should look at the **ratio** of the two numbers, rather than the difference. The only problem with this approach is that the concept of ratio is difficult to understand fully. Developing this concept requires time and exposure to many experiences. We deal with this problem in two ways. First, instead of using ratios, we use a related concept—percent. Second, instead of calculating specific percentages (another difficult concept), we make comparisons to certain benchmark percentages, such as 10%. Using 10% as a benchmark for closeness, we see that $1 is not close to $2 since $2 is more than 10% bigger than $1 (in fact, it's 100% bigger). On the other hand, if we compare $30,000 and $30,001 we see that the difference, $1, is a lot less than 10% of $30,000.

> The most fundamental idea about closeness is that it is a **relative** idea.

In Example 1, the one in which many students measured the head circumference of one person, most measurements fell between 47 and 49 centimeters. A rough estimate for 10% of these numbers is 4 cm. Now the difference between 47 cm and 49 cm is 2 cm, so there is clearly less than 10% variation between the largest and smallest measurement. We can safely say these measurements are "close." On the other hand, the student who got 37.5 cm was almost 10 cm less than 47 cm. This is nowhere close to being within 10% of the other measurements, so we should suspect a mistake in that measurement. In Example 2, students took three measurements of the bounce height of a ball—41 cm, 45 cm, and 44 cm. Again, the variation is less than 10%. Finally, in Example 3, when students measured the volume of a marble, most obtained a value between 7 cc and 8 cc, while a few measured 67 cc. Now, 10% of 7 or 8 cc is less than 1 cc, so the students who measured 67 cc are nowhere close to the others. It should be pointed out that in situations such as Example 3, we do not decide who had the correct measurements by taking a majority vote. While the majority is usually right, it is not always right. The different results are a warning flag telling us to seek out the reasons for the discrepancies. Someone is making a mistake, but we can only find out who by looking more closely. Once we find the mistake, then we discard the incorrect information.

The 10 Percent Solution

It's natural to ask why we use 10% as a standard of closeness. We have a variety of reasons:

1. It's easy to find 10% of a number, or at least to estimate it. Just divide by 10. For whole numbers bigger than 10, the simplest estimate for 10% is obtained by dropping the last digit. Thus 10% of 187 is about 18 (it's between 18 and 19) and 10% of 5623 is about 562.
2. In many of the *Math Trailblazers* hands-on experiments, 10% is about the accuracy we can expect from students using the equipment they have, while 10% accuracy is still good enough for seeing the patterns in the data on graphs.
3. Psychologically, 10% is near the limit of our visual estimating ability. For example, if a person sees two drawings in sequence, one an enlargement of the other, in most cases that person will have difficulty distinguishing pictures that are less than 10% different in size, but will be able to distinguish figures that are much more than 10% different in size. Of course, this 10% borderline is not exact, and the point at which different people will be able to make distinctions is different.

Estimating the Magnitude of a Measurement

The basic measurement variables in the *Math Trailblazers* curriculum are length, area, volume, mass, and time. While much of the discussion that follows will apply to any type of measurement, it is a good idea to keep these few variables in mind. The examples given in this section will use these five variables.

There are two important types of knowledge used in many measurement estimation exercises. First, you need to know the measurements of some objects to use as a reference point. Second, you must know how to estimate unknown measurements by comparison with things you know. Very often this will involve some kind of proportional reasoning. The first type of knowledge is gained from experience. Therefore, students should have a wide variety of hands-on experiences as well as knowledge gained from external sources. For example, students should know the height of an average adult in English and metric systems ($5\frac{1}{2}$–6 feet, 160–185 cm), the length of their feet, and the width of their hands. We would hope that students have a general idea of the width of the continental United States from east to west (3000 miles) and from north to south (1000 miles). These facts can be used to make other estimates. For example, what is the area of the United States? The continental United States looks as though it would fit in a rectangle that is 3000 miles long and 1000 miles wide. This gives us an estimate of 3 million square miles. The actual area is close to 3.6 million square miles. To estimate the height of a three-story building (Figure 3), we could first estimate the height of one floor. Looking at an adult standing in the room, we might estimate that the distance from floor to ceiling is twice the height of the person. If the person is about 6 feet tall, then we get an estimate of 12 feet from floor to ceiling. If there are three floors, then the total height of the building is approximately $3 \times 12 = 36$ feet high.

Figure 3: *Estimating the height of a three-story building*

Accuracy and Precision

The accuracy required in a measurement depends on how we are going to use the measurement. By its very nature, any measurement we make in the real world is an estimation. What does it mean to say that a sheet of paper is 21.6 cm wide? How does one find this out? One way is to put the 0 cm mark on the ruler even with the left-hand edge of the paper and see that the right-hand edge of the paper is even with the 22.6 cm mark. If the paper is really 22.61 cm wide, we could not tell this with our ruler, which is only divided into tenths of a centimeter. So the measurements we make are really estimates that are accurate to the nearest tenth of a centimeter. Measuring the width of a piece of paper to an accuracy of more than a tenth of a centimeter would probably not make sense, since the sides cannot be perfectly even and measuring the width in different places would give different answers (like 22.613 cm and 22.615 cm). In any case, a measurement of 22.6 cm is probably more than sufficient for our purpose.

By its very nature, any measurement we make in the real world is an estimation.

Dealing with Decimal Digits

One important fact to note is that in the course of solving a problem we can end up with a number that has many digits, most of which do not make sense in the real world (although they make mathematical sense). For example, suppose we wanted to share 16 ounces of orange juice among three students. When I divide 16 by 3 on my calculator, I get 5.3333333333. It makes no sense at all to say that we should give each student 5.3333333333 ounces of juice, since, with the tools we have, we cannot measure more accurately than to the nearest tenth of an ounce. In fact, when we say that we want to share 16 ounces of orange juice, we do not mean that we have exactly 16 ounces of juice. Unless we were using unusually sensitive measuring instruments, it would only make sense to say that we would give each student 5.3 ounces or $5\frac{1}{3}$ ounces of juice. Although 5.3 and $5\frac{1}{3}$ are not equal, they are approximately equal in this context.

Estimating "How Many"

In this type of estimation, we estimate the number of objects in some collection. It could be the number of trees in the United States, the number of students in a school district next year, or the number of beans in a jar. This class of problems has a lot in common with the estimation problems we have already discussed. Many problems that require estimating "how many" are similar to estimating a measurement in that they involve knowing how many objects there are in some known set and then comparing the unknown with the known. Here are some examples:

Example 1: Students are asked to estimate the number of peanuts in a jar. If students have no previous experience with peanuts or jars, this is not really an estimate, but rather a guess. Answers will vary widely because students do not have any idea of what the answer might be and no strategies to use to get a sensible answer. A more reasonable exercise is to give them a small jar and have them count how many peanuts can fit in the jar. If they are now given a larger jar, they should be able to make a sensible estimate by comparing the large jar to the small one. How many small jars would they think fit in the large jar? If the small jar holds 10 peanuts and it appears that 12 small jars fit in the large one, what is a reasonable estimate for the number of peanuts that fit in the large jar?

Example 2: How many students are in your school? The reference set here can be the number of students in a class. Students should know how many students are in their class. They should also be able to estimate the number of classes in the school. This gives an estimate for the number of students in the school (using multiplication).

Example 3: How many total hours of television were watched by all the children in the school? We can find the *exact* answer by asking every student how much they watched and then adding the number of hours. The answer can be *estimated* using a very important technique called sampling. Take a survey of some of the children in the school (say one class or two students in each class) and then scale up.

Example 4: We have a picture of the crowd at a basketball game. How can we determine the number of people at the game? It would be tedious to count the number of people in the picture. We could draw a square on the picture and count the number of people in that square. Then multiply that result by the number of such squares needed to cover the crowd. Figure 4 from the *Math Trailblazers* fourth-grade curriculum shows a picture used to pose a similar problem.

Figure 4: *Picture of a basketball game crowd*

Example 5: Will more people vote for Fred or Amy in the next election? This is another example of a kind of problem that frequently occurs in the real world. The common technique for estimating the answer is to take a sample of the voters and use the sample to predict the results for the whole population. For example, if 40% of the sample says they will vote for Fred and 60% says they will vote for Amy, we might predict that Amy will win. We might even predict that Fred will get 40% of the vote and Amy 60%. We know from real life that predictions like this are not always accurate. Some things that affect the accuracy of such estimates are the size of the sample (compared to the whole population) and the randomness of the sample (how well the sample represents the whole population).

Example 6: How many households are there in the United States? We can only make this estimate if we know enough facts about the population of the United States. We know that the population of the United States is about 250 million people and that the average family has 2.3 children. If we think that some households have only one person, while others have several generations living together, we might say that the average household size is about 4 or 5 people. Using a household size of 5 for our estimate (since 5 goes evenly into 25) we get a figure of 50 million households.

Conclusion

We hope that this tutor gives you an overview of the way estimation is treated in the *Math Trailblazers* curriculum. Naturally, it could not deal with all the types of estimation situations and all kinds of estimation strategies. The best way to become a good estimator is to estimate. The best way for children to learn to be good estimators is to be given meaningful situations that require estimation and to be given the opportunity to discuss their strategies with others. As with all mathematics instruction, the teacher plays a valuable role by moderating discourse and by adding new strategies when appropriate.

> *The best way to become a good estimator is to estimate.*

References

Schoen, Harold L., and Marilyn J. Zweng (eds.). *Estimation and Mental Computation—1986 Yearbook.* National Council of Teachers of Mathematics, Reston, VA, 1986.

Sowder, J., "Estimation and Number Sense," in *Handbook of Research on Mathematics Teaching and Learning.* Douglas A. Grouws (ed.). Macmillan Publishing Co., New York, 1992.

Threadgill-Sowder, J. "Computational Estimation Procedures of School Children." *Journal of Educational Research,* 77 (6), 1984.

Webster's Eleventh New Collegiate Dictionary. Merriam-Webster, Inc., Springfield, MA.

Functions

Introduction

Function is one of those words with a mathematical meaning that is not the same as its everyday meaning. In everyday life, a function can be an important celebration, a role someone or something has, or the purpose for something. In mathematics and science, a function is a special and very important kind of relationship between variables. Discovering functional relationships between variables is what science is all about.

In mathematics and science, a function is a special and very important kind of relationship between variables. Discovering functional relationships between variables is what science is all about.

Three Blind Men and an Elephant. There is a story about three blind men who encounter an elephant. The first comes up against one of the elephant's legs and says, "An elephant is like a tree." The second touches the side of the elephant and says, "No, no. An elephant is like a wall." The third blind man finds the elephant's trunk and claims, "You're both wrong. An elephant is like a big snake."

Each blind man has some notion of what an elephant is. The story doesn't tell whether they eventually resolve their differences and come to a proper understanding of elephants; we can only hope so. Our approach to functions will be similar: We will begin with three different views of functions. This, we hope, will lead to a fuller and more proper understanding of functions.

Tables

Many functions are displayed as tables. For example, consider this data table from the experiment *Mass vs. Number,* shown in Figure 1.

N Number of <u>Erasers</u>	M Mass (in gm)
1	39 gm
2	79 gm
4	158 gm

Figure 1: Mass vs. Number *data table*

This table displays a functional relationship between the variables N and M. For each value of N we have a value of M; we say that the mass is a function of the number of erasers. That is, if we know what N is, then we can find M. This is the essence of a function: knowing one variable's value enables us to find the corresponding value of the other variable. In this example, the data has a distinctive pattern: within experimental error, doubling one variable causes the other to double. *N* and *M* are said to be (directly) proportional.

Many functions we encounter in everyday life come to us as tables. You can think of stock tables, for example, as functions: one variable is the company, the other is the closing price. If you know the company, you can look up the price. Almanacs are filled with tables of information, most of which you can think of as functions: one variable is the name of the country, the other is the population, and so on. The sports pages are filled with tabular functions of team standings and individual statistics.

Many functions come to us first as tables, and some, like batting averages or almanac information, are normally given only as tables. Tables of numbers, however, can be very difficult to understand. Patterns in the data can go undetected—patterns that might help us better understand the function. One of the best ways to get a handle on patterns is to make a visual image of the data in the form of a graph.

Graphs

If a picture is worth a thousand words, a graph is worth a billion numbers. The graph of the *Mass vs. Number* data, seen in Figure 2, is a good example.

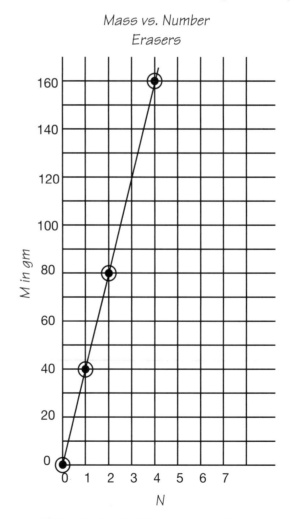

Figure 2: *Graph of* Mass vs. Number *data*

The key thing about this graph is that the data points lie on a straight line through (0,0). This confirms that N and M are proportional: we can fit a straight line through (0,0) if and only if the variables are proportional. Many other types of functions besides direct proportion are characterized by their graphs.

Often, experimental error obscures the nature of the relationship between the variables until the data is plotted. Like taking multiple measurements and averaging, graphing the data and fitting a curve can help control error. With error minimized, the true nature of the relationship between the variables may become clearer. Stock analysts graph their data to spot trends in order to make predictions (and money); such trends are unlikely to be noticed in the stock tables. Scientists graph their data almost as soon as they get it because the graph is so much more likely to be revealing than the raw data.

The graph is a crucial step on the road from the concrete apparatus to formal understanding. Sometimes, this formal understanding can be distilled in a few symbols, as in a formula.

The graph is a crucial step on the road from the concrete apparatus to formal understanding.

Formulas

A more abstract way to consider a function is as a formula. In our *Mass vs. Number* example, we can exploit the fact that when variables are proportional, their ratio is constant. The value of this constant ratio is the slope of the best-fit line. So,

$$\frac{M}{N} = \frac{39.5 \text{ gm}}{1 \text{ eraser}} .$$

This can be rewritten to give a formula for M as a function of N:

$$M = \frac{39.5 \text{ gm}}{1 \text{ eraser}} \times N$$

Such formulas are very useful when they can be found. When we do manage to obtain a formula, it allows us to solve problems quickly and accurately. We can also use formulas to ascend to higher levels of abstraction. This movement to ever greater abstraction and generality is the driving force behind much of science and mathematics.

G Number of Generations	A Number of Ancestors
1	2
2	4
3	8
4	16

Figure 3: *Ancestors data table*

Often students are not able to understand formulas, but they are, nevertheless, able to continue a pattern in a data table or devise a rule that works. For example, the pattern in the table shown in Figure 3 is easy to extend. Five generations back, you have 32 ancestors: each further generation doubles the number of ancestors (ignoring the inevitable overlap). Extending patterns like this is a first step towards formulas. Later, the students may be able to give a rule for a data table. For example, consider the table in Figure 4, the number of fence posts needed for a given length of fence.

L Length of Fence in _feet_	N Number of Fence Posts
10	2
20	3
30	4
40	5

Figure 4: _Fence posts data table_

The rule may be stated: the number of fence posts is just one more than $\frac{1}{10}$ the number of feet in the fence.

$$N = \frac{L}{10} + 1$$

It is not much harder for us to express this sentence as a formula, but this type of expression may be confusing to a third-grader. Often, a rule stated in ordinary language is more accessible.

Formulas are the most powerful way to look at functions but are often not appropriate for elementary school students. The great temptation is to move to formulas as quickly as possible. This sometimes leads to quick gains, but over the long run it is often problematic. Pushing formulas at children is like building a house of cards: students need to build a conceptual foundation by handling apparatus, gathering data, and graphing and analyzing it. Only after students develop an understanding of the relationship of the variables is it proper to distill that understanding into a formula. Extending patterns and figuring out rules are excellent alternatives for younger students moving towards higher levels of abstraction.

What Is a Function?

A **function** is a special kind of relationship between variables that can often be expressed as a data table, graph, or formula. One variable is the manipulated (or independent) variable; the other is the responding (or dependent) variable.

But not every relationship is a function. The main requirement for a relationship to be a function is that for each value of the manipulated variable, there is only one value of the responding variable. For example, suppose the manipulated variable is the edge length of a cube and the responding variable is the surface area. Then, for each given edge length there is exactly one surface area: if the edge is 3 cm, then the surface area is 54 sq cm, and so on. Or consider the manipulated variable to be the company and the responding variable to be the closing price: each stock has exactly one closing price each day. Notice that many stocks may have the same closing price; that's okay. The requirement says only that each value of the manipulated variable must have exactly one value of the responding variable. Values of the responding variable may repeat, and often do. One way to visualize this requirement is to think about functions as mappings. Figure 5 shows a map of a squaring function.

> . . . not every relationship is a function. The main requirement for a relationship to be a function is that for each value of the manipulated variable, there is only one value of the responding variable.

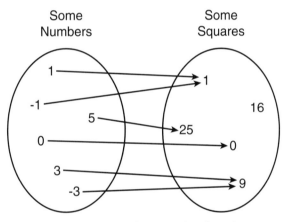

Figure 5: *Map of a squaring function*

Every number has exactly one square; this corresponds to the single arrow leaving each number on the left above. Notice that more than one arrow can end at a single number; the requirement is only that exactly one arrow leave each of the starting numbers. The mapping in Figure 6 is not a function because two arrows leave each number.

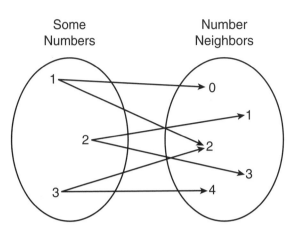

Figure 6: *Map of a relationship that is not a function*

But you may object, saying that when we do experiments we often have several different values of the responding variable for each value of the manipulated variable. Isn't there a functional relationship between variables like the drop height and the bounce height in *The Bouncing Ball?* In a word, yes. But with real data, things get more complicated. Experimental error creeps in; there are other uncontrolled variables; there is uncertainty inherent in all our measurements.

One useful way to think about the situation is to suppose there is some "true" value of the responding variable that we cannot measure exactly. So, instead we measure the responding variable several times and then take the average as our best estimate of the true value.[1] Then we have a function: for each value of the manipulated variable there is exactly one *true* value of the responding variable. The only trouble is, in most real-world situations, we usually don't know what that true value is.

Mathematicians have precise and abstract definitions of function. We could go on and on describing more precisely the requirements a relationship must have to be a function. We could spell out the meanings of technical terms having to do with functions—terms like *domain, range, one-to-one, many-to-one,* and so on. For most purposes, however, thinking about functions in the terms outlined above is enough.

Functions in the Classroom

The concept of a function is a powerful one for organizing and extending mathematical ideas. From time to time, we have activities that deal with functions, for example, *Function Machines* in second grade. The best approach to functions, however, is just doing the *Math Trailblazers* lessons. As your students do TIMS Laboratory Investigations and other activities, they will move naturally from the apparatus to the data table, graph, and questions. Much of the data analysis is designed to help children see how changes in one of these correspond to changes in the others. Thus, in each experiment the students will deal with specific functions in several guises and will gain facility in moving between different representations of functions. This is the best possible preparation for the explicit study of functions later in high school and beyond.

> *As your students do TIMS Laboratory Investigations and other activities, they will move naturally from the apparatus to the data table, graph, and questions. Much of the data analysis is designed to help the children see how changes in one of these correspond to changes in the others. . . . This is the best possible preparation for the explicit study of functions later in high school and beyond.*

[1]See the TIMS Tutor: *Averages.*

Journals

We at TIMS embrace the idea of writing across the curriculum. We see helping students to write better as part of every teacher's job.

By writing in mathematics and science class, students improve their communication skills and develop their subject-matter understanding. Writing about mathematics and science helps students consolidate ideas, see connections between school and life, and think more abstractly.

Writing about mathematics and science helps students consolidate ideas, see connections between school and life, and think more abstractly.

Another reason to have students write about mathematics and science lessons is so you can gain insight into how those lessons are being received and what the students are learning. Collecting and saving students' writing is also an excellent way to document long-term student progress.

We incorporate writing into *Math Trailblazers* in several ways. We often ask for students to write a short or extended answer to a question and we may also ask students to explain how they obtained their solutions. Students may be asked to write about problems they solved in cooperative groups.

Journals are another effective way to use writing in mathematics and science. Typically, a journal is a small, bound book in which students write regularly. The writing can be in response to various prompts, or it can be rather undirected. Because each student responds at his or her own level and rate, journal writing is accessible to all students.

The teacher reads students' journals regularly, possibly responding in writing to what students wrote. Usually journal writing is not corrected for grammar, spelling, and punctuation—the focus is on the content of the writing, not the form.

The physical form of the journal is not important. A cloth-covered bound book, a spiral notebook, or even several sheets of paper stapled together all work just fine.

We urge you to have your students write regularly, every day or at least every week. Start with short periods and gradually extend the amount of time.

Journal Prompts

We urge you to have your students write regularly, every day or at least every week. Start with short periods and gradually extend the amount of time. When a student fills up one journal, give him or her another. Students will also enjoy reading their writing aloud and discussing it.

Your students' journal writing should take a variety of forms. Here are some suggestions for assignments ranging from highly structured to rather open-ended.

Sentence Completion

Give part of a sentence and ask students to complete it (Azzolino, 1990). For example, you might ask students to complete sentences like these:

"A shape is symmetric when . . ."
"Today we learned . . ."
"Before you use an equal-arm balance it's important to . . ."

A variation of this activity is to give one or more complete sentences and then to ask students to continue.

Explanations of Procedures

Ask students to explain how to measure the area of a leaf, how to use an equal-arm balance, how to add two three-digit numbers, or how to make a graph of some data. This may require an explanation of an entire procedure or only of certain steps.

Answers to Specific Questions

Sometimes you may pose a specific question about a lesson. For example, ask students to describe the shape of the graph for a certain experiment and to explain why the graph has that shape. Many *Math Trailblazers* lessons include questions that require some writing; these questions can be answered in the journals.

A question to ask sometimes is, "How did working in your group turn out?" You may get valuable information that can help you improve the dynamics of your small groups.

Descriptions of Solutions

There are usually many ways to solve a mathematics problem; it is often worth exploring multiple solutions. To correct the common misconception that there is usually only one way to solve a problem, students need to learn that the process of problem solving is often as important as the answer. In *Math Trailblazers,* they see connections by comparing different solutions. They learn that mathematics makes sense because their own ideas are validated. They are exposed to advanced ideas through other students' solutions, but without undue stress if they fail to understand those advanced ideas.

One way to encourage multiple solutions is to ask students to write about how they solved a problem. Ask them to describe all the ways they solved a problem or to describe a single way in depth. Ask them to write about failed solutions or what they did when they got stuck. Such assignments will encourage students to see such efforts not as failures but as periodic by-products of the problem-solving process.

Definitions

Ask students to define a key concept like area or volume. You may be surprised at some of their answers.

Advice to Adventure Book Characters

Often the characters in the *Adventure Books* and other activities encounter problems that yield to the techniques the students have been learning in the labs and activities. You might stop part way through an *Adventure Book* story and ask your students to write some advice, perhaps in the form of a letter, to the hero. When you finish the book, compare what the hero actually did to the students' advice.

Reactions

Ask students what they liked or didn't like about a certain lab, activity, or adventure book. Or, ask what they learned or what confused them.

Word Banks

Supply a list of words or phrases and ask students to use those words in a piece of writing (Azzolino, 1990). For example, you might supply the following words, "ten, hundred, thousand, less than, seven, more than, nine."

Problems

Students enjoy writing their own problems. Ask them to write another problem like a given problem; to write an addition, subtraction, or sharing problem; to write a number riddle; or to make up any problem that classmates would find interesting to solve.

Free Writing

Other times, simply tell students to write whatever they want about a certain lesson.

Some Tips for Getting Started

- Start with brief periods of writing and gradually extend the amount of time.
- Encourage pictures, data tables, graphs, number sentences, and other mathematical and scientific forms of communication.
- Vary the prompt. Sometimes be very specific; other times make the assignment more open-ended.
- Do not worry about grammar, spelling, and punctuation. Focus on content.

One way to encourage multiple solutions is to ask students to write about how they solved a problem. Ask them to describe all the ways they solved a problem or to describe a single way in depth. Ask them to write about failed solutions or what they did when they got stuck.

Conclusion

The name of our project—TIMS (Teaching Integrated Mathematics and Science)—expresses our conviction that the teaching of mathematics and science should be integrated. But we also believe strongly that integration should not stop there; language arts and social studies can and should be integrated with mathematics and science. Journals are one way to use writing in mathematics and science. Reading and writing are too important to be confined to language arts lessons.

References

Azzolino, A. "Writing as a Tool for Teaching Mathematics: The Silent Revolution." In *Teaching and Learning Mathematics in the 1990s: 1990 Yearbook.* T.J. Cooney and C.R. Hirsch, Eds. National Council of Teachers of Mathematics, Reston, VA, 1990.

Burns, Marilyn, and Robyn Sibley. "Incorporating Writing into Math Class." *So You Have to Teach Math? Sound Advice for K–6 Teachers.* Math Solutions Publications, Sausalito, CA, 2000.

Countryman, Joan. *Writing to Learn Mathematics.* Heinemann, Portsmouth, NH, 1992.

Math Facts

Students need to learn the math facts. Estimation, mental arithmetic, checking the reasonableness of results, and paper-and-pencil calculations require the ability to give quick, accurate responses when using basic facts. The question is not if students should learn the math facts, but how. Which teaching methods are most efficient and effective? To answer this question, we as authors of *Math Trailblazers* drew upon educational research and our own classroom experiences to develop a comprehensive plan for teaching the math facts.

Philosophy

The goal of the *Math Trailblazers* math facts strand is for students to learn the basic facts efficiently, gain fluency with their use, and retain that fluency over time. A large body of research supports an approach that is built on a foundation of work with strategies and concepts. This not only leads to more effective learning and better retention, but also to development of mental math skills. Therefore, the teaching and assessment of the basic facts in *Math Trailblazers* is characterized by the following elements:

- *Early emphasis on problem solving.* Students first approach the basic facts as problems to solve rather than as facts to memorize. Students invent their own strategies to solve these problems or learn appropriate strategies from others through class discussion. Students' natural strategies, especially counting strategies, are explicitly encouraged. In this way, students learn that math is more than memorizing facts and rules that "you either get or you don't."
- *De-emphasis of rote work.* Fluency with the math facts is an important component of any student's mathematical learning. Research shows that overemphasizing memorization and frequent administration of timed tests are counterproductive. Both can produce undesirable results (Isaacs and Carroll, 1999; Van de Walle, 2001; National Research Council, 2001). We encourage the use of strategies to find facts, so students become confident they can find answers to fact problems they do not immediately recall.
- *Gradual and systematic introduction of facts.* Students study the facts in small groups they solve using similar strategies. Students first work on simple strategies for easy facts and then progress to more sophisticated strategies and harder facts. By the end of the process, they gain fluency with all required facts.
- *Ongoing practice.* Work on the math facts is distributed throughout the curriculum, especially in the Daily Practice and Problems (DPP), Home Practice, and games. This practice for fluency, however, takes place only after students have a conceptual understanding of the operations and have achieved proficiency with strategies for solving basic fact problems. Delaying practice in this way means that less practice is required to achieve fluency.

- *Appropriate assessment.* Teachers assess students' knowledge of the facts through observations as they work on activities, labs, and games as well as through the appropriate use of written tests and quizzes. Beginning in first grade, periodic, short quizzes in the DPP naturally follow the study of small groups of facts organized around specific strategies. As self-assessment in Grades 3–5, students record their progress on *Facts I Know* charts and determine which facts they need to study. Inventory tests of all facts for each operation are used sparingly in Grades 2–5 (no more than twice per year) to assess students' progress with fact fluency. The goal of the math facts assessment program is to determine the degree to which students can find answers to fact problems quickly and accurately and whether they can retain this skill over time.
- *Multiyear approach.* In Grades 1 and 2, *Math Trailblazers* emphasizes strategies that lead to fluency with the addition and subtraction facts. In Grade 3, students gain fluency with the multiplication facts while reviewing the addition and subtraction facts. In Grade 4, students achieve fluency with the division facts and verify fluency with the multiplication facts. In Grade 5, the multiplication and division facts are systematically reviewed and assessed.
- *Facts are not gatekeepers.* Students are not prevented from learning more complex mathematics because they do not perform well on fact tests. Use of strategies, calculators, and other math tools (e.g., manipulatives, hundred charts, printed multiplication tables) allows students to continue to work on interesting problems while still learning the facts.

Expectations by Grade Level

The following goals for the math facts are consistent with the recommendations in the National Council of Teachers of Mathematics *Principles and Standards for School Mathematics:*

- In kindergarten, students use manipulatives and invent their own strategies to solve addition and subtraction problems.
- By the end of first grade, all students can solve all basic addition and subtraction problems using some strategy. Fluency is not emphasized; strategies are. Some work with beginning concepts of multiplication takes place.
- In second grade, learning efficient strategies for addition and especially subtraction continues to be emphasized. Work with multiplication concepts continues. By the end of the year, students are expected to demonstrate fluency with all the addition and subtraction facts.
- In third grade, students review the subtraction facts. They develop efficient strategies for learning the multiplication facts and demonstrate fluency with the multiplication facts.
- In fourth grade, students review the multiplication facts and develop strategies for the division facts. By the end of year, we expect fluency with all the division facts.
- In fifth grade, students review the multiplication and division facts and are expected to maintain fluency with all the facts.

This is summarized in the following chart:

Grade	Addition	Subtraction	Multiplication	Division
K	• invented strategies	• invented strategies		
1	• strategies	• strategies		
2	• strategies • practice leading to fluency	• strategies • practice leading to fluency		
3	• review and practice	• review and practice	• strategies • practice leading to fluency	
4	• assessment and remediation as required	• assessment and remediation as required	• review and practice	• strategies • practice leading to fluency
5	• assessment and remediation as required	• assessment and remediation as required	• review and practice	• review and practice

Table 1: *Math Facts Scope and Sequence*

Strategies for Learning the Facts

Students are encouraged to learn the math facts by first employing a variety of strategies. Concepts and skills are learned more easily and are retained longer if they are meaningful. By first concentrating on concepts and strategies, we increase retention and reduce the amount of time necessary for rote memorization. Researchers note that over time, students develop techniques that are increasingly sophisticated and efficient. Experience with the strategies provides a basis for understanding the operation involved and for gaining fluency with the facts. In this section, we describe possible strategies for learning the addition, subtraction, multiplication, and division facts. The strategies for each operation are listed roughly in order of increasing sophistication.

Strategies for Addition Facts

Common strategies include counting all, counting on, doubles, making or using 10, and reasoning from known facts.

Counting All

This is a particularly straightforward strategy. For example, to solve 7 + 8, the student gets 7 of something and 8 of something and counts how many there are altogether. The "something" could be beans or chips or marks on paper. In any case, the student counts all the objects to find the sum. This is perhaps not a very efficient method, but it is effective, especially for small numbers, and is usually well understood by the student.

Counting On

This is a natural strategy, particularly for adding 1, 2, or 3. Counters such as beans or chips may or may not be used. As an example, consider 8 + 3. The student gets 8 beans, and then 3 more, but instead of counting the first 8 again, she simply counts the 3 added beans: "9, 10, 11."

Even if counters are not used, finger gestures can help keep track of how many more have been counted on. For example, to solve 8 + 3, the student counts "9, 10, 11," holding up a finger each time a number word is said; when three fingers are up, the last word said is the answer.

Doubles

Facts such as 4 + 4 = 8 are easier to remember than facts with two different addends. Some visual imagery can help, too: two hands for 5 + 5, a carton of eggs for 6 + 6, a calendar for 7 + 7, and so on.

Making a 10

Facts with a sum of 10, such as 7 + 3 and 6 + 4, are also easier to remember than other facts. Ten frames can create visual images of making a 10. For example, 8 is shown in a ten frame like the one in Figure 1:

Figure 1: *A ten frame*

This visual imagery helps students remember, for example, that 8 + 2 = 10.

Using a 10

Students who are comfortable partitioning and combining small numbers can use that knowledge to find the sums of larger numbers. In particular, there are many strategies that involve using the number 10. For example, to find 9 + 7, we can decompose 7 into 1 + 6 and then 9 + 7 = 9 + 1 + 6 = 10 + 6 = 16. Similarly, 8 + 7 = 8 + 2 + 5 = 10 + 5 = 15.

Reasoning from Known Facts

If you know what 7 + 7 is, then 7 + 8 is not much harder: it's just 1 more. So, the "near doubles" can be derived from knowing the doubles.

Strategies for Subtraction Facts

Common strategies for subtraction include using counters, counting up, counting back, using 10, and reasoning from related addition and subtraction facts.

Using Counters

This method models the problem with counters like beans or chips. For example, to solve 8 − 3, the student gets 8 beans, removes 3 beans, and counts the remaining beans to find the difference. As with using the addition strategy "counting all," this relatively straightforward strategy may not be efficient but it has the great advantage that students usually understand it well.

Counting Up

The student starts at the lower number and counts on to the higher number, perhaps using fingers to keep track of how many numbers are counted. For example, to solve $8 - 5$, the student wants to know how to get from 5 to 8 and counts up 3 numbers: 6, 7, 8. So, $8 - 5 = 3$.

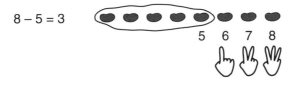

$$8 - 5 = 3$$

5 6 7 8

Figure 2: *Counting up*

Counting Back

Counting back works best for subtracting 1, 2, or 3. For larger numbers, it is probably best to count up. For example, to solve $9 - 2$, the student counts back 2 numbers: 8, 7. So, $9 - 2 = 7$.

$$9 - 2 = 7 \qquad 9 \quad 8 \quad 7$$

Figure 3: *Counting back*

Using a 10

Students follow the pattern they find when subtracting 10, e.g., $17 - 10 = 7$ and $13 - 10 = 3$, to learn close facts, e.g., $17 - 9 = 8$ and $13 - 9 = 4$. Since $17 - 9$ will be 1 more than $17 - 10$, they can reason that the answer will be 8, or $7 + 1$.

Making a 10

Knowing the addition facts that have a sum of 10, e.g., $6 + 4 = 10$, can be helpful in finding differences from 10, e.g., $10 - 6 = 4$ and $10 - 4 = 6$. Students can use ten frames to visualize these problems as in Figure 4. These facts can then also be used to find close facts, such as $11 - 4 = 7$.

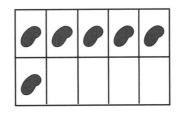

$$10 - 4 = 6$$

Figure 4: *Using a ten frame*

Using Doubles

Students can use the addition doubles, e.g., $8 + 8 = 16$ and $6 + 6 = 12$, to learn the subtraction "half-doubles" as well: $16 - 8 = 8$ and $12 - 6 = 6$. They can then use these facts to figure out close facts, such as $13 - 6 = 7$ and $15 - 8 = 7$.

Reasoning from Related Addition and Subtraction Facts

Knowing that $8 + 7 = 15$ would seem to be of some help in solving $15 - 7$. Unfortunately, however, knowing related addition facts may not be so helpful to younger or less mathematically mature students. Nevertheless, reasoning from known facts is a powerful strategy for those who can apply it and should be encouraged.

Strategies for Multiplication Facts

Common strategies for multiplication include skip counting, counting up or down from a known fact, doubling, breaking a product into the sum of known products, and using patterns.

Skip Counting

Students begin skip counting and solving problems informally that involve multiplicative situations in first grade. By the time they begin formal work with the multiplication facts in third grade, they should be fairly proficient with skip counting. This strategy is particularly useful for facts such as the 2s, 3s, 5s, and 10s, for which skip counting is easy.

Counting Up or Down from a Known Fact

This strategy involves skip counting forwards once or twice from a known fact. For example, if children know that 5×5 is 25, then they can use this to solve 6×5 (5 more) or 4×5 (5 less). Some children use this for harder facts. For 7×6, they can use the fact that $5 \times 6 = 30$ as a starting point and then count on by sixes to 42.

Doubling

Some children use doubling relationships to help them with multiplication facts involving 4, 6, and 8. For example, 4×7 is twice as much as 2×7. Since $2 \times 7 = 14$, it follows that 4×7 is 28. Since 3×8 is 24, it follows that 6×8 is 48.

Breaking a Product into the Sum of Known Products

A fact like 7×8 can be broken into the sum $5 \times 8 + 2 \times 8$ since $7 = 5 + 2$. See Figure 5. The previous two strategies are special cases of this more general strategy.

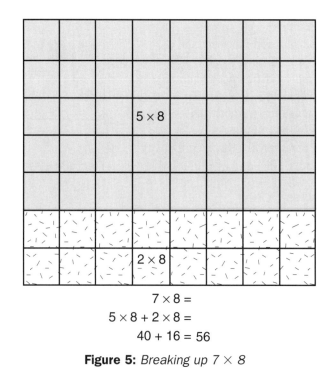

$$7 \times 8 =$$
$$5 \times 8 + 2 \times 8 =$$
$$40 + 16 = 56$$

Figure 5: *Breaking up 7×8*

Patterns

A. Perhaps the best-known examples of patterns are the nines patterns:

1. When the nines products are listed in a column, as shown below, it is easy to see that the digits in the tens place count up by one (0, 1, 2, 3, . . .) and that the digits in the ones place count down by one (9, 8, 7, . . .).

   9
   18
   27
   36
   45
   54
   63
   72
   81

2. The sums of the two digits in each of the nines products above are all equal to nine. For example, the sum of the digits in 36 is $3 + 6 = 9$; the sum of the digits in 72 is $7 + 2 = 9$. Adding the digits of a number to see whether they add up to nine can be a strategy in remembering a nines fact. For example, a student might think, "Let me see, does 9×6 equal 54 or 56? It must be 54 since $5 + 4$ is 9, but $5 + 6$ is not 9."

3. The digit in the tens place in a nines fact is one less than the number being multiplied. For example, $4 \times 9 = 36$, and 3 is one less than 4. This can be combined with the previous pattern to derive nines facts. For example, 3×9 is in the twenties. Since $2 + 7$ is 9, 3×9 must be 27.

4. Nines can easily be computed using the counting down strategy. Nine times a digit is the same as 10 times the digit, minus the digit. For example, 9×6 is $10 \times 6 - 6 = 54$.

B. Other patterns.

   Other patterns that are useful in remembering other special facts:

1. 0 times a number equals 0.
2. 1 times a number equals the number.
3. 2 times a number is double the number.
4. 5 times a number ends in 0 or 5; even numbers times 5 end in 0 and odd numbers times five end in 5.
5. 10 times a number is the same number with a 0 on the end.

Sequencing the Study of Multiplication Facts

In kindergarten, children solve word problems involving multiplication situations. Beginning in first grade, the curriculum develops a conceptual foundation for multiplication through a variety of multiplication models, including repeated addition, the array model, and the number-line model. Fluency with the multiplication facts is expected by the end of third grade. Strategies are often introduced in specific, third-grade lessons. Practice is continued in subsequent lessons and especially in the Daily Practice and Problems and Home Practice. We do not introduce the multiplication facts in the order in which they are traditionally taught (first learning the 2s, then the

3s, then the 4s, etc.). Rather, we emphasize thinking strategies for the facts, introducing fact-groups in the following order:

2s, 3s, 5s, and 10s. The 2s, 3s, 5s, and 10s are easily solved using skip counting.

Square numbers such as $3 \times 3 = 9$, $4 \times 4 = 16$, and $5 \times 5 = 25$. These are introduced by arranging tiles into square arrays.

Nines. Students explore patterns for nines.

Last six facts. After students have learned the facts listed above and their turn-around facts ($9 \times 6 = 6 \times 9$), there are only six more facts to learn: 4×6, 4×7, 4×8, 6×7, 6×8, and 7×8.

Strategies for the Division Facts

The main strategy for learning the division facts is to think of the related multiplication fact. Therefore, students review the multiplication facts and develop fluency with the division facts by working with fact families. (Fact families are groups of related facts. An example of a fact family is $3 \times 4 = 12$, $4 \times 3 = 12$, $12 \div 3 = 4$, and $12 \div 4 = 3$.)

Using the Right Strategy

Different strategies appeal to different students. Students should not feel overburdened with the need to determine which is the "correct" strategy for a given fact. We do not intend to give them a new layer of things to learn. For example, when asked to explain a strategy for a fact, a student may say, "I've used it so much that now I just remember it." "Just remembering" is obviously an efficient strategy. The purpose of suggesting and discussing various strategies is to give students other, perhaps helpful, ways of learning the facts and to give them the confidence to think problems through when necessary. Students should have the opportunity to choose the strategies that work best for them or to invent their own.

Math Facts Lessons

The *Math Trailblazers* math facts program pervades most of the curriculum's components. Work with math facts are in different kinds of lessons. These are described in this section.

Figure 6: *Discussing fact strategies*

Everyday Work

As students work on problems in the labs and activities, encourage them to use and discuss various strategies for solving math facts problems. A number of important goals can best be reached through such discussions.

One goal is to legitimize all valid strategies, even those that may be less efficient. When students see their intuitive methods recognized and validated, they tend to perceive mathematical knowledge as continuous with everyday knowledge and common sense. We thus hope to avoid the unfortunate tendency of many students to separate their knowledge of mathematics from their knowledge of the real world.

By discussing strategies as they arise in context, students and teachers can explore how the strategies work and can verify that they are being used properly. Students should come to realize that a fact strategy that gives wrong answers is not very useful.

A second goal of our approach is to encourage students to communicate mathematical ideas. There are several reasons to stress communication: Students can learn from one another; communicating a method requires higher orders of thinking than simply applying that method; and skill at communicating is important in itself. We are social creatures. Mathematics and science are social endeavors in which communication is crucial.

A third goal of encouraging discussions of various methods is to give the teacher opportunities to learn about how students think. Knowing more about students' thinking helps the teacher ask better questions and plan more effective lessons.

Strategy Lessons

We feel that occasionally it is appropriate for lessons to focus on certain strategies that are developmentally appropriate for most students. Our plan is to begin with simple strategies that should be accessible to all students and to progress gradually to more complex forms of reasoning. For example, in the fall of first grade, we have several lessons that stress counting on to solve certain addition problems. Later, we explicitly introduce making a 10 and other, more sophisticated, strategies.

In general, you should expect your students to come up with effective strategies on their own. Our strategy lessons are intended to explore how and why various strategies work and also to codify and organize the strategies the students invent. They are not meant to dictate the only appropriate strategy for a given problem or to discourage students from using strategies they understand and like. They should be seen as opportunities to discuss strategies that may be appropriate for many students and to encourage their wider use.

Practice

Our ultimate goal is to produce students who can think mathematically, who can solve problems and deal easily with quantified information, and who enjoy mathematics and are not afraid of it. It is easier to do all of the above if one has fluency with the basic math facts. Practice strengthens students' abilities to use strategies and moves students towards fluency with the facts. Practice that follows instruction that stresses the use of strategies has been shown to improve

As students work on problems in the labs and activities, they should be encouraged to use and to discuss various strategies for solving math facts problems.

Our ultimate goal is to produce students who can think mathematically, who can solve problems and deal easily with quantified information, and who enjoy mathematics and are not afraid of it. It is easier to do all of the above if one has fluency with the basic math facts.

students' fluency with the math facts. We recommend, and have incorporated into the curriculum, the following practice to gain this fluency.

Practice in Context

The primary practice of math facts will arise naturally for the students as they participate in the labs and other activities in the curriculum. These labs and activities offer many opportunities to practice addition, subtraction, multiplication, and division in a meaningful way. The lessons involve the student visually with drawings and patterns, auditorily through discussion, and tactilely through the use of many tools such as manipulatives and calculators.

Pages of problems on the basic facts are not only unnecessary, they can be counterproductive. Students may come to regard mathematics as mostly memorization and may perceive it as meaningless and unconnected to their everyday lives.

Structured Practice

Student-friendly, structured practice is built into the curriculum, especially in the DPP, Home Practice, and games. One small group of related math facts is presented to the students at a time. The practice of groups of facts is carefully distributed throughout the year. A small set of facts grouped in a meaningful way leads students to develop strategies such as adding doubles, counting back, or using a 10 for dealing with a particular situation. Furthermore, a small set of facts is a manageable amount to learn and remember.

Beginning in the second half of first grade and continuing through fifth grade, a small group of facts to be studied in a unit is introduced in the DPP. Through DPP items, students practice the facts and take a short assessment. Beginning in second grade, students use flash cards for additional practice with specific groups of facts. Facts are also practiced in many word problems in the DPP, Home Practice, and individual lessons. These problems allow students to focus on other interesting mathematical ideas as they also gain more fact practice.

Games

A variety of games are included in the curriculum, both in the lessons and in the DPP items of many units. A summary of the games used in a particular grade can be found in the Games section. Once students learn the rules of the games, they should play them periodically in class and at home for homework. Games provide an opportunity to encourage family involvement in the math program. When a game is assigned for homework, a note can be sent home with a place for the family members to sign, affirming that they played the game with their student.

Figure 7: *Playing a game*

Use of Calculators

The relationship between knowing the math facts and the use of calculators is an interesting one. Using a multiplication table or a calculator when necessary to find a fact helps promote familiarity and reinforces the math facts. Students soon figure out that it is quicker and more efficient to know the basic facts than to have to use these tools. The use of calculators also requires excellent estimation skills so that one can easily check for errors in calculator computations. Rather than eliminating the need for fluency with the facts, successful calculator use for solving complex problems depends on fact knowledge.

When to Practice

Practicing small groups of facts often for short periods of time is more effective than practicing many facts less often for long periods of time. For example, practicing 8 to 10 subtraction facts for 5 minutes several times a week is better than practicing all the subtraction facts for half an hour once a week. Good times for practicing the facts for 5 or 10 minutes during the school day include the beginning of the day, the beginning of math class, when students have completed an assignment, when an impending activity is delayed, or when an activity ends earlier than expected. Practicing small groups of facts at home involves parents in the process and frees class time for more interesting mathematics.

> *Practicing small groups of facts often for short periods of time is more effective than practicing many facts less often for long periods of time.*

Assessment

Throughout the curriculum, teachers assess students' knowledge of the facts through observations as they work on activities, labs, and games. In Grades 3–5, students can use their *Facts I Know* charts to record their own progress in learning the facts. This type of self-assessment is very important in helping each student to become responsible for his or her own learning. Students are able to personalize their study of facts and not waste valuable time studying facts they already know.

In the second half of first grade, a sequence of facts assessments is provided in the Daily Practice and Problems. A more comprehensive facts assessment program begins in second grade. This program assesses students' progress in learning the facts, as outlined in the Expectations by Grade Level section of this tutor. As students develop strategies for a given group of facts, short quizzes accompany the practice. Students know which facts will be tested, focus practice in class and at home on those facts, then take the quiz. As they take the quiz, they use one color pencil to write answers before a given time limit, then use another color to complete the problems they need more time to answer. Students then use their *Facts I Know* charts to make a record of those facts they answered quickly, those facts they answered correctly but with less efficient strategies, and those facts they did not know at all. Using this information, students can concentrate their efforts on gaining fluency with those facts they answered correctly, but not quickly. They also know to develop strategies for those facts they could not answer at all. In this way, the number of facts studied at any one time becomes more manageable, practice becomes more meaningful, and the process less intimidating.

Tests of all the facts for any operation have a very limited role. They are used no more than two times a year to show growth over time and should not be given daily or weekly. Since we rarely, if ever, need to recall 100 facts at one time in everyday life, overemphasizing tests of all the facts reinforces the notion that math is nothing more than rote memorization and has no connection to the real world. Quizzes of small numbers of facts are as effective and not as threatening. They give students, parents, and teachers the information needed to continue learning and practicing efficiently. With an assessment approach based on strategies and the use of small groups of facts, students can see mathematics as connected to their own thinking and gain confidence in their mathematical abilities.

Conclusion

Research provides clear indications for curriculum developers and teachers about the design of effective math facts instruction. These recommendations formed the foundation of the *Math Trailblazers* math facts program. Developing strategies for learning the facts (rather than relying on rote memorization), distributing practice of small groups of facts, applying math facts in interesting problems, and using an appropriate assessment program—all are consistent with recommendations from current research. It is an instructional approach that encourages students to make sense of the mathematics they are learning. The resulting program will add efficiency and effectiveness to your students' learning of the math facts.

References

Ashlock, R.B., and C.A. Washbon. "Games: Practice Activities for the Basic Facts." In M.N. Suydam and R.E. Reys (eds.), *Developing Computational Skills: 1978 Yearbook.* National Council of Teachers of Mathematics, Reston, VA, 1978.

Beattie, L.D. "Children's Strategies for Solving Subtraction-Fact Combinations." *Arithmetic Teacher,* 27 (1), pp. 14–15, 1979.

Brownell, W.A., and C.B. Chazal. "The Effects of Premature Drill in Third-Grade Arithmetic." *Journal of Educational Research,* 29 (1), 1935.

Carpenter, T.P., and J.M. Moser. "The Acquisition of Addition and Subtraction Concepts in Grades One through Three." *Journal for Research in Mathematics Education,* 15 (3), pp. 179–202, 1984.

Cook, C.J., and J.A. Dossey. "Basic Fact Thinking Strategies for Multiplication—Revisited." *Journal for Research in Mathematics Education,* 13 (3), pp. 163–171, 1982.

Davis, E.J. "Suggestions for Teaching the Basic Facts of Arithmetic." In M.N. Suydam and R.E. Reys (eds.), *Developing Computational Skills: 1978 Yearbook.* National Council of Teachers of Mathematics, Reston, VA, 1978.

Fuson, K.C. "Teaching Addition, Subtraction, and Place-Value Concepts." In L. Wirszup and R. Streit (eds.), *Proceedings of the UCSMP International Conference on Mathematics Education: Developments in School Mathematics Education Around the World: Applications-Oriented Curricula and Technology-Supported Learning for All Students.* National Council of Teachers of Mathematics, Reston, VA, 1987.

Fuson, K.C., and G.B. Willis. "Subtracting by Counting Up: More Evidence." *Journal for Research in Mathematics Education,* 19 (5), pp. 402–420, 1988.

Fuson, K.C., J.W. Stigler, and K. Bartsch. "Grade Placement of Addition and Subtraction Topics in Japan, Mainland China, the Soviet Union, Taiwan, and the United States." *Journal for Research in Mathematics Education,* 19 (5), pp. 449–456, 1988.

Greer, B. "Multiplication and Division as Models of Situations." In D.A. Grouws (ed.), *Handbook of Research on Mathematics Teaching and Learning: A Project of the National Council of Teachers of Mathematics* (Chapter 13). Macmillan, New York, 1992.

Hiebert, James. "Relationships between Research and the NCTM Standards." *Journal for Research in Mathematics Education,* 30 January, pp. 3–19, 1999.

Isaacs, A.C., and W.M. Carroll. "Strategies for Basic Facts Instruction." *Teaching Children Mathematics,* 5 May, pp. 508–515, 1999.

Kouba, V.L., C.A. Brown, T.P. Carpenter, M.M. Lindquist, E.A. Silver, and J.O. Swafford. "Results of the Fourth NAEP Assessment of Mathematics: Number, Operations, and Word Problems." *Arithmetic Teacher,* 35 (8), pp. 14–19, 1988.

Myers, A.C., and C.A. Thornton. "The Learning-Disabled Child—Learning the Basic Facts." *Arithmetic Teacher,* 25 (3), pp. 46–50, 1977.

National Research Council. *Adding It Up: Helping Children Learn Mathematics.* National Academy Press, Washington, DC, 2001.

Principles and Standards for School Mathematics. National Council of Teachers of Mathematics, Reston, VA, 2000.

Rathmell, E.C. "Using Thinking Strategies to Teach the Basic Facts." In M.N. Suydam and R.E. Reys (eds.), *Developing Computational Skills: 1978 Yearbook.* National Council of Teachers of Mathematics, Reston, VA, 1978.

Rathmell, E.C., and P.R. Trafton. "Whole Number Computation." In J.N. Payne (ed.), *Mathematics for the Young Child.* National Council of Teachers of Mathematics, Reston, VA, 1990.

Swart, W.L. "Some Findings on Conceptual Development of Computational Skills." *Arithmetic Teacher,* 32 (5), pp. 36–38, 1985.

Thornton, C.A. "Doubles Up—Easy!" *Arithmetic Teacher,* 29 (8), p. 20, 1982.

Thornton, C.A. "Emphasizing Thinking Strategies in Basic Fact Instruction." *Journal for Research in Mathematics Education,* 9 (3), pp. 214–227, 1978.

Thornton, C.A. "Solution Strategies: Subtraction Number Facts." *Educational Studies in Mathematics,* 21 (1), pp. 241–263, 1990.

Thornton, C.A. "Strategies for the Basic Facts." In J.N. Payne (ed.), *Mathematics for the Young Child.* National Council of Teachers of Mathematics, Reston, VA, 1990.

Thornton, C.A., and P.J. Smith. "Action Research: Strategies for Learning Subtraction Facts." *Arithmetic Teacher,* 35 (8), pp. 8–12, 1988.

Van de Walle, J. *Elementary and Middle School Mathematics: Teaching Developmentally.* Addison Wesley, New York, 2001.

Portfolios

A portfolio is a purposeful collection of a student's work that provides evidence of the student's skills, understandings, or attitudes. If the portfolio includes work collected over time, then it may also reflect the student's growth.

This tutor outlines reasons portfolios may be useful and provides some guidance for getting started and going further. A bibliography includes suggestions for additional reading.

Why Portfolios?

Portfolios can help teachers:

- better assess student learning;
- foster student autonomy;
- communicate the goals of instruction to students and parents; and
- improve their own teaching.

Student Assessment

Since a portfolio contains direct samples of student work, it may, for certain purposes, be superior to indirect indicators like grades. For example, an actual graph shows a student's skill at graphing better than a grade; and the juxtaposition of two graphs, one from September and the other from January, documents learning over time much more accurately than two grades could ever do.

Portfolios can assess many outcomes that are hard to assess by more conventional methods . . . They also can help you learn about how students think and track the development of that thinking.

Portfolios can assess many outcomes that are hard to assess by more conventional methods—communication, reasoning, problem solving, confidence, perseverance, flexibility, and so on. They also can help you learn more about how students think and track the development of that thinking.

Student Autonomy

Portfolios can encourage students to assess their own learning. Students become more self-directed and motivated by examining and reflecting on their own work and the work of their peers.

Communication

Concrete examples of student work reveal much that is not easily conveyed in grades or comments. Parents and others can see progress and achievement for themselves.

The examples of student work in a portfolio also convey the content and goals of the curriculum in a specific way that complements the generalities of curriculum philosophies and scope and sequence charts. Portfolios focus on the work students actually do, not on ideology or wishful thinking. You can enhance communication between students and their parents, teachers, and peers by having particular examples to discuss.

Portfolios can help establish public norms for mathematics achievement. Focusing assessment on tests and grades communicates a narrow concept of what is valuable in mathematics. When assessment is more broadly based, it promotes a broader vision of mathematics.

Improvement of Instruction

Student portfolios are useful both for making instructional decisions and for evaluating and improving instruction.

Certainly, better understanding of how students think and feel can help you make better decisions about directions for future instruction. But portfolios can also help teachers improve their teaching more generally. Portfolios can facilitate discussions with professional colleagues about different approaches to the same topic; they can reflect the range of instructional opportunities offered; and they can indicate the use of manipulatives, group work, and technology in an implemented curriculum.

Student portfolios might be included in a Teaching Portfolio that a teacher can use for self-evaluation. You can refine your own teaching by collecting and examining several years of student portfolios. Some benefits that portfolios promise for students—collegiality, establishment of public norms, improvement of higher-level skills—may thus become available to teachers.

Getting Started

> The beginnings of all things are small.
>
> —Cicero

There is no single right way to do portfolios.

There is no single right way to do portfolios. The suggestions offered below have worked for others and may work for you, but you should expect to learn by trial and error and to rely on your own judgment. If you have used portfolios for writing or some other subject, then your experience will be invaluable. If you possibly can, work with a colleague as you implement portfolios for the first time.

Starting small, with modest goals, is a good idea. For example, you may organize your portfolio program around one well-defined area that is hard to assess by more traditional methods. For instance, choose one of the following areas as a theme for the portfolios:

- measurement,
- graphing,

- drawing pictures and diagrams, or
- communicating solution methods.

Besides starting small, start early so you have a baseline of student attitudes and achievement. Before and after comparisons are useful, but impossible without early samples. All materials in a portfolio must be dated.

A box with a file folder for each child's work is a simple way to start. If the box is easily accessible, then the portfolios are more likely to fit into classroom routines. Anticipate the need for more room as items are added to the portfolios.

What goes in the portfolios is a key decision. Figure 1 shows some kinds of materials you might include in a portfolio, although clearly no real portfolio will have such a wild collection. Figure 2 is a table of contents for a possible third-grade portfolio.

You might aim for balance in the selection of materials: group vs. individual assignments; short problems vs. longer projects; real life vs. purely mathematical problems; on-demand vs. no-deadline tasks; attitude vs. skill vs. concept-oriented work; and so on. The number of pieces should not be so few that there is not enough evidence about important outcomes, nor so many that there is no judgment about what is important or worthwhile. About eight to ten pieces might be enough for a semester.

You must also decide how to pick what to put in the portfolios. We suggest that students select items subject to constraints imposed by the teacher. Constraints might range from requiring particular items, to selecting items that meet certain criteria, to allowing complete freedom of choice by students. The amount of latitude you allow will depend on your class and goals. Younger children, for example, usually need more direction. Putting fewer constraints on what goes in the portfolios may foster student autonomy, but may result in portfolios with few overlapping items so comparisons between students are difficult, or may even yield useless collections of random scraps.

> *The number of pieces should not be so few that there is not enough evidence about important outcomes, nor so many that there is no judgment about what is important or worthwhile. About eight to ten pieces might be enough for a semester.*

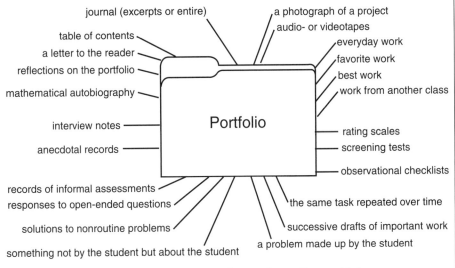

Figure 1: *Possible items for mathematics portfolios*

One way to organize the selection process is to have two folders for each child—a collection folder and the portfolio proper. Then, from time to time (once every several weeks or so), students can harvest the collection folder and add a few select items to the portfolio. At the same time, they can weed the portfolio so the total number of items does not become too large. Students can do this selection in small groups or pairs subject to teacher constraints as described above. Keep remaining items in the collection folder or send them home.

Eight to ten well-chosen and chronologically arranged pieces of work are most useful. You will have specific examples that communicate at parent conference time what your curriculum is and how your students are progressing; you will have a sampling of the products of your instruction so you can critically examine your teaching; and your students will see a cross section of their own work so they can attain greater self-awareness and autonomy. You have accomplished much even if your portfolios are no more than this.

Going Further

There are, however, other things you might want to try as you gain experience with portfolios, especially if you are working with older students. Periodic reviews of the portfolios, writing about the portfolios, and assessing the portfolios are worth considering.

	Jarrett's Portfolio • Table of Contents	
Item	**Description**	**Date**
Letter to Reader	My letter tells what my portfolio shows about my math work this semester.	9/22
Journal	A few times a week we write about math in our journals. Mine has 35 pages so far!	
Spinning Differences	I used a spinner to make subtraction problems and then graphed how many times I got each difference.	9/27
The Better "Picker Upper"	I used water to make spots on different kinds of paper towels. Then I counted square cm to find the areas of the spots.	10/25
Joe the Goldfish	Joe needed a raincoat and I figured out how much cloth he would need to make it.	11/1
Palindromes	A palindrome is a number that is the same frontwards and backwards. I used addition to make numbers into palindromes.	11/10
Lemonade Stand	This was the first line graph I ever made.	11/15
Mass vs. Number	I measured the mass of different numbers of marbles. Then I made a line graph and used it to make some predictions.	12/5
Stencilrama	This was my favorite. We made stencils out of index cards and then used the stencils to make designs. We had to figure out how many times we would have to move the stencil to make a border around the bulletin board.	1/15

Figure 2: *Sample third-grade portfolio with an emphasis on graphing*

Portfolio Review

Most teachers will be hard-pressed to find time to meet with individual students to review portfolios. Whole-class discussion and peer consultations, however, can accomplish many of the same goals.

For example, ask students to look through their collection folders for their best graphs to add to their portfolios. First, through whole-class discussion, help students identify characteristics of a good graph. Then in small groups or pairs, students can examine their collections to pick out the best graphs. This opportunity for students to examine one another's work can help establish public norms for excellence.

Portfolio Writing

Asking students to write about the contents of their portfolios encourages reflection and self-assessment. This writing can take a variety of forms.

The most basic writing is a table of contents with the name of each piece, a brief description, and the date it was completed. Students can also include who chose the piece and why, who worked on the piece, and what was learned or liked or hard about the piece.

You might ask students to write a letter to the reader of the portfolio. The letter can identify favorite pieces and explain why they are favorites, or best work, or work that shows the most progress. The letter might show you what the portfolio reveals about the student as a learner of mathematics.

Assessing the Portfolios

You do not have to assess the portfolios. Most likely you already graded the work included in them, and the collection is itself a direct indicator of achievement and attitude. This indicator may be sufficient for your purposes.

Assessing the portfolios, however, can have advantages, especially if you are working with older students. For one, it shows that you care about the portfolios and so communicates to students that they should take them seriously. It can also model processes you want students to apply in peer- and self-assessment of the portfolios.

If you do intend to grade the portfolios, you should make your expectations known to the students in advance. The establishment of such public criteria for excellence, like the TIMS Student Rubrics, will help students know what they should aim for so their work can be better focused. You might concentrate on how well the portfolios are organized—table of contents, correct chronological order, completeness, etc.—or on the quality of the reflective writing about the portfolio. You may encourage a balanced selection of items, documentation of improvement over time, clarity of communication, accuracy of self-assessment, neatness, or something else. As long as your students know the criteria and you have the time to do it, such grading can be useful.

Conclusion

Portfolios will not solve all the problems of mathematics education. And there are some costs for using them. Using portfolios as part of an assessment program will certainly take extra time and can be difficult, especially at first. Getting students to reflect on their own learning is particularly hard. But despite such pitfalls, portfolios offer great promise for improving your teaching and your students' learning. The basic idea is simple: collect, select, reflect.

References

Crowley, Mary L. "Student Mathematics Portfolio: More Than a Display Case." *Mathematics Teacher,* 86 (7), pp. 544–547, 1993.

Kuhs, Therese. "Portfolio Assessment: Making It Work for the First Time." *Mathematics Teacher,* 87 (5), pp. 332–335, 1994.

Lambdin, Diana V., and Vicki L. Walker. "Planning for Classroom Portfolio Assessment." *Arithmetic Teacher,* 41 (6), pp. 318–324, 1994.

Mumme, Judith. *Portfolio Assessment in Mathematics.* (A publication of the California Mathematics Project.) University of California, Santa Barbara, CA, 1990.

Stenmark, Jean Kerr, ed. *Mathematics Assessment: Myths, Models, Good Questions, and Practical Suggestions.* National Council of Teachers of Mathematics, Reston, VA, 1991.

Word Problems

> In fact, word problems should not just be integrated into the mathematics curriculum; they should form the basis of the curriculum.
>
> —CARPENTER, FENNEMA, AND PETERSON, 1987

Although word problems are not the basis of the *Math Trailblazers* curriculum, we do agree that students should confront a wide variety of challenging word problems and exercises. Word problems can highlight applications of the mathematics students are learning. They can introduce, motivate, and develop new mathematics in meaningful contexts.

This tutor provides teachers with a summary of research and background information about word problems. It outlines the theoretical and practical frameworks that underlie the extensive use of word problems in *Math Trailblazers.*

Problem Representations

Problems are presented to us in different ways. Sometimes a problem arises from a real situation; other times we give problems in words, pictures, or symbols. These different ways are sometimes called modes of representation.

Real Situations

Consider this problem: "Jessica and Meri Joy baked 36 cookies. Then, Meri Joy dropped 12 cookies on the floor. How many were left?" Now this problem has a basis in reality: Jessica and Meri Joy are the daughters of two members of the *Math Trailblazers* development team; they really did bake cookies; some cookies really were dropped and spoiled. Note that Meri Joy and Jessica could answer the question simply by counting the cookies that were not dropped.

Such real-life situations are the most concrete level of problem representation. People rarely go wrong when they solve such problems. (Resnick, 1987)

Concrete Model

If, however, some time has passed and the cookies are no longer at hand, we can still ask and answer the question. One way is to get some beans and to pretend they are cookies. To solve the problem, we can count out 36 beans, separate 12, and count how many remain.

This use of beans to represent cookies is one step up the ladder of abstraction: a concrete model represents a real situation. Good evidence exists that even kindergarten students can handle complex problems that are represented by concrete models. (Carpenter, Ansell, Franke, Fennema, and Weisbeck, 1993)

Figure 1: *Twelve of 36 cookies dropped*

Pictures

Another way to approach the problem is via pictures. Each cookie can be represented by a circle. We can solve the problem by drawing 36 circles, crossing out 12, and counting those left.

This sort of pictorial representation is often useful in mathematics and science. Even when the picture does not lead immediately to a solution, it often helps us understand the problem situation and starts us on the road to a solution.

Verbal Representations

Most school problems are stated in words. This is often necessary (How else could we present our cookie problem in this essay?) and builds on a well-developed set of skills your students have—their language skills.

Language is the first and most powerful symbol system we learn. The recent emphasis on discourse and communication in learning is based at least in part on a recognition of the importance of language in human thought.

Symbols

We can also represent Jessica and Meri Joy's cookies in symbols:

$$36 - 12 = \Box$$

Such symbolic representations are abstract and powerful. Much of the explosive growth of mathematics in the last 400 years is due to the invention of more efficient symbol systems.

Unfortunately, for too many students, mathematical symbolism is a code they never crack. Such students do not see the marks on paper as meaningful or related to the real world in any way. Instead, they see the marks as part of an arcane game.

When writing number sentences, it is important to use units. Of course, constantly writing the units can be tedious. One compromise is to omit the units in the middle of a sequence of symbolic representations, but be sure to include them at the beginning and again at the end.

> *Even when the picture does not lead immediately to a solution, it often helps us understand the problem situation and starts us on the road to a solution.*

We want students to learn to write, read, and understand mathematical symbolism, especially number sentences. Here, word problems can be particularly useful. The situations in many word problems are straightforward enough that the corresponding number sentences are simple.

Usually, several number sentences are appropriate for each problem. Consider, for example, the following problem: "Janice had 9 stickers. Then her mother gave her some more. Now Janice has 16 stickers. How many stickers did Janice's mother give her?"

An adult might see this as a subtraction problem and write

$$16 - 9 = 7 \tag{a}$$
or
$$16 - 9 = \Box \tag{b}$$

These number sentences are in the normal or "canonical" form. That is, the known quantities are on the left-hand side of the equals sign and the unknown or the answer is on the right-hand side.

Many students, however, write something like

$$9 + \Box = 16 \tag{c}$$
or
$$9 + 7 = 16 \tag{d}$$

These "non-canonical" forms reflect the students' way of thinking about the problem: Janice had 9 stickers, then she got some more, and now she has 16 stickers. Often a student who writes (c) or (d) will solve the problem by counting on from 9 to 16 rather than by subtracting 9 from 16. We consider these non-canonical number sentences to be as correct as the canonical forms. They can also be more understandable for the students.

Translations between Representations

So we have a hierarchy of levels of representation: real objects, physical models, pictures, words, symbols.

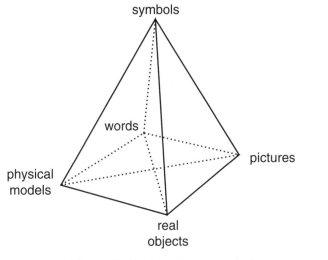

Figure 2: *Modes of representation*

But perhaps "hierarchy of levels" is not quite the right phrase; it may be better to consider that there are a number of different modes of representation, each of which has certain strengths and weaknesses. Recent cognitive theory indicates that the ability to translate from one representation to another is a crucial part of conceptual understanding and problem-solving skill. Connecting symbols with real referents, for example, permits one to understand symbolic manipulations and results in terms of real situations. Earlier, we saw how translating a problem from a real or verbal presentation to a concrete model could yield a solution by an elementary method.

Unfortunately, too much instruction in mathematics focuses exclusively on symbols. While symbolic representations are compact and powerful, they cannot stand alone. Our goal is to have students create mental "two-way streets" between symbols, words, concrete models, pictures, and real situations. Word problems are an excellent vehicle for reaching this goal.

Solving Problems

One view of problem solving is that the most critical step is developing the right representation: when we see the problem in the correct light, then the solution is obvious. Of course, the right representation for me might not be right for you. Accordingly, just as multiple representations should be part of the mathematics curriculum, so should multiple solutions. Estimation and attention to the reasonableness of results must also be part of instruction in problem solving.

Multiple Solutions

Many students think the main thing in mathematics is to get the right answer. Incorrect or partial answers are seen as failures, and re-solving a problem in a different way is considered futile.

On the contrary, students can learn much by solving problems in several ways. When different methods yield the same answer, students gain confidence both in the answer and in the various methods. This can be particularly useful for students learning more abstract and powerful methods: if a more powerful method gives the same answer as a more familiar method, then students are more likely to understand and trust the powerful method.

Students can also see connections within mathematics by comparing the points of view that generate different solutions to a problem. Making such connections is a key goal of the National Council of Teachers of Mathematics *Principles and Standards for School Mathematics* (NCTM, 2000). If students share their solution methods, then not only do they learn new methods from one another, but they also learn to communicate mathematically, another *Principles and Standards* goal.

Even incorrect or partial answers can be useful. Wrong answers are almost always the result of a student's honest attempt to get the problem right. Examining and discussing wrong answers and the procedures that generated them can make students' thinking explicit so that misconceptions can be identified and cleared up.

Sometimes a partial answer is the best we can reasonably hope for. In fact, many practical problems are impossible or prohibitively expensive to solve exactly. In some real situations, a partial answer may be all that is required.

A partial solution may be based on an idea that can be modified or extended to yield a complete solution. If a problem is hard, then making progress towards an answer is perfectly respectable, and certainly far better than giving up.

One way to get the most out of partial solutions is to encourage students to talk and write about the problem even if they cannot solve it. This will also help students stay with difficult problems longer.

Estimation

A common reason for estimating is that an exact answer is not necessary. If we have $5 and want to buy milk, bread, and eggs, a quick estimate will tell us if we have enough money. Sometimes an estimate must serve because an exact answer is impossible or impractical to obtain. The exact number of piano tuners who live in Chicago, for example, can only be estimated.

Another reason to estimate an answer is to verify the accuracy of a result obtained in some other way. This is especially important in our age of computing machines—if we do not have some idea what the answer should be, then we may be at a loss to know whether the answer the machine gives us is reasonable.

A less commonly recognized reason to make an estimate is as a step on the way to an exact answer. As one of our favorite teachers used to say, "Never solve a problem until you know the answer." We think he meant that finding an approximate answer can help in the search for the exact answer. By estimating an answer, we come to understand the problem better.

Learning to estimate builds number sense and encourages students to rely on their common sense rather than on rote procedures. Making a good estimate requires a flexible combination of common sense, experience, rules of thumb, and specific knowledge. Estimation is a high-level skill that takes a long time to develop. Estimation is, accordingly, built into *Math Trailblazers* from the beginning.

Reasonableness of Results

How often have you seen a student's paper with patently absurd answers? Such answers indicate that the student is not working at a meaningful level. Rather some procedures—half-understood, half-remembered—were carried out and something was produced, but the relationship of that product to the problem at hand is far from clear. No connection exists in the student's mind between the real situation and the symbolic manipulations.

Looking back when an answer is obtained, mapping the result of symbolic or other manipulations back onto the original problem statement, is a crucial part of the problem-solving process. George Polya, in his famous book *How to Solve It* (1957), included looking back as one of four basic steps in solving a problem. (Polya's other steps are to understand the problem; to make a plan to solve the problem; and to carry out the plan.)

When students look back at a solution, they should assess whether it is reasonable and correct. They can also look for ways to improve the solution, simplify it, or generalize it. By comparing their solution to other solutions, they can obtain further evidence of correctness and they have an opportunity to make connections between different approaches.

Addition and Subtraction Problem Types

Children typically use many varied methods to solve word problems. This, in part, relates to the fact that there is an underlying variety of problem types. Educational researchers in the last 20 years or so have explored the different problem types extensively. Several different examples are discussed here. Additional discussion about the methods children use to solve problems are in the TIMS Tutor: *Math Facts*.

Students should experience solving many different types of word problems. It is important to note, however, that in discussing the different problem types, we are not suggesting a new level of material for children to learn, i.e., we do not expect nor want children to have to learn about the different types of problems as a study in and of itself. Rather, we discuss the diversity in problem types so teachers recognize that this variety exists and subsequently are better prepared to present their students with a rich and varied collection of word problems.

Thomas Carpenter and his colleagues (Carpenter, Fennema, and Peterson, 1987; Carpenter, Carey, and Kouba, 1990; Carpenter, et al., 1999) have devised a classification scheme for problems that most adults would solve by simple addition or subtraction. They identify four general types of situations that give rise to 11 different kinds of addition or subtraction problems. (Other researchers have devised similar schemes. See, for example, Riley, Greeno, and Heller, 1983, and Rathmell and Huinker, 1989.)

Join Situations

Carpenter begins with "join" situations. Here, something is joined to a beginning quantity so a new quantity results. We think of these situations like this:

$$\text{start} + \text{change} = \text{result}$$

If the result is unknown, then we have an addition situation. Otherwise, we have a subtraction situation. Children often have more difficulty with problems in which the start is unknown than those in which the change is unknown.

Join/Result Unknown
Erick had 8 action figures. Then his father gave him 3 new ones. How many does he have now?

Join/Change Unknown
Janice had 9 stickers. Then her mother gave her some more. Now Janice has 16 stickers. How many stickers did Janice's mother give her?

Join/Start Unknown
Maria had some pennies. Then she found 3 more. Now she has 12 pennies. How many pennies did Maria have at first?

Separate Situations

Adults most often think of these situations as take-away problems:

$$\text{start} - \text{change} = \text{result}$$

If the result or change is unknown, then we have a subtraction (or take-away) situation. Otherwise, we have an addition situation.

Separate/Result Unknown
Thomas had 8 cookies. Then he ate 6. How many cookies does he have left?

Separate/Change Unknown
Leah had 12 dolls. She gave some of her dolls away. Then she had 7 dolls left. How many dolls did Leah give away?

Separate/Start Unknown
Michael had some marbles. He lost 5 of his marbles. Then he had 7 marbles. How many marbles did Michael have at first?

Part-Whole Situations

Carpenter's third category is part-whole. Here, a single whole is broken into two parts:

$$\text{part} + \text{part} = \text{whole}$$

This is similar to the join situation. The difference is that part-whole situations are static, the two parts coexisting from the beginning, whereas in join situations, two things are put together to form a new whole.

If the whole is unknown in a part-whole situation, then we have an addition situation. Otherwise, we have a subtraction situation.

Part-Whole/Whole Unknown
Ian has some action figures. He has 8 good guys and 3 bad guys. How many action figures does Ian have altogether?

Part-Whole/Part Unknown
There are 14 children who live in Clayton's building. Five of the children are boys. How many girls live in Clayton's building?

Compare Situations

Carpenter's last category is "compare." Here, two independent quantities are being compared:

$$q_1 - q_2 = \text{difference}$$

If the difference or q_2 is unknown, then we subtract. If q_1 is unknown, we add.

Compare/Difference Unknown
Samantha has $14. Kristin has $5. How much more money does Samantha have?

Compare/Q$_2$ Unknown
Jason has 13 crayons. Angela has 6 fewer than Jason. How many crayons does Angela have?

Compare/Q_1 Unknown

Lamar has some markers. Robin has 15 markers. Robin has 7 fewer markers than Lamar. How many markers does Lamar have?

Compare problems seem to be the hardest for children to solve. The other three types—join, separate, and part-whole—all involve a whole with parts in situations that are either static or dynamic. In compare problems, on the other hand, there is no whole. Rather, there are two independent quantities and a difference between them.

Need for Diversity in Problem Types

Traditionally, just two of these 11 kinds of problems have dominated American elementary mathematics textbooks, a dominance that contrasts sharply with customary practice abroad (Stigler, Fuson, Ham, & Kim, 1986; Fuson, Stigler, & Bartsch, 1988). These favored problem types, moreover, are the easiest to solve. Most of the subtraction problems are take-away situations (separate/result unknown). Most of the addition problems are join/result unknown. By presenting such a limited variety of problems, these texts give students a wrong impression about what addition and subtraction are. Carpenter's four situations—join, separate, part-whole, and compare—and the various types of problems reflect a much wider conception of addition and subtraction. In *Math Trailblazers,* we present this full range of addition and subtraction problems beginning in the earliest grades.

Diversity in Strategies

The description of the various problem types identified addition and subtraction situations. However, students may approach the problems in different ways. For example, while adults may immediately subtract when they encounter a take-away situation (8 cookies − 6 cookies = 2 cookies) some children may choose to use an addition strategy and count up. (Thomas ate 6 cookies and he has 2 left. Two more than 6 is 8 cookies.) Both are valid strategies.

Types of Multiplication and Division Problems

Researchers who have studied multiplication and division have identified different types of multiplication and division problems. While students do not need to be able to identify these different types of problems by name, it is important that they encounter and solve them. The different types of multiplication and division problems are outlined below.

Problems Involving a Number of Equivalent Sets

These sets can be groups of objects, arrays, or jumps on the number line. An example: Ask a class of 20 students to stand in a group. Instruct them to break into teams of four.

Using this situation, three different questions emerge. One question is interpreted as a multiplication problem, the other two as division problems.

The Unknown Is the Total Number in All the Groups

If there are 5 teams with 4 members on each team, how many players are there in all? There are two known factors and a missing product. Using established knowledge, students often interpret this correctly as a repeated addition problem (4 + 4 + 4 + 4 + 4 = 20). Through classroom experiences with many such problems, they can connect the repeated addition sentence to a multiplication sentence (5 × 4 = 20).

The Unknown Is the Number of Groups

Twenty members of a class are divided into teams of four members each. How many teams are there? The problem gives the total number in all the groups and the measure or size of each group. This aspect of division is called *measurement division.*

The Unknown Is the Number in Each Group

Twenty members of a class are divided equally into five teams. How many students are on each team? The problem gives the total number of students and the number of partitions or groups. This aspect of division is known as *partitive division.*

Jumps on a number line and arrays provide additional experience with the multiplication and division of equivalent sets. Successive jumps of equal size on a number line provide a model for multiplication as repeated addition and division as repeated subtraction. In *Math Trailblazers,* we model this situation using mythical creatures called "mathhoppers." For example, a +2 mathhopper starts at 0 and hops 4 times. On what number will it land? (8)

An array is a group of objects arranged in rows and columns. For example, a candy box that contains 5 rows with 6 pieces in each row is a 5 × 6 array. One virtue of the array model is that it makes it very clear that 5 × 6 = 6 × 5. You can rotate the box 90 degrees to form a 6 × 5 array. Another advantage is that it creates a visual image for both multiplication and division problems.

Problems Involving Scale Factors

This type of problem is often found in TIMS Laboratory Investigations. For example, after students have rolled different cars down a ramp, they might be asked if one car rolled three times as far as another. Similarly, when finding the mass of objects, they may be asked if the mass of one object is one-half the mass of another object.

A Cartesian Product

This problem involves two sets of objects (such as shirts and pants) that must be joined into pairs (shirt-and-pant sets). The answer for this type of problem then becomes the number of unique pairs that students can form from these two sets. While this type of problem is difficult for young children, they are able to solve it using manipulatives and diagrams.

Experiences with many types of problems should provide a strong conceptual foundation not only for multiplication and division, but for fractions, ratios, and proportional reasoning as well.

Problem Contexts

Most word problems in *Math Trailblazers* are embedded in a larger context; this is often an advantage since situational problems are more meaningful to students than abstract problems. Sometimes, however, providing a context is constraining or distracting. Also, problems may come to us without context; often, we have to provide extra information to make sense of a problem. Accordingly, in an attempt to provide a balance between problems embedded in situations and problems that are self-contained, we often provide free-standing word problems.

Teaching Word Problems

A variety of approaches to teaching word problems can be useful and stimulating. Here are several:

Whole Class, Then Small Groups

First, present a sample problem to your whole class. Discuss the problem and ask students to estimate the answer. Also ask students to explain how they made their estimates. Neither the estimates nor the explanations are likely to be very good, but this is only the beginning.

Next, ask students to solve the problem in groups of two or three students. Tell them you want (1) an answer for the problem, (2) an explanation of how they obtained the answer, and (3) a number sentence for the problem.

Require students who need help to seek it first from other students in their groups. Clearly, this is beneficial for the students who need the help, but those who give the help also benefit since they must make explicit what they may understand only implicitly. You will also be freed up since your students will be helping one another instead of depending so much on you.

As students work, move among the groups, listening to the various strategies. Use your judgment about what questions to ask and how much help to give, but try to restrain yourself. It is often better if students struggle on their own and find a solution themselves.

When the groups have answers, reconvene the whole class and ask students to explain their solutions and number sentences for the problem. Be sure they assess the reasonableness and correctness of their results. During these discussions, emphasize that every student is responsible for understanding his or her group's solution. One way to accomplish this is to call on random students to explain each group's work.

Encourage students to solve problems in more than one way by accepting only novel solutions during class discussions. This will motivate students to search for multiple solutions so they can contribute to the class discussion.

Small Groups, Then Whole Class

As your students gain experience, you can abbreviate or eliminate the whole-class introduction to the problem. Again, a whole-class discussion of solutions is appropriate.

Individual Work, Then Small Groups

Another approach is for students to work individually first and then to come together in pairs or small groups to compare solutions. Then, the small-group solutions can be shared with other groups during a class discussion.

Other Suggestions

Find some word problems appropriate for homework or for individual seatwork. Other problems may be so hard that no student is able to solve them; use such problems for whole-class investigations. You may use certain problems to introduce new mathematics like multiplication and division. Use an interesting problem as an "opener" when students arrive or when math class begins.

TIMS Tips

- If students cannot solve a problem, ask them to describe the problem and to restate it in their own words or ask them to draw a picture. This may lead to a better understanding of the problem and then to a solution.
- Do only a few problems at a time. Distributed practice will be more effective than bunched practice.
- Vary the format: individual, small group, whole class, homework.
- Be sure to discuss multiple solution strategies. Compare and contrast strategies, and point out advantages of each, but accept all correct strategies.
- Discuss several number sentences for each problem. Ask students to explain how a given number sentence fits the problem situation.
- Ask students to explain why their answers are reasonable.
- Provide manipulatives and calculators to each group. Just having them available in the room may not be enough—these resources should be immediately at hand.

Conclusion

As your students work word problems and share solutions, they will be applying mathematics they already know and learning new mathematics. Word problems deserve a prominent place in your mathematics lessons.

References

Carpenter, T.P., E. Fennema, M.L. Franke, L. Levi, and S.E. Empson. *Children's Mathematics: Cognitively Guided Instruction.* Heinemann, Westport, CT, 1999.

Carpenter, T.P., E. Fennema, and P. Peterson. "Cognitively Guided Instruction: The Application of Cognitive and Instructional Science to Mathematics Curriculum Development." In *Developments in School Mathematics Education Around the World,* I. Wirszup and R. Streit, eds. National Council of Teachers of Mathematics, Reston, VA, 1987.

Carpenter, T.P., D. Carey, and V. Kouba. "A Problem-Solving Approach to the Operations." In *Mathematics for the Young Child,* J.N. Payne, ed. National Council of Teachers of Mathematics, Reston, VA, 1990.

Carpenter, T.P., E. Ansell, M.L. Franke, E. Fennema, and L. Weisbeck. "Models of Problem Solving: A Study of Fourth Grade Children's Problem-Solving Processes." *Journal for Research in Mathematics Education,* 24 (5), pp. 428–441, 1993.

Fuson, K.C., J.W. Stigler, and K. Bartsch. "Grade Placement of Addition and Subtraction Topics in Japan, Mainland China, the Soviet Union, Taiwan, and the United States." *Journal for Research in Mathematics Education,* 19 (5), pp. 449–456, 1988.

National Council of Teachers of Mathematics. *Principles and Standards for School Mathematics.* National Council of Teachers of Mathematics, Reston, VA, 2000.

Polya, G. *How to Solve It.* Princeton University Press, Princeton, NJ, 1957.

Rathmell, E.C., and D.M. Huinker. "Using Part-Whole Language to Help Children Represent and Solve Word Problems." In *New Directions for Elementary School Mathematics,* P.R. Trafton, ed. National Council of Teachers of Mathematics, Reston, VA, 1989.

Resnick, L.B. "Presidential Address: Learning In School and Out." *Educational Researcher,* 16 (9), pp. 13–20, 1987.

Riley, M.S., J.G. Greeno, and J.I. Heller. "Development of Children's Problem-Solving Ability in Arithmetic." In *The Development of Mathematical Thinking,* H.P. Ginsburg, ed. Academic Press, New York, 1983.

Stigler, J.W., K.C. Fuson, M. Ham, and M.S. Kim. "An Analysis of Addition and Subtraction Word Problems in American and Soviet Elementary Mathematics Textbooks." *Cognition and Instruction,* 3 (3), pp. 153–171, 1986.

The TIMS Laboratory Method

Math Trailblazers is a comprehensive mathematics program that ... many important scientific ideas. Scientific concepts often provide contexts for developing and practicing math concepts and skills. The tools and processes of science are integral to mathematical problem solving throughout the curriculum.

This tutor expands upon the *Math Trailblazers* connection with science. It outlines the Teaching Integrated Math and Science (TIMS) Project's view of science and describes the TIMS Laboratory Method, a version of the scientific method. This method forms a framework throughout the curriculum for students to explore science in much the way scientists work.

The TIMS View of Science

Traditionally, school science has focused on the results of science. Students learn about parts of the body, types of rocks, the solar system, evolution, and so on. Knowing basic facts of science is seen as part of being educated, today more than ever. However, the facts of science, important and interesting as they are, do not alone comprise a comprehensive and balanced science curriculum.

The great educator and philosopher John Dewey expressed this idea some 100 years ago. In 1910, he wrote:

> *At times, it seems as if the educational availability of science were breaking down because of its sheer mass. There is at once so much of science and so many sciences that educators oscillate, helpless, between arbitrary selection and teaching a little of everything.*
>
> *Visit schools where they have taken nature study conscientiously. This school moves with zealous bustle from leaves to flowers, from flowers to minerals, from minerals to stars, from stars to the raw materials of industry, thence back to leaves and stones.*
>
> *Thus,. . . . science teaching has suffered because science has been so frequently presented just as so much ready-made knowledge, so much subject-matter of fact and law, rather than as the effective method of inquiry into any subject-matter.*

Surely if there is any knowledge which is of most worth it is knowledge of the ways by which anything is entitled to be called knowledge instead of being mere opinion or guess-work or dogma.

Such knowledge ... is not information, but a mode of intelligent practise, an habitual disposition of mind.

In 1996, the National Research Council (NRC) published the *National Science Education Standards* for K–12 science education. Among the many recommendations of the NRC document is a direction for decreased emphasis on teaching scientific facts and information, and increased emphasis on teaching for understanding of scientific concepts and developing abilities of inquiry. The NRC *Standards* state:

Emphasizing active science learning means shifting away from teachers presenting information and covering science topics. The perceived need to include all the topics, vocabulary, and information in textbooks is in direct conflict with the central goal of having students learn scientific knowledge with understanding.

These points of view underlie the TIMS approach to science. If we were to describe the TIMS approach in the most concise way possible, we would choose two words, *variable* and *experiment*. The essence of modern science, as it is practiced by scientists, is to understand the relationships among variables. Out of the great sea of variables we have selected those that we feel are fundamental to the understanding of all areas of science, namely: length, area, volume, mass, and time. These variables might be considered the fundamental vocabulary of science. They are integral to the everyday work of biologists, chemists, physicists, astronomers, and earth scientists. The more a child explores these variables, the greater will be his or her command of scientific language and the more complete will be his or her ability to take up the adventure of science.

We have therefore made these variables the focus of experiments and activities in Grades K through 5 of *Math Trailblazers*. Explorations in kindergarten are conceptual in nature. As the curriculum progresses through the grades, students revisit the variables many times in increasingly more sophisticated ways. In Grade 5, students are able to move on to compound variables such as density and velocity, which involve two of the basic variables. For example, density involves both mass and volume while velocity involves both length and time. To understand these compound variables, it is important that students are first familiar with the more basic variables. Through repeated investigation of the variables in different contexts, fundamental science concepts and skills become generalized.

> *If we were to describe the TIMS approach in the most concise way possible, we would choose two words, variable and experiment.*

PART II   Variables in Scientific Experiments

A **variable** is a quantity that may assume any one of a set of values. The variable is the heart and soul of science because the variable is to scientific investigation what the word is to language—its foundation and the basis of its structure. All experiments center around at least two variables, and the ability to measure these variables satisfactorily will determine the success or failure of the experiment.

Variables and Values

Variables fall into two broad categories: categorical and numerical. Would you say that a person's hair color is a categorical or a numerical variable? Would you say that a person's height is a categorical or numerical variable? A **numerical variable** is one that may assume a numerical set of values. In contrast, a **categorical variable** is one that does not assume numerical values.

Color, then, which can take on values such as red, blue, or yellow, is a categorical variable. Other categorical variables are shape, kind of object, and type of material the object is made of. In each case, you have the broad classification, the variable, and then the values the variable can assume.

The simplest kind of numerical variable is the number of objects in a set. For example, if we were studying the number of students who came to class each day, the variable would be "Number of Students," and the possible values of the variable would be 0 students, 1 student, 2 students, etc. A second category of numerical variable involves measurement. The basic measurement variables stressed in *Math Trailblazers* are length, area, volume, mass, and time. The values for these variables are what we measure during the course of an experiment. For example, if we are investigating the variable length, the values might be the number of meters, centimeters, millimeters, or other appropriate unit of length. When the variable is area, the values might be the number of square centimeters. Or if volume is the variable, the value might be the number of cubic centimeters, and so on. The variable is the broad classification; the **values** for the variable describe what we are counting or measuring for that variable.

One point in studying variables that will take repeated practice for your students to master is the regular use of units of measure. In science, we never deal with numbers without understanding what their units are. For example, say that we tell you that Mary dropped a ball from a height of 30. A question your students will learn to ask is, "Thirty what?" Was it 30 centimeters, 30 feet, or 30 miles? The name after the number 30 is what we call the unit of measure, and every variable has a set of them. $5 + 4 = 9$ can be meaningless unless we know 5 of what. 5 apples + 4 apples = 9 apples, but 5 apples + 4 pears does not equal either 9 apples or 9 pears. The sum is equal to 9 pieces of fruit. Invariably, children will give you the numerical value of the variable and leave off its unit. Learning to use units is merely a matter of discipline; that is, using them correctly so often that you feel uncomfortable when you either forget them or use them incorrectly. Developing this discipline in your students will help them later in their schooling as they examine more complicated scientific concepts.

Manipulated and Responding Variables in Controlled Experiments

In an experiment, a scientist tries to find a relationship between two variables. Where possible, the experimenter chooses ahead of time the values of one of the variables. This variable is called the **manipulated variable.** The values of the second variable are determined by the results of the experiment—something that the experimenter does not know ahead of time. We shall call the variable whose values result from the experiment, the **responding variable.**

For example, consider the following situation from a fourth-grade experiment, *The Bouncing Ball.* In this experiment, children study how high a ball bounces. They drop a ball from various heights and measure how high it bounces. As the experimenters, they decide what drop heights they want to use in the experiment, say 40 cm, 80 cm, and 120 cm. The drop height is the manipulated variable. But the height to which the ball bounces can only be determined after you drop the ball. It is not known ahead of time. So, the bounce height is the responding variable.

Or, say you fill a plastic jar with different-colored blocks and choose red, yellow, and blue as the colors of your blocks. You then ask a child to reach in and pull out as many pieces as he or she can in one grab, sort the blocks by color, and count them. Color is the manipulated variable in this experiment. The number of each color that he or she pulls out is the responding variable. You choose the values of the colors that go in but you have no choice over the number of each color that comes out.

Beginning in the first grade of *Math Trailblazers,* the experimental variables are identified in all laboratory experiments. This is an essential part of conducting any scientific experiment. It is not until fourth grade, however, that we introduce the formal terms "manipulated" and "responding."

Note that in *Math Trailblazers,* we have elected to use the terms "manipulated" and "responding" to describe experimental variables. We have found manipulated and responding to be less abstract for children (and adults) and easier to understand than the more commonly used terms for variables, "independent" and "dependent."

Fixed Variables in Controlled Experiments

Experiments often have more than two variables. In an ideal experiment, more easily realized in the laboratory than in the real world, a scientist focuses on only two variables—the ones we have called manipulated and responding—and strives to hold all others constant. If too many variables change simultaneously in an experiment, obtaining meaningful results can be difficult or impossible.

Consider a laboratory experiment done in second grade, *Rolling Along in Centimeters.* Students roll different kinds of cars down a ramp and use metersticks to measure the distance each car rolls. Here, the "type of car" is the manipulated variable and the distance each car rolls is the responding variable. The height of the ramp, the starting line, the floor onto which the cars roll, and the method for releasing the car are all held constant each time a car is rolled down the ramp. We refer to these as the **fixed variables** (or controlled variables) in the experiment. Children intuitively understand this as "keeping things fair" while the data are collected during the course of the experiment.

In many situations, some variables in an experiment are hidden; that is, they are not immediately obvious, although changing them will greatly alter the results of your experiment. Consider an experiment in which you collect data on the kinds of pets owned by each child in the classroom. The kind of pet is the manipulated variable and the number of each kind of pet is the

In an ideal experiment, more easily realized in the laboratory than in the real world, a scientist focuses on only two variables—the ones we have called manipulated and responding—and strives to hold all others constant. If too many variables change simultaneously in an experiment, obtaining meaningful results can be difficult or impossible.

responding variable. If you think about it, you can see that your results depend on where the pet owners live—in a high rise or a single-family house, in the city or a farm community, and even in which country. Thus the variable, "location," can drastically change the results.

One of the reasons cancer research is so difficult is because there are so many variables which are either difficult or impossible to control (such as environmental factors, personality traits, multitudinous viruses) that it is hard to pinpoint the variables that might be the cause of cancer. It is the complexity of biological and sociological systems that makes doing repeatable experiments in these areas very difficult.

Nonetheless, children can learn how to deal with simple physical systems where three or four variables are present. They should learn how to recognize the different variables involved and understand the importance of controlling all but two—the manipulated and the responding variable.

The TIMS Laboratory Method

Throughout *Math Trailblazers,* children carry out quantitative investigations in which they explore the relationships between variables. Each investigation is carried out with the same general format, which we call the TIMS Laboratory Method. One may call this our version of the scientific method. There are four phases: beginning the investigation and drawing the picture, collecting and organizing the data, graphing the data, and analyzing the experimental results. We discuss these four phases below, illustrating our discussion with references to *The Bouncing Ball* experiment described above and to *Marshmallows and Containers,* a second-grade experiment in which children study the number of marshmallows that fit into different-sized jars.

Phase 1: Beginning the Investigation and Drawing the Picture

Most investigations begin with a question. The question does not have to be momentous, but it must be meaningful to children. If the question connects in some authentic way with their experience, children will need no flashy inducements to want to find the answer. This is illustrated in the following classroom anecdote involving *Marshmallows and Containers.*

> As class begins, students sit together in groups of three. Each group has three different containers: a margarine tub, a 100 cc graduated cylinder, and a small paper cup. The teacher shows the class a bag of miniature marshmallows and asks, "Which container will hold the most marshmallows? Why do you think so?"

> The teacher encourages the groups to discuss their predictions and explanations and to record their ideas in their journals. When the groups report to the class, many groups think that the graduated cylinder will hold the most because it is the tallest. One boy explains that he thinks the cylinder holds the most because even if he could stretch the plastic in the bowl so it was tall like the cylinder, it still would not be as tall and would not hold as much. Other groups choose the tub because it is fatter than the other containers.

The teacher then asks, "How could you find out which container holds the most marshmallows?" This question leads naturally to an experiment: The students will fill each of the containers with marshmallows, count them, and record the numbers in a data table.

Once a suitable question has been posed—and posing such questions is far from trivial—then you must identify variables related to the question. *Marshmallows and Containers* examines the kind of container and the number of marshmallows. The size of the marshmallows and the method for packing the marshmallows into the jars is held fixed. In *The Bouncing Ball,* students measure the drop heights and bounce heights of a ball, while holding fixed the type of ball, the floor on which the ball is dropped, and the method for dropping the ball.

Through class discussion, the original question has been refined into a precise query about the relationship between two variables. These variables become defined well enough so children know how to gather information about them. Drawing a picture is an excellent way to summarize and communicate this beginning phase, and also to plan what is to come.

Figure 1: *Picture for* Marshmallows and Containers

Scientists often make sketches in experimental situations. In the TIMS Laboratory Method, drawing pictures helps children understand and organize what they are to do. A sketch gives the child time to think, to see relationships between variables, to place diverse relationships in a compact form, and to "explain" the experiment or problem to someone at a glance. Pictures also help teachers assess whether students are ready to proceed. Figure 1 shows one student's picture for

Figure 2: *Picture for* The Bouncing Ball

Marshmallows and Containers. The picture indicates the student's understanding of the experimental variables and the procedure. Note that the student is using an egg carton to make groups of 10 when counting marshmallows. Figure 2 shows a picture from *Bouncing Ball,* indicating the manipulated and responding variables (the drop height and the bounce height) and the procedure for the experiment. The students who drew these pictures are ready to go on to the next step, gathering data.

Phase 2: Collecting and Organizing the Data

In Phase 2 of the TIMS Laboratory Method, children gather the data and organize it in a table. To illustrate, we return to our classroom anecdote involving *Marshmallows and Containers:*

On the next day, the children use their pictures to review the experiment before beginning the data collection. Each group receives a two-column data table, fills in the column headings, and writes the names (or draws pictures) of the containers in the first column. The teacher emphasizes the need for accuracy in counting, and the children discuss various methods for grouping and counting the marshmallows. As students begin to collect the data, the teacher circulates among the groups, coaching and assessing.

After the children complete their data tables (Figure 3), the teacher leads a discussion in which the groups compare their results. This discussion centers on whether the groups' results are reasonable or not. Most groups report about 130 marshmallows in the graduated cylinder. Students agree that numbers close to 130, but not exactly 130, are acceptable. Based on this discussion, a group that had recorded only 110 marshmallows for the cylinder decides to refill the cylinder and count again.

Container	N Number of Marshmellow _{units}
Graduated cylinder	133
Cup	121
bowl	181

Figure 3: *Data table from* Marshmallows and Containers

Tennis Ball

D Drop Height in cm	B Bounce Height in cm			
	Trial 1	Trial 2	Trial 3	Average
40	27	22	21	22
80	50	40	43	43
120	72	62	68	68

Figure 4: *Data table from* The Bouncing Ball

Figure 3 shows a student's data table for *Marshmallows and Containers.* Figure 4 is a student's data table from *The Bouncing Ball.* The name of a variable, including units if appropriate, heads each column.

When creating data tables, scientists and mathematicians generally place the manipulated variable in the left column and the responding variable in the right column. Since the experimenter chooses values for the manipulated variable before the experiment begins, the first column of the data table can be filled out prior to the experiment. Values of the responding variable can only be filled in as the experiment is conducted.

Data tables are tools for organizing data. In a real laboratory experiment, scientists have to record the data clearly and correctly the first time, during the experiment. It has to be recorded in such a way that not only you can read it, but also your colleagues and even a stranger. A story is told about the Nobel Prize-winner James Watson, who helped discover DNA. His teacher at Indiana University was asked if he suspected that Watson might go on to great things when he graduated. Yes, he answered. Watson would go far. Why? The teacher replied that although Watson did not take great care of his personal appearance, and his desk was a mess, he kept a neat notebook. That is a lesson that even young children can understand.

The data table is also useful in controlling error and identifying patterns. Children can detect blunders when a measurement deviates too much from established patterns (as in the *Marshmallows and Containers* anecdote above), and they can control inevitable measurement error by averaging several trials.

Note that in *The Bouncing Ball* lab, the students performed three trials for each measurement. In other words, to answer the question of how high does the ball bounce when dropped from 40 centimeters, they dropped the ball three times from 40 centimeters and recorded the bounce height, in this case (Figure 4), 27, 22, and 21 centimeters. The students then take the average (they used the median for the average) bounce height for their value of the bounce height. This is done to minimize the effect of measurement and experimental error on the experiment. (See the TIMS Tutors: *Averages* and *Estimation, Accuracy, and Error.*)

Phase 3: Graphing the Data

Graphing is the heart of scientific analysis. Graphs are powerful communication tools that create a picture of the data and "tell its story." They allow you to compare, predict, and infer. If there is a pattern in the relationship between the variables, you are more likely to see it clearly in a graph. Being able to read a graph and produce a graph from data should be a major goal of school science. Graphing cuts across many disciplines: biology, chemistry, sociology, and economics. Students using *Math Trailblazers* work extensively with graphs from kindergarten on.

Bar Graphs vs. Point Graphs
In *Math Trailblazers,* data are mostly graphed as either a bar graph or a point graph; these two types of graphs will thus be the focus of our discussion in this section. Since a graph is a visual representation of the relationship between variables, the type of graph used depends upon the types of variables studied in the experiment.

When both variables are numerical, a point graph is often (though not always) appropriate. In *The Bouncing Ball,* for example, both variables—the drop height and the bounce height—are numerical. Since the values for these variables are numbers and are not discrete—that is, there are values between the data points that make sense, such as 52.5 cm—it is possible to use points and lines on the graph instead of bars to represent the data. Drawing a line or a curve makes sense only when the variables are numerical and there is a pattern in the data. Figure 5 shows a student's graph from *The Bouncing Ball.*

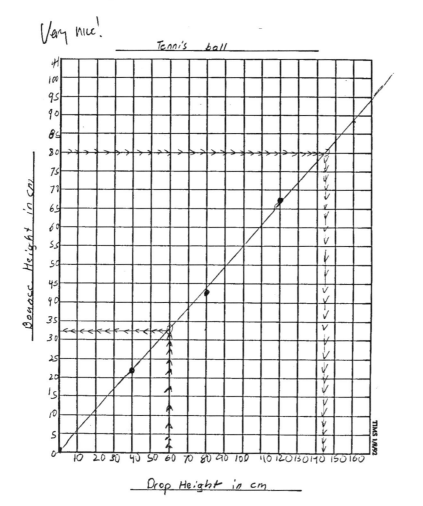

Figure 5: *Point graph from* The Bouncing Ball *showing best-fit lines, interpolation, and extrapolation*

Point graphs are introduced in *Math Trailblazers* in third grade and are used to represent a variety of different mathematical situations as well as to display data from laboratory experiments.

A bar graph is usually best when one of the variables is categorical (qualitative). In *Marshmallows and Containers,* for example, the type of container is a categorical variable and the number of marshmallows is numerical. Figure 6 shows the graph for *Marshmallows and Containers.* There are no values that make sense between the types of containers. Thus it does not make sense to connect them on the graph with a line. A bar graph, therefore, is appropriate for these kinds of situations.

> *A bar graph is usually best when one of the variables is categorical (qualitative).*

Although point graphs are most often used when both experimental variables are numerical, that is not always the case. For example, in the experiment *First Names* from third grade, students collect data about the number of letters in the first names of classmates. The two primary variables in this experiment are the number of letters (the manipulated variable) and the number of names (the responding variable). A graph for the experiment is shown in Figure 7. While both variables in this experiment are numerical, they are also discrete—that is, it is not meaningful to speak of $6\frac{1}{2}$ letters in a name or $3\frac{1}{4}$ people who have that number of letters in their names. Thus, we can see why a point graph, in which values between the data points are represented, would not be appropriate in this case. Instead, the data is best represented on a bar graph.

Figure 6: *Bar graph from* Marshmallows and Containers

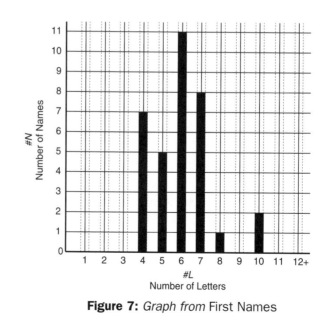

Figure 7: *Graph from* First Names

Labeling the Axes

With most types of data, it is conventional in science to place the manipulated variable along the horizontal axis and the responding variable along the vertical axis. The horizontal axis is labeled with a word or letter describing the manipulated variable and the vertical axis with a word or letter describing the responding variable. In Figure 7, for example, the horizontal axis—the manipulated variable—is labeled "#L, Number of Letters" and the vertical axis—the responding variable—is labeled "#N, Number of Names."

Once the axes are in place, the children can label the axes with the values for each variable. In the case of the *Marshmallows and Containers* in Figure 6, the student wrote in labels to represent the different kinds of containers.

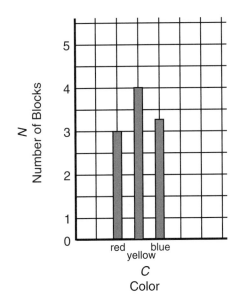

Figure 8: *Common errors in labeling the axes*

A common error in labeling axes is illustrated in Figure 8. This graph shows irregular spacing on both axes. The vertical axis in Figure 8 is incorrect with one space between 0 and 1 and two spaces between the other numbers. Technically, the categorical variables displayed on the horizontal axis do not have to be equally spaced, but it is a good idea to get your students into the habit of spacing their bars across the axis in regularly spaced intervals. This is because when dealing with numerical data, the values *must* be equally spaced.

Scaling the axes for numerical data requires an analysis of the range of the data and comparing it with the number of available intervals on your particular graph paper. Scaling by ones, two, fives, tens, or other numbers might be appropriate depending on the data for a particular experiment. What is essential, however, is that the intervals are all equal along a given axis. Students will learn that it is best to determine the appropriate interval ahead of time. Otherwise they will end up plotting their initial data points and later discovering that other points will not fit on the graph.

In most cases, the scale on the horizontal axis is independent of the scale on the vertical axis. Students should number the axes in ways that make sense for the data. For example, the horizontal axis in *The Bouncing Ball* graph

(Figure 5) is scaled by tens but the vertical axis is scaled by fives. One exception to this is when making scale maps. Here, using different scales for the different axes would create a distorted image and make it difficult to find distances on the map.

As scientists do, students using the TIMS Laboratory Investigations often use their graphs to make predictions about physical phenomena. When making point graphs, therefore, we often encourage students to scale their axes to allow room for extrapolation. (See the section below entitled *Predictions from Point Graphs: Interpolation and Extrapolation* for information about extrapolation.)

Bar Graphs in *Math Trailblazers*

As early as kindergarten, students using *Math Trailblazers* work on graphing concepts, including making and interpreting simple graphs. A quick way to make bar graphs of classroom data is to place self-adhesive notes on a labeled graph. An example of this with *First Names* is illustrated in Figure 9. In this graph, each student placed a self-adhesive note with the data for his or her name on the graph. The data are clearly represented. The one-to-one correspondence between data points and the number of students in the class is particularly apparent in this type of graph, which we use primarily in kindergarten, first, and second grades.

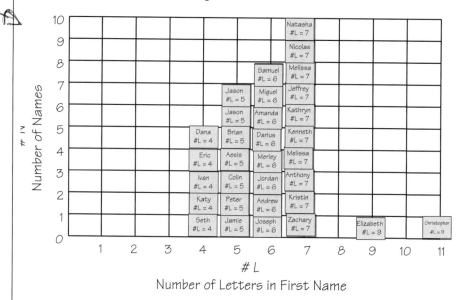

Number of Names — # N

L
Number of Letters in First Name

Figure 9: First Names *graph using self-adhesive notes*

In first grade, we introduce a graphing protocol that is different in *Math Trailblazers* than in some other programs. When making bar graphs, we encourage students to create their bars along the vertical lines in the graph rather than in the spaces between the lines. (See Figures 6, 7, and 9.) This does not affect the data or the reading of the graph. Rather it prepares students for making point graphs, where data points are plotted at the intersection of lines extending from the horizontal and vertical axes.

To assist students with this, we have created a special graph paper for making bar graphs. A version of this graph paper is shown in Figure 10. The dark vertical grid lines across the page are where the data for the manipulated variable is plotted. These lines are surrounded on both sides by a pair of dashed guide lines. Students make bars by coloring in the space on either side of the dark vertical lines. The result is a straight bar that is centered along a vertical line. The values for the manipulated variable are indicated on the horizontal axis directly below each bar.

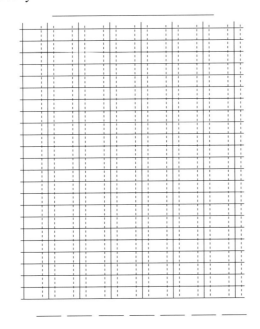

Figure 10: *TIMS bar graph paper*

The benefit of making bar graphs in this manner is most apparent in third grade as students make the transition to creating point graphs. To simplify students' initial attempt at creating a point graph, they first graph a data set as a bar graph and then convert the bar graph to a point graph. This is shown in Figure 11.

Figure 11: *Transition from bar graphs to point graphs in third grade*

Point Graphs: Fitting Lines and Curves

With point graphs, the data are plotted at the junction of the values of each variable. Once the data are plotted, we look for patterns. If the data points form a line or close to a line, we try to fit a line through the points. If the data form a curve, we try to fit a smooth curve through the points.

Figure 11 shows a graph in which the data points lie exactly on a straight line. Fitting a line to these data points is simply a matter of laying down a ruler and connecting the points.

For most experiments, we cannot expect the data to be so precise. In these experiments, the data may lie close to, but not exactly on a straight line. The "zigzags" in the data are due to experimental error. (See the TIMS Tutor: *Estimation, Accuracy, and Error.*) To average the error, one fits a line that comes as close to the data points as possible even though the line may not pass through any of these points. To assure a good fit, you would like as many points above the curve as below. You do not want to force the line through two points while missing the third by a mile. It is better to miss them all but come close to all than be too far from any one point.

As shown on *The Bouncing Ball* graph in Figure 5, you can fit a line to the data points, not by using some complicated statistical procedure, but simply "by eye." The student uses a clear ruler or a thread and moves it around until it fits the data points as closely as possible. This best-fit line is useful for minimizing error and making predictions.

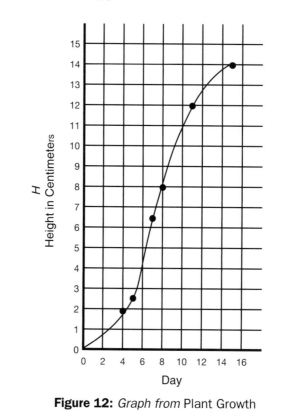

Figure 12: *Graph from* Plant Growth

Of course, not all experimental relationships result in data that yields straight lines on graphs. In *Math Trailblazers,* we also explore data that exhibits other kinds of patterns. Figure 12 shows the graph from a fourth-grade experiment, *Plant Growth,* where the data shows a pattern, but not a straight line.

When you can fit a smooth curve through the data points, you have uncovered one of nature's secrets—that the variables are related, that there is a predictable pattern to the data. We are then not restricted only to our specific data points, but can now use the pattern to predict what the value of the responding variable will be for any value of the manipulated variable.

Predictions from Point Graphs: Interpolation and Extrapolation

A major goal of mathematics and science is to find patterns in data and to use the patterns to make predictions. Interpolating and extrapolating on a point graph are two ways to do this.

Using the graph to find data points that lie between those in your data table is called **interpolation.** *Inter* means between or among. The simplest situation is when the pattern of data points produces a straight line. In the graph in Figure 5, the student interpolated to predict that a ball dropped from 60 cm would bounce about 32 cm. Note that in Figure 5 the student showed how she made her interpolation by starting at 60 cm on the horizontal axis, drawing a line (with arrows) up to the best-fit line, and then drawing a horizontal line to find the corresponding value of the bounce height—about 32 cm.

Extrapolation is an attempt to predict information beyond the last data point. *Extra* means outside or beyond. To extrapolate, we must extend the line into a region where there is no data. You can do this easily by laying a ruler on the straight line, extending the line, and reading off your prediction. In Figure 5, the student extrapolated to predict that a ball that bounced 80 cm was dropped from a height of about 144 cm. Here, the student began with values on the vertical axis (the bounce height) and predicted a value on the horizontal axis (the drop height). It is possible to interpolate and extrapolate in either of two directions: from values on the horizontal axis to values on the vertical axis or vice versa.

Having used these techniques to make predictions, it is important to have the children check their predictions experimentally and see how close their new data comes to the curve. This is one of the joys of science—to see that nature is often regular and predictable and that you can make predictions that come true! Checking predictions, though time-consuming, is worthwhile because it reinforces connections between mathematical abstractions and the real world.

Phase 4: Analyzing the Data

After making the graph, students explored the relationship between the variables in four ways: with the physical materials, in the picture, in the data table, and in the graph. The last phase of the TIMS Laboratory Method is the analysis of the entire situation, where students explore the relationship quantitatively and represent it symbolically (i.e., with numbers).

> *A major goal of mathematics and science is to find patterns in data and to use the patterns to make predictions. Interpolating and extrapolating on a point graph are two ways to do this.*

One way to structure this analysis is to ask a series of questions. The questions usually begin on the literal level: *Did the tallest container hold the most marshmallows? How high did the tennis ball bounce when dropped from 60 cm?* More demanding questions require prediction: *How many marshmallows would two bowls hold? If a ball bounced to 45 cm, what height was it dropped from?* Asking what would happen if one of the fixed variables is changed can build a broader understanding of the situation: *What would happen if we used large instead of miniature marshmallows? What would happen if we used a Super ball instead of a tennis ball?* This quantitative analysis of the data is one place in *Math Trailblazers* where students regularly practice and reinforce arithmetic and other math skills.

The end of the investigation may be a completely satisfying answer to the original question, but, more often than not, the end is another question that can lead to further investigations. *Marshmallows and Containers,* for example, might lead to an investigation of the liquid capacities of other short and tall containers. After an initial experiment with tennis balls in *The Bouncing Ball,* children carry out an investigation using another type of ball and compare the results from the two experiments.

Picture, Table, Graph, and Questions: Putting It Together

Each of the four phases previously described may require one or more class periods. In addition, you may spend time becoming familiar with the equipment at the beginning and on further experiments at the end. Thus, a lab is an extended activity that may last a week or even longer. This is much longer than a typical mathematics or science lesson, but there are significant benefits.

First, the four phases simplify the scientific method enough for children to use, but not so much that it fails to resemble what scientists do. Identifying variables, drawing pictures, measuring, organizing data in tables, graphing data, and looking for patterns are part of many scientists' work. Students are thus inducted via this method into the authentic practice of science.

The method fosters children's sense-making. Children handle numbers they have generated themselves by counting or measuring, numbers that are thus meaningful to them. As they deal with experimental error, they develop number sense and estimation skills. As they look for patterns in their tables and graphs, they make sense of the numbers before them. Arithmetic in context is more understandable.

The approach is multimodal, which has benefits for both individual students and heterogeneous groups of students. The multiple representations of relationships between the variables permit problems to be solved in more than one way, allowing different students to approach the same content in ways they understand. The container that holds the most marshmallows, for example, can be found from the graph, from the data table, or from the marshmallows themselves. A prediction about a bounce height might be obtained by extrapolating on the graph or by extending patterns in the data table, and can then be verified using the apparatus. Students can compare these various approaches, thus helping them make connections within mathematics as well as between the informal mathematics of their everyday experience and more formal mathematics.

Identifying variables, drawing pictures, measuring, organizing data in tables, graphing data, and looking for patterns are part of many scientists' work. Students are thus inducted via this method into the authentic practice of science.

Mathematics in Context

Two principles underlie the TIMS Laboratory Method. First, an investigation should begin within the children's own experiences. Children use objects from their everyday lives to investigate a familiar situation. Children's everyday knowledge, like a scientist's theory, provides a framework for interpreting the results of the investigation. Without that framework, the investigation would remain hollow and meaningless.

The second principle is that an investigation should also transcend children's everyday experiences. The exploration must go somewhere; it must lead the children both to a better understanding of the immediate situation and to improved skills, understandings, habits, and attitudes. The concepts can then be extended and transferred to new contexts.

Balancing these principles requires teacher judgment. The key is to enable students to follow their own ideas, but with the intention that those ideas will lead somewhere. How much scaffolding to provide, how much to guide students in directions that are fruitful rather than sterile, must be decided by the teacher in context. The goal is that students should advance not only in skill and understanding, but also in autonomy and perseverance. Just how much structure to provide along the way is perhaps a teacher's most important and difficult job.

The TIMS Laboratory Method helps children connect their everyday experiences with formal mathematics. As they investigate everyday situations quantitatively, children handle variables, explore relationships between variables, master a few powerful techniques for representing these relationships, and use these multiple representations to generate a wide variety of problem solutions. By beginning and ending in familiar situations, the abstractions of mathematics are linked to children's everyday knowledge. As students master this method, they become increasingly autonomous and flexible in its application. Then we can truly say they understand the fundamentals of *doing* science.

References

Archambault, Reginald D. (ed.), *John Dewey on Education: Selected Writings.* Modern Library, 1964.

Bruner, Jerome S. "The Course of Cognitive Growth." *American Psychologist* 19 (1), pp. 1–15, 1964.

Dewey, John. "Science as Subject-Matter and as Method." *Science* 31 (787), pp. 121–7, January 28, 1910.

Goldberg, Howard, and F. David Boulanger. "Science for Elementary School Teachers: A Quantitative Approach." *American Journal of Physics* 49 (2), pp. 120–124, 1981.

Goldberg, Howard, and Philip Wagreich. "Focus on Integrating Science and Math." *Science and Children* 2 (5), pp. 22–24, 1989.

Goldberg, Howard, and Philip Wagreich. "A Model Integrated Mathematics and Science Program for the Elementary School." *International Journal of Educational Research* 14 (2), pp. 193–214, 1990.

Hiebert, James. "A Theory of Developing Competence with Written Mathematical Symbols." *Educational Studies in Mathematics* 19, pp. 333–355, 1988.

Isaacs, Andrew C., and Catherine Randall Kelso. "Pictures, Tables, Graphs, and Questions: Statistical Processes." *Teaching Children Mathematics* 2 (6), pp. 340–345, 1996.

Isaacs, Andrew C., Philip Wagreich, and Martin Gartzman. "The Quest for Integration: School Mathematics and Science." *American Journal of Education* 106 (1), pp. 179–206, 1997.

Lesh, Richard, Thomas Post, and Merlyn Behr. "Representations and Translations among Representation in Mathematics Learning and Problem Solving." In C. Janvier (ed.), *Problems of Representation in the Teaching and Learning of Mathematics.* Lawrence Erlbaum Associates, Hillsdale, NJ, 1987.

National Research Council. *National Science Education Standards.* National Academy Press, Washington, DC, 1996.

Silver, Edward. "Using Conceptual and Procedural Knowledge: A Focus on Relationships." In J. Hiebert (ed.), *Conceptual and Procedural Knowledge: The Case of Mathematics.* Lawrence Erlbaum Associates, Hillsdale, NJ, 1986.

The Concept of Length

Units

In dealing with scientific problems, we must often know such things as the location of an object, the distance between objects, how tall or wide an object is, or how fast it is moving. Central to all these ideas is the concept of length. In this tutor, we shall examine the various disguises in which length can appear.

First, however, we must note the messy problem of units. The kinds of units chosen for length were for a long time quite arbitrary. The cubit, used by several ancient civilizations, was the length of a forearm between the tip of the middle finger and the elbow. The fathom was the width of a Viking sailor's embrace. (Fathom that!)

The foot was a convenient length defined as the length of a person's foot. Of course, everyone has a different-sized foot, so if we want to use, say, the king's foot as a standard, we will have to mark it permanently; we cannot very well lug the king around! Since the king is the ruler of the land, it was both rational and proper to call this marker a ruler as well. To show students the chaos caused by not having a standard length, have them measure the length of their desks in cubits or the width of the room in feet with each child using his or her own body measurements. You will have as many different values as measurers.

> *The foot was a convenient length defined as the length of a person's foot. Of course, everyone has a different-sized foot, so if we want to use, say, the king's foot as a standard, we will have to mark it permanently; we cannot very well lug the king around! Since the king is the ruler of the land, it was both rational and proper to call this marker a ruler as well.*

Nonstandard Units

At first, we have the children measure length using nonstandard units, often links. A link is shown in Figure 1 along with a chain of links. The measurement of the object shown is $4\frac{1}{2}$ links. The reasons we go to links are: (1) to make counting the unit length easy and (2) to keep the numbers manageable. Rather than dealing with hundreds of cm, we can count 50 links. And to count a link is easy since they are so large.

By alternating link colors (2 reds, 2 whites, 2 reds, etc.), one can make the counting even easier by skip counting by 2s. If you want to have the children skip count by 5s, then have a chain with 5 blues, 5 yellows, 5 blues, etc.

With links, it is also easy to round off to $\frac{1}{2}$ link as shown in Figure 1. If the edge we are measuring is near the middle, then the length is $4\frac{1}{2}$ links. If shorter, then the length is 4 links; if longer, the length is 5 links.

$4\frac{1}{2}$ links

Figure 1: *Links*

The Metric System

Of course, links are not a commonly used standard of measure. In the United States, it is feet. Unfortunately, many objects are smaller than a foot. This means one must subdivide the standard unit. For some miserable reason, the smaller unit, the inch, is $\frac{1}{12}$ of a foot. Who likes to divide by 12? So, the French scientific community at the time of the French Revolution (c. 1790) chose as the standard unit of length a distance that they called a meter.

It was chosen so that 10^7 (10 million) metersticks laid end to end would just fit between the North Pole and the equator, as shown in Figure 2. A platinum-iridium rod was constructed with two marks a meter apart and stored in a vault near Paris. Every meterstick, albeit indirectly, comes from this standard. Having defined the meter, the French were smart enough to define all subsequent subdivisions of the meter as integral powers of ten. The foot is divided into $\frac{1}{12}$s and $\frac{1}{48}$s, and other equally horrible numbers; for the meter, the divisions are $\frac{1}{10}$s, $\frac{1}{100}$s, and $\frac{1}{1000}$s. We shall now explore this point further.

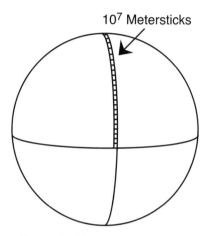

Figure 2: *Metersticks from the North Pole to the equator*

For measuring ordinary objects in the classroom, the meter is divided into three other units; the millimeter, the centimeter, and the decimeter (although the latter is rarely used). Without being specific as to the size of each unit, we can order them using the greater than (>) or less than (<) sign. Starting with the smallest, we have:

1 millimeter < 1 centimeter < 1 decimeter < 1 meter.

Reversing the order and starting with the largest, we have:

1 meter > 1 decimeter > 1 centimeter > 1 millimeter.

It is important that students know at least this much before going on to more exact relations.

The key to the subdivision of the meter is the prefix *milli*. Milli is related to the word mile. Mile was the distance it took a Roman soldier to step off 1000 paces, a pace being two steps. Since an average pace is approximately 5 feet (try it and see), a mile would be approximately 5000 feet. The crucial point is the number 1000 as related to the word mile. Milli is the prefix for "$\frac{1}{1000}$ of." Thus, a millimeter is one-thousandth of a meter. There are 1000 millimeters in a meter just as there are 1000 paces in a mile. In each case, we have a subunit that is one-thousandth of the main unit. The word mile is to remind us that there are 1000 paces in a mile. The word millimeter is to remind us that there are 1000 millimeters in a meter. One should try to picture this in one's mind. Millimeters are tiny; it takes a lot of them to make up any macroscopic length. (By macroscopic, we are referring to something one can see unaided versus microscopic where one would need a magnifying glass or microscope to see it.) On the other hand, because a meter is large, a millimeter is usually a fraction of most lengths one would measure in the lab. Thus, it is reasonable that a third-grader knows how to measure the length of his thumb as 3 cm or 30 mm, but not as 0.03 m.

How are mm, cm, dm, and m related? Let's start with the smallest and see how many mm are in a cm, a dm, and a meter.

1 centimeter contains 10 mm;
1 decimeter contains 100 mm;
1 meter contains 1000 mm.

Based on these relationships, we should be able to figure out how many centimeters are in a decimeter or in a meter. Here, however, the French have made it easy for us; the prefix for each word gives the answer away. *Centi* stands for 100th and *deci* stands for one-tenth. Thus one centimeter is one-hundredth of a meter; there are 100 cm in a meter. A decimeter is one-tenth of a meter; there are 10 dm in a meter. What this boils down to then is the following:

1 decimeter contains 10 cm;
1 meter contains 100 cm;
1 meter contains 10 dm.

Everything depends upon the size of the meter. Once that is fixed (by our rod in Paris), the sizes of all other metric units are determined.

Measuring Length

The simplest way to get started in the metric system is to count, using a meterstick, the number of mm or cm (and if they do not equal fractions, dm or meters) in a given length. Say we measure the width of the sheet of paper in cm. Then depending upon the accuracy of the meterstick (a cheap one could be off a bit) and the judgment of the student, one can see that there are between 21 and 22 cm across the page. If you stick to cm, then for students who are not yet comfortable with fractions or decimals, this is all you can say. As they begin to learn decimals, the children can determine the width as 21.6 cm. However, you can get still better accuracy even without decimals by going to mm instead of cm. Here, all one has to be able to do is count beyond 100. Thus, the width is 216 mm. In fact, one of the neat things about the metric system is that you can always choose a set of units to obtain almost any accuracy you want without going to fractions or decimals. On the other hand, you can purposely choose units that will give decimal or fractional answers. As we just saw, in cm units, the width of the page is a decimal, 21.6 cm. We could have asked for the width in meters. Since the width is less than a meter, we are dealing with fractions. In this case, the width is 0.216 meters or roughly $\frac{1}{5}$ of a meter. Clearly, there is great potential in the metric system for teaching math and linking this to scientific measurement.

With regard to addition, when adding numbers they must always have the same units. For example:

(a) 5 cm + 6 m = ? This is a "no-no"; the units are mixed.

(b) 5 cm + 600 cm = 605 cm. This is okay—we are adding the same units.

(c) 8 mm + 50 cm = ? We should convert the cm to mm and get:

8 mm + 500 mm = 508 mm.

Thus, if we ask a student to measure the length of his arm by separately measuring his hand (say in mm), his lower arm (say in cm), his upper arm (say in decimeters), and then adding them, he will first have to convert to a set of consistent units that he or she can handle. If you do not choose to have the students work with fractions, the students can change the units to millimeters as shown above. If you want to give the students a chance to work on decimal fractions, they can change the units to centimeters.

$$.8 + 50 \text{ cm} = 50.8 \text{ cm}$$

This brings us to another point—how to use a ruler. At first it seems quite apparent: just place the end of the ruler at the end of the object and read the length directly (Figure 3). However, a better test of whether students really understand how to use a ruler as well as a test of their ability to subtract is to place the object in the center of the ruler. Clearly, the length of the object should not depend upon its position vis-a-vis the ruler, but we have found that many young people (and even a few at our university) have trouble understanding how to find the length in the latter case.

Figure 3: *How to use a ruler*

Since we do not always have a ruler handy, a few "natural" rulers might be fun to discuss and use. For example, say the length of a person's upper thumb from knuckle to tip is generally about 3 cm while his spread-out fingers span about 20 cm, as shown in Figure 4. Either can now be used to measure the length of an object. Of course, as shown in Figure 3, there is the foot, a convenient measure for stepping off distances. This person's foot, without his shoes, is 23 cm or about 9 inches. Anyway, you should have the children measure a few objects using natural rulers and have them compare their results with that of a meterstick.

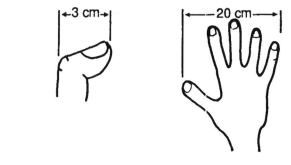

Figure 4: *Natural rulers*

The Concept of Area

Defining Area

The area of a shape or object can be defined in everyday words as the "amount of stuff" needed to cover the shape. Common uses of the concept of area are finding the amount of tile needed to cover a floor, the amount of wallpaper needed to cover a wall, and the amount of paint needed to cover a ceiling. You can often directly compare areas of different objects without measurement. For example, if one piece of carpet completely covers another, we know the top piece has more area.

Just as with length, to measure area we need a unit of measure. Many different units have been used throughout history. The acre is still used as a measure of land area, along with square miles. The square inch, square foot, and square yard are area units in the English system. For example, square yards is the unit of area measure for carpeting in the United States. Most of the world and all scientists use the metric system. For the classroom, the most frequent metric unit of area is the square centimeter. It is defined as the amount of flat surface within a square that is 1 cm on a side. This is illustrated in Figure 1.

Figure 1: *Units of length and area*

A note on terminology: Scientists often use the term "centimeters squared" in place of "square centimeters." This may be due to the fact that one way of writing the symbol for square centimeters is cm^2. We prefer to use sq cm for square centimeters. On occasion, the use of cm^2 can confuse students. Since 7 squared is 49, they may reason that 7 centimeters squared is 49 square centimeters. Unfortunately, the symbols $7\ cm^2$ and $(7\ cm)^2$ sound the same when spoken, if you say cm^2 as "centimeters squared." For that reason, we stick to "square centimeters" and sq cm.

Measuring Area by Counting Square Centimeters–Part I

One way to find an area is to count the number of sq cm needed to cover a surface. To count the number of sq cm, you can construct unit squares within the desired area. For example, the rectangle in Figure 2 is 3 cm wide and 4 cm high. You can find its area by completing the following steps.

Figure 2: *A rectangle*

1. Draw a grid of lines so that each square in the grid is 1 cm on a side. (Figure 3.)

Figure 3: *A rectangle tiled with centimeter squares*

2. Count the number of sq cm enclosed in the rectangle. (Figure 4.)

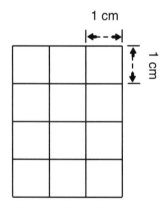

Figure 4: *Counting square centimeters*

There are 12 sq cm in a rectangle that is 3 cm wide and 4 cm high. So the area of the rectangle is 12 sq cm.

Why Not Use Length × Width?

You may be wondering why we did not use the formula *length × width* to find the area of the rectangle. After all, 4 × 3 = 12. The formula works. Indeed, the reason the formula works is precisely because the rectangle can be represented by an ordered array of squares, 3 squares in each row and 4 rows of 3 squares each.

In any ordered array, you can count the total number of elements by multiplying the number of rows by the number of columns. Figure 5 shows 24 apples arrayed in 6 rows. Instead of counting each apple, we take advantage of the array and multiply 4 × 6 to obtain 24 apples. Using the length times width formula does give the area of a rectangle, but we delay teaching the formula for two reasons. First, we want students to build a mental image of the concept of area. Premature use of the formula for area of rectangles leads to rote use of the formula without understanding. In particular, many students are led to believe that the definition of area is length times width and that this formula works for any shape. While there are formulas for the areas of rectangles, circles, and other geometric shapes, there is no formula for the area of a leaf!

Premature use of the formula for area of rectangles leads to rote use of the formula without understanding. In particular, many students are led to believe that the definition of area is length times width and that this formula works for any shape.

Figure 5: *An array of apples*

Furthermore, using the formula can be harder than counting square centimeters when the sides of the rectangle are not whole numbers.

For example, what is the area of the rectangle, $3\frac{1}{2}$ cm wide and $2\frac{1}{2}$ cm high, shown in Figure 6? We asked a group of sixth-graders to find the area of this rectangle. Even though the students knew the length × width formula, 80 percent could not find the area. They were not able to multiply fractions. It is likely that these students would have been able to find the area by counting sq cm, as we shall see in the next section.

Figure 6: *Another rectangle*

Counting Square Centimeters–Part II

In Figure 7, we set up the square cm grid. To keep track of the sq cm, we first number the whole square centimeters. There are six whole sq cm in the rectangle. Next, we turn to the fractions of sq cm. Students can manipulate sq cm pieces of paper to complete the task. The two half sq cm on the right make up the seventh sq cm and so both are numbered 7. The two half sq cm along the bottom make up the eighth sq cm and are numbered 8. One half sq cm and one fourth square cm make up the remaining areas. The area is $8\frac{3}{4}$ sq cm.

1	2	3	7	
4	5	6	7	
8	8	$\frac{1}{2}$	$\frac{1}{4}$	

Figure 7: *Whole and part centimeter squares*

Most students can count squares to find area—no multiplication is necessary. But what if there is no "order" to the figure? The shape in Figure 8 has no unique length or width; the formula *length* × *width* does not apply. The only way to find the area is to count the number of sq cm contained within the boundary of the figure.

Figure 8: *A blob*

First, construct a sq cm grid to fit over the shape of Figure 8. It's often easier if the horizontal and vertical boundary of the grid each touch the figure at one point. The grid should extend beyond the figure. The completed grid would look similar to the grid in Figure 9.

Figure 9: *Finding area by counting centimeter squares*

Next, count and number the whole sq cm. There are four. Now estimate which fractions of grid squares add together to form one square centimeter. For example, square centimeter number 5 is a big piece upper left and a little piece farther to the right. Number 6 is two pieces, a big piece on the left and a smaller piece in the lower right corner. Square centimeter number 7 is two pieces, each around a half square cm. Square centimeter 8 is made up of a $\frac{3}{4}$ and $\frac{1}{4}$ square cm piece. So is square centimeter 9. Three pieces make up square centimeter 10, two half square cm pieces and a smaller piece to the right.

Now all the shape is covered and counted in square centimeters. The shape has an area of about 10 square cm. While the method does not give an exact area, the result is usually close. And the primary benefit of this method is that students will have the opportunity to "see" area, aiding their understanding of this important mathematical concept.

Surface Area

Often, students who understand area quite well seem to have difficulty with the notion of surface area. One problem may be that they were led to believe that area and surface area are two different things. This is not surprising, since we use two different words. However, area and surface area are identical; a measure of the number of sq cm (or square units) needed to cover an object. Customarily, the term "surface area" is usually used for three-dimensional shapes and "area" for two-dimensional shapes.

To measure the surface area of a three-dimensional object, we count the number of square centimeters needed to cover it, just as with flat shapes. In some cases, this is easy as in the case of a rectangular box (since it is made up of flat pieces). Another easy example can be made by taking a sheet of flat paper and rolling it to make a cylinder (Figure 10). As long as the edges do not overlap, the surface area of the outside of the cylinder will be the same as the flat piece of paper. Another way to find the area of a cylinder is to cover it with one square centimeter "stamps." As with flat shapes, you may need some fractional pieces. With more complex shapes, like a sphere, it is hard to get an exact measurement of the surface area, but we can approximate the surface area by covering the object with square centimeters or smaller squares.

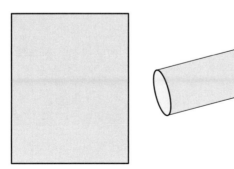

Figure 10: *Paper flat and rolled*

The Concept of Volume

Defining Volume

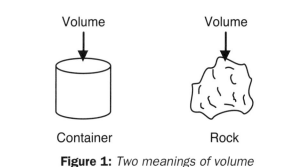

Figure 1: *Two meanings of volume*

Figure 1 shows a container and a rock. The space that the container surrounds (and is occupied by air) and the space that the rock takes up (and is occupied by elements such as oxygen, silicon, and aluminum) are both called **volume.**[1] The concept of volume is tricky. Two objects (like our container and rock) might occupy the same volume but contain totally different amounts of matter. Children often confuse the amount of matter, which we call mass, with the space occupied, which we now know is volume. Thus children tell us that a "heavy" object has more volume than a "light" object even though the latter may actually occupy more space. Indeed, volume is so oversimplified in the elementary schools that many eighth-graders we asked thought of volume as length × width × height, no matter what the shape of the object. Others told us that volume was length squared. Misconceptions such as these are a result of a curriculum that emphasizes memorization of formulas without attention to the conceptual foundations of volume.

Figure 2: *Units of length, area, and volume*

---

[1]Sometimes, the space inside a container is called the capacity of the container. For simplicity, we prefer to use one term, volume, to denote both "space inside" and "space occupied."

Units

As with length and area, if we wish to measure volume, we need to decide on a unit of measure. In the metric system, the metric unit of length is the centimeter (Figure 2a), and the unit of area is the square centimeter (the extent of the plane surface that is bounded by a square 1 cm on a side) (Figure 2b), so it is not unreasonable that we take as our unit of volume the space occupied within a cube that is 1 cm on a side (Figure 2c). The volume occupied by such a cube is defined as 1 cubic centimeter whether that volume is occupied by a solid object (Figure 3a) or by empty space (Figure 3b).

Figure 3: *Full and empty cubic centimeter*

Unlike area, it is very hard to divide an object up and count cubic cm. We can't trace the volume the way we trace areas on square cm paper. In theory we could slice it up into 1 cubic cm pieces, but this process will destroy the object. Therefore, learning to understand and measure volume can be more difficult than understanding and measuring area.

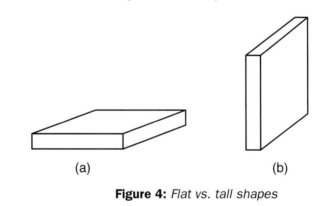

Figure 4: *Flat vs. tall shapes*

In everyday life, we are accustomed to a variety of other units of volume measure. Gallons, quarts, pints, and fluid ounces are one set of units, usually used to measure the capacity of a container. Cubic feet and cubic inches are also frequently used. For example, in the United States, air conditioners are often rated on the volume of space they can cool, measured in cubic feet. The remainder of this tutor uses metric units of measure, but many of the same underlying ideas apply to any system of measure.

Problem of Dimensionality

Another great difficulty in understanding volume is that the concept deals with three dimensions. As Piaget pointed out, it is much easier, and therefore usual, for a child to focus on one dimension. They will decide that a tall object has lots of volume because they only focus on the height and fail to take into account the other two dimensions to make a proper estimate. In Figure 4, the two objects have the same volume, but because (a) is flat and (b) is upright, young children will tell you that (b) has the greater volume.

Volume is an extremely important scientific variable. The way it is related to area and to mass and the manner in which it may change with time are all intrinsic to every area of scientific investigation. It is well worth our time to do a good job on volume.

Measuring Volume–Early Activities

Kindergarten students explore volume by filling containers with rice, water, pasta, sand, or beans. Another way to deal with volume in the primary grades is to have the children make figures out of a set of cubes. In first and second grade, we usually use connecting cubes that are about $\frac{3}{4}$-inch on a side. At the end of second grade, we start using standard centimeter linking cubes. For example, you can give each child 10 cubes and ask him or her to make a figure whose volume is 10 cubic units. You will get a variety of shapes, all of which have the same volume. This will begin to impress upon the children the idea that many different shapes can have the same volume.

Another centimeter cube activity to build the children's understanding at this level involves building shapes with different volumes. Give each child a few (3–10) centimeter cubes. Have each child make a shape with his or her centimeter cubes. Then have the children sort themselves into groups according to the volume of their shapes.

You can bring in some simple solid shapes, like a piece of chalk, a match box, a pile of washers, etc., and have the children make figures out of cubic units that approximate the volume (size and shape) of these objects. In this way, they can estimate the volume of the original object by keeping track of the number of cubic cm they used. An example is given in Figure 5 of a marking pen and cubic cms linked together to make a shape of approximately the same volume.

Figure 5: *A marker and a cm cube model*

> Another great difficulty in understanding volume is that the concept deals with three dimensions. As Piaget pointed out, it is much easier, and therefore usual, for a child to focus on one dimension. They will decide that a tall object has lots of volume because they only focus on the height and fail to take into account the other two dimensions to make a proper estimate.

The next step would be for you to make several cube models and have children count the number of unit cubes in each. Pictures of three typical models, each a bit more complex than the previous, are given in Figures 6a, b, and c. There are two potential problems here. The children may confuse surface area and volume and count the faces of the cubes calling each face a cubic cm. A subtle problem, exemplified by Figure 6c, is when there are one or more "hidden" cubic centimeters buried inside the figure.

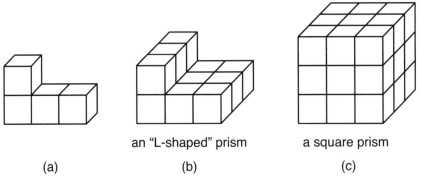

an "L-shaped" prism   a square prism

(a)   (b)   (c)

Figure 6: *Shapes made from centimeter cubes*

We want the children to learn to be systematic, look for patterns, and use simple addition and multiplication to count the cubic cm.

A very basic problem is learning to count the cubic centimeters properly. It is relatively easy to pick up 12 cubic centimeters, make a figure, and say the volume is 12 cc. It is quite another to hold a centimeter cube figure like that in Figure 6b, turn it over, and keep track of all the centimeters. We want the children to learn to be systematic, look for patterns, and use simple addition and multiplication to count the cubes. For example, Figure 6a is easy since it is only 4 cc. Figure 6b is made up of three layers, each of which is exactly like Figure 6a. Your students can then use addition to see that the volume is 4 cc + 4 cc + 4 cc, or use multiplication, 3 × 4 cc. Likewise in Figure 6c, it would be difficult to find and keep track of each cubic cm. A systematic approach allows the children to solve the problem easily. There are 9 cc in the top layer, and there are three layers; therefore the volume is

$$9 \text{ cc} + 9 \text{ cc} + 9 \text{ cc} = 27 \text{ cc}.$$

Note that Figures 6b and 6c are labeled as prisms. This means they are made of a number of identical layers. Figure 6b has three "L-shaped" layers and 6c has three "square-shaped" layers. It is important to know that these are prisms. Otherwise, there might be some hidden cubes behind the object that we cannot see, or there might be missing cubes "inside" the object.

A more difficult skill is finding the volume of an object directly from a perspective drawing, without actually building the object. You can develop this kind of spatial visualization skill by first having students build cube models from pictures. Students as early as first grade can build simple models from pictures. As the models get more complex, this task can become quite difficult. One important subtlety is that pictures such as 6b and 6c do not give enough information to reconstruct the model. For example, there might be some unexpected cubes hidden behind the model in Figure 6c (see Figure 7).

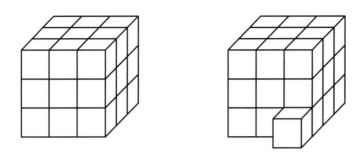

Front View   Rear View

Figure 7: *Front and rear views of Figure 6c*

For example, in Figure 7 we see what appears to be a 3 × 3 × 3 cm cube from the front, but when we view the model from the rear, we see there is an "extra" cube stuck on.

Finally, and hardest of all, you can ask the children to try to draw a figure with a given number of cubic centimeters. It is very hard for anyone to draw a cube, and a figure with several cubic centimeters is harder still. Nevertheless, it is worth a try since doing so will help them improve their spatial perception and will force them to think in three dimensions.

Let's review the four steps we just described:

1. Make figures out of a given number of centimeter cubes.
2. Count cubic centimeters in a cube model.
3. Count cubic centimeters in the drawing of a cube model—usually prisms.
4. Draw a figure with a given number of cubic centimeters.

This discussion covers volumes of objects made from cubes. The most important tool, however, for determining volume will be the graduated cylinder which we will discuss in the section after next. But first we want to talk about how to calculate the volume of prisms.

Calculating Volume—An Upper Grade Exercise

The volume of a rectangular prism made of cubic centimeters can be found using multiplication. The number of cubic centimeters in the top layer is just the product of 3 × 6 since there are 3 rows of 6 cubic cm (see Figure 8). Thus, in each layer there are 18 cc. Because there are 5 layers, the total number of cubic centimeters is 5 × 18 cc = 90 cc. As often written in math books, this type of counting is expressed as

$$V = l \times w \times h.$$

You should interpret this as the number of cubic cm in the top layer (given by the value of $l \times w$) times the number of layers (given by the value of h).

Figure 8: *A rectangular prism*

If the top layer is not rectangular but the figure is a right solid (sides perpendicular to top and bottom), then we can still find the volume by the above technique. The formula *length × width × height* will no longer work since the layers are not rectangular. However, since each horizontal slice has the same shape (see Figure 9), all we have to do is find the number of cubic cm in the top layer and multiply this by the number of layers. To find the number of cubic centimeters in the top layer, we have to find the number of square centimeters in the top surface, since each square centimeter of the surface is attached to a cubic centimeter in the top layer. Thus, if in Figure 9 by counting square cm we find that there are 22 sq cm on the top surface, then there must be 22 cubic cm in the top layer and in each subsequent layer. The total volume, then, is:

$$\frac{22 \text{ cubic cm}}{1 \text{ layer}} \times 5 \text{ layers} = 110 \text{ cubic cm}$$

for the object shown in Figure 9. As a general formula we have:

$$V = A \times h,$$

where the area A of the top tells us the number of cc in the top layer, and the value of h tells us the number of layers. Children should not just memorize each formula; they should understand what is behind the formulas.

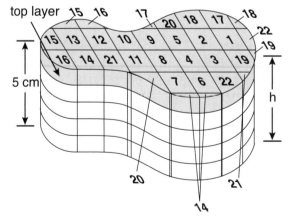

Figure 9: *A right solid*

When using a formula like $l \times w \times h$, the old bugaboo of units reappears. Since l, w, and h are all measured in centimeters, it is tempting to say that the units of volume are centimeters cubed written as $(\text{cm})^3$. And indeed this is what is often done in scientific texts. Yes, it's technically correct to write $(\text{cm})^3$ or cm^3, but again it can be misleading for children just as "centimeter squared" can be misleading for area. If we say a volume is 7 centimeters cubed, is that $(7\text{ cm})^3 = 343$ cc? We can avoid this confusion by writing what we mean; that the volume is 7 cubic centimeters or 7 cc.

Figure 10: *Graduated cylinders*

Clearly, the ability to calculate volume is rather limited to certain special shapes. An irregularly shaped container or object will require a different approach.

A Volume Measurer: The Graduated Cylinder

We have seen that a ruler which is calibrated in cm can be used to measure length. There is no comparably simple device for measuring area, but there is one for measuring volume. It is the graduated cylinder calibrated in cubic centimeters. Two graduated cylinders are shown in Figure 10. They can be made of glass or Pyrex, both of which are breakable, or plastic, which is not. The cylinder most suitable for classroom use would be calibrated in 1 cc, 5 cc, or 10 cc divisions and have a capacity of 100 to 150 cc. When filled with a liquid (usually water) or a fluid substance like sand or salt, one can read the volume of the material off the side of the graduated cylinder. One cannot use this device to directly measure the volume of a number of marbles since the marbles piled in the cylinder will leave an unknown volume of air spaces between them. This is illustrated in Figure 11b. As we shall see in the next section, we can find the volume of solid objects like marbles by the method of displacement. The rest of this section will discuss using the graduated cylinder for finding the volume of liquid, particularly water.

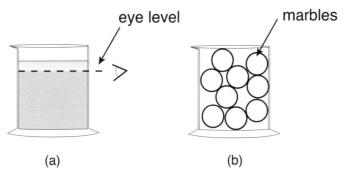

Figure 11: *Liquid and marbles in graduated cylinder*

To read the volume of water in a graduated cylinder, your eyes must be level with the liquid, as shown in Figure 11a. Since water is pulled up at the sides of the cylinder into a curved surface called a meniscus, one must measure the water level at the center of the cylinder. This is done by using the lower of the two lines that one sees (Figure 12) when looking at the water from the side. The top line is due to the pulled up water and should be ignored. (This phenomenon tends to be more pronounced when using glass rather than plastic graduated cylinders.)

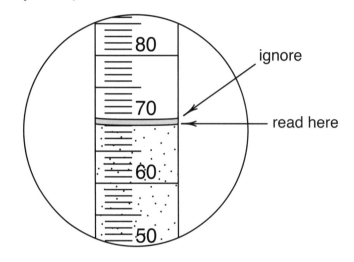

Figure 12: *The meniscus*

One must be careful about what one puts into a graduated cylinder. A tall, narrow one will generally have 1 cc divisions and thus can be used for accurate measurements. The trouble is, that because it is narrow, you can use only small objects. Many a time a student has misjudged the size of an object and found it stuck in the narrow cylinder never to come out again.

Chalk off one cylinder. A good general size that we like is one about 4 cm in diameter with a 150 cc capacity and made of plastic. The divisions are usually 5 or 10 cc. We shall discuss in the next section how to use a "big" graduated cylinder to measure the volume of small objects.

Many graduated cylinders that you purchase will have several different scales along the sides. This is due to the diversity of units for liquid measurements. Many cylinders will have a scale for fluid ounces and another for milliliters. The metric unit of volume is the milliliter, which is defined to be 1 cubic cm:

$$1 \text{ ml} = 1 \text{ cc}.$$

The liter is often encountered in daily life (for example, soda bottles are often 1 or 2 liters). It is exactly 1000 ml.

One of the first exercises the children can do with a graduated cylinder is simply to fill the cylinder to a specified level—10 cc, for example. An eyedropper is handy for getting the volume exactly right, since by pouring one usually overshoots or undershoots the mark. Whatever the divisions of the cylinder are, choose some volumes that fall right on a major division and some that fall between divisions, where the children will have to interpolate. An example is shown in Figure 13 for a cylinder with 10 cc divisions.

Figure 13: *A graduated cylinder exercise*

Once the second- or third-graders are good at reading the scale, they can use the graduated cylinder to find the capacity or volume of a set of three jars (Figure 14). You should build up a collection of jars of all shapes and volumes, from small baby food jars, through peanut butter containers, to large coffee jars. Exotic shapes are nice. To find the volume of a jar, one can either fill the jar to the brim and then keep pouring the water into the graduated cylinder, or one can keep filling the graduated cylinder and pour the water into the jar until it is filled. Either way, the children have to keep track of the number of times the graduated cylinder is filled and the total volume of water accumulated this way. This activity appears as a lesson called *Fill 'er Up* in third grade.

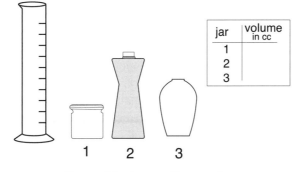

Figure 14: *A capacity exercise*

Volume Measurement by Displacement

How would you measure the volume of a small rock? This problem is dealt with in lessons on volume beginning in Grade 2. The technique is illustrated in Figure 15. First, you fill the graduated cylinder with a convenient amount of water, for example, 40 cc rather than 43 cc. Then you place the rock in the graduated cylinder without losing any water (there must be enough water in the cylinder initially to cover the object). You then read the new volume V. Since the volume of water V_{water} stays constant, the volume V is due to the water plus the rock. The rock displaces, or pushes aside, its volume in water and the water level rises. Thus, we have:

$$V_{rock} = V - V_{water}.$$

For example, in Figure 15 the volume of the rock is 22 cc. Note that subtraction is easier if you start with a multiple of ten for the volume of water. The technique works for any solid object no matter what its shape. To start with, then, ask children to find the volume of a wide variety of objects, some spheres, cubes, rocks, coins, washers, etc.

V_w $V = V_{rock} + V_{water}$

Figure 15: *Volume by displacement*

But what if the object is too big to fit into the graduated cylinder? If a bigger graduated cylinder isn't handy, then use your graduated cylinder to calibrate a large jar, and then away you go. One word of warning: When you place a large object in a graduated cylinder or jar, a considerable amount of water may splash out, even though you are very careful. You can get around this by placing the object in the graduated cylinder first and then pouring in a known amount of water V_w, and then read $V = V_{rock} + V_{water}$ off the scale. An alternative method is to find a large container and fill it with water to the brim. When the object is carefully placed in the container, it overflows, and the volume of the overflow liquid is equal to the volume of the object. If you catch all the overflow liquid in a second container, you can then use a graduated cylinder to find the volume of that liquid.

Finding the volume of small objects is also a problem, since the object may be so small you can't see the water level rise. Of course, you can always use a smaller graduated cylinder, one with 1 cc divisions instead of 5 or 10 cc divisions. The trouble is that sometimes even 1 cc per division is too large. The only way out is to measure the volume of several of the small objects at once (Figure 16b). (The volume of the several objects are identical.) For example, suppose you have 10 identical objects. To find the volume of one object, subtract the volume of the water and divide by 10. In this fashion, children can find the volume of small washers, paper clips, pins, and so on. Using 10 objects is a good idea since it is easy to divide by 10.

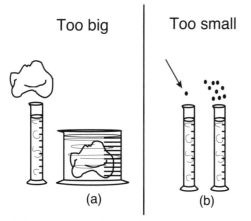

Too big   Too small

(a)   (b)

Figure 16: *Finding volumes of large or small objects*

Obtaining Accurate Results

A few words about accuracy are appropriate here. Most of the time you have to interpolate between divisions in order to read the volume. This usually leads to a reading error of about 20% of the value between the scale marks. Thus, if your graduated cylinder has 10 cc divisions, you might expect an error (i.e., children will get readings that differ) by up to 2 cc. This is illustrated in Figure 17a. If the object has raised the water level several divisions, then this 20% per division uncertainty is not a serious problem. For example, our rock changed the water level from 40 cc to 62 cc. If a reading error is up to 2 cc, then three children who read the same graduated cylinder might read 62 cc, but possibly 61 cc or 63 cc (if they are careful; maybe even more if they are not). But the volume of the rock is 62 cc − 40 cc = 22 cc for one child, but 23 cc for another, and 21 cc for the third. Thus we have a spread in reading of about 2 parts in 22 or 10%. A bigger rock, with a volume of, say, 46 cc would still have the same reading error of 2 cc, but its volume error would only be 2 parts in 46 or about 5%.

$V = 62 - 40$ cc $= 22$ cc
or
$V = 63 - 40$ cc $= 23$ cc
or
$V = 61 - 40$ cc $= 21$ cc

$V = 105$ cc or 106 cc or 107 cc

$$V = \frac{105 - 40 \text{ cc}}{3} = \frac{65}{3} = 21.67 \text{ cc}$$

$$V = \frac{106 - 40 \text{ cc}}{3} = \frac{66}{3} = 22.0 \text{ cc}$$

$$V = \frac{107 - 40 \text{ cc}}{3} = \frac{67}{3} = 22.33 \text{ cc}$$

(a)   (b)

Figure 17: *Measurement error*

A good rule of thumb is that your reading will not be accurate unless the object raises the water level by more than one division. There are two ways to achieve this. One, use a narrow graduated cylinder, or two, use several identical objects if they are available. In the case of the latter, you find the volume of one object by dividing by the number of identical objects, as we did above for very small objects. For example, three objects would still produce a reading error of 2 cc but a volume error of only 2 cc/3 = 0.67 cc. This is illustrated in Figure 17b where three marbles give a volume spread of only 0.67 cc in 22 cc or 3%, compared to 10% for one marble. Of course, this would not work for finding the volume of a rock, since it would be difficult to find three identical rocks.

If the object floats, you have to push it under in order to measure its volume. In this situation, what is important is how you push it under. If you use your finger, then what you measure is the volume of the object plus the volume of your submerged finger. Since the volume of your finger may be comparable to the volume of the object, this is clearly not a good idea. What you need is a pusher whose volume is much less than the volume of the object. A straightened paper clip or a pin will do (Figure 18).

Figure 18: *Finding the volume of something that floats*

Two Misconceptions

Early on, the children should come to grips with two important ideas concerning volume:

1. The volume of an object is independent of the material it is made of.
2. The volume of an object does not change when its shape changes.[2]

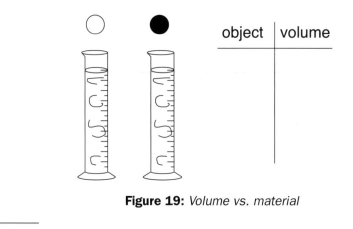

Figure 19: *Volume vs. material*

---

[2]Usually. See later discussion.

As to the first point, you can study spheres of the same volume but made of a wide variety of materials (steel, lucite, glass, even wood). The children should discover that their volumes are the same. As illustrated in Figure 19, students can fill two identical cylinders to the same level with water, carefully place both objects in, and see that the volume displaced is the same. Initially, many children will say that the heavier object has more volume and that the water will go up higher in its graduated cylinder. They are confusing mass and volume. If you take a clay cube and mash it into a thin disk, many children will say that the disk has less volume than the cube. Here they confuse one dimension, thinness, with volume: they mistakenly assume all thin objects have a small volume. Again, using the graduated cylinder the child can see that the volumes are the same. Figure 20. They can make all kinds of shapes out of a single piece of clay and determine that they all have the same volume. Indeed, the only way they can change its volume is to tear off a piece.

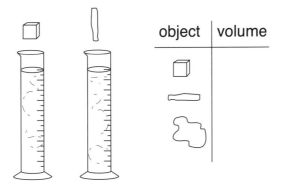

Figure 20: *Volume vs. shape*

The Concept of Mass

Defining Mass

Mass is one of the most difficult variables to understand. It is also one of the most important. Length, area, and volume have straightforward definitions. The volume of an object, for example, is defined as a measure of the space it occupies. Does mass have a similar straightforward definition? In a sense it does and in a sense it does not. Basically, **mass** is a measure of the quantity of matter in an object. That is its simple definition. Unfortunately, that begs the question. One can ask, what is matter, and we are back to where we started. So we have to look more closely at mass. And that is where things get difficult. Mass is defined through what it *does,* and this sets it apart from length, area, and volume. Moreover, mass does two things which means, in a sense, it has two definitions.

> *Basically, **mass** is a measure of the quantity of matter in an object.*

One of the things that mass does is absolutely crucial for the existence of our universe. Mass is the cause of the force of gravity. Without mass, there would be no gravity, and without gravity, matter would not have clumped into galaxies and stars and us. Since mass causes gravity, we can define mass through the pull of gravity—the greater the pull, the greater the mass an object has.

The other thing that mass does has to do with the motion of an object. All other variables being equal, the mass of an object determines how much the velocity of an object will *change* when subject to a given force. In layman's terms, the larger the mass of an object, the harder you have to push to change its speed. Since we are not ready to study motion, we will not discuss the details of this aspect of mass. Nevertheless, we might note that it was Einstein's contemplation of both properties of mass (gravity and motion) that led him to his general theory of relativity.

One way, then, to determine which of two objects has more mass is to determine which one is pulled on more strongly by the Earth's gravitational force. One possible way to do this is to drop two objects, as shown in Figure 1, and see which reaches the ground first. You might suppose, since the more mass an object has, the bigger the force of gravity, that the more massive object would fall faster and reach the ground first. If you do this exercise, however (as Galileo did), you will find that

Figure 1: *Dropping two objects*

both objects reach the ground at the same time! What went wrong? Well, we are breaking one of our cardinal rules, which is keeping variables fixed. When the objects fall, we not only have gravity pulling on them, but their velocity is changing as well. Therefore, both definitions of mass are involved and the overall effect is no longer obvious. It appears that in some way the effects cancel!

So we need a way of measuring the pull of gravity (i.e., using definition 1) without having the object move (i.e., eliminating definition 2). As we shall see in the next section, we can do this with a two-pan balance.

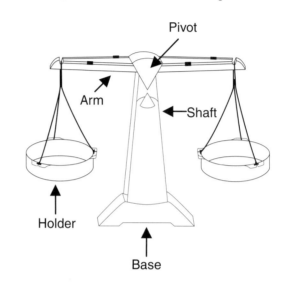

Figure 2: *A balance*

Equal Arm Balance

The equal arm, or two-pan, balance is the key to our operational definition of mass for children. If two objects balance, they have the same mass. If the arm tilts to one side, the object in the lower of the two pans has more mass than the object in the other pan.

Basically, the balance is a stick that is pivoted at its center and has two holders that are mounted on at points which are equidistant from the pivot (hence the name equal arm balance). Figure 2 pictures a balance that we often use in *Math Trailblazers*. It is quite sturdy and accurate enough for use in the elementary classroom. The tall shaft and long arms of the balance make it very useful in a variety of balancing experiments. If you would like to make your own, you can use a block of wood (Figure 3a) or a book to hold the pivot rod (Figure 3b). A ruler can act as the arm and the bottom of paper cups as pans. These latter pieces can be attached to the arm with string and paper clips.

The equal arm, or two-pan, balance is the key to our operational definition of mass for children. If two objects balance, they have the same mass. If the arm tilts to one side, the object in the lower of the two pans has more mass than the object in the other pan.

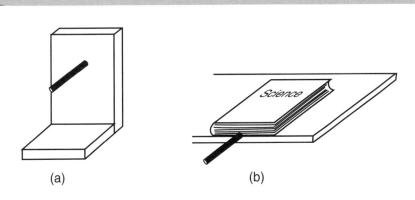

Figure 3: *Making a balance*

Once you have put your two-pan balance together, it must be zeroed. That is, the arm must be level before any masses are added. We suggest that you zero each balance and then have the children check to see that it is level before and during each experiment.

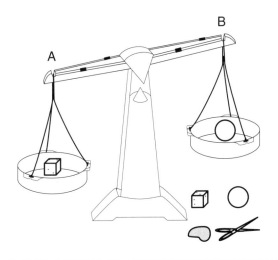

A	B	More Mass
Cube	Ball	Cube
Scissors	Ball	Scissors

Figure 4: *Comparing masses*

We are now ready to find out which of two objects, A or B, has greater mass. One is placed in each pan. Since the object with more mass will experience the bigger gravitational pull, the balance will tilt either one way or the other. If A has more mass it will tilt to the left, as shown in Figure 4, while if B has more mass it will tilt to the right. If the masses in the pans are equal, the pull of gravity on both is the same and the balance will remain level. One word of caution, though: If the masses are the same and the arm is tilted when the masses are placed on the balance, then the ruler will often remain tilted. Thus, to be sure, bring the arm back to level and see if it remains there.

One of the first exercises you can do with children in kindergarten through second grade is to have them compare, two at a time, the masses of a wide variety of objects. Then they should order the objects from the most massive to the least massive (see *Putting Masses in Order* in Grade 2 Unit 10). You can use a washer, connecting cube, small scissors, steel ball, and so on. Notice that the two-pan balance does away with the motion definition of mass since the balance is at rest when the measurement is made. Thus, the balance allows us to relate the object's mass directly to the pull of gravity.

Measuring Mass: The Mass Standard

The above is fine for comparing masses, but how do we measure *the* mass of an object? In other words, how do we assign a number to the mass of our object? Just as when we measure length, area, and volume, we need to decide on a unit. Say that we take as our standard masses a set of identical washers (paper clips would do as well). Let's call the mass of each washer 1 *ugh*. Then, if our object is balanced by 4 washers, its mass is 4 ughs, as shown in Figure 5. If the mass of the object is between 4 and 5 ughs, then the balance will not level out but tilt one

way for 4 washers and the other way for 5. In this way, the child can assign unique masses to a wide range of objects. Clearly, the smaller the washer, the more accurately one can determine the mass of an object.

But washers are not a very satisfactory standard. The washers in your class may not have the same mass as those used in another school in your district, much less in another city or another country. What we need is a universal standard that is accepted by the entire scientific community. This problem was recognized by scientists a long time ago and was resolved when the Paris Academy of Sciences submitted a report to the French National Assembly in which 1 cc of

*The Paris Academy of Sciences submitted a report to the French National Assembly in which 1 cc of water was defined to have a mass of 1 gm, the **gram** being the name chosen for the unit of mass.*

Object	Number of Washers	Mass in ughs
Ball	4	4
Cube	2	2

Figure 5: *Measuring masses*

water was defined to have a mass of 1 gm, the **gram** being the name chosen for the unit of mass. Then, using this definition, a platinum cylinder was made and declared to be the standard for 1000 grams. In 1875, an international treaty was signed by most "civilized" nations which established an International Bureau of Weights and Measures in Sevres, France, near Paris. The international prototype kilogram, made of platinum iridium alloy, is kept there. If you want your own kilogram, you have to go to Paris with an equal arm balance and some material and hack away at the material until it balances the platinum iridium standard. The National Bureau of Standards in Washington, DC, has an accurately constructed copy as do other governments throughout the world.

For small measurements, one needs a mass that is smaller than a kilogram, just as one needs a length that is smaller than a meter. The gram, like the centimeter, is perfect for this. Most objects you will deal with in the elementary school science program will have masses between 1 and 100 grams. Masses are commercially available, usually in 1-, 5-, 10-, 20-, 50-, 100-, 200-, 500-, and 1000-gram pieces. It might be a good idea to have one good set of very accurate standard masses for your school (locked in a closet marked "Paris," of course), but they are expensive. For general classroom use, there are less expensive sets of plastic masses available. However, since the plastic masses may not be as accurate, you may wish to compare them to a good set of standard masses or find their mass using a triple beam balance or other accurate scales.

The cheapest standard mass is a nickel. It has a mass very close to 5 grams! But alas, a dime does not have a mass of 10 grams. There are two ways to get around having to buy sets of expensive standard masses. To determine the mass of a small object, measure the mass of several of the objects and then divide the total mass by the number of objects. For example, if it turns out that 10 small objects balance a 5-gram piece, then each object will have a mass of 0.5 grams. (5 grams ÷ 10 objects = 0.5 grams per object.)

1 gm   2 gm   5 gm

5 gm   8 gm

Figure 6: *Using washers as standard masses*

If you go to a hardware store and make a pest of yourself— bring your two-pan balance—you can usually find washers that have "nice" masses, like 1, 2, 5, 8 grams, etc. Figure 6 shows such a collection that can be used as standard masses. Once you have the washers, give each child several of each and a lot of objects whose mass you want them to determine. A good data table is a big help since you want to keep track of the number of different washers it takes to balance the object.

Then, as shown in Figure 7, a little multiplication and addition is necessary to obtain the final mass in grams. In the example above, the total mass is:

$$m_{total} = 3 \times 1 \text{ gm} + 1 \times 2 \text{ gm} + 2 \times 5 \text{ gm} + 2 \times 8 \text{ gm} = 31 \text{ gm}.$$

Finding masses in grams is a great way to practice multiplication, addition, and mental math.

Object	Number of Standard Masses				Mass in gm
	1 gm	2 gm	5 gm	8 gm	
Plastic Cylinder	3	1	2	2	31

Figure 7: *Finding mass using washers*

A second way to get around using expensive standards is again to use washers but place them in packages of sets of 1, 5, 10, 20 grams, etc. The package can be composed of several washers wrapped in masking tape with enough tape or small washers to make an even 5 gm, 10 gm, and so on. Either way, the cost of a washer is small enough that children can have a set of masses for a few dollars.

Mass vs. Weight

In everyday language, we talk about the weight of an object rather than its mass. Are these two words for the same thing? Technically, weight and mass are distinct concepts. In scientific terms, the **mass** of an object is the amount of matter in the object. Mass is measured in kilograms and grams in the metric system and in pounds and ounces in the English system. The **weight** of an object is the measure of the pull of gravity on that object. Sir Isaac Newton first explained the importance of gravity for the motions of the planets and for the fall of an object more than 300 years ago.

Because of the awareness of space travel, most children know that the pull of gravity is different on different planets and that there is essentially no gravity in outer space. Many museums and planetariums have exhibits that show your weight on the moon and various planets. For example, since the moon's gravity is weaker than the Earth's, the pull on an individual object would be less. Thus, a human being would weigh less on the moon than on Earth.

How is the mass of an object affected by gravity? The mass of an object remains constant regardless of space travel since gravity does not influence mass. Since we use a two-pan balance to measure mass, both sides of the balance are equally affected by gravity. If an 11-gram pencil balances one 1-gram and two 5-gram standard masses on Earth, it will balance those same masses on the moon.

However, since most of us are likely to spend our lives on Earth, the distinction between mass and weight may be lost on many students.

We suggest two pedagogical alternatives with regard to the distinction between mass and weight:

1. Ignore it. This point is fairly subtle and eludes many adults.
2. Provide a simple explanation, but don't worry about it too much.

Building the *Math Trailblazers* Classroom

This section focuses on establishing a flexible and challenging learning environment for all students. Strategies include addressing classroom culture, effectively grouping students, managing manipulatives, and pacing instruction.

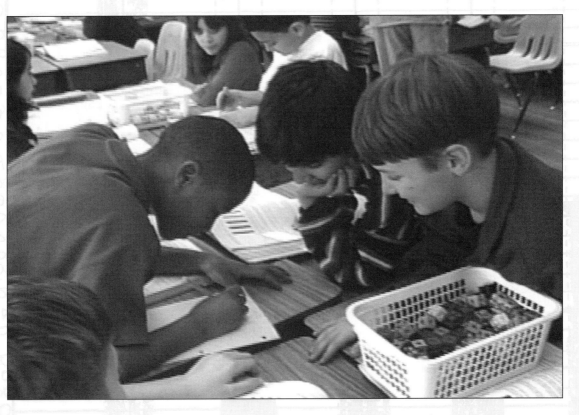

Students work effectively in groups assisted by easy access to math manipulatives.

Building the *Math Trailblazers* Classroom

Using strategies like those described here enables students to develop confidence and expertise in problem solving.

Two factors essential to student learning are the curriculum and a classroom environment that supports and challenges students (NCTM, 2000; Reys & Bay-Williams, 2003). Data on classroom implementation of the *Math Trailblazers* curriculum came from pilot test results, classroom observations, videos of lessons, and teacher feedback. From these sources, effective classroom management and teaching strategies emerged. These strategies enable students to develop confidence and expertise in problem solving. This section summarizes the following teaching and classroom management strategies: addressing classroom culture, student grouping, organization and management of manipulatives, and curriculum pacing.

 PART I

Classroom Culture

Creating a classroom culture that promotes thinking and learning requires an explicit focus on high student expectations and cooperation. The following strategies result in high performance among students (Kersaint, 2007) and should become part of *Math Trailblazers* classrooms:

- *Allow time for students to reason mathematically.* While many teachers may think they have high expectations, their well-intentioned actions can lower the difficulty level of students' work (Smith, Stein, Henningson, & Silver, 2000). For example, a teacher may model a detailed solution path for a challenging problem. However, when students mimic the teacher's solution path, they lose the opportunity to think about the problem and attempt their own strategies. This reduces the challenge of the problem. Instead, develop a challenging classroom culture that encourages mathematical reasoning by allowing students to discuss their strategies and ideas with classmates prior to starting the problem.

- *Provide opportunities for students to freely discuss mathematical understandings.* One noticeable characteristic of an effective *Math Trailblazers* classroom is the nature of the discussion that takes place consistently. When discourse is part of the classroom culture of learning, students are confident in sharing their ideas and questioning other students' contributions. Good classroom discourse is vital to the implementation of *Math Trailblazers.* "Academically Productive Talk" (Chapin & O'Connor, 2007) is the vehicle through which students make sense of new concepts. The Language in the *Math Trailblazers* Classroom section explores the connection between classroom discourse and learning.

- *Have students explain how they solve problems.* Teachers can encourage students to persevere in the problem-solving process by having them try different approaches or seek help from their classmates. Support students' thinking and classroom discourse by asking them to reflect on earlier completed tasks. References to previously completed tasks helps students make connections in their learning and in their problem-solving processes. Once students have drawn parallels in their learning, have them communicate their understandings in writing or share their ideas in class discussions.

- *Let students be responsible for their own learning.* One indicator of a classroom culture that supports and challenges students is that students realize they alone are responsible for solving problems. The teacher only provides the tools that assist students in solving problems. Students further understand that the teacher is not the owner of answers. Students should solve problems and offer explanations, not the teacher. The following two anecdotes are examples of students taking responsibility for their learning:

Jeremy, a fifth grader, whispered to a math coach who came regularly to his classroom, "I think you've known the answers all year! But you want us to figure them out!"

Hannah, a second grader, raised her hand to answer a question the teacher had posed. She paused and before responding, asked, "Will I have to explain my answer?" When the teacher assured her she would have to explain, she said, "Then let me think about it a little longer."

Use of the above strategies results in students who value mathematics, increase their persistence in solving a problem, become confident in their ability to do mathematics, become mathematical problem solvers, and believe that mathematics makes sense.

Establishing Classroom Norms

PART II

Establishing a classroom culture that promotes high expectations and inquiry means establishing classroom norms for participation. When you enter a classroom that "works" it seems effortless. The students and teacher respect each other's ideas. There is a true sense of collaboration and exploration. To create such an environment requires intentional and ongoing effort on the part of the teacher. The following recommendations represent ideas from numerous effective *Math Trailblazers* teachers.

> *To create an environment of true collaboration and exploration requires intentional and ongoing effort on the part of the teacher.*

- *Set clear expectations and remind students of them daily.* Some teachers use a "Rights and Responsibilities" approach to classroom rules. These rights and responsibilities can be framed in a positive way and encourage student ownership. Some examples include:

  1. I have the right to be heard when speaking.
  2. I will speak clearly.
  3. I will not interrupt others.
  4. I will listen carefully when others speak.
  5. I have the right to learn.
  6. I will ask questions when I do not understand.
  7. I will not distract others from learning.

Chapin and O'Connor (2007) use the concept of "obligations" when considering students' participation in classroom discourse. Regardless of the rules you select, or whether you negotiate those rules with students or set them yourself, it is essential that you teach and model those expectations for students. In the beginning of the year, dedicate time each day to teaching and practicing students' rights and responsibilities. Take easy tasks and use them to teach desired behaviors. Be explicit and let students know which outcomes are being practiced. Some teachers discuss the expectations and post them in the front of the room. The investment in the beginning of the year and daily reminders are powerful in creating a risk-taking learning environment. For video examples of how some teachers prepare for and begin the year with *Math Trailblazers* go to www.Trailblazers.com.

- *Teach children to be mathematicians.* Provide opportunities for students to work in groups, struggle to find a solution path, argue their mathematics solution, and settle differences. These opportunities mirror the work of mathematicians.

- *Create a flexible and dynamic classroom environment.* Allow opportunities for further exploration or extensions of a topic. Often as students explore new problems, they make connections to other mathematical teaching opportunities.

Grouping Students for Effective Instruction

Working with a partner or in small groups enhances students' opportunities to communicate about mathematics in a nonthreatening environment. Students learn from and help each other. However, selecting and managing effective groups requires important considerations. They include:

- Do I group heterogeneously?
- What size groups should I use?
- Do I just choose names randomly?
- Do I plan groups that mix students by ability, temperament, or both?
- Do I give students in a group "jobs" to ensure that everybody works?
- What individual accountability measures can I use?
- Will each student prepare a product, or will the group produce one shared product?

There are many ways to group students to ensure success. Some important considerations in grouping and facilitating group work follow.

Grouping needs to be flexible. Flexibility in grouping means that the number of people in the group changes based on the task. Also, sometimes pairing students with like abilities makes more sense then pairing a struggling learner with a very strong student. It may be effective to establish cooperative groups of three to four students that remain constant for a period of time, such as one month or one unit. Some days students may work in their cooperative group and other days they may be in a new partnership, based on your decision of what size group will best support student thinking and engagement.

The following are appropriate ways to group students for instruction:

- Small groups of two, three, or four students seem to be the most successful. In primary classrooms, pairs are the most effective groupings with the occasional exception of bringing two strong pairs together to form a group of four. Sometimes groups of three work best depending on the task. For example, in third grade, the *The Better Picker Upper* lab compares the absorbency of three types of paper towels. In this case it is best to assign each member of the group the responsibility of examining one type of paper towel. When it comes to grouping in your classroom, the important idea is to keep groupings flexible and to stress the importance of cooperation and respect no matter the group size.

Flexibility in grouping means that the number of people in the group changes based on the task.

- Teach pair-sharing where students turn quickly to a partner and discuss new concepts, strategies, or new vocabulary with a classmate. This breaks up teacher talk time and allows students to scaffold ideas for one another.
- Pick names randomly from a hat or jar when you want to increase the flexibility of students' working relationships.
- Have children choose partners.
- Place children in groups that match how they best work—the quiet ones all in one group and the boisterous all together.
- Assign groups by ability, heterogeneous or homogeneous when targeting specific skills with specific students.
- Keep the whole class together in one group.

While whole-class instruction and working individually are not often considered grouping strategies, both are appropriate and essential in learning mathematics. Whole-class instruction is especially useful when explaining the day's problem, introducing a new manipulative, correcting a common mistake, or summarizing the lesson. Whole-group instruction is most effective when it is brief, focused, and the information applies to all students. Clarity is enhanced when teachers provide a few minutes for pairs to discuss new ideas.

Working alone is powerful and effective as well. Giving students time to reflect and record their strategies before joining the group increases participation and helps students assess their own needs. When students do begin group time, they are able to focus on the lesson's goals and contribute thoughtfully to the discussion. In concluding the lessons, individual reflection in the form of journal writing can be a powerful assessment tool. Teachers can keep close tabs on student thinking as they develop from each day's lesson and also help catch any misinformation before big gaps in learning take place (DeBellis & Rosenstein, 2007).

Giving students time to reflect and record their strategies before joining the group increases participation and helps students assess their own needs.

Room Arrangement Matters. Seating students at tables or with desks pulled together does not necessarily guarantee that students will work well together, but sitting in rows and columns makes cooperation much more difficult. Have students sit around a group of desks that may be pulled together as a work surface to facilitate discussion and focus.

Build in Individual Accountability. Individual accountability is also important when students work in groups. To balance individual responsibility with cooperation, some teachers adopt a procedure that numbers students in each group 1, 2, 3, 4. The teacher prompts the class by saying, "3s may start the conversation at each table" or "odds talk to each other" or "1s and 3s talk and 2s and 4s listen." The important things to remember are that all students are held accountable and that the questions for groups are rich enough to push understanding.

Group members also need to be accountable to each other. They need to use one another as a resource before consulting the teacher. Be disciplined and not answer questions from group members unless they have carefully consulted each member. It is especially when working together on laboratory investigations that it is the group's responsibility to make sure all members have appropriate and accurate data tables and graphs. Students need to learn to rely on and trust one another for group work to be successful.

Here is a summary of how a *Math Trailblazers* classroom might use different student groupings:

- Students work independently giving each child a chance to think through a question and come up with a way to problem solve.

- Students turn to a partner to rehearse their answers or to make their answers more complete.

- Students work in groups to complete a task. They share ideas, responsibilities, and materials. These tasks would be difficult to complete independently. There are many ways to choose groups so that all students benefit from working with others.

- Students work as a whole class evaluating peer problem-solving strategies or receiving direction from the teacher.

Managing Math Manipulatives

Most *Math Trailblazers* lessons suggest or require the use of manipulatives. Manipulatives facilitate student learning, but effective manipulative use requires attention to their management. The following suggest ways to manage manipulatives within the classroom:

Manipulatives need to be prepared and organized ahead of time.

- When appropriate, the "Preparing for Upcoming Units" section of the Unit Planner identifies a manipulative to be used in the next unit. Gather manipulatives in advance and place them in a center for exploration.

- At the appropriate grade, have laminated copies of full-size or desk-size ten frames, *100* or *200 Charts,* and multiplication tables available for students.

- Store commonly used materials such as laminated flash cards and base-ten boards in accessible locations such as pocket charts. Make copies of these for students and allow them to take home their originals for practice.

- Allow students to explore manipulatives during indoor recess or center time. This casual experience helps them to be more focused when the lesson begins.

- Try all the manipulatives yourself before using them with students. Some grade levels use common planning time to try the lab activities together.

- Prepare and store copies of frequently-used items such as data tables and graphs. These can be copied in bulk before the school year saving both time and money.

Store manipulatives with easy access for students in mind.

- Have the most frequently used manipulatives, such as connecting cubes, links, coins, and base-ten pieces, available all year at student desks, on counters, or stored in nearby tubs for quick availability.

- If sharing a manipulative kit between teachers, develop a system to catalog manipulatives for easier accessibility.

- Store manipulatives in clear plastic bags, boxes, or cartons. Organize them so there are enough pieces in each bag or box for partners or whole tables. Have students who needs practice counting arrange links and connecting cubes in sets of ten by color.

- When working in groups with manipulatives, assign one person in each group the responsibility of collecting and returning items to their original location.

- Create a personal Daily Practice and Problem (DPP) manipulative kit for students to use when solving their DPPs each day. These kits include manipulatives frequently used to solve DPP problems. They may include things like links, coins, and connecting cubes at the primary grades, and base-ten pieces and pattern blocks at the middle grades.

- Label manipulative kits with quantities of materials to help prevent their loss. A label such as "This kit should contain 4 rulers, 4 calculators, and 4 sets of base-ten pieces" will help students (and teachers) track all materials before they are stored.

- Easy accessibility and visibility are key to efficient use of storage devices. Organizers, such as those with clear plastic shoe pockets designed to be hung on a door are a good resource for storing calculators or other manipulatives. By adding students' names to the outside of each pocket, you can tell quickly who has or has not returned their manipulatives.

Use manipulatives in instruction to promote understanding.

- Introduce each manipulative and discuss its use. For example, when students first use graduated cylinders, say, "What do you see when you look at a graduated cylinder?" Or for a balance ask, "What do you notice about this balance?" The conversations that groups have first and then share with the whole class are rich and exciting. Students often see interesting things that teachers may not.

- Include calculators as an option for students. As with most tools, the more they use them, the more commonplace they become. Be open about discussing when calculators are an appropriate choice.

- Post a list of the day's manipulatives to be used for each lesson. Make older students responsible for retrieving and returning their own supplies according to that list.

- Designate a "hands off" area on the desk or table for manipulatives to be kept while listening to a student or teacher.

Above all, remember that the more experience students have with manipulatives, the more equipped they will be for solving problems.

Ideas on the Pacing of *Math Trailblazers* Lessons

Teach math 60 minutes per day, every day. The National Council of Teachers of Mathematics established a standard of 60 minutes per day of mathematics instruction for children beginning in grade 1. *Math Trailblazers* is designed to be used for 60 minutes per day, every day. Sequence activities that follow the day's schedule and the children's ability to focus. For example, you can begin the day with a Daily Practice and Problem item, do a math activity that keeps the children working in groups at tables, and do an activity that has the children walking around to gather data later in the day. Not all 60 minutes of instruction need to be offered continuously.

Use manipulatives in instruction to promote understanding.

The National Council of Teachers of Mathematics established a standard of 60 minutes per day of mathematics instruction for children beginning in grade 1.

The early units in each grade contain many opportunities for teachers to get to know the children and to assess their math abilities from the first day. Encourage your colleagues to join you in reaching the goal of a full hour of math, every day.

Use the Pacing Suggestions in the *Unit Resource Guide*. Suggestions for pacing are given within each *Unit Resource Guide* at the beginning of the lessons and Unit Outlines. They are also in the Overview section of the *Teacher Implementation Guide*. Often the suggestions will recommend omitting or adding certain lessons if this is your first year with *Math Trailblazers*. For example, pacing suggestions for fifth grade will sometimes direct you to add a lesson from fourth grade or skip sections of the unit if your students are new to *Math Trailblazers*.

Use the multidisciplinary structure of *Math Trailblazers* to your advantage. Teach the lessons involving *Adventure Books* during literature blocks or read aloud times. Pull the science-heavy lessons or units into your science time. The lessons involving "Mr. Origin" can be completed during Social Studies lessons to address map skills. There are many creative ways to incorporate more mathematics into each day.

If this is your first year teaching *Math Trailblazers,* work towards teaching as much of the material as possible. This is especially true for teachers at grades 3–5. Teachers in the primary grades often complete all the lessons as outlined in the *Unit Resource Guide* with little trouble. To do this, teachers must start on the first day of school and dedicate an hour to math instruction each day through the last day of school. Completing all the lessons in the primary grades greatly impacts students at grades 3–5.

Teachers in the upper grades should strive to complete more and more of the curriculum each year. However, there is more content in grades 4–5 than can be taught in one school year. *Math Trailblazers* is aimed at a national audience. Because content expectations vary from state to state, some content included in grade 4 may be taught in grade 5 in your district. Thus, you and your colleagues need to carefully choose what content to teach at what time.

Upper-grade teachers in their first year with *Math Trailblazers* should teach the lessons as described and try not to stay too long on any one concept. Although this may be the first time your students see concepts presented in this way, they will have several opportunities to explore the ideas. Each lesson is not designed to be taught for mastery. The concepts will spiral back throughout the year in the Daily Practice and Problems and later units. Each time a concept is presented, the approach is slightly different. If students struggled the first time, they will have more opportunities as the year progresses to acquire the concept or skill.

Respecting differences in classrooms. Some schools or districts establish a pacing chart for each grade so classrooms stay together and all students will receive the same mathematics instruction. Asking teachers to move through a curriculum at exactly the same rate is very difficult to implement. Sometimes individual teachers find that students need more time with one concept and less time with another. We find that schools and districts with the best implementations recommend the lessons and units that need to be completed within a quarter and allow teachers some flexibility in the weekly pacing of the materials.

Rearranging lesson order. If changes must be made to the order of the lessons, make decisions as a grade level in a school or district. These decisions should be made with the advice of a math specialist or coordinator who understands the development of the mathematics content within and across grades. It is very important to the integrity of the curriculum that individual teachers not make pacing decisions on their own. Sometimes the timing of state tests determines when a particular unit should be covered. In these cases, teachers benefit from cross-grade level discussions.

Whole-group decisions can consider timing of the math facts program and Daily Practice and Problems. Teachers can use the *Facts Resource Guide* at grades 2–5 to keep on track with the math facts while making adjustments to other content. When making decisions as a school, teachers from one grade to the next can adjust for gaps in learning when items are missed or altered. It is very helpful to have at least one person with access to the entire curriculum to help guide these types of discussions for your school or district. If you do not have a qualified person in your district contact Kendall/Hunt for additional resources.

This section is just the beginning of what the *Math Trailblazers* classroom can be. The conversation continues with other sections of the *Teacher Implementation Guide.* Sections on classroom discourse, working with parents, and meeting the needs of individual students add to the information presented here. Also the online communities at Mathtrailblazers.com and the listserv give you direct access to teachers in the field. To join the *Math Trailblazers* Listserv, send a note to TIMS@uic.edu.

References

Chapin, Suzanne H., and Catherine O'Connor. "Academically Productive Talk: Supporting Students' Learning in Mathematics." *The Learning of Mathematics*. Portia C. Elliot, W. Gary Martin, and Marilyn E. Strutchens, eds., pp. 113–128. National Council of Teachers of Mathematics, Reston, VA, 2007.

Curriculum and Evaluation Standards for School Mathematics, National Council of Teachers of Mathematics, Reston, VA, 1989.

DeBellis, Valerie A., and Joseph G. Rosenstein. "Creating an Equitable Learning Environment for Teachers of Grades K–8 Mathematics." *The Learning of Mathematics*. Portia C. Elliot, W. Gary Martin, and Marilyn E. Strutchens, eds., pp. 271–288. National Council of Teachers of Mathematics, Reston, VA, 2007.

Kersaint, Gladis. "The Learning Environment: Its Influence on What is Learned." *The Learning of Mathematics*. Portia C. Elliot, W. Gary Martin, and Marilyn E. Strutchens, eds., pp. 83–96. National Council of Teachers of Mathematics, Reston, VA, 2007.

Principles and Standards for School Mathematics, National Council of Teachers of Mathematics, Reston, VA, 2000.

Reys, B.J., and J.M. Bay-Williams. "The Role of Curriculum Materials In Implementing the Curriculum and Learning Principles." *Mathematics Teaching in the Middle School.* 9(2), pp. 120–124, 2003.

Stein, M.K., M.S. Smith, M.A. Henningson, & E.A. Silver. *Implementing Standards-based Mathematics Instruction: A Casebook for Professional Development.* Teacher's College Press, New York, 2000.

Teaching the *Math Trailblazers* Student: Meeting Individual Needs

This section concentrates on meeting the needs of individual students, specifically focusing on the needs of English Language Learners, special education students, and talented or gifted students as they access the rigorous mathematics in *Math Trailblazers*.

Student and teacher working together to access the rigorous mathematics in Math Trailblazers.

Teaching the MTB Student

Teaching the *Math Trailblazers* Student: Meeting Individual Needs

Today's world is increasingly more diverse, and educators frequently need to attend to this diversity. New issues, ideologies, and calls for accountability surface almost daily, highlighting the need for teachers to address all forms of diversity within their classrooms. It may be surprising to some, but every classroom is diverse in some ways. Students vary in their prior knowledge, interests, and learning styles, among other things. Many classrooms have students from different cultures or ethnic groups. Within a student group, some may have special learning needs while others are gifted or talented in mathematics. All have the right to access the rigorous mathematics in *Math Trailblazers*.

The importance of making rigorous mathematics available to all students is articulated in the Equity Principle in the *Principles and Standards for School Mathematics* (NCTM, 2000). The Equity Principle states:

> Excellence in mathematics education requires equity—high expectations and strong support for all students. . . . All students, regardless of their personal characteristics, backgrounds, or physical challenges must have opportunities to study and support to learn mathematics. Equity does not mean that every student should receive identical instruction. . . . All students need access each year to a coherent, challenging mathematical curriculum taught by competent and well-supported mathematics teachers. (p. 12)

From its inception, the *Math Trailblazers* writers intended to design a curriculum that would support all learners. According to Robert Marzano (2003), the school-level factor that has the most impact on student achievement for all students is a "guaranteed and viable curriculum." Marzano defines a guaranteed and viable curriculum as one in which students are provided with both the opportunity to learn and the time in which to learn. This means that the sequence and organization of the curriculum must support students as they learn.

Math Trailblazers materials (lessons, labs, games, and assessments) include a variety of strategies that address the needs of students of differing learning styles, cultural and linguistic differences, and mathematical abilities. To assist teachers in creating a flexible learning environment, these strategies as well as some of the opportunities for meeting the needs of a wide variety of learners are identified in the Unit Outline in grades 1–5.

While the design of *Math Trailblazers* makes great strides in supporting a wide range of learners, it is still important to consider the unique needs of learners and adapt lessons appropriately. English Language Learners, for example, benefit from the use of the language that is part of the *Math Trailblazers* design, but these learners will be more successful when teachers implement additional language support. Gifted learners certainly benefit from the challenging open-ended tasks that are found throughout the curriculum, but can learn more when these tasks include extensions or

> All students, regardless of their personal characteristics, backgrounds, or physical challenges must have opportunities to study and support to learn mathematics.

adaptations. Special education students are supported with the language, models, and strategies used throughout the curriculum, but additional scaffolding and reading and writing support can enhance their experience.

This section was created for teachers to understand how the curriculum design supports specific groups of learners *and* to provide ideas for additional strategies that can further support each learner. The populations addressed in this section are:

Part 1. English Language Learners

Part 2. Special Education Students

Part 3. Talented and Gifted Students

These sections are not a review of all research in the field nor are they intended to be exhaustive lists of appropriate strategies. Instead they are an overview of some math-specific issues that are likely to be true in many classrooms. They also include some tried and true strategies that *Math Trailblazers* teachers have found to support their efforts to provide a challenging and supportive learning environment for their students.

Resources

Marzano, Robert. *What Works in Schools: Translating Research into Action.* Association for Supervision and Curriculum Development, Alexandria, VA, 2003.

Principles and Standards for School Mathematics. National Council of Teachers of Mathematics, Reston, VA, 2000.

Using *Math Trailblazers* with English Language Learners

A. Introduction

Mathematics classrooms no longer operate within a universal environment of "just numbers." Students are now expected to reason, explore, justify, and record their strategies for solving complex problems. This shift in practice, while excellent in rigor, presents a different challenge for students who are learning English. Their needs are unique and, therefore, warrant special attention.

Whether your district has adopted a small group instruction model or a mainstream classroom model for English Language Learners (ELLs), they deserve access to the rich mathematics presented throughout *Math Trailblazers.* If you teach in a district that has adopted or is considering adopting *Math Trailblazers,* be prepared to instruct all students with this curriculum. You can be confident that students with special needs, whether linguistic or academic, will benefit immensely from the hands-on, concept-based instruction provided in *Math Trailblazers.*

Whether your district has adopted a small group instruction model or a mainstream classroom model for English Language Learners (ELLs), they deserve access to the rich mathematics presented throughout Math Trailblazers.

With the move away from isolated computation as the primary focus of mathematics instruction, it is important to ask, "How can I help English Language Learners succeed in a language-rich math class?" Rather than seeing the amount of listening, reading, writing, and speaking in *Math Trailblazers* as an obstacle, consider it as an opportunity for ELLs to learn and use their new language in a meaningful way. In fact, the only way they will learn English and mathematics is if they have the opportunity to use language in their math class.

The section in the *Teacher Implementation Guide,* titled Language in the *Math Trailblazers* Classroom, provides many ideas for supporting language use in general. In this section, the focus is on the unique needs of ELLs. While certainly not exhaustive, the ideas presented in this section offer a starting point for further thought, discussion, and collaboration. The section begins with a brief overview of research and theory related to language learning. It identifies and discusses tools already in the structure of *Math Trailblazers* and shares additional strategies that will increase access to the content.

B. Second Language Learning: Theory in Review

Early theories of second language learning were rooted in behaviorist theories of education. Behaviorists believed that language was learned through exposure to controlled grammar and language structure with minimal thought to social or cultural impact. (Ricard-Amato and Snow, 2005) In a time when much of education was decontextualized and rote, language instruction was no different.

From research in the field of second language learning starting in the late 1970s, we now know that second languages are not "learned" through rules and structures. Rather, they are acquired through context-embedded interactions much as children learn their first language. The work of Stephen Krashen, James Cummins, and others greatly shape our current views of how children acquire a language (*Schooling and Language Minority Students: A Theoretical Framework* Pp. 3–79, 1991).

Krashen (ibid, 1991) proposes that children acquire a second language naturally as they are exposed to comprehensible input through a low affective filter. In other words, as students interact in a safe, concrete environment they are able to understand and take risks in language. Through high motivation and purposeful use of the new language over time, students move towards proficiency in that language.

Cummins (ibid, 1991) adds further insight into second language learning by documenting the amount of time it takes most students to become proficient in the target language as described above. According to his research, it takes approximately two years for a student to master face-to-face, context-embedded communicative fluency. This level of competency is necessary to succeed in day-to-day social conversations such as those on the playground for example.

Ease at simple exchanges by ELLs, however, is often mistaken for advanced fluency in the new language. Therefore, Cummins (1984) identified an important distinction between the ease of social language and the unique demands required to succeed in the classroom's academic environment. To become proficient in the cognitively demanding language of the classroom, students need five to seven years to reach the level of their native English-speaking peers. That means even though students seem proficient in everyday conversations, they have years of academic language to master. The distinction between the two language proficiencies is crucial in ensuring the success of English Language Learners in our schools. The distinction allows teachers and researchers to identify and address the unique demands of academic language instruction.

Donaldson (1978) predated Cummins in her identification of "embedded and disembedded thought and language." By expanding on Donaldson's ideas, Cummins developed a framework for defining language use in the classroom. Cummins (1984) cites her framework when explaining why students acquire conversational language more rapidly due to the embedded contextual clues and high motivation of face-to-face communication. In addition, the framework reiterates the difficulty experienced by students in completing the cognitive demands of abstract tasks within the classroom. Cummins articulates the major aim of schooling as developing students' abilities to manipulate and interpret abstract texts. Therefore, the more we can do as educators to relate the abstract, academic world to the concrete, familiar world of students, the more accessible that knowledge becomes.

C. Tools in *Math Trailblazers* to Support English Language Learners

By using *Math Trailblazers* you are already well on your way to providing ELLs access to rigorous mathematics. This curriculum has numerous effective tools for making the abstract come to life. As you plan your lessons using the *Unit Resource Guide* consider the following features:

- Abundance of visuals
- Extensive use of manipulatives
- Graphic organizers
- Labs
- Problem solving from everyday life
- Connections to literature
- Group and partner work
- Opportunities to write and read in English

Math Trailblazers uses many of these features daily. Simply implementing all aspects of the curriculum will increase the support of your English Language Learners.

By using Math Trailblazers *you are already well on your way to providing English Language Learners access to rigorous mathematics.*

D. Language-rich Approach to Instruction

We now know that English Language Learners develop skills in listening, speaking, reading, and writing at the same time, although we once believed they progressed in a linear fashion (Richard-Amato and Snow, 2005). Therefore, every lesson should provide meaningful opportunities for English Language Learners to experience and use language. *Math Trailblazers* provides excellent opportunities for students to use and learn language in a safe environment. Language is two-way communication: receptive (listening and reading) and productive (speaking and writing). This section takes each of these four domains and explains what is built into *Math Trailblazers* along with a discussion of the related needs and strategies of English Language Learners.

Every math lesson should provide meaningful opportunities for English Language Learners to experience and use language.

Listening. *Math Trailblazers* provides problem solving in motivating scenarios. In these tasks, students listen to others in their groups as they work on solutions. For example, students sell lemonade and plan class parties in third grade. They track the weather and investigate healthy eating habits in first grade. They take trips to famous places to study mathematical concepts. They consider the height of the Sears Tower and the circumference of the large Ferris wheel at Navy Pier in Chicago. They even predict the number of pennies in a stack from Earth to the moon!

Students listen to original or adapted literature in the *Adventure Book* and trade books recommended in the curriculum. The *Unit Resource Guides* and the *Teacher Implementation Guides* list literature selections that are either suggested or essential to completing each unit. Research is overwhelming as to the benefits of daily read alouds for all students, especially English Language Learners (Krashen, 1993; Trelease, 2001). If you are unable to read each selection to the students, add math-related titles to your listening center, or for high motivation, your podcasting center.

For English Language Learners it is essential that you monitor their abilities to listen and comprehend what they hear, whether it is listening to you or their peers. Use strategies like "numbered heads together" where each group member is assigned a number for the teacher to use in monitoring participation or drawing names from a cup to ensure that all students share. Be careful, of course, to allow generous wait time for ELLs to form their thoughts, and even allow them to share in alternative ways like drawings or motions. Allow students to be the teacher as they share their strategies for solving problems. By limiting the sharing of duplicate strategies, you also encourage students to listen carefully and evaluate each other's ideas.

There are teacher actions that can improve the listening and comprehension skills of English Language Learners. These include:

- As you speak to your English Language Learners, use clear language with lots of expression and movement.
- Be your own dictionary, always explaining difficult words as you use them.

- Use Art Costa's 10/2 principle. Do not speak for more than 10 minutes without giving students at least 2 minutes to process and make connections with the new information (Brechtel, 1998).

- Familiarize students with the process of turning quickly to their neighbor and interacting with what they are hearing.

- Allow students time to draw a picture or do a quick write.

However you manage it, just give students time to connect the new learning to a familiar idea.

Reading. Math class is a great opportunity for students to apply all their reading skills in a different context. English Language Learners benefit from paired reading especially when paired with strong English readers. (Diaz-Rico and Weed, 2002) They also benefit when expository texts, such as the *Student Guide,* are reworded into summary statements. (Echevarria and Graves, 2003) These strategies encourage groups of students to rewrite each paragraph or section using one sentence. Summarizing helps English Language Learners focus on the important information and not get lost in the details.

Again, use all the reading resources in the curriculum:

- Use the literature in the Literature Connections and the *Adventure Book* in addition to the *Student Guide.*

- Transfer key sentences from the *Student Guide* to sentence strips for English syntax examination.

- Omit key words for vocabulary development or "cloze" activities where students use the context of the sentence to find the missing key term or terms.

- Consider using math-related words in your spelling or vocabulary program.

- Do NOT focus on teaching key words like "in all" or "how many left" as indicators of certain operations. These terms can mislead and distract students from thinking about the whole problem. Instead teach students to read the problem carefully by focusing on its action or by considering the picture it creates.

Speaking. Use cooperative groups to put English Language Learners into situations where they can use their language and hear other native speakers. The Lesson Guides suggest ways for students to work in groups. Keep the groups flexible while varying their size and purpose. Students may work in groups to complete labs or in pairs to share strategies for problem solving. Because students need constant guidance and encouragement when working with others, spend the time needed to create a classroom environment of constructive student-to-student relationships. Give children the language needed to help each other or clarify ideas. Be sensitive to cultural and dominance issues that hinder equity among students. Do not be discouraged if it takes longer than you expect for students to work well together. Suggestions include:

- Provide sentence frames and sentence starters for discussion.

- Teach new vocabulary. (For more information and teaching ideas refer to the end of this section.)

- In primary classes use a key term as the "word of the day." Each time you transition within the lesson use the new term as a signal to move or begin work. You may even want to associate a physical movement or sound with the term to further involve the children with the new concept. (Brechtel, 1998)

- Encourage students to share their thinking by refusing to be the only expert in the room.

- Foster a safe environment where students are not ridiculed for making mistakes in English (or in math). For more information on establishing classroom norms, see the Building the *Math Trailblazers* Classroom section.

- Try numbering the participants in each group to encourage each student to speak. Use numbers or other identifiers as triggers to begin conversations. For example, "Twos, begin the conversation on prime numbers." Or "Fours, be ready to report back to the class at the end of your discussion." Using numbers or other identifiers in this way provides gentle accountability for all students.

- Keep in mind that the less time you talk, the more time students will have to talk.

- Set time for students to 1) work alone, 2) work in small groups before coming together in a whole-group discussion. This gives students a chance to think about the problem and test their ideas with a few others, before sharing with the whole class.

Writing. Take advantage of the many opportunities for children to write that exist in *Math Trailblazers*. English Language Learners need to see good writing modeled for them everyday, especially in math class. Even native speaking English students struggle to express their thinking and strategies for problem solving. All students need the language of thought. They need words for what is happening in their head. Therefore, encourage the use of terms such as counting on, skip counting, and regrouping. Use this vocabulary in class, not as words to be tested, but rather as language that gives meaning to the solution paths that students present. In the beginning you do the drawing and the writing; students give the ideas. Little by little as students become more confident, encourage them to draw, and later write, about their solutions. Save student work and show problem-solving examples to your students. You can score those just as you would score formal writing pieces in other subjects.

In addition, consider the following suggestions for improving writing for English Language Learners:

- Use the journal prompts. Make the journal prompts interactive by responding to the students in writing whenever possible.

- Model mathematical language by using shared writing strategies in which you and your students write together (McCarrier, Pinnell, and Fountas, 2000).

- Use the writing required in *Math Trailblazers* to support good writing in general. For example, reinforce transition words in strategy explanations as you would in expository writing.

- Use sentence frames or sentence starters to help English Language Learners model correct structure.

- Develop a respectful safe environment for students to share their strategies, so that English Language Learners will have more opportunities to develop that inner sense of what "sounds right" in English.

E. Issues Frequently Raised in Discussions with Teachers of English Language Learners

Planning Lessons When Some or All of the Students are ELLs

Use the *Unit Resource Guide* in planning your lessons. This component remains the center of each daily activity. The *Unit Resource Guide* outlines the content goals for each lesson. For the English Language Learners in your room, it is extremely important that the grade-level content goals are as close to the goals of their peers as possible. Not only do they need access to the same rich mathematics, for English Language Learners each new lesson is another opportunity for language growth as well. Therefore every lesson now needs to accomplish two goals: learning rigorous mathematics content and improving English skills (Echevarria, Vogt, and Short, 2000).

The following lesson from Grade 2 Unit 3 is an example of one way you might adapt a *Math Trailblazers* lesson to accommodate English Language Learners. This level of detail is NOT necessary for each lesson, but might be useful in getting started. Once you become more familiar with these strategies, the lesson planning will become second nature. You will be more confident making the adaptations right from the *Unit Resource Guide*.

English Language Learners need access to the same rich mathematics as their classmates, and each new lesson is another opportunity for language growth as well.

Teacher:	Grade 2 Unit 3 Lesson 3	Date:

Envision Outcomes:

Content Goals:
- Sorting objects by size.
- Collecting and recording data in a table.
- Making and interpreting bar graphs.

Posted goal for students:

"Students will sort buttons into groups by size, record the numbers in each group in a data table, and study them in a graph"

Language Goals:
- "There are __ (small, medium, large) buttons in our handful."
- _____ buttons are the most common in our handful.
- _____ buttons are the least common in our handful.
- See Journal Prompt.
- Student pairs discuss how to sort their piles of buttons.
- Students review their graph at the end of class focusing on trends in the data.

Vocabulary:

sort	size*
button	small
medium	large
data table	graph
label	handful
most/least	common
tally	

*Word of the day

Enlist Help:

Consult the TIMS Tutor: *The TIMS Laboratory Method.* Ask adult helpers, if available, to monitor partner discussions.

Equip the Learners:
- Ask partners to identify a small, medium, and large object in the room and share with their table. Report a few examples to the class.
- Break down the word "handful." Ask students to predict its meaning from its construction.
- Bring in a soup can to show an example of a label. Discuss the function of a label.
- Review the pictures from *The Button Box* by M. Reid read in Unit 3 Lesson 1.

Engage Motivation:
- Give student pairs a handful of buttons and ask them to sort them into three groups: small, medium, and large. Show the transparency and model with a small group of buttons.
- Remind students of the sentence starters listed in the "Language Goals" they can use for discussion.
- Walk around and observe students as they work together. Praise appropriate use of mathematical language and cooperative behavior.

Execute the Lesson:
- Using the data table as a visual, remind students how to fill out the bottom of page 57 in their *Student Guide.* Ask pairs how they can record "Number of Buttons."
- If no groups suggest it, remind them how to draw tallies to keep track of the buttons.
- On a transparency or chart paper, review the parts of a graph. Pay close attention to the "labels" on each axis. Remind them of the soup can.
- Ask students to graph their data.
- Refer to the sentence frames to help students discuss their graphs with the class. Encourage student pairs to share.

Evaluate the Progress:
- Use the addition and subtraction problems suggested on page 34 of the *Unit Resource Guide* to continue problem solving in pairs.
- Have groups compare and contrast their graphs using sentence starters like, "Our group had ____ more/less buttons than…" or "Our graph looks like a _____, while their graph looks like a _____."
- Place graphs in portfolios to use as a baseline for future activities.
- Interact with the students' entries in their math journals.
- Record observations as groups work together. (See the Assessment section.)

Teacher: **Grade __ Unit __ Lesson __ Date:**

Envision Outcomes:

Content Goals:	**Language Goals:**	**Vocabulary:**

Enlist Help:

Equip the Learners:

Engage Motivation:

Execute the Lesson:

Evaluate the Progress:

Effective Lesson Planning for English Language Learners using the *Unit Resource Guide:*

ENVISION OUTCOMES:

Content Goals: These should be clear and posted for students at the beginning of the lesson. They may be in the form of a question that students will answer or a task they can complete. The Key Content section of the Lesson Guide is a good place to start formulating your goals. Regardless of their form, review them before the lesson begins and as you progress to help the students (and you) keep focus.

Language Goals: Here is the major adjustment needed for English Language Learners. As you review the lesson in the *Unit Resource Guide,* consider what language needs will arise for your students. Identify the English structure or vocabulary you must address as you proceed through the lesson. Be direct and explicit as you teach the language lessons. See below for more ideas on teaching new vocabulary.

ENLIST HELP:

Connect with other teachers in your building if you need help making your goals accessible to English Language Learners. If you have staff trained specifically in providing instruction to English Language Learners, ask them to team teach with you on occasion. If they work with some of your students in a small group either outside or inside the classroom, have them build background knowledge for your upcoming lessons. Be careful, however, to keep them from giving direct instruction before students have a chance to develop the concepts for themselves. Consult the *Teacher Implementation Guide* for any content-related questions involving the curriculum. You can also use the Background and Content Notes in the *Unit Resource Guides* to review the mathematics for yourself.

EQUIP THE LEARNERS:

Take a few minutes at the beginning of the lesson to awaken the background knowledge of your students. This is a great time to use picture or literature books recommended in the *Unit Resource Guide.* Also, as you review the *Unit Resource Guide* record any new vocabulary words that might pose a challenge to English Language Learners. This includes at least the Key Vocabulary section, but most likely additional terms as well. Remember to highlight new definitions of familiar terms or homophones relating to math. Take time to introduce new vocabulary before you begin the lesson as long as it does not take away from student exploration and discovery. (See the vocabulary section for more ideas.)

ENGAGE MOTIVATION:

Motivate students by providing manipulatives or engaging them in a real-life problem-solving scenario. Again the *Unit Resource Guide* is your best source for ideas regarding appropriate manipulatives for each lesson. Remind students of previous work they have done related to this topic. The *Student Guide* includes many opportunities for problem solving that relate to students.

EXECUTE THE LESSON:
Teach the lesson once the students are engaged. Use lots of visuals and graphic organizers to increase comprehension. For every ten minutes of instruction, give two minutes of process time. Remember to keep focused on the goals, language, and content that were introduced at the beginning of the lesson. Help the students remember the important, not just the interesting.

EVALUATE THE PROGRESS:
Finish the lesson by checking for understanding. Review the goals and check students' progress. Use response journals or pictures. Ask students to monitor their own learning as to how well they met the lesson's goals. Consult the lesson's Assessment section in the *Unit Resource Guide* for suggestions on assessment activities.

Strategies to Help English Language Learners Remember all the New Academic Language

The amount of new academic vocabulary can be overwhelming. As teachers we want to make every effort to familiarize the students with new vocabulary within the context of the lesson (Coggins, et al. 2007). This is not a directive for isolated vocabulary instruction.

- Help students to see new words all over the classroom.
- Include them in spelling lists and on word walls.
- Use a "word of the day" to signal transition times between activities.
- Create personal dictionaries that students update daily with pictures and descriptions of new terms.
- Remember that many terms specific to mathematics have multiple meanings from common words. For example, mean, average, foot, product, and difference are a few of the words that have new meanings related to math content. Other words are homophones like sum, whole, plane, or weight that have common definitions when spelled differently. It is important to acknowledge these nuances in meaning when it comes to content-specific vocabulary.

Help English Language Learners explore new words on a deeper level:
- Look for patterns between words and how words relate to each other.
- Uncover root words and prefixes to predict meanings.
- Map words according to their relationship to other words.
- Compare and contrast words.
- Consider non-examples as a way to define unfamiliar terms.
- Take words out of their original sentences or paragraphs to help students focus on context clues. This familiar technique is referred to as a "cloze" exercise, and it has been effective for years at helping students uncover meanings of new words from their surroundings.

Ultimately, students will leave your classroom and have to take responsibility for their own learning:

- Move students toward independence by teaching them to use available tools.

- Teach them to use the glossary or index section at the back of their *Student Guides.*

- Remind them that when they look up an unknown term in a standard dictionary, the definition relating to math may not be the first one mentioned.

- Help students assess their knowledge when they come across familiar or unfamiliar words. Teach them to ask themselves questions like, "Where have I heard that term before?" or "How is this familiar word being used in a new way?" Then, they can evaluate where they need to go for more information.

Strategies to Increase Use of Nonverbal Communication in the Classroom

Math Trailblazers includes many opportunities for students to discover knowledge and content through experience. Capitalize and extend those daily opportunities. For example, in the first-grade activity called *Sharing Cookies,* bring in a box of cookie-shaped cereal for the students to use instead of cubes. Use cardboard pizzas in third grade for the *Pizza Problems.* Have kids make a paper T-shirt to decorate for *T-shirt Factory Problems,* also in third grade. Collect actual coins for money problems. Whenever possible, use real or close to real objects in presenting lessons.

If the objects are too hard to gather, bring in pictures, videos, or online images to show new concepts. Save old magazines and laminate pictures to use for vocabulary development. Make your own Shape Book using digital photography during the first-grade *Shape Walk* activity. Enlist the help of older classes to make resources for the younger grades. Video and internet services like UnitedStreaming.com can also be useful for collecting visuals. Save your work in an organized file from year to year to make the task more manageable.

Help build background knowledge by setting up an exploratory center of the coming unit. Use the Preparing for Upcoming Lessons section of the *Unit Resource Guide* to give you ideas of what is coming. Have your English Language Learners explore some of the new vocabulary with a native speaking peer. Just try not to give direct instruction robbing the learner of the joy of future discovery.

In this growing field of education stay connected to current research through national organizations such as the National Council of Teachers of Mathematics, TODOS: Mathematics for All, and National Association of Bilingual Education.

> Math Trailblazers *includes many opportunities for students to discover knowledge and content through experience.*

References

Blachowicz, Camille, and Peter J. Fisher. *Teaching Vocabulary in All Classrooms.* Pearson Education, Upper Saddle River, NJ, 2002.

Brechtel, Marcia. *Bringing the Whole Together: An Integrated Whole Language Approach for the Multilingual Classroom.* Dominie Press, Carlsbad, CA, 1998.

Coggins, Debra, et al. *English Language Learners in the Mathematics Classroom.* Corwin Press, Thousand Oaks, CA, 2007.

Cummins, James. "Language Proficiency, Bilingualism, and Academic Achievement." *Academic Success for English Language Learners: Strategies for K–12 Mainstream Teachers.* Patricia A. Richard-Amato, and Marguerite Ann Snow, eds., pp. 76–86. Pearson Education, White Plains, NY, 2005.

Donaldson, Margaret. *Children's Minds.* Collins, Glasgow, 1978.

Diaz-Rico, L., and K. Weed. *The Crosscultural, Language, and Academic Development Handbook.* Allyn & Bacon, Needham Heights, MA, 2002.

Echevarria, Jana, and Anne Graves. *Sheltered Content Instruction: Teaching English-Language Learners with Diverse Abilities.* Allyn & Bacon, Boston, MA, 2003.

Echevarria, Jana, MaryEllen Vogt, and Deborah J. Short. *Making Content Comprehensible for English Language Learners: The SIOP Model.* Allyn and Bacon, Boston, MA, 2000.

Herrell, Adrienne, and Michael Jordan. *Fifty Strategies for English Language Learners.* Pearson Education, Upper Saddle River, NJ, 2004.

Hill, Jane D., and Kathleen M. Flynn. *Classroom Instruction That Works with English Language Learners.* Association for Supervision and Curriculum Development, Alexandria, VA, 2006.

Krashen, Stephen. "Bilingual Education and Second Language Acquisition Theory." *Schooling and Language Minority Students: A Theoretical Framework.* Charles F. Leyba, ed., pp. 51–79. Evaluation, Dissemination and Assessment Center, Los Angeles, CA, 1991.

Krashen, Stephen. *The Power of Reading.* Libraries Unlimited, Englewood, CO, 1993.

Leyba, Charles F, ed. *Schooling and Language Minority Students: A Theoretical Framework.* Evaluation, Dissemination and Assessment Center, Los Angeles, CA, 1991.

McCarrier, Andrea, Gay Su Pinnell, and Irene C. Fountas. *Interactive Writing: How Language and Literacy Come Together, K–2.* Heinemann, Portsmouth, NH, 2000.

Ortiz-Franco, Luis., et al., eds. *Changing the Faces of Mathematics: Perspectives on Latinos.* National Council of Teachers of Mathematics, Reston, VA, 1999.

Richard-Amato, Patricia A., and Marguerite Ann Snow, eds. *Academic Success For English Language Learners: Strategies for K–12 Mainstream Teachers.* Pearson Education, White Plains, NY, 2005.

Trelease, Jim. *The Read Aloud Handbook.* Penguin Books, New York, NY, 2001.

PART II | Using *Math Trailblazers* with Special Education Students

A. Introduction

Finding appropriate strategies for working effectively with students who receive special education services is a challenge in any classroom. Depending on a student's disability, he or she may struggle with some or many aspects of mathematics instruction. This section highlights strategies designed to help all students, including those who experience difficulties with mathematical concepts, access the mathematics concepts and skills as presented in the *Math Trailblazers* curriculum.

In particular, this section focuses on issues related to using *Math Trailblazers* with students who have mathematics learning disabilities. You may find the information useful for other students who do not have a diagnosed disability but are experiencing learning difficulties in mathematics.

The 2004 reauthorization of the *Individuals with Disabilities Education Act* (IDEA) and associated regulations on implementing the law outline the parameters that schools must follow in providing specially designed instruction for students with disabilities. This includes the provision that students with disabilities must receive education in the least restrictive environment possible, where they have access to the general education curriculum and role models of typically developing classmates. This often means that students with disabilities have opportunities to learn challenging curricula alongside their peers without disabilities.

As part of the *No Child Left Behind Act* (NCLB) of 2001, school districts are held accountable for ensuring that all students, including those with special needs, make adequate yearly progress in reading and mathematics. The combination of IDEA and NCLB regulations has created new challenges for teachers and schools. With special-needs students being assessed on the full mathematics curriculum and schools being held accountable for the progress in mathematics of most students with disabilities, schools and districts are exploring new ways to ensure that all students including those with disabilities have access to the district's general mathematics curriculum.

Math Trailblazers was developed with a strong commitment to providing high-quality mathematics instruction for all students, including those with special needs. As such, the authors of *Math Trailblazers* incorporated approaches and tools into the curriculum to address the diverse learning needs of a wide range of students and to assist teachers with the task of differentiating their instruction. The authors of *Math Trailblazers* have designed this section to provide greater detail about strategies to support teachers to effectively plan their *Math Trailblazers* lessons for use by students in need of additional support in mathematics.

> *This section highlights strategies designed to help all students, including those who experience difficulties with mathematical concepts, access the mathematics concepts and skills as presented in the* Math Trailblazers *curriculum.*

The following section (Part B) highlights how the approaches used in *Math Trailblazers* align with the best practice research on differentiating mathematics instruction for students with disabilities. Part C includes additional resources developed by the Addressing Accessibility in Mathematics Project at Education Development Center (EDC) that can help teachers develop appropriate accommodations for students who have special learning needs in mathematics. References are included at the end of Part II.

B. *Math Trailblazers* Instruction and Special Education Research

The study of mathematics learning disabilities is relatively new when compared with research into reading disabilities (Geary, 2005; Gersten et al., 2004). Much of the work with mathematics learning disabilities has focused on simple arithmetic competencies, with little research on more complex arithmetic and other mathematical domains (Geary, 2004). While more research is needed, there is a research base of modifications and accommodations that can support (or inhibit) a student with learning disabilities. Some of the most promising strategies are shared here.

There is no single method or approach you can adopt for all students with disabilities or even all those with a specific disability. By definition, appropriate services for students with disabilities must be individualized. An essential element of working effectively with a student struggling with mathematics is identifying the source(s) of the student's difficulties. Accurately diagnosing mathematics learning disabilities is tricky (Ginsburg, 1997; Geary, 2005; Gersten et al., 2005). Different cognitive competencies are required for counting, recalling basic facts quickly; developing effective arithmetic procedures with whole numbers, fractions, and decimals; and learning mathematics that requires visual or spatial understandings, such as geometry or data representation. Students may have disabilities in one domain but function well in another.

It is also true that a student with significant language-based disabilities may appear to have a mathematical-based disability. It is therefore important that the full range of available assessment data be utilized to determine appropriate accommodations for each child.

However, there are general research-based teaching practices that seem to enhance learning for children with some mathematics learning disabilities. This section discusses those practices in relation to *Math Trailblazers*.

Strategies used within *Math Trailblazers* for all students are consistent with approaches researchers recommend for students who either are struggling with mathematics or those receiving special education services. As a result, accommodations for many special needs students will not likely require the development of drastically different approaches or lessons. Rather, teachers will need to examine lessons in relation to the learning preferences and needs of individual students, and highlight the specific approaches and strategies from within *Math Trailblazers* that make good instructional sense for the individual child. Good instruction for children with special needs ultimately depends upon reflective, knowledgeable, and flexible teachers who plan lessons carefully (Kilpatrick et. al., 2001).

Good instruction for children with special needs ultimately depends upon reflective, knowledgeable, and flexible teachers who plan lessons carefully.

Math Facts and Computation

Many students who are diagnosed with mathematics learning disabilities also have memory-related difficulties. Memory deficits can impact students' abilities to quickly recall math facts or routinely follow multiple steps in arithmetic procedures, but memory demands differ with the task. For example, the memory demands required for retrieval of math facts differ from those required for the recall of steps in a multistep procedure or to learn geometric shapes and properties.

Students with memory difficulties must use effective strategies to work around rote memorization of facts, procedures, or definitions. Following are examples that show how the design of the curriculum supports students with special needs.

Math Trailblazers interweaves conceptual understanding with development of procedural competency.

1. Instruction on the math facts focuses on patterns and connections among and between facts. _Math Trailblazers_ approach for teaching and learning math facts is an example of how a strategies-based approach can assist some students who are not able to memorize the math facts. For those children, explicitly teaching strategies for figuring out the answers to math facts can be helpful. Such instruction connects the learning of one fact with knowledge of another. Research has consistently affirmed that carefully constructed, explicit instruction on problem-solving strategies provides students with learning disabilities more opportunities to figure out the correct answer and can dramatically improve their computation skills (Bottge, 2001; Gersten and Chard, 2001). See the TIMS Tutor: _Math Facts_ for more information on this strategies-based approach.

2. _Math Trailblazers_ interweaves conceptual understanding with development of procedural competency. This aligns with best-practice recommendations for instructing students with learning disabilities (Bottge et al., 2001; Thorton & Jones, 1996; Rittle-Johnson et al., 2001; Ginsburg, 1997). The _Math Trailblazers_ approach to teaching arithmetic operations draws attention to tools within the curriculum that can assist special-needs learners to develop the needed conceptual understanding of the operations in order to gain fluency with the procedures.

3. Students use a variety of strategies for doing computation. The introduction of more than one valid procedure for each arithmetic operation offers students alternative options that might align better with their learning strengths. The regular use of calculators may be of great assistance and is a common accommodation for students who can effectively set up problems but have difficulty developing facility with paper-and-pencil procedures.

4. Extensive and ongoing use of multiple representations of arithmetic operations, such as manipulatives (e.g., connecting cubes and base-ten pieces), pictures (e.g., tallies, base-ten shorthand), and other visual representations (e.g., mathhoppers, rulers and number lines, part-part-whole mats) support students with special needs by providing different "entry points" for understanding the operations.

Use of multiple representations or alternative procedures are not panaceas in and of themselves. Most learners, but especially those with learning disabilities, will require instruction that explicitly helps them connect the various models and visual representations with the symbolic (numerical) representations of the concept (Fuson, 1992; Ginsberg, 1997). Students with learning disabilities often have difficulty making choices when multiple options are presented, and they often need more practice than other students. Introducing too many representations or alternative procedures may make it difficult for some students to make effective use of the information (Gersten & Chard, 2001). A lesson adaptation may include more explicit guidance identifying which procedures and representations are best suited to individual students at different times.

5. Daily Practice and Problems (DPPs) provide additional opportunities to practice. Once an appropriate method is identified as best suited for an individual student, additional practice is important. Most times, the practice opportunities are within the DPP or simple extensions of problem-solving contexts in daily lessons. Occasionally, the teacher may need to seek other resources for the extra practice.

Facts about Practice

- Arithmetic worksheets with many practice problems may not be helpful to many students with learning disabilities.
- Shorter, carefully constructed problem sets may be more effective in helping students with special needs develop fluency with facts and procedures (Diezman et al., 2003).
- In their meta-analysis of research on learning disabilities, Swanson and Deshler (2003) stated, "Although intensive practice of newly learned information in the early stages of learning is necessary, the cognitive intervention literature suggests that distributed practice is better for retention. Several studies have also suggested that the long-term retention of all kinds of information and skills is greatly enhanced by distributed practice" (p. 129).

Problem Solving

A fundamental assumption in *Math Trailblazers* is that students learn mathematics more effectively if they are using mathematics in meaningful contexts to solve problems. Engagement in mathematical problem solving is particularly important for students with special needs. Rich problems add context that may help such students make sense of the mathematics, build upon their previous knowledge, and judge the reasonableness of results. The problems also provide a source for the extra practice that students may require. As such, researchers caution against holding off problem solving because some basic skills are not yet in place (Bottge et al., 2001; Ginsburg, 1997; Gersten & Chard, 2001). The games and puzzles included in every grade of *Math Trailblazers* provide another source of motivation and practice that can be used effectively with special needs students.

Engagement in mathematical problem solving is particularly important for students with special needs.

Problem-solving situations in *Math Trailblazers* require students to transfer their mathematical knowledge to new situations. While these situations may be challenging for some students with learning disabilities, researchers emphasize that these students not be excluded from this important part of the mathematics curriculum. The kinds of mathematics problems they will encounter in *Math Trailblazers* can be successfully solved by the great majority. Some recommendations for supporting students are offered here:

1. Explicitly teach strategies for solving different kinds of problems (Fuchs and Fuchs, 2002; Fuchs and Fuchs, 2003; Baker et al., 2002; Swanson and Deschler, 2003). Such instruction often offers a series of steps that help students navigate through a problem, find the relevant information, and connect the problem with previous learning.

2. Consistently use tools such as advance organizers, picture-based models, or other explicit learning strategies that help students successfully work through complicated problems (Swanson and Deschler, 2003).

3. Help students make connections between varied aspects of instruction. Students with learning disabilities may need extra assistance making the connection between problem-solving experiences, concrete representations, and formal procedures (Gersten and Baker, 1998; Gersten and Chard, 1999; Ginsburg, 1997). They also will likely require additional, specific assistance with decision making, information use, vocabulary, sequencing, and patterning (Bley and Thorton, 1995).

4. Explicitly connect current or upcoming lessons with previous learning in the form of advance organizers. This may also be helpful, particularly with older students (Swanson and Deshler, 2003; Gersten and Baker, 1998).

Communication about Mathematics

Regular communication of mathematical ideas using different representations is a hallmark of instruction with *Math Trailblazers*. Classrooms that encourage students to discuss their solution strategies and justify their answers enable students with learning disabilities to communicate their mathematical understandings in ways that align with their strengths—using actions, symbols, words, or manipulatives. Students with learning disabilities are more likely to understand and retain concepts when they:

- rephrase problems in their own words;
- describe solution approaches and results; and
- summarize what others have reported. (Diezman et al., 2003).

Multiple modes of classroom communication also provide teachers with richer data to assess student progress and offer regular feedback to students. Evidence suggests that students with learning disabilities tend to overestimate their academic performance and therefore depend even more than

---

Classrooms that encourage students to discuss their solution strategies and justify their answers enable students with learning disabilities to communicate their mathematical understandings in ways that align with their strengths—using actions, symbols, words, or manipulatives.

Communication Strategies

Deizmann et al. (2003) suggest the following communication strategies, among others, to assist students with learning difficulties:

- Allow students to communicate their thinking and solution strategies in ways that align with their preferred learning styles and strengths, using actions, symbols, words, or manipulatives.
- Use a buddy system or other means to highlight the links between what is said, manipulated, and written during a task.
- Ask students to rephrase a task or problem in their own words because virtually all these students need to hear themselves so they can understand and retain ideas; ask them to repeat the solution strategies shared by other students in the class.
- Break tasks into smaller parts and require students to report in as each part is finished.
- Ask students to write on a slate or the board as opposed to paper.

other students on consistent feedback from teachers about their progress (Heath and Glenn, 2005; Bottge, 1999).

The balance in *Math Trailblazers* of whole class instruction, small group interactions, and individual work is well-suited to promoting the communication and learning needs of students with learning disabilities. Many special needs educators recommend varying group sizes to provide students with a range of opportunities for participation. Smaller groups also allow students with learning difficulties to experiment with ideas prior to sharing with a larger group.

Homework

Homework in *Math Trailblazers* presents special challenges because it often is atypical of parents' own experiences with mathematics homework. Parents may feel ill-equipped to assist with math homework and will likely need additional, explicit discussions about expectations for mathematics learning, homework policies, and ways to assist their children. Students with learning disabilities will benefit from strong, at-home homework support structures (parents, siblings, other relatives or adults, peers). The following suggestions may be helpful as teachers plan their homework assignments for students with learning disabilities. (ERIC/OSEP, 2001).

- Be sure the homework is meaningful and focuses on the essential mathematics that students must learn.
- The assignment should be clear and doable.
- Communicate clearly, taking extra time to explain assignments and use various means to remind students about the homework and due dates.
- Adjust the length of the assignment; assign the homework in small units.
- Adapt the assignment to address the individual needs and strengths of students; allow alternative methods for students to turn in their work, e.g., audio taping rather than writing assignments.
- Provide learning tools, such as calculators or manipulatives; don't assume those tools will be available at home.
- Identify a peer tutor or assign the student to a study group.
- Use various methods to communicate with parents about homework assignments; try to develop at-home homework support structures (e.g., parents, siblings, peers, other adults).

Homework that prepares students for an upcoming lesson may be particularly useful for those with learning disabilities. Such homework may review previously taught concepts and skills needed in the upcoming lesson or preview some individual pieces of the upcoming lesson giving students some extra time prior to class to think about and process parts of problems they will see in class.

C. Lesson Planning Tools

The preceding section underscored two major points:

- The instructional approaches used regularly in *Math Trailblazers* align with the prevailing research on teaching students with learning disabilities.
- The curriculum already has many embedded tools and structures that can help students with mathematics learning disabilities succeed in mathematics.

Careful lesson planning is the cornerstone of effective work with students who have mathematics learning disabilities. The Addressing Accessibility in Mathematics Project, based at the Education Development Center, has developed a lesson planning process and a set of tools that can assist teachers using *Math Trailblazers.* The project's goals are to make mathematics curricula and instruction more accessible to students with disabilities and to promote collaboration between mathematics teachers and special needs educators.

The Project's lesson planning process provides a framework for thinking proactively about the kinds of barriers that students may encounter in a lesson. Like many suggested planning routines for working with special needs students, the concept behind the Addressing Accessibility in Mathematics Project lesson planning process is that once barriers are identified, they can be addressed by providing the scaffolding and support that students need to reach the mathematics goals.

As part of the lesson planning, the Project suggests that teachers begin by considering instructional practices, such as pairing students or using large visuals, before deciding to alter the curriculum materials. They caution that some strategies can go too far and lose the integrity of the mathematics content and pedagogy or set expectations too low for students (Brodesky et al., 2004).

The steps in the Addressing Accessibility in Mathematics Project lesson planning process are summarized in the following table. Keep the guiding questions in mind as you plan. Making lessons accessible is a combination of proactive planning and on-the-spot decision-making. The expectation is not to make an individual lesson plan for each student; the goal is for teachers to create one lesson plan with accessibility strategies built in, recognizing that additional accommodations will be needed for some individuals. By examining the lesson through an accessibility lens, teachers can anticipate potential barriers for their students, plan strategies, and "keep them in their back pockets" to use as needed.

| Addressing Accessibility in Mathematics Project Lesson Planning Process[1] ||
Step	Guiding Questions
1. Focus on the mathematics of the lesson.	• What are the mathematics goals? What are the tasks? • What is most important for *all* students to learn?
2. Focus on the students.	• What are the student's strengths and weaknesses?
3. Identify potential barriers.	• What is the match or mismatch between the lesson's mathematics content and tasks and the student's strengths and weaknesses?
4. Consider accessibility strategies.	• What strategies might meet the student's needs and enable them to reach the mathematics goals?
5. Plan and implement the lesson.	• How do I integrate the accessibility strategies into my lesson plan? • How do I collect evidence to see if the strategies were effective?
6. Plan follow-up actions.	• Did the student achieve the mathematics goal for the lesson? Did the accessibility strategies help? How do you know? • How do the results of this lesson impact planning for future lessons?

[1] Adapted from Brodesky et al., 2004.

Tools for Planning Lessons

To assist *Math Trailblazers* teachers, we include several tools here that were developed by the Addressing Accessibility in Mathematics Project. These documents are reprinted here with permission from the Education Development Center for use by *Math Trailblazers* teachers. Teachers and school and district-based staff developers may make up to 10 copies. ***For all other uses, please contact Fred Gross (fgross@edc.org) for permission.*** These and other documents can also be accessed in electronic format from the Addressing Accessibility in Mathematics web site (http://edc.org/accessmath/).

• *Instructional Strategies to Increase Accessibility*
  This one-page document lists strategies to consider for planning and teaching accessible lessons. It is a good introduction to a more detailed resource developed by the Addressing Accessibility in Mathematics Project: the *Accessibility Strategies Toolkit for Mathematics,* which is available from the project web site (http://edc.org/accessmath/resources/strategies.asp).

The goal of the *Accessibility Strategies Toolkit for Mathematics* is to provide an organized list of strategies for making mathematics more accessible to students with disabilities. Students' strengths and needs in six areas—conceptual processing, language, visual-spatial processing, organization, memory, and attention—are examined. For each of these six areas, the authors identified common types of tasks in *Standards*-based mathematics curricula, student needs and challenges, and corresponding teaching strategies for promoting accessibility.

- *Accessibility Planners*

  The Accessibility Planners are templates that provide guiding questions for identifying mathematical goals, potential barriers, and strategies to enable students to reach the goals. The planners are typically used in professional development workshops and with groups where teachers work together to analyze lessons and brainstorm accessibility strategies. They can, however, be used by individual teachers. Two different Planners are included here. Additional Planners are available from the Addressing Accessibility in Mathematics web site (http://edc.org/accessmath/resources/planners.asp).

  - *Individual Focal Student Planner*

    This planner is designed for recording observations on the strengths and weaknesses of an individual student. There is a space for listing accessibility strategies that are helpful for the student.

  - *Lesson Planner*

    This template can be used to plan accessibility strategies for individual lessons.

Instructional Strategies to Increase Accessibility

Helping Students Understand Tasks

- Reword directions or questions
- Have students paraphrase directions and questions
- Provide visual *and* auditory directions
- Preview vocabulary
- Have students highlight key information
- Change context to make it more familiar or appealing to students
- Show examples of the finished product

Helping Students Access Math in Varied Ways

- Build on students' prior math knowledge
- Make connections across math topics
- Move from concrete to representational to abstract
- Use multiple representations
- Provide additional examples
- Offer manipulatives
- Use technology strategies
- Use visuals like charts or projected images
- Offer alternative ways for students to show what they know
- Provide kinesthetic learning opportunities

Building Student Independence

- Offer timers to help students with pacing
- Teach highlighting and color-coding
- Use "think alouds" and other metacognitive strategies
- Teach *and* model strategies for:
  - Organization
  - Self-questioning and self-monitoring
  - Problem-solving
  - Memory (such as mnemonics)
- Clarify expectations (use rubrics)

Providing Tools and Handouts

- Provide study guides with key information to reduce copying and note-taking
- Offer calculators and multiplication charts
- Provide resource sheets
- Provide templates for tables, graphs, writing, and other tasks
- Use graphic organizers
- Provide practice problems
- Provide a word bank with key vocabulary words and visuals

Promoting Understanding through Discourse

- Have students work in pairs or small groups
- Use cooperative learning
- Keep class discussions short and focused
- Provide timely and constructive feedback
- Check in frequently with students
- Use questions, prompts, and hints

Helping Students Manage Tasks and Organization

- Reformat handouts to provide more workspace
- Reduce amount of copying
- Provide a checklist
- Provide time management cues
- Set up a notebook organizational system
- Provide project organizers to help the students keep track of tasks
- Offer tools such as highlighters and post-its to help students focus

Adjusting Tasks to Student Needs

- Adjust level of difficulty
- Use friendlier numbers
- Break complex tasks into smaller parts
- Adjust amount of time for tasks
- Adjust amount of work
- Create multiple versions of a problem, in order to offer alternatives to a range of learners
- Adjust pacing to optimize attention

Creating a Supportive Environment

- Post and reinforce classroom expectations
- Post homework assignments in a consistent location
- Seat students strategically, based on needs like vision or hearing. Seat distractible students away from windows or doors.
- Use nonverbal signals to cue attention or behavior
- Use consistent and familiar routines
- Provide easy access to manipulatives, templates, and other tools in the classroom

Teaching the MTB Student

Observations and Strategies for Focal Student: _____

	Student's Strengths	Student's Difficulties
Conceptual		
Language		
Visual-Spatial		
Organization		
Memory		
Attention		
Other		
Helpful Strategies for this Student		

Lesson Planner for _____

Math Goals: _What are the priorities?_		
Lesson Demands _What's involved for students?_ _Consider tasks and content._	**Potential Barriers & Student Difficulties** _What difficulties do you anticipate?_	**Accessibility Strategies** _What strategies would you_ _use to meet students' needs?_

References

Baker, S., R. Gersten, and D. Lee. "A Synthesis of Empirical Research on Teaching Mathematics to Low-achieving Students." *The Elementary School Journal,* 103(1), pp. 51–74, 2002.

Bley, N.S., and C.A. Thornton. *Teaching Mathematics to Students with Learning Disabilities.* Pro-Ed, Austin, TX, 1995.

Bottge, B.A. Reconceptualizing Mathematics Problem Solving for Low-achieving Students. *Remedial and Special Education,* 22(2), pp. 102–112, 2001.

Bottge, B.A., M. Heinrichs, S.Y. Chan, and R.C. Serlin. "Anchoring Adolescents' Understanding of Math Concepts in Rich Problem-solving Environments." *Remedial and Special Education,* 22(5), pp. 299–326, 2001.

Brodesky, A.R., C. Parker, M. Murray, and L. Katzman. *Accessibility Strategies Toolkit for Mathematics.* Education Development Center, Newton, MA, 2002.

Brodesky, A.R., F.E. Gross, A.E. McTigue, and C.C. Tierney. "Planning Strategies for Students with Special Needs: A Professional Development Activity." *Teaching Children Mathematics,* 11(3), pp. 146–154, 2004.

Diezmann, C.M., C.A. Thornton, and J.J. Watters. "Addressing the Needs of Exceptional Students Through Problem Solving." F.K. Lester & R.I. Charles, eds. *Teaching Mathematics Through Problem Solving: Prekindergarten–Grade Six*, pp. 169–182. National Council of Teachers of Mathematics, Reston, VA, 2003.

ERIC/OSEP Special Project. "Homework Practices That Support Students with Disabilities." *Research Connections in Special Education No. 8.* (EC 308348), Spring 2001.

Fuchs, L.S., and D. Fuchs. "Enhancing the Mathematical Problem Solving of Students with Mathematics Disabilities." H.L. Swanson, K.R. Harris, and S.E. Graham, eds. *Handbook on Learning Disabilities,* pp. 306–322. Guilford, New York, 2003.

Fuchs, L.S, and D. Fuchs. "Mathematical Problem-solving Profiles of Students with Mathematics Disabilities with and without Comorbid Reading Disabilities." *Journal of Learning Disabilities,* 35(6), pp. 563–573, 2002.

Fuson, K.C. "Research on Learning and Teaching Addition and Subtraction of Whole Numbers." G. Lenihardt, R. Putnam, and R. Hattrup, eds. *Analysis of Arithmetic for Mathematics Teaching.* Lawrence Erlbaum Associates, Hillsdale, NJ, 1992.

Geary, D.C. "Mathematics and Learning Disabilities." *Journal of Learning Disabilities,* 37(1), pp. 4–15, 2004.

Geary, D.C. "Role of Cognitive Theory in the Study of Learning Disability in Mathematics." *Journal of Learning Disabilities,* 38(4), pp. 305–307, 2005.

Geary, D.C., M.K. Hoard, J. Byrd-Craven, and M.C. DeSoto. "Strategy Choices in Simple and Complex Addition: Contributions of Working Memory and Counting Knowledge for Children with Mathematical Disability." *Journal of Experimental Child Psychology,* 88, pp. 121–151, 2004.

Gersten, R., and D. Chard. "Number Sense: Rethinking Arithmetic Instruction for Students with Mathematical Disabilities." *The Journal of Special Education,* 33(1), pp. 18–28, 1999.

Gersten, R., N.C. Jordan, and J.R. Flojo. "Early Identification and Interventions for Students with Mathematics Difficulties." *Journal of Learning Disabilities,* 38(4), pp. 293–304, 2005.

Gersten, R., and S. Baker. "Real World Use of Scientific Concepts Integrating Situated Cognition with Explicit Instruction." *Exceptional Children,* 65(1), pp. 23–25, 1998.

Ginsburg, H.P. "Mathematics Learning Disabilities: A View from Developmental Psychology." *Journal of Learning Disabilities,* 30, pp. 20–33, 1997.

Heath, N., and T. Glen. "Positive Illusory Bias and the Self-protective Hypothesis in Children with Learning Disabilities." *Journal of Clinical Child and Adolescent Psychology.* 34 (2), pp. 272–281, 2005.

Kilpatrick, J., J. Swafford, and B. Findell, eds. *Adding It Up: Helping Children Learn Mathematics.* National Academy Press, Washington, DC, 2001.

Lovin, L., M. Kyger, and D. Allsopp. "Differentiation for Special Needs Learners." *Teaching Children Mathematics,* pp. 158–167, 2004.

Marolda, M.R., and P.S. Davidson, eds. "Assessing Mathematical Abilities and Learning Approaches" C.A. Thornton and N.S. Bley, eds. *Windows of Opportunity: Mathematics for Students with Special Needs,* pp. 41–60. National Council of Teachers of Mathematics, Reston, VA, 1994.

McGilly, K., ed. *Classroom Lessons.* Bradford, Cambridge, MA, 1994.

Rittle-Johnson, B., R.S. Siegler, and M.W. Alibali. "Developing Conceptual Understanding and Procedural Skill in Mathematics: An Iterative Process." *Journal of Educational Psychology,* 93(2), pp. 346–362, 2001.

Smith, D.D., ed. *Introduction to Special Education: Teaching in an Age of Opportunity* (5th ed.). Pearson Education, Inc., Boston, MA, 2004.

Swanson, H.L., and D. Deshler. "Instructing Adolescents with Learning Disabilities: Converting a Meta-analysis to Practice." *Journal of Learning Disabilities,* 36(2), pp. 124–35, 2003.

Thornton, C.A., and N.S. Bley, eds. *Windows of Opportunity: Mathematics for Students with Special Needs.* National Council of Teachers of Mathematics, Reston, VA, 1994.

Thornton, C.A., and G.A. Jones. "Adapting Instruction for Students with Special Learning Needs, K–8." *Journal of Education,* 178(2), pp. 59–69, 1996.

Womack, D. *Special Needs in Ordinary Schools: Developing Mathematical and Scientific Thinking in Young Children.* Cassell Educational Limited, London, 1988.

Teaching the MTB Student

Meeting the Needs of the Mathematically Gifted or Talented Student in the *Math Trailblazers* Classroom

A. Introduction

> *The design of* Math Trailblazers *is well aligned with the needs of talented or gifted students, and the curriculum provides many opportunities for extending and differentiating instruction.*

Talented or gifted students are quite different from other students in the classroom. For example, they remember things easily, needing very little review. They like to be engaged in problem solving, can work with abstract concepts beyond the scope of their peers, and approach problems in novel ways (Wilkens, Wilkens, & Oliver, 2006). A teacher's challenge with talented or gifted students is unique; rather than finding ways to make the content comprehensible to students, the teacher must move beyond the curriculum to provide additional challenge. Given this fact and that high stakes assessments focus on bringing low achieving students up to proficient levels, attention has shifted away from the talented or gifted student. Fortunately, the design of *Math Trailblazers* is well aligned with the needs of talented or gifted students, and the curriculum provides many opportunities for extending and differentiating instruction.

According to Zaccaro (2006), mathematically gifted children need to be given material that truly and appropriately challenges them. Assouline and Lupkowski-Shoplik (2005) list key elements of a curriculum that supports mathematically talented or gifted students. These elements include a broad scope of content studied in depth and at a high level with problem solving at the core of the instruction. Students solve problems, communicate solution strategies, represent problem situations in a variety of ways, and reflect on the efficiency of their problem-solving methods. Students should discover mathematical content that connects to real life as well as to other subjects.

The *Math Trailblazers* curriculum was developed with a commitment to both equity and excellence for all students, including the talented or gifted student. The following are some *Math Trailblazers* features that align with the needs of talented or gifted students:

- Students construct new knowledge as well as practice mathematical concepts through rigorous and authentic problem-solving situations.
- Students are frequently asked to communicate their solution strategies orally and in writing.
- Students solve problems using multiple problem-solving processes and provide multiple representations for their solutions.
- Students are encouraged to reflect and evaluate the efficiency of both their problem-solving strategies and the strategies of others.

B. Talented or Gifted Students in Mathematics

The following topics explore issues related to teaching talented or gifted children. Information includes insights from research, work with teachers, and how the structure of *Math Trailblazers* addresses these issues.

Identifying Talented or Gifted Students

One prevailing myth about mathematically talented students is that only students identified for a gifted program can be mathematically talented. There are a range of ways to identify students as gifted, some based on IQ scores (above 130) or on standardized test scores (above 95%). These types of criteria, however, can eliminate a student who has a special talent in one area and average or above average abilities in other areas. As a result a mathematically talented student may not meet the criteria for his or her school's gifted program (Assouline and Lupkowski-Shoplik, 2005).

> The National Association for Gifted Children (NAGC) calls for a more comprehensive definition of a gifted student. They describe a gifted person as:
>
> . . . someone who shows, or has the potential for showing, an exceptional level of performance in one or more areas of expression.
>
> Some of these abilities are very general and can affect a broad spectrum of the person's life, such as leadership skills or the ability to think creatively. Some are very specific talents and are only evident in particular circumstances, such as a special aptitude in mathematics, science, or music. The term giftedness provides a general reference to this spectrum of abilities without being specific or dependent on a single measure or index. It is generally recognized that approximately five percent of the student population, or three million children, in the United States are considered gifted.
>
> A person's giftedness should not be confused with the means by which giftedness is observed or assessed. Parent, teacher, or student recommendations, a high mark on an examination, or a high IQ score are not giftedness; they may be a signal that giftedness exists. Some of these indices of giftedness are more sensitive than others to differences in the person's environment.
>
> (http://www.nagc.org/index.aspx?id=574)

In this discussion, we consider the talented or gifted student as those formally identified as gifted in the area of mathematics through assessment procedures and those students not formally identified as talented, but whom a teacher determines, through assessments, observations, and classroom assessments to be talented in mathematics.

Content Note

Although students are referred to as being either talented or gifted, programs developed for such students use the title Talented and Gifted.

While every student is different, talented or gifted students in mathematics commonly exhibit particular traits in a mathematics classroom. They begin to grasp mathematical concepts at an early age. Many of these students enter school having established their own theories of number sense, computational strategies, problem solving, and patterns. Teachers describe these children as being able to see connections among topics and ideas without formal instruction. They are often able to discern answers with unusual speed and accuracy. Also, due to their intuitive understanding, they may skip steps and be unable to explain how they arrived at their answer (Rotigel & Fello, 2005). According to Sheffield (1999), students who demonstrate giftedness in mathematics may demonstrate uneven understanding of mathematical concepts. These students are frequently less interested in the computational "how to," preferring to engage in problem solving that is both challenging and interesting (Zaccaro, 2006).

Though these students are usually able to understand difficult mathematical concepts more readily than their same age peers, these same students may also appear to be disinterested or unmotivated in a one-size-fits-all classroom. Diezmann and Watters (2005) identify boredom as a major concern for gifted students, which results from a lack of challenging academic tasks and from a perception that the learning experience has limited value to them. This lack of challenge may be furthered when teachers try to address the needs of these students by: simply increasing the amount of work the students are to complete without addressing the complexity of the task; assigning these students to help others who are still working; or asking them to work on something else quietly while they wait for others to finish (Tomlinson, 1999; Diezmann and Watters, 2005). Both the *Principles and Standards* (NCTM, 2000) and Zaccaro (2006) caution educators that the practice of simply pushing students through the curriculum at a faster pace is not the answer.

The NCTM *Principles and Standards* states:

> One traditional way for students to learn additional mathematics in which they have a particular interest is differential pacing—allowing some students to move rapidly through the mathematical content expected of all so that they can go on to additional areas. However, some alternatives to differential pacing may prove advantageous. For example, curricula can be offered in which students can explore mathematics more deeply rather than more rapidly. This model allows them to develop deep insights into important concepts that prepare them well for later experiences instead of experiencing a more cursory treatment of a broader range of topics. (p. 369)

Zaccaro (2006) explains that expecting more work from students increases the likelihood that gifted students will develop a lack of interest. More work does not nurture the student's passion for mathematics. He compares this to "teaching all scales and no music." (p. 3)

This model (differential pacing) allows them [students] to develop deep insights into important concepts that prepare them well for later experiences instead of experiencing a more cursory treatment of a broader range of topics.

Teaching Talented or Gifted Students: Classroom Learning Community

Providing the best classroom support for talented or gifted students begins with a classroom learning community that focuses on deep understanding of important mathematics for all learners. Hiebert et al. (1997) explain that effective learning means providing rich environments for developing deep understanding of mathematics through collaboration, communication, and the creation of cognitive conflict. Having these foundations in place allows the teacher to facilitate the most effective work with talented or gifted students.

The literature suggests that there are some common foundations present in a healthy classroom learning community. They include:

- Ideas and methods expressed by all students deserve and are given respect.

- Students are encouraged to work out their own methods and communicate them with understanding to others.

- Teachers help students make their own sense of ideas and methods.

- Teachers provide high expectations and the necessary scaffolding to move each child to his or her next learning benchmark.

- Mistakes are seen as sites for learning. Challenge and frustration are a part of learning and life and should be viewed as part of the learning process.

- The authority for determining whether something is correct and sensible lies with the logic of the subject rather than with the status of the teacher. The teacher strives for student independence. (Hiebert, et al., 1997; Tomlinson, 1999; Zaccaro, 2006; Kilpatrick, Swafford, & Findell, 2001)

For additional information on establishing and maintaining effective classrooms, see the Building the *Math Trailblazers* Classroom section.

Teaching Talented or Gifted Students: Homogeneous and Heterogeneous Grouping

Appropriate grouping of students in math class is often a concern of both new and experienced teachers. In an attempt to meet the needs of all learners, educators have often separated students by achievement, grouping them with students who have similar achievement levels. Many educators believed that these homogeneous classrooms would allow students to learn at their own pace and would allow teachers to meet the needs of the students more consistently. According to the National Research Council, however, data from international comparisons (especially Asia) support the assumption that all students can achieve important mathematical learning goals within heterogeneously grouped classrooms. Tomlinson (1999) further argues that students learn best in a heterogeneous classroom only when teachers create "effective communities of learning in which all learners are specifically and systematically addressed." (p. 22) She further states that classroom learning communities grounded in best-practice and that are responsive to the diverse needs of the learners benefit all students through differentiation of instruction.

> *Providing the best classroom support for talented or gifted students begins with a classroom learning community that focuses on deep understanding of important mathematics for all learners.*

Math Trailblazers is designed for heterogeneous grouping and contains the strategies described above to support and challenge talented or gifted students. The tasks within lessons are challenging and involve problem solving and reasoning—curriculum qualities appropriate for the talented or gifted child. In addition, tasks are solved using a range of strategies, which allows those more advanced to implement more sophisticated strategies. *Math Trailblazers* lessons provide the support for discussion about math concepts. These supports help students learn to be effective communicators and to work collaboratively. Many of the lessons involve working in pairs or small groups. This sets the stage for providing the differentiation and individualization that may not occur in classrooms that are more teacher directed or designed exclusively for whole class instruction.

Tasks That Support the Learning of Mathematically Talented or Gifted Students

According to Doyle (1983, 1988) students learn from the kind of work they do. The tasks students are asked to complete determine the nature of that work. When designing mathematical tasks for talented or gifted students, Diezmann and Watters (2005) identify four defining characteristics, each of them at the heart of the *Math Trailblazers* curriculum.

Defining Characteristics of Curriculum that Challenges and Supports Talented or Gifted Students (Diezmann and Watters 2005)

1. The tasks are authentic. Students are able to emulate the practices of mathematicians at an appropriate level.

2. The tasks develop mathematical abstract reasoning. These allow the student who is gifted mathematically to explore patterns and relationships, produce holistic and lateral solutions, and work abstractly.

3. The tasks develop meta-cognitive skills. Hiebert et al. (1997) describes this as knowing how to use information as a result of understanding how it is connected or related to new knowledge or skills. Additionally, meta-cognition is being able to decide when to use a strategy by judging whether or not it is efficient.

4. The tasks increase motivation and passion for mathematics. Tasks that are challenging and meaningful allow mathematically talented students to construct meaning and develop autonomy as a learner.

One of the unique strengths of the *Math Trailblazers* curriculum is its integration with science and language arts. This interdisciplinary approach to problem solving allows students to emulate the real-world work of mathematicians and scientists. Throughout the curriculum, students are involved in scientific investigations of everyday phenomena that develop and apply mathematical skills and concepts to generate meaningful situations.

The laboratory experiments in *Math Trailblazers* are examples of authentic tasks, crucial to the success of talented or gifted students. In each experiment, students identify variables, draw pictures of their methodology, collect and organize data in tables and graphs, and look for and use patterns to analyze their data. For example, in second grade, students compare the distance different vehicles can roll. Students are introduced to the concept of "multiple trials" in an investigation and to the use of the median as a way to average their data.

Students in fifth grade first explore the geometry of circles informally and then formally. Students use collected data to find an accurate approximation for the ratio of the circumference to diameter of a circle. Discussion ensues to cement the connection between this investigation and the constant pi (π). Students then use the constant to find a formula for the circumference of a circle. In each activity, the context of authentic tasks helps the talented or gifted students make connections between previous learning and new information. Students are able to apply what they have learned in a new or different context. According to the *Principles and Standards* (NCTM, 2000), students develop deeper and more lasting understanding when they can identify the rich connection among mathematical topics in contexts they can relate to other subjects, their own interests, and their experience. For a more in-depth discussion about *Math Trailblazers* integration with science and language arts, refer to the Foundations of *Math Trailblazers* section.

Communication is also an integral part of the *Math Trailblazers* curriculum. Students increase their understanding of mathematics by discussing the mathematics they are doing. Students are expected to share their strategies for problem solving during classroom discourse and through written explanations. Journal and discussion prompts are standard features in the lesson guide for many lessons. You can use these prompts to focus classroom discussions. Asking talented or gifted students to communicate the results of their thinking to others provides them an opportunity to clarify and deepen their understanding. Students become better able to justify their solution paths to others, especially when there are divergent solution paths. For a more in-depth discussion about communication in the *Math Trailblazers* classroom refer to the Language in the *Math Trailblazers* Classroom section.

The *Math Trailblazers* curriculum also emphasizes problems that have multiple solution paths. These problems give students opportunities to talk about their own thinking in both small group and whole-class discussions. As students share their problem-solving strategies with their classmates and teacher, and as they listen to the strategies of others, they become more reflective about mathematics. The consistent inclusion of opportunities for reflection helps the talented or gifted student think about his or her own learning and leads to more efficient strategies for problem solving.

Problems with multiple solutions give students opportunities to talk about their own thinking in both small group and whole-class discussions.

A Sample Task from *Math Trailblazers*

This sample task from *Math Trailblazers* includes the components discussed above, especially the importance of communication between student and teacher. Sharing such a task with parents, teachers of talented or gifted students, or administrators can illustrate the opportunities and challenge in this curriculum that make it appropriate for the talented or gifted student.

To develop an understanding of the base-ten number system, the students in first grade are asked to fill in numbers on an empty 50's chart, consisting of

5 rows of 10 squares per row, as shown in Figure 1. The students begin by choosing a number from a deck of digit cards. They then use a variety of strategies to determine where to record the selected number. Students continue this way until all the cards are used.

								9	
						17			
		24							
	43								

Figure 1: *A partially completed 50's chart*

This activity provides a launching point for developing important concepts in mathematics. The classroom described at left demonstrates that, when students are given the opportunity to construct meaning through open-ended problem solving and when they are provided the opportunity to reflect on and share their thinking with others, they are able to discover patterns and relationships, and deepen their understanding of mathematics.

Lessons are designed to encourage students to develop efficient strategies for problem solving as they build deep conceptual understandings of the mathematics.

C. Planning for Instruction

The *Math Trailblazers* curriculum was developed to provide high quality, rigorous mathematics for all students. Lessons are designed to encourage students to develop efficient strategies for problem solving as they build deep conceptual understandings of the mathematics. The teacher's role is integral to this process as he or she designs complex instruction with the needs of each learner in mind. Complex instruction is defined by Cohen (1994) as, "a rich strategy developed to deal with the sorts of academic ranges that frequently exist in classrooms that are academically, culturally, and linguistically heterogeneous." (p. 68)

Cohen's definition creates the underlying foundation for differentiated classrooms. In education, differentiation is defined as a teacher's responsive reaction to the needs of the learners in the classroom. In other words, differentiation is responding to individual or small group needs as opposed to teaching as if the class were a singular unit in which all students are alike.

50's Chart: From the Classroom

First graders were observed completing the task described above. They used a variety of problem-solving strategies to determine where to place the number represented on the selected card. Some students made a representation of that number using trains (or groups) of connecting cubes. The cubes were made into groups of tens and leftovers. The students placed the cubes directly onto the 50's chart to help them identify the correct box in which to record the number. Other students counted the squares, placing the number in the correct box. Still other students used the strategy of counting by tens and then by ones to identify where to place the number.

As the students continued to work, one child began to see a pattern emerging on the chart and was able to use this pattern to place the numbers. For example, he recognized that the number 47 would go in the same column as 17 only down 3 rows because 4 is 3 more than 1. This student may have been beginning to develop an abstract understanding of the value of 10 and using this to understand the relationship between the various numbers on his chart. He then asked the teacher, "Does this always work?" He was trying to make sense of the situation, make connections to what he knew, and devise a rule that explained how this system worked. The teacher continued to stretch this child's understanding by encouraging him to try to think about numbers greater than 50 asking, "Where would the number 93 fit on your chart?" He pointed to 43 and said, "Under this number, just more tens."

The goal of differentiation is maximum student growth and individual success (Tomlinson & Allen, 2000).

In the differentiated classroom, effective instruction begins with teacher planning. Tomlinson (1999) identifies the following three critical elements of the curriculum that must be linked for effective instruction:

- Content—The content is what we want students to know, understand, or do as a result of instruction. The content is the "input" for instruction.
- Process—The process includes the activities or tasks that allow a student to make sense of the content.
- Product—The product is the "output." The product represents the way in which a student demonstrates what he or she understands and can do as a result of learning.

The lessons in the *Math Trailblazers* curriculum are designed and organized to clearly focus on the content, the process, and the products so students develop understandings of the key concepts, guiding principles, essential skills, and necessary facts of mathematics. For the talented or gifted student, the teacher must consider if the content, processes, and products are appropriately challenging, and when necessary, to adapt the lesson.

Instructional Strategies for Differentiation in the *Math Trailblazers* Classroom

In any lesson plan, a teacher needs to consider three important questions: What should be differentiated? For what purpose? And, how will this be accomplished? (Tomlinson, 1999)

When considering what to differentiate, a teacher needs to remember the three critical elements of the curriculum: content, process, and product. Additionally the teacher needs to consider the learning profile of each student, student interest, and student readiness. Another aspect that can be differentiated is the physical learning environment. Differentiating the physical learning environment might include the classroom configuration, use of specific grouping strategies, use of manipulatives both real and virtual, and student choice of product.

There are many effective instructional strategies for working with talented or gifted students in a heterogeneous setting. Centers, stations, and using tiered lessons provide the greatest flexibility since the teacher can use these instructional strategies to differentiate instruction for all students in the classroom.

There are many effective instructional strategies for working with talented or gifted students in a heterogeneous setting. Centers, stations, and using tiered lessons provide the greatest flexibility since the teacher can use these instructional strategies to differentiate instruction for all students in the classroom.

Key Principles of a Differentiated Classroom

- The teacher is clear about the key concepts of the unit.
- The teacher is clear about which skills are fundamental to supporting conceptual learning.
- The teacher understands, appreciates, and builds upon student differences.
- Assessment and instruction are inseparable.
- The teacher adjusts content, process, and product in response to student readiness, interests, and learning profile.
- All students participate in respectful work.
- Students and teachers are collaborators in learning.
- Goals of a differentiated classroom are maximum growth and individual success.
- Flexibility is the hallmark of a differentiated classroom. (Tomlinson, 1999)

Centers. There are two types of centers that a teacher may use in a classroom to provide differentiation of instruction. The first, a learning center, is an area of the classroom that contains activities designed to teach, reinforce, or extend a skill or concept. Teachers can design classroom centers to focus on current instruction, review past instruction, or preview and explore an upcoming concept or skill set. The second type is the interest center. This center is designed to increase a student's motivation by providing opportunity to explore topics of interest to the student. In general a center provides students with materials and activities that address a wide range of instructional levels and learning styles. Center activities can vary from structured to open-ended, and promote individual learning toward a defined goal.

In the *Math Trailblazers* classroom, teachers can use centers effectively with talented or gifted students. A teacher may set up learning or interest centers with activities or materials that focus on practice or extension of a core concept or skill. Configuring a center for talented or gifted students is more than just giving them more work. The skillful use of centers permits the teacher to challenge talented or gifted students with content appropriate to their levels of understanding.

Stations. While similar to a center, stations provide a structure in which teachers can assign students to specific areas of the room to complete different tasks. The tasks can be varied according to the ability level of students assigned to that station. Stations invite flexibility in the classroom in that not all students need to go to every station. Stations may also be used sequentially to build desired skills or conceptual understandings.

Teachers in a *Math Trailblazers* classroom may develop stations in which all students are working on the same content but where each station represents a different entry point into the content. For example, at one station, students may work with manipulatives to construct concrete models for problem solving while at another station students might be asked to solve problems using more abstract representations for their solutions. The essential consideration in doing such lesson design is that each station is still focused on the goals of the lesson and of the unit. It is inappropriate to have stations that are limited to more trivial expectations—this interpretation of differentiated lessons has resulted in the propagation of inequities in the classroom.

In grades 3–5, the task and challenge items in the Daily Practice and Problems can be a rich resource for both centers and stations. The items identified as a task are designed to take about 15 minutes to complete, and often expand a concept or provide extra practice on a skill. Challenge items are designed to be more thought provoking and to stretch a student's problem-solving skills.

Tiered Lessons. Using tiered lessons is a differentiation strategy that allows teachers to develop multiple pathways for students to take as they address the same concept or skill. Although much of the content in *Math Trailblazers* is intentionally structured as tiered lessons, understanding how a tiered lesson is structured helps teachers more efficiently and effectively reach the talented or gifted student. Teachers can identify the challenge of each of the defined tiers in a lesson to determine which best meets the learning needs of the students in the classroom (Kingore, 2006; Pierce & Adams, 2005; Kettler & Curliss, 2005; Tomlinson, 1999).

Factors that Influence the Complexity of Tiered Learning Experiences

Degree of Assistance and Support
- Teacher directs instruction
- Teacher as facilitator
- Small group support
- Individual autonomy

Degree of Structure
- Clearly defined parameters
- Open ended

Complexity of Activity or Task
- Process and product are concrete
- Process and product involve abstract thinking

Complexity of Process
- Pacing
- Number and complexity of steps
- Simple to high levels of thinking
- Sophisticated research skills are required

Complexity of Product
- Simple, correct answers
- Varied and complex responses
- Integration of advanced skills and concepts is required

Adapted from Kingore (2006)

While there are several different models for developing a tiered lesson, some general characteristics span them all. The following list, which describes the tiered structure found in *Math Trailblazers* is adapted from Tomlinson (1999); Kingore (2006); and Pierce & Adams (2005).

1. Identify the key concepts, skills, or generalizations that are the focus of the lesson. Ask yourself the following: What do I want students to know and be able to do as a result of this lesson?

2. Think about the students in your classroom. Keep in mind that tiered lessons assume that all children are able to learn the same essential concepts, skills, or generalizations in different ways. The groups of students working at each tier should be flexible depending on the

content, process, and products assigned at each tier. As you define your groups consider the range of readiness in your classroom, as well as the interests, talents, and learning styles of each student.

3. Determine the complexity of the activity along a continuum from least complex to greatest complexity. In other words, will the task challenge your most talented or gifted students, your students working at grade level, or your less advanced students. Once you determine where this activity falls on the continuum you can determine if the task meets the needs of all in your classroom. One example of a lesson's tiered structure is that in the laboratory experiments, the questions are successively more difficult.

4. If you find that this activity does not meet the level of your most talented or gifted student, identify who needs another version of the learning experience.

5. Only when necessary, create a different version of the task to address the learners in your classroom. You will find that different *Math Trailblazers* lessons have different quantities of tiers depending on the concepts and skills.

6. Use appropriate assessment for the lesson. Assessments will vary depending on the tier.

Math Trailblazers was designed with many of its lessons structured according to the characteristics of tiered lessons. Lessons begin by clearly identifying the key content that is the focus for all students. Throughout the lesson students are presented with tasks and questions that allow for multiple solution paths that vary in complexity. The following is an example of a tiered lesson from *Math Trailblazers*.

In the fourth-grade lesson *Perimeter vs. Length,* students explore the relationship between the area and perimeter of a rectangle as the area is increased in a specified way. Students first create the rectangles with square inch tiles. They then record the rectangle on grid paper. This lesson is tiered because students are asked increasingly more complex questions about the area and perimeter of the rectangle. Students are provided multiple entry points to the problems presented. Some students will use the square-inch tiles to build concrete models to represent each figure and count the number of tiles to determine either the area or the perimeter. Other students will create representations of the figures using grid paper and rely on the figures they draw to solve the problem. Still others will begin to use mathematical formulas to find the area or perimeter of the figures as they build them.

Because this lesson is already "tiered," it allows children to access the mathematics in ways that make sense to them and to push their understanding as far as possible. The talented or gifted students engaged in this lesson are likely to apply mathematical formulas to find the area or perimeter of geometric figures. These learners are more likely to see that they can decompose more complex figures into simpler geometric shapes. For example they may decompose a trapezoid into a rectangle and two triangles. These students may also see the relationship between shapes, for example two triangles might make a square. These learners benefit from lessons such as this one that contain challenges that are an integral part of the curriculum.

D. Resources for Teachers

Meeting the needs of all learners in the classroom can be challenging but also very exciting. The *Math Trailblazers* curriculum provides many resources for teachers in the *Teacher Implementation Guide* (TIG). This resource includes information for teachers that explores mathematical concepts and ideas addressed in the curriculum.

To learn more about working with students identified as talented or gifted in the classroom the following websites may be helpful:

National Association for Gifted Children (NAGC) The NAGC has been in existence for more than 50 years. This organization is dedicated to serving professionals who work on behalf of gifted children. NAGC publishes a journal for professionals entitled, Gifted Child Quarterly.
http://www.nagc.org

The Association for the Gifted (TAG) TAG is a special interest group of the Council for Exceptional Children (CEC).
http://www.cec.sped.org

American Association for Gifted Children (AAGC) The AAGC is the oldest organization dedicated to advocacy for gifted children.
http://www.aagc.org

Hoagies Gifted Education Page An extensive listing of conferences, resources, articles, and support for teachers.
http://www.hoagiesgifted.com

References

Assouline, S., and A. Lupkowski-Shoplik. *Developing Mathematical Talent: A Guide for Challenging and Educating Gifted and Advanced Learners in Math.* Prufrock Press, Waco, TX, 2005.

Diezmann, C., and J. Watters. "Catering for Mathematically Gifted Elementary Students." *Math Education for Gifted Students.* S. Jensen and J. Kendrick, eds., pp. 33–46. Prufrock Press, Waco, TX, 2005.

Hiebert, J., T. Carpenter, E. Fennema, K. Fuson, D. Wearne, H. Murray, A. Olivier, and P. Human. *Making Sense Teaching and Learning Mathematics with Understanding.* Heinemann, Portsmouth, NH, 1997.

Kettler, T., and M. Curliss. "Mathematical Acceleration in a Mixed-Ability Classroom." *Math Education for Gifted Students.* S. Jensen and J. Kendrick eds., pp. 83–92. Prufrock Press, Waco, TX, 2005.

Kilpatrick, J, J. Swafford, and B. Findell, eds. *Adding it Up: Helping Children Learn Mathematics.* National Research Council (NRC), Washington, DC, 2001.

Kingore, B. "Tiered Instruction: Beginning the Process." *Teaching for High Potential.* NAGC, winter 2006.

Pierce, R., and C. Adams. "Tiered Lessons." *Math Education for Gifted Students.* S. Jensen and J. Kendrick, eds., pp. 49–60. Prufrock Press, Waco, TX, 2005.

Principles and Standards for School Mathematics. National Council of Teachers of Mathematics, Reston, VA, 2000.

Reed, C. "Mathematically Gifted in the Heterogeneously Grouped Mathematics Classroom." *Math Education for Gifted Students.* S. Jensen and J. Kendrick, eds., pp. 17–31. Prufrock Press, Waco, TX, 2005.

Rotigel, J., and S. Fello. "Mathematically Gifted Students How Can We Meet Their Needs?" *Math Education for Gifted Students.* S. Jensen & J. Kendrick, eds., pp. 3–16. Prufrock Press, Waco, TX, 2005.

Sheffield, L.J., ed. *Developing Mathematically Promising Students.* National Council of Teachers of Mathematics, Reston, VA, 1999.

Shore, B.M., and M.A.B. Delcourt. "Effective Curricular and Program Practices in Gifted Education and the Interface with General Education." *Journal for the Education of the Gifted* 20(2), pp. 138–154, 1996.

Tomlinson, C. *The Differentiated Classroom Responding to the Needs of all Learners.* Association for Supervision and Curriculum Development, Alexandra, VA, 1999.

Wilkins, M.M., J.L. Wilkins, and T. Oliver. "Differentiating the Curriculum for Elementary Gifted Mathematics Students." *Teaching Children Mathematics,* 13(1), pp. 6–13, 2006.

Zaccaro, E. "The Seven Components of Successful Programs for Mathematically Gifted Children." *Teaching for High Potential,* NAGC, winter 2006.

Language in the
Math Trailblazers Classroom

This section focuses on the use of language while students read, write, speak, and listen in the *Math Trailblazers* classroom. Students' language abilities increase while using a curriculum rich in opportunities to communicate mathematically.

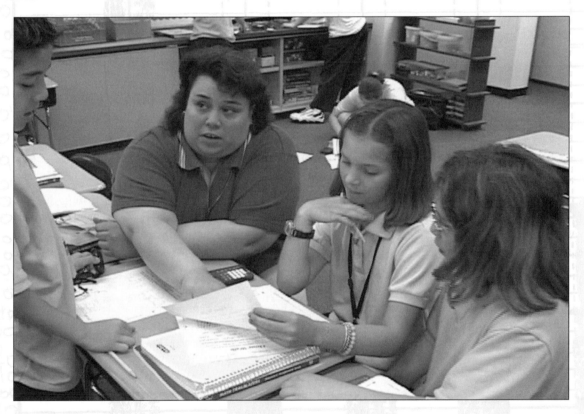

A teacher helps students solidify their understanding of mathematical concepts by listening to their explanations, helping them read the problems, and write their solutions.

Language in the Math Trailblazers Classroom

The use of language—listening, reading, speaking, and writing—is emphasized throughout the *Math Trailblazers* curriculum. This enables students to consider and communicate ideas and solidify their understanding of mathematical concepts. In the past, many mathematics textbooks and lessons limited students' use of language. Parents, administrators, and other teachers may not understand the need for so much reading and writing in a mathematics class. Moreover, getting students to read, write, speak, and listen, while crucial to the learning process, is sometimes a challenge.

This section offers support for developing language use in your classroom. Part I provides a brief rationale of why language is important and how it is used in *Math Trailblazers*. This information is useful in working with colleagues and parents who may not understand the need for reading and writing in mathematics class. Part II provides additional background and support for incorporating language into your daily lessons. Specifically, support is provided on three overlapping areas of language use: reading, writing, and discourse strategies.

Listening, reading, speaking, and writing enable students to consider and communicate ideas and solidify their understanding of mathematical concepts.

Incorporating Language into Mathematics Lessons

Using language to learn mathematics is grounded in learning theory and research. While there are many reasons to incorporate reading, writing, listening, and speaking into mathematics instruction, we discuss issues that may arise when discussing language with parents, administrators, and other teachers.

Reasons to Focus on Language in Mathematics Lessons

Language can help students understand mathematics. The value of studying mathematics is to learn both processes and skills necessary for solving real-life problems. In *Math Trailblazers,* students investigate and solve mathematical problems in real-world contexts. They design accurate and efficient strategies. Discussing possible approaches during the problem-solving process and presenting various solution strategies broadens and deepens students' understanding. It also solidifies their ideas as they learn to use mathematics language.

The context of many mathematics lessons are language-dependent. *Math Trailblazers* uses real-life contexts to develop mathematical concepts in a concrete, visual manner. The contexts actually help students understand math concepts and promote student interest in the math lessons. The contexts provide meaning and concrete examples for thinking about abstract concepts.

Incorporating problem-solving contexts into the lessons, however, requires increased use of language in the text and in implementing of the lesson (through speaking, listening, and writing). For example, second-grade students use the context of a car moving through a neighborhood to develop initial concepts of geometry known as slides, flips, and turns. Without this context, which requires students to both read and listen as they solve the problems, the lesson would not be accessible to all learners. In later grades, these language-dependent contexts provide an opportunity for students to make sense of symbolic representations; e.g., 9×4 becomes 9 groups of 4 boxes, and so on. While tempting to remove the contexts to reduce the language demands, such adaptations interfere with a student's ability to make sense of what they are doing. The contexts also connect ideas within mathematics and between mathematics and their world.

Using language in mathematics results in improved literacy. Some teachers, parents, or principals may believe that the increased use of language interferes with the learning of mathematics. This is most often suggested for English-language learners and students with language-related learning disabilities. While such students may need additional support in interpreting the language in the problem, having a familiar context to ground thinking is more often a support to students, not a hurdle. In addition, English-language learners will only learn the language of mathematics if there is significant use of productive (speaking and writing) and receptive (listening and reading) forms of language. Language use in a mathematics classroom has the benefit of not just improving students' abilities to communicate mathematically, but to communicate in general. Everyday language is improved while using it within the context of math class.

Proficiency in mathematics language is essential for success in mathematics. There are three types of language involved in mathematical discourse. The first is conversational language used for giving instruction, explaining a process, and so on. The second is discrete language used for understanding symbols such as $+$, $-$, $\times$, $\div$, and the words and meaning attached to symbols. The third is mathematical language, which includes terms such as *range, product,* and *sample.* These have definitions specific to mathematics that are different from everyday usage. All three types of mathematical language are important to effectively communicate. Since mathematical language is not often a part of students' experiences outside the mathematics classroom, it is particularly important to make them a regular part of their mathematics learning.

Where Students Encounter Language in the *Math Trailblazers* Curriculum

In *Math Trailblazers,* students engage in all facets of language use including:
- reading introductory vignettes at the start of many lessons,
- explaining the process they used to solve a problem,
- listening to and comparing solution strategies,
- working collaboratively with classmates,
- writing responses to open-ended problems,
- reporting observations either orally or in writing, and
- reading and discussing the trade books and *Adventure Books.*

PART II | Assisting Students with Reading, Writing, and Discourse

Reading

Only if students comprehend the text can they begin to understand the problem and engage in doing mathematics.

Reading Comprehension: Background

George Polya (1973) outlined a 4-step problem-solving process. "Understand the problem" is the first step, followed by devising a plan, carrying out the plan, and looking back. Understanding first involves comprehending the text and then understanding what the mathematics is within the text. If students do not comprehend the text, they can't begin to understand the problem, therefore they cannot engage in doing mathematics. This is true even for reading symbolic expressions as simple as $8 \div 2 = 4$. At the beginning of the problem-solving process, it is important to realize the complexity of reading in mathematics. Mathematics text is different from other text; it is very dense, containing more ideas per sentence than any other type of text (Kenney, 2005). In addition, it can contain words as well as numeric and nonnumeric symbols. Students may have to comprehend illustrations that relate to the text, including tables, graphs, charts, pictures, and coordinate axes. Finally, the syntax of mathematics story problems is different from everyday language. Making these distinctions explicit supports reading comprehension for all students and is absolutely essential for those struggling with language or learning English.

Reading Comprehension: Strategies

The following strategies can increase students' reading comprehension:

1. Help students understand the goal of the lesson. Understanding the lesson's goal helps them with reading comprehension.
2. Find out whether the context is familiar to students. Bring meaning to that context. For example, students may not know the meaning of sampling a population. Ask, "Can you share how you have heard the word 'sampling' used?" Students may report on sampling food, samples of wallpaper or paint, or other experiences. If not, share a personal experience such as when you participated in a survey.
3. Model the process of interpretation through "think aloud." This includes articulating what dilemmas or questions arise as you read and what words and phrases help you figure out what to do.
4. Ask students what difficulties they have understanding the problem. As students try to find words to describe what they don't understand, they often solve the problem themselves. Sometimes, other students offer helpful input.
5. Restate the problem in an interactive manner. Ask students to use the pair-share strategy: one partner tells what the problem is about (e.g., finding volunteers to work at the science fair) and the other partner tells the question they will need to answer (e.g., how many people will be needed).

6. Help students with phrases and their meanings. For example, consider the question: "Which group has twice as many small lids as large lids?" Ask students to think about what that phrase "twice as many . . . as" means and then describe how they know. Add these phrases to a journal or math word wall. Note that this helps students see how the meaning of words are influenced by other words around them. This is very different from a key-word approach, which can result in limited comprehension (see the section on using key words later in this document).

7. Allow students time to read aloud and time to listen to others read aloud. Follow with "What is this question asking you to do?" and "How did you know?" Asking "how" makes explicit the connection between words and mathematical concepts and procedures.

To support students as they read (or listen to) children's books connected to *Math Trailblazers* lessons, we recommend the following strategies:

- Preview or review vocabulary that may be problematic.
- Ask students to predict or summarize story contents.
- Ask questions related to the story, but beyond the discussion prompts.

Grades 1–5 in *Math Trailblazers* each has a series of *Adventure Books,* short stories written like graphic novels (comic book style) or illustrated, connected text. The stories are used to illustrate a math or science concept with children as the problem solvers.

You can share these stories in a variety of ways:

1. Read the story as students follow along.
2. Read the story, then have students read it with a partner.
3. Students read the story with a partner.
4. Assign the story for homework the night before for students to pre-read with family members.
5. Students read the story in a reader's theater format.
6. Record the story and place it in a listening center with accompanying questions for students to answer.

Reading Levels

In any classroom there is a range of reading abilities. While the curriculum is written to be accessible to all students, struggling readers or nonreaders may need additional support. One way is to read the text first as a whole class. Another is to group the nonreaders with the teacher at the start to be sure they understand the text. Heterogeneous grouping can support nonreaders or reluctant readers, especially if you insist that when you visit the group every student can explain the task. The following story demonstrates how one second-grade teacher organized her classroom with reluctant and nonreaders to provide access to all students.

A Classroom Example of Accommodating Different Reading Levels

(This second-grade lesson deals with making a map on the x- and y-axis with Mr. Origin (a referent object) at the origin of the coordinate plane.)

The room is full of second graders with varying degrees of reading abilities. I had planned the Mr. Origin lab for one class period, but didn't think we would get to the questions about the map. But these kids were wonderful and finished making their maps and measuring with ease. So, since they were in groups, I said to each group as they finished, "Go ahead and start answering the questions about your map."

There were groans, but each group began to read the questions and respond to them. One group put their heads together and answered all the questions. A second group got started but one child asked to be excused for a moment (a nonreader). A third group immediately split into two pairs and began answering questions (but didn't finish). When group 4 was stuck, I asked one boy to read the questions to the group. There was a nonreader in that group and he wouldn't listen to the questions being read. So, I asked him to read. He read the words but obviously couldn't read for meaning (yet). The first boy read it one more time and then the group answered the questions. Before they were finished they had read the question a total of 6 times and then answered the question.

Afterwards, I reflected on the lesson, in particular how the students were able to answer the questions. I thought that pairs might be better than larger groups for tasks involving reading.

I also thought about which child needed to be paired with which child during a reading part of a math lesson. One idea I had was to pull my nonreaders together and read to them before having them work in pairs on the questions.

When I looked at the papers, I found that only two children had not answered all or most of the questions successfully, both nonreaders. I made a mental note that I need to ask each nonreader to respond to me orally to check for understanding.

Working together, the students had helped each other understand the questions and respond to them successfully.

Caution: Key-Word Approach Can Limit Comprehension

Some reading strategies can inhibit learning. In mathematics, the most common is searching the story problem for key words that indicate a specific operation. Research shows that while teachers help identify what are sometimes called "key words" to support student thinking, students use these words to abandon reasoning about the problem (Kenney, Hancewicz, Heuer, Metsisto, Tuttle, 2005; Sowder, 1988). The reasons why a "key-word approach" can be detrimental to comprehension include:

1. Key words often have multiple meanings.
2. The list of key words continues to grow over the years making it difficult to remember.
3. The key words might indicate an operation, but the question may be asking for more than the response to a computation.
4. Key-word search doesn't help students understand the meaning of the problem.
5. For problems involving multiple steps, it doesn't work and students are then ill-prepared to read for understanding. Instead, students need opportunities to find meaning in the reading.
6. Phrases can shift the meaning of words in the phrase. For example "how," "many," and "how many" signify different things in mathematics.
7. Addition of (or removal of) a single letter changes meaning (e.g. "percent of" versus "percent off," "ten" versus "tens").

Appropriate Attention to Key Words

It is important to develop vocabulary that is specific to mathematics. Although, this point may seem to contradict the previous section, there is an important distinction. In the "keyword" approach, students memorize that a word (e.g., difference) means to "subtract" regardless of the content of the sentence; in a precision-of-vocabulary approach, students become familiar with the common phrases (e.g., more than) and relationships among words (e.g., if-then) and how they interact with the rest of the sentence. As a teacher, one way to support student-reading skills is to make explicit some of these vocabulary considerations specific to mathematics. Some common examples of the subtleties in mathematics language follow:

1. Here are two problems using the term *more than,* one requiring subtraction (or counting down) and one requiring addition (or counting up):
   - Jenny has 9 apples. She has 3 *more than* Linda. How many apples does Linda have?
   - Jenny has 9 apples. Linda has 3 *more than* Jenny. How many does Linda now have?
2. Here are two problems in which "by" indicates two different operations:
   - Linda had four cats in her stuffed animal collection. After her birthday, the number of cats *increased by* three. How many cats does Linda have?
   - Linda had four cats in her stuffed animal collection. After her birthday, the number of cats was *multiplied by* three. How many cats does Linda now have?

3. In this example, the operation is the same, but a different response is required for each:
   - The third grade went on a field trip. There are 50 students in the third grade. Twenty students fit on each bus. How many buses were needed?
   - The third grade went on a field trip. There are 50 students in the third grade. Twenty students fit on each bus. How many buses were full?
4. In these statements the key word *of* is used in different ways:
   - What is the area *of* a triangle? (indicating find the space inside)
   - What is one-half *of* 24? (indicating $\frac{1}{2} \times 24$ or $24 \div 2$)
   Find the perimeter *of* the rectangle. (indicating where the perimeter is).

Writing

Writing: Background

The value of having students write in math is quite simply that writing improves learning. Pugalee (2005) explains:

As students write, they manipulate, integrate, and restructure knowledge through using and reflecting on what they know and believe. This process facilitates the development of meaningful understanding: the more a student works with ideas and concepts, the more likely those ideas and concepts will be understood and remembered. (p. xii)

Writing can allow more flexibility in how much time a student has to describe a solution and provides the opportunity for reflection and correction. If students struggle with the words to explain, they can supplement or replace with illustrations. While writing has clear benefits, it is also very challenging. Students are learning to write as they are learning mathematics, so the thought processes are demanding, the precision required in communicating mathematically increases the difficulty of this task, and even students willing to share orally, may be reluctant to share their ideas in writing. Because writing does improve learning, but is difficult, it is essential that students have ample opportunity and support for writing.

Math Trailblazers offers many opportunities for students to write. Just as in a writing lesson, students benefit when they submit a written explanation, receive input from the teacher, and then revise the explanation based on feedback. In the early grades, writing might include a simple process of asking students to tell in words or sentences how many objects they found altogether. Teachers can help primary students learn to write by having them dictate their thinking to an adult or by drawing pictures. Teachers at all grade levels, including kindergarten, should expect students to submit written work, even if the thoughts are incomplete or inaccurate. Students become better writers by writing. As noted earlier, as students improve their writing in mathematics, they improve their writing skills in general. Math class is just one of many situations in which students need to learn effective written communication.

Writing: Strategies

Because writing may be the most difficult literacy skill, it is important to explicitly teach students to write (or illustrate) their work. Here are some ways teachers support student writing:

1. Use and display the *Math Trailblazers* Student Rubrics in grades 3–5. If students have the rubrics in front of them as they work, they will produce better products. If you use a sample, have students collectively respond to whether the sample meets the expectations in the *Telling* or other rubrics. Students will learn how to be more clear and thorough in their writing. For more information on rubrics, see the Assessment section.

> **TIMS Tip**
>
> Post enlargements of the rubrics in the classroom where they are easy to point to and read.

2. Prior to writing, ask students to verbally summarize the important concepts of the lesson. You can even list key points on the board so students can synthesize the information into complete sentences in their own way. Sharing key points can serve as a good review and an opportunity for speaking and reading that further solidifies the concept for students.

3. For students having trouble beginning, sentence starters are a good tool. Another related tool is a graphic organizer with sections where students are prompted to write the question, process, and solution. Some teachers use Polya's (1973) 4-step problem-solving process as a guide, asking students to (1) state the problem, (2) tell what approach they used, (3) explain what solution they got, and (4) tell how their solution answers the original problem.

4. Incorporate creative writing prompts that engage your students. For example, use a genre introduced in language arts, like poetry, fables, or persuasive narratives.

5. Ask students to draw pictures, diagrams or, for older students, concept maps of what they later explain in words. Using pictures can support writing and help you to see what they are trying to explain.

6. Have students keep a math journal of the written summaries of lessons or problems. In this way students can see their improvement in explaining mathematics and have a resource for looking up information they might have forgotten. See the TIMS Tutor: *Journals* for a range of prompts and tips on keeping a math journal.

7. Make a transparency of a well-written response to share with students. To preserve anonymity, use a sample from another class or save samples from year to year.

8. Ask students to fold a paper in half, solve the problem on the first half, and then open the paper and write the steps on the second half.

Regardless of the strategies you use, it is important to remember that the goal is to capture students' ideas and thinking. Creativity and novel solutions are important, and writing opportunities should not impose ways for students to begin or solve a problem.

Discourse

Discourse: Background

Those who start teaching with a *Standards*-based curriculum like *Math Trailblazers* often see a change in their classroom discourse. Because *Math Trailblazers* engages students in problem solving and inquiry, there are opportunities for students to approach a problem differently and share different solution strategies. Students learn from hearing others' approaches, and such conversations allow teachers to help students focus on key mathematical ideas. This is different from asking questions to get students to a particular teacher-determined endpoint, a model of questioning often referred to as funneling, where the teacher uses questions to funnel students to a particular formula, approach, or term (Herbel-Eisenmann and Breyfogle, 2005).

Post-exploration discussions are essential to the learning process. As Chapin, O'Conner, and Anderson (2003) write, "When a teacher succeeds in setting up a classroom in which students feel obligated to listen to one another, to make their own contributions clear and comprehensible, and to provide evidence for their claims; that teacher has set in place a powerful context for student learning." (p. 9)

Discourse is not only a concluding activity in a lesson, however, but is important as student work is in progress. This can help stimulate new ideas across working groups. Whitin & Whitin (2000) call this "rough draft thinking" and argue that it allows classmates and the teacher to get a glimpse into other students' thought processes and to revise one's own thinking (p. 220).

Having classroom discourse means establishing norms for how students interact with each other. Hiebert, et al. (1996) describe four critical features of establishing a social culture for learning mathematics, shared in brief here:

Ideas are the currency of the classroom. Ideas, expressed by any participant, have the potential to contribute to everyone's learning and consequently warrant respect and response.

Students have autonomy with respect to the methods used to solve problems. Students must respect the need for everyone to understand their own methods and must recognize that there are often a variety of methods that will do the job.

The classroom culture exhibits an appreciation for mistakes as learning sites. Mistakes afford opportunities to examine errors in reasoning and thereby raise everyone's level of analysis. Do not cover up mistakes; use them constructively.

The authority for reasonability and correctness lies in the logic and structure of the subject, rather than in the social status of participants. The persuasiveness of an explanation or the correctness of a solution depends on the mathematical sense it makes, not on the popularity of the presenter. (pp. 9–10)

Discourse: Strategies

Facilitating discourse improves with practice. As students become more accustomed to explaining their thinking, listening to others, and asking their own questions, knowing what questions you should ask and when to ask them is an important skill. Discourse that "focuses" rather than "funnels" is less predictable and requires skills on your part. Some strategies to support effective discourse include the following:

1. Allot time for students to share and compare strategies and solutions at the end of the lesson, even if it is not the end of the period. It takes time for students to articulate their ideas. If you are running out of time, build it into the next day. Reflecting about the lesson helps children develop an understanding of math concepts and helps you to understand what it is they learned.

2. Shift classroom procedures from general ones like "listen to one another" to specific ones, such as "We need to listen and understand what the speaker is saying. We all have an obligation to ask questions when we don't understand."

3. Focus on the important mathematical concepts in the lesson. If these objectives are written on the board it helps both you and students keep the dialogue focused.

4. Ask good questions. Interesting questions that have answers not already known support good classroom discussions. Use questions that prompt students to listen to each other. For example, "Can you repeat in your own words what you just heard?" "How is this strategy similar to or different from your strategy?" and "What can you add to what was just said?" "Do you agree or disagree with it? Why or why not?" In all cases, the response is neither punitive nor evaluative. If the student who is asked these questions cannot answer, he or she can always ask, "I didn't understand, could you please repeat what was said?" These questions communicate to students that you expect them to listen and learn from each other. Good questions for facilitating discourse are offered in *Professional Standards for Teaching Mathematics* (NCTM, 1991) or can be accessed through Public Broadcasting Service Teacherline.

5. Engage all students in discussion. Participation is not optional. If students are sharing with the whole group, stop at times and ask them to share their thoughts with a partner. Ask students to write an idea on paper or in their journals so they are ready to share.

6. Focus on student understanding. Kenney, et al. (2005) characterize three types of discourse. First, the traditional, in which the teacher and several students talk. Second is a "probing" discussion, where the teacher is still generating the questions, but the questions are more open-ended. Third, is "discourse-rich," where students are working together toward mathematical understanding. An important distinction in the third type is the student-to-student and student-to-class interactions.

7. Decide when to guide students and when to wait, when to ask a student for further elaboration and when to elicit input from others. Quiet pauses should not be uncomfortable dead time, but "think time" for all students to think about what was just said, process it, and then respond.

In addition to these strategies, Easley (1990) offers guidelines for establishing an environment that fosters discourse (see below).

Ten Suggestions for Practice in Communication

From *Dialogue and Conceptual Splatter in Mathematics Classes* by Jack Easley

1. Try to maintain an atmosphere of freedom in the classroom, that is, an atmosphere that encourages students* to feel free to express themselves.
2. When in doubt, remain silent! Give students a chance to work through their mathematical difficulties.
3. Don't paraphrase because paraphrasing is usually a technique for pushing the students too quickly towards the teacher's point of view. Let the students' words stand by themselves. Ask students to clarify the expression of their own thoughts rather than comply with your thoughts.
4. Encourage constructive arguments. For example, ask, "Do you believe that?" "Do you agree or disagree?" "How do you know?" or say, "Tell me what you mean."
5. Play dumb, but avoid condescension. Let the students teach you as well as each other.
6. Don't focus on "right" answers. Alternative answers can create a tension that leads to lively and fruitful interaction. In addition, many good problems have more than one right answer, or at least more than one possible solution technique.
7. Let students have time to work on a problem as individuals before you ask them to share their thoughts in a small or large group, thereby encouraging each student to get involved in the problem.
8. No best way exists to form small groups. For example, you can group students at random or on the basis of ability levels or of their conflicting opinions.
9. Dialogue groups, whether small or large, can be called "meetings." Take time to model expected etiquette for the meetings.
10. Save the written work of the students to evaluate and substantiate their learning. Record the classroom dialogues on videotapes, audiotapes, and in your own journal of the activities; share these recordings with the students. And finally, bring continuity to the dialogues by basing future sessions on your evaluation of the conceptual splatter that has been expressed. (p. 36)

*Students is used here to replace "pupils," which was used in the original publication.

Arithmetic Teacher by Jack Easley. Copyright 1990 by National Council of Teachers of Mathematics. Reproduced with permission of National Council of Teachers of Mathematics in the format Textbook via Copyright Clearance Center.

For further information on developing a language-rich classroom for English Language Learners, see the Teaching the *Math Trailblazers* Student: Meeting Individual Needs section.

References

Assessment Standards for School Mathematics. National Council of Teachers of Mathematics, Reston, VA, 1995.

Burrill, G. "Changes in your Classrooms: From the Past to the Present to the Future." *Mathematics Teaching in the Middle School,* 4(3), pp. 184–190, 1998.

Chapin, S.H., C. O'Conner, and N.C. Anderson. *Classroom Discussions: Using Math Talk to Help Students Learn.* Math Solutions Publications, Sausalito, CA, 2003.

Cummins, J. "Supporting ESL Students in Learning the Language of Mathematics." *Research Says: Issues and Trends in Mathematics.* Pearson Education, New York, 2007.

Cuoco, A., E.P. Goldenberg, and J. Mark. "Habits of Mind: An Organizing Principle for Mathematics Curricula." *Journal of Mathematical Behavior,* 15, pp. 375–402, 1996.

Curriculum and Evaluation Standards for School Mathematics (1st ed.). National Council of Teachers of Mathematics, Reston, VA, 1989.

Easley, Jack. "Research into Practice. Dialogue and Conceptual Splatter in Mathematics Classes." *Arithmetic Teacher,* 37(7), pp. 34–37, 1990.

Galima, L., and T. Hirsch. "Making Mathematics Accessible to English Learners." Paper presented at the National Council of Teachers of Mathematics (NCTM) annual meeting, Atlanta, GA, March 2007.

Herbel-Eisenmann, B.A., and M.L. Breyfogle. "Questioning our Patterns of Questioning." *Mathematics Teaching in the Middle School,* 10(9), pp. 484–489, 2005.

Hiebert, J., et al. *Making Sense: Teaching and Learning Mathematics with Understanding.* Heinemann, Portsmouth, NH, 1997.

Kenney, J.M., E. Hancewicz, L. Heuer, D. Metsisto, and C.L. Tuttle. *Literacy Strategies for Improving Mathematics Instruction.* Association for Supervision and Curriculum Development, Alexandria, VA, 2005.

McIntosh, M.E. "500 Writing Formats." *Mathematics Teaching in the Middle School,* 2(5), pp. 354–358, 1997.

Polya, G. *How to Solve It: A New Aspect of Mathematical Method.* Princeton University Press, Princeton, NJ, 1973.

Principles and Standards for School Mathematics. National Council of Teachers of Mathematics, Reston, VA, 2000.

Professional Standards for Teaching Mathematics. National Council of Teachers of Mathematics, Reston, VA, 1991.

Pugalee, D.K. *Writing for Mathematical Understanding.* Christopher Gordon Publishers Norwood, MA, 2005.

Sowder, L. "Children's Solutions of Story Problems." *Journal of Mathematical Behavior* 7, pp. 227–238, 1988.

Van de Walle, J.A. *Elementary and Middle School Mathematics: Teaching Developmentally.* Pearson Education, New York, 2007.

Whitin, D.J., and P. Whitin. "Exploring Mathematics Through Talking and Writing." M.J. Burke, and F.R. Curcio, eds. *Learning Mathematics for a New Century: 2000 Yearbook,* pp. 213–222. NCTM, Reston, VA, 2000.

Wood, T. "Alternative Patterns of Communication in Mathematics Classes: Funneling or Focusing?" H. Steinbring, M.B. Bussi, and A. Sierpinska, eds. *Language and Communication in the Mathematics Classroom,* pp. 167–178. NCTM, Reston, VA, 1998.

Working with *Math Trailblazers* Parents and Families

The Parents and *Math Trailblazers* section provides suggestions and tips to help parents participate in their child's understanding of *Math Trailblazers* and to enhance its benefits for their children.

A teacher, student, and parent work together to solve a problem.

Working with *Math Trailblazers*
Parents and Families

 PART I

Math Trailblazers Features

Parents' understanding and support of your mathematics curriculum plays an important role in its successful implementation and can be a key factor in children's success with mathematics. This section provides suggestions and tips to help parents understand the *Math Trailblazers* curriculum. It is arranged in three parts. The first part describes several built-in features to help you communicate with parents. The second part gives advice on preparing two types of special programs: math nights for families and parent presentations at school or district meetings. The third part provides blackline masters to copy and distribute to parents.

Parents want assurances that the content and approaches of the school's mathematics program will not only educate and interest their children now, but also benefit them later when test scores and school admissions become serious realities. Most adults experienced a mathematics curriculum that focused almost exclusively on teaching facts and standard procedures for computing. In contrast, *Math Trailblazers* maintains a careful balance between developing skills, underlying mathematical concepts, and problem solving. Parents need to understand this balance. Moreover, parents must understand the importance of teaching the other mathematics strands (algebra, geometry, measurement, and data analysis and probability). As you work with parents throughout the year, communicate the following:

- Varied contexts for solving problems in *Math Trailblazers* help children learn to use mathematics in meaningful ways;

- The activities in *Math Trailblazers* are designed to provide children with the skills they will need in the workplace of the 21st century.

- Current research supports the approaches used in *Math Trailblazers* for teaching mathematics. In regard to computation and facts, the approaches in *Math Trailblazers* allow students to gain fluency with less drill and memorization than former methods and with better retention;

- Practice with skills and procedures is distributed between homework, Daily Practice and Problems, and within most problem-solving activities in the program;

- *Math Trailblazers* encourages students to develop varied ways to solve problems—not just the solutions that adults might select; and

- Mathematical ideas are represented with manipulatives, pictures, tables, graphs, and numbers—and how these representations allow children to access the mathematics in varied ways.

Parents need to understand the careful balance that Math Trailblazers *maintains between developing skills, underlying mathematical concepts, and problem solving.*

Communicating with Parents

Gaining parent support early will save effort in the long term. Anticipate potential parental concerns about a new math program and address them proactively through an ongoing parent education effort.

Math Trailblazers includes a parent brochure, letters home, homework notes, and parent information blackline masters to help you communicate about the curriculum.

Parent Brochure

The parent brochure provides an introduction to the curriculum. Blackline masters of this brochure (in English and Spanish) are at the end of this section. They are designed for you to send home at the beginning of the year or use as a handout at a fall parent meeting.

Letters Home

Parent letters are included at the beginning of each unit to give specific information about what children will study. These letters describe the concepts presented in each unit and how parents or family members can provide follow-up and encouragement at home. A sample Letter Home is shown in Figure 1.

Figure 1: *Sample letter home from Grade 1*

Homework Notes

Many homework assignments, especially in grades K–3, include a separate explanation for family members, outlining the activity's purpose and providing hints for assisting with the assignment. An example of such a note is shown in Figure 2. These explanations are to help parents feel comfortable with the curriculum's content and goals. We encourage you to supplement the parent instructions with your own notes and to provide a way for parents to get their homework questions answered (e.g., via emails, phone, or after school).

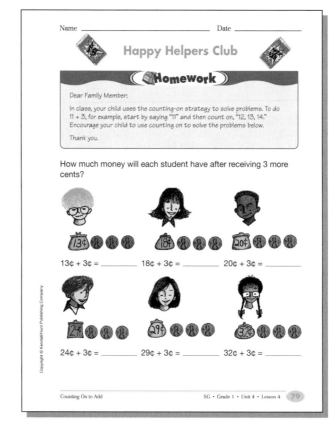

Figure 2: *Sample Grade 1 homework note for parents*

Parent Information Blackline Masters

Additional information on selected topics is available to be copied for parents at the end of this section. Topics include:

• Math Facts Philosophy

• Multiplication Methods in *Math Trailblazers*

• Long Division in *Math Trailblazers*

• Internet Resources for Families of *Math Trailblazers* Students

Roles for Parent Volunteers

Parent volunteers can support the implementation of *Math Trailblazers* in a variety of capacities.

Parent volunteers can be an important support to the implementation of Math Trailblazers *in a variety of capacities.*

Math Trailblazers incorporates many hands-on activities. In addition to the commercially purchased manipulatives such as base-ten pieces, many activities call for materials such as jars, container lids, paper towel cores, and so on. Parent volunteers can ease the job of gathering and managing these materials.

Parent volunteers also can assist with classroom activities. They can work on special projects or lesson extensions with small groups. Some teachers periodically invite several parents to assist with station activities, where student groups rotate from station to station. Often it is helpful to have an extra set of hands and eyes in the classroom to assist as needed.

Parents can assist students during a lesson. Assign parents to work with particular groups of students or with individual students who need extra assistance. With guidance on appropriate ways to support student thinking, this can be a great support for students, as well as educate parents in the instructional approaches used in *Math Trailblazers*.

You can obviously tailor the roles parents play in providing support to your needs and the interests and capabilities of individual parents. There is little doubt, however, that parent volunteers are a valuable asset as you work with *Math Trailblazers*.

Special Programs for Families and Parents

One way to help parents understand and support the goals and philosophy of *Math Trailblazers* is to organize special math-related programs for parents and families. One type of program is a math night, during which parents participate in math activities with their children. Another is a more formal presentation given by a teacher or other curriculum leader at a school parent night or special informational meeting. Many schools combine both types of programs by giving a short presentation as part of a math night. The following are suggestions to help you plan parent and family programs for your school.

Family Math Nights

A typical math night involves families coming to school to participate together in math activities. A variety of successful math night formats include:

- **Math Night Carnival**
  Families move from one math activity to another at their own pace. This format is typically held in a large space such as a gymnasium or lunchroom.

- **Teacher-Led Math Night**
  Families visit their child's math classroom and work together through grade-level specific activities and games.

- **Math Night Classroom Rotation**
  Families rotate through a series of classrooms. Each classroom presents a specific math activity or game. Families may encounter activities from a variety of grade levels.

One way to help parents understand and support the goals and philosophy of Math Trailblazers *is to organize special math-related programs for parents and families.*

The best format of any math night differs from school to school and even from year to year within the same school. The following is what happened at one school.

The school invited parents and students to a math night designed as a carnival, held in the gym. Students and parents played a game at each booth and got a prize when they finished. As the evening progressed though, parents congregated in the middle of the gym while their children played the games alone. This event did not meet the goal of getting parents involved with and learning about Math Trailblazers.

The next year, the staff decided to reorganize the math night to keep parents involved in Math Trailblazers *activities with their children. In preparation for the math night, teachers chose primary and intermediate activities and planned them to be held in classrooms. They made a display about the activity that included information on how the activity aligned with the state and NCTM Standards. Teachers also hung estimation activities in the hallways to keep families busy as they moved through the school. As families worked their way from the primary to the middle grades, they saw how the mathematics develops across the grades. Parental involvement on this math night was a big improvement over previous years.*

Suggested Activities

When planning a math night, choose activities that illustrate key ideas from the *Math Trailblazers* curriculum and engage parents. For example, choose activities that focus on problem solving, address a range of mathematical content, or have connections to science.

Doing parts of one of the labs is an effective way for parents to experience how mathematics in the curriculum is embedded in meaningful contexts. Consider using labs you have already done in class. That way, students can lead their parents. Students won't mind repeating the lab, since in many cases, the data will be new to them.

Following is a list of activities that worked well in math night programs. We chose these activities because the concepts underlying them are easily understood, and require minimum preparation. They also show the impact of *Math Trailblazers* work with the scientific method and ways for children to practice computation in a context.

Kindergarten:
- sorting apples from *Data Collection* in the *Ongoing Content* section
- *A Garden's Area,* Month 7 Lesson 4

Grade 1:
- *Pockets* activities in Unit 3 (selected pieces)
- *More or Less Than 100,* Unit 9 Lesson 2

Grade 2:
- *High, Wide, and Handsome,* Unit 4 Lesson 1 (selected pieces)
- *Tile Designs,* Unit 2 Lesson 1
- *Marshmallows and Containers,* Unit 6, Lesson 5 (selected pieces)

Grade 3:
- *First Names,* Unit 1 Lesson 10
- *The Better "Picker Upper,"* Unit 5 Lesson 3
- *Floor Tiler,* Unit 11 Lesson 5

Grade 4:
- *Arm Span vs. Height,* Unit 1 Lesson 5 (selected pieces)
- *Investigating Area and Perimeter,* Unit 2 Lesson 1

Grade 5:
- *Three in a Row,* Unit 8 Lesson 2
- *Factor 40,* Unit 11 Lesson 1
- *Fraction Cover All,* Unit 5 Lesson 3

Tips for Math Nights

The following list of recommendations reflects the experiences of teachers in many different settings. The list is intended to help you make decisions for your own Math Night, but not all may be appropriate in your setting.

- Hold more than one math night, with different grade levels (e.g., K, 1–2, 3–5) grouped together. If you target multiple grades, families with children in different grades can participate together. On the other hand, if you offer grade-level classes, parents can learn more about their child's particular grade.

- Require that students come with an adult. Explain that this is not just a program for children, but a chance for families to enjoy mathematics together.

- If using the teacher-led classroom format, make sure there is enough room for everyone. Some schools divide participants into groups of eight to ten families, so there are about 25 people per class.

- Consider offering babysitting for younger siblings, so parents can devote their attention to their school-age children.

- Ask families to register in advance so you will know how many people to plan for. This also lets you know whether you need further recruitment efforts. However, some schools believe that asking families to register discourages some from attending.

- Involve as many people as you can. Include groups such as the parent-teacher organization. Ask high school students to help as volunteers—some schools offer credit for volunteer service.

- Involve parent volunteers in planning the event and leading the activities. This gives parents a first-hand look at the curriculum and makes the planning more manageable. Parents who are not comfortable leading activities can help with registration, shop for supplies, arrange for food, and babysit.

- Advertise. Send home fliers, have students make invitations for their parents, feature articles in school newsletters, put up posters.

- Offer rewards for coming, such as packages of manipulatives or math games that can be played at home. Offer a reward to the class that has the highest attendance.

- Provide food. Find local sponsors or ask the parent organization for donations of food or beverages.

- Have a raffle. Items can be donated by local businesses. Include information about the raffle in the flyer. Math trade books and gift certificates make great prizes.

- Be sure to try the activities yourself before leading them.

- Use manipulatives in the activities so parents can see how their children use them for meaningful math activities.

- Use one or more of the math facts games to illustrate one way to engage students in practicing math facts.

- Send home a packet of games so families can continue to play at home.

- Hand out an evaluation form to help plan for future programs.

- Have a math day, instead of math night. Parents can visit their children's math classes and stay for lunch. Or set up math stations around the school and have students as tour guides.

Here are some additional tips for programs that use a carnival or classroom rotation format:

- Hand out "passports." Ask families to get "stamped" at each station and enter their completed passports in a prize drawing.

- If you want participants to spend equal amounts of time at each station, then plan a second activity or open-ended task at short stations.

- Include stations that feature brief sessions on various aspects of *Math Trailblazers,* for example, how to use strategies to learn math facts, the TIMS Laboratory Method, and so on.

Other Resources for Planning Math Nights

- *Family Math* is an excellent resource for planning a math program for families. It describes stimulating math games and activities for a series of classes in which parents and children participate together. Included are an early childhood book and a K–8 book, and translations into Spanish. The goals of *Family Math* complement the goals of *Math Trailblazers* and as a result, parents who participate in *Family Math* are likely to have a good understanding of the approach used in *Math Trailblazers.* Whether you plan a one-night event to introduce *Math Trailblazers* or a longer series of classes, *Family Math* gives practical advice to help you plan. It also has useful handouts on topics such as math and careers that are interesting to families. For more information about the program, including training for Family Math workshop leaders, or to order a book, contact:

Family Math
Lawrence Hall of Science
University of California at Berkeley
Berkeley, CA 94720-5200
www.lhs.berkeley.edu/equals

Content Note

Getting the most from your work with parents
Just as teachers ask students to reflect on their learning, be sure to ask parents what they learned from any *Math Trailblazers*-related parent activities. Invite parents to think about a question as the final activity. This can help provide insights into what parents have learned, but also provide feedback for the next parent session.

- As part of their continued professional development and support for *Math Trailblazers* users, Kendall/Hunt Publishing Company offers assistance in planning math nights tailored to the needs of your school. You may contact them at 1-800-542-6657.

Presentations to Parents

Since the *Math Trailblazers* program is different from what is familiar to most parents and grandparents, curriculum presentations and the reasons your school selected it can help build support. These range from formal presentations at district-wide or school-wide meetings to less formal discussions at classroom parent nights. Some schools hold monthly meetings that focus on different grade levels or different topics. Others schedule one district-wide or school-wide presentation that gives an overview of the program. Suggestions of topics to include in a presentation are discussed below. Additional resources for preparing your presentation are at the end of this section.

> **Suggested Topics for a Parent Presentation**
>
> - Description of *Math Trailblazers*
> - Your District's Implementation
> - A Closer Look
> - Computation and Math Facts in *Math Trailblazers*

Description of *Math Trailblazers*

The following are ways to describe *Math Trailblazers*. For further elaboration, see the Foundations section.

- *Math Trailblazers* is a *Standards*-based curriculum. It follows the recommendations of the *Principles and Standards for School Mathematics*, developed by the National Council of Teachers of Mathematics (NCTM, 2000) to improve the teaching and learning of mathematics. These recommendations outline a vision for school mathematics that includes:
  - a mathematically challenging curriculum that covers a broad range of mathematical content;
  - a strong focus on engaging students in mathematical problem solving;
  - instruction that is conceptually oriented and stresses thinking, reasoning, and the application of appropriate uses of calculators and computers; and
  - a strong commitment to promoting success in mathematics among all students—not only those who traditionally do well.

- *Math Trailblazers* is a research-based curriculum. The first edition was the result of more than six years of work by the Teaching Integrated Math and Science Project (TIMS) at the University of Illinois at Chicago, including extensive pilot- and field-testing of the materials. In developing *Math Trailblazers,* the authors drew upon research findings from a wide variety of sources, as well as from the broad experiences of the authoring group, which included mathematicians, scientists, and former teachers. The National Science Foundation funded development of *Math Trailblazers* and has continued to support research on the impact of *Math Trailblazers* on student achievement and research-based development of revised editions.

- *Math Trailblazers* is a problem-solving curriculum. A fundamental principle is that mathematics is best learned through active involvement in solving real problems. Problem solving in *Math Trailblazers* is not a distinct topic, but one that permeates the entire program, providing a context for students to apply the mathematics they know and learn new

> Since the Math Trailblazers *program is different from what parents and grandparents are familiar with, presentations about the curriculum and the reasons your school selected it can help build support.*

mathematics. For example, in a third grade laboratory experiment, *The Better "Picker Upper,"* students investigate which paper towel is more absorbent. They explore the absorbency of various brands of paper towels by dropping water onto each and comparing the areas of the resulting spots. In the process, they learn about area, fractions, averaging, and computation. As students work on problems such as these, they develop skills, procedures, and concepts.

- *Math Trailblazers* is a full mathematics curriculum, with a focus on science and language arts. It uses science as a context for much of the problem solving built into the program. In Kindergarten students collect and analyze data at least once every week, and in each of grades 1–5, students engage in eight to ten laboratory investigations that serve as a rich source of real-world mathematics problems. In these investigations, students identify variables, draw pictures, take measurements, organize data in tables, graph data, and look for and use patterns—all important mathematics skills that are used by scientists. *Math Trailblazers* also focuses on language arts, with lessons that emphasize reading, writing, and oral communication. Collections of original math-related stories are found in the *Math Trailblazers Adventure Book.* Math trade books are recommended to accompany many lessons.

Your District's Implementation of *Math Trailblazers*

Include some of the following as you discuss your district's implementation:

- **Selection process.** Assure parents that a careful and thoughtful process was used to select the curriculum. Consider inviting a representative from the selection committee to describe the process.

- **Reasons for choosing *Math Trailblazers* over other curricula.** Describe the features of the program that appeal to the selection committee. How does *Math Trailblazers* help meet the goals of your school? If your district pilot-tested the curriculum before adoption, discuss feedback from teachers who have piloted the program. Invite one or more of those teachers to share their experiences.

- **Professional development.** Explain the program your district has in place to assure that teachers are trained to use the curriculum effectively. Describe the professional development opportunities teachers have had or will have to support their implementation.

- **Evidence of success.** If your district has used the program for a few years, describe teacher and student experiences with it. If you are new to the program, report on some of the experiences of other districts. Information on the success of *Math Trailblazers* around the country is available on the Kendall/Hunt web site, http://www.kendallhunt.com/mtb3.

- **Examples of what students are doing.** A good way to communicate to families that their children are learning more than just computational skills is to show examples of student work. Pick samples that illustrate how students solve complex multistep problems.

A Closer Look at *Math Trailblazers*

To help parents understand some of the strengths of *Math Trailblazers,* show them examples of specific lessons. If possible, ask them to solve a problem or play a game so they can experience firsthand the problem-solving approach to *Math Trailblazers.* Debrief from the activity in the way that you would with students. Ask parents to reflect on the lesson's content, how it compares to their experience, and what this means in terms of opportunities for students to learn. Consider using student work to show the kinds of problems *Math Trailblazers* students solve. Use work collected from your own students or samples available in the *Math Trailblazers* support material.

One source of student work examples is a component of *Math Trailblazers* called the Teacher Enhancement Resource Modules (TERMs). The TERMs were designed to help staff developers assemble workshops for teachers, but portions can also be presented to parents. They contain a guide for presenters with blackline masters, explanatory text, and discussion questions and answers. A set of TERMs is usually available in each district. Check with your principal or district office or call Kendall/Hunt at 1-800-KH-Books.

Most TERMs also include videos showing *Math Trailblazers* teachers and students engaged in activities from the curriculum. These streaming videos are available through the Kendall/Hunt website, mymathtrailblazers.com. Check with your principal or district office for information on how to access these resources.

Another source of appropriate sample student work, video, and explanatory text are from a grade 2 activity, *Measuring Volume.* This source contains a selection of relevant text, blackline masters, and the video you can use to develop a presentation for parents. These materials are available on the web, www.mymathtrailblazers.com.

The following are modules that can be adapted for use with parents (found in TERMS Set #1):

- **Why Reform?**
  This TERM presents information to introduce *Standards*-based mathematics. It includes a video *How Many in the Bag?* that shows students talking with their partners about their solutions to subtraction problems that arise from pulling handfuls of cubes from a bag. The interaction of the students talking about the problems shows how communication helps students clarify their thinking, correct mistakes, and hear different strategies from fellow students.

  A selection of text, blackline masters, and the video of one TERM, *Why Reform?* is available for download at www.mymathtrailblazers.com

- **Operations: Meaning, Invention, Efficiency, Power**
  Use this TERM to help guide the discussion of how the concept of division develops across grades K–5 and to describe the *Math Trailblazers* philosophy of computation. This TERM also shows how this philosophy applies to the development of other operations and to teaching the math facts.

- **Area: A Look Across the Grades**

  Use the *Area* TERM to help parents see how science is a rich context for applying and learning mathematics. This TERM includes representative area activities from each grade to show growth in mathematics and development of the concept of area through the grades.

- **Computation and Math Facts in *Math Trailblazers***

  Many parents think of computation when they think of mathematics, so it is natural for them to be curious about the way *Math Trailblazers* teaches computation. Explain that a balanced approach fosters the development of both mathematical concepts and skills. The following points might be useful in talking with parents about computation and basic math facts.

  1. Computation. In today's world, students compute using paper-and-pencil algorithms, calculators, and mental arithmetic. They need to get exact answers to problems as well as make and recognize reasonable estimates. *Math Trailblazers* helps students develop efficient and accurate methods for computation with the four basic operations. The treatment of each operation proceeds in the following stages:

     - Developing meaning for the operation

     - Inventing procedures for solving problems

     - Becoming more efficient at carrying out procedures

     - Developing mathematical power

  2. "Mathematical power" means that students understand when to apply the operation and how to use varied computational methods to solve problems. Students practice using the operations in activities, games, and laboratory investigations. More practice is provided in the Daily Practice and Problems in Grades 1–5 and in the Home Practice in Grades 3–5. Flexible thinking and mathematical power are our goals. The above computation stages are discussed more thoroughly in the Math Facts and Whole-Number Operations section.

  3. The paper-and-pencil algorithms for multiplication and long division taught in *Math Trailblazers* are probably somewhat different from those that parents learned in school. We introduce the "all-partials method" for multiplication first since many children find it easier to learn. Then we introduce the more efficient "compact method," the algorithm traditionally taught. (See Figure 3.)

All-Partials Method	**Compact Method**
15	15
× 22	× 22
10 (2 × 5)	30 (2 × 15)
20 (2 × 10)	+ 300 (20 × 15)
100 (20 × 5)	330
+ 200 (20 × 10)	
330	

Figure 3: *Paper and pencil algorithms for multiplication*

For division, we teach the "forgiving method" because many students find it easier to learn than the traditional method. While this method involves making estimates about the quotient, as does the traditional method, the forgiving method encourages the use of "easy" numbers, such as division by 10 or 100 in the estimates. The forgiving method also allows underestimates so it doesn't involve as much erasing and re-calculating as done by some children when using the traditional method. In the case where the highest possible estimate is made, the two methods are essentially the same. (See Figure 4.) Parent information sheets that describe the multiplication and division algorithms used in *Math Trailblazers* are at the end of this section.

Forgiving Method		Traditional Method
335		335
5) 1675	300 (estimate quotient 1675 ÷ 5)	5) 1675
− 1500		− 15
175	30 (estimate quotient 175 ÷ 5)	17
− 150		− 15
25	5 (25 ÷ 5)	25
− 25		− 25
0	335	0

Figure 4: *Paper and pencil algorithms for division*

4. Math Facts. The goal of the *Math Trailblazers* math facts program is for students to learn the basic facts efficiently, gain fluency with their use, and retain that fluency over time. A large body of research supports an approach that is built on a foundation of work with strategies and concepts. This leads not only to more effective learning and better retention, but also to the development of mental math skills.

   The *Math Trailblazers* math facts program is characterized by the elements below. These are summarized in the *Math Facts Philosophy* Blackline master at the end of this section.
   • Early emphasis on problem solving
   • Use of strategies to find facts and the de-emphasis of rote work
   • Gradual and systematic introduction of the facts
   • Ongoing practice
   • Appropriate assessment
   • Facts are not gatekeepers
   • Multiyear approach

As you discuss the math facts program, give parents a few examples of math fact strategies such as the subtraction strategies of "counting up" and "using a ten." Other strategies are discussed in the *Math Facts* Tutor. This tutor is available to parents on the Kendall/Hunt website, as are several other TIMS Tutors.

Other Resources for Planning Your Presentation

The *Family* section of the Kendall/Hunt Website http://www.mymath trailblazers.com has several links to documents that can help you plan your presentation. Here are a few:

- *An Introduction for Families* includes answers to the following questions:

  What is in the *Math Trailblazers* curriculum?

  What is a *Math Trailblazers* classroom like?

  What connections does *Math Trailblazers* make with other school subjects?

  Why is my child using calculators with *Math Trailblazers?*

  How can parents talk with their children about math?

- *Frequently Asked Questions* includes answers to the following questions:

  How is *Math Trailblazers* different from other mathematics curricula?

  What is the opinion of the scientific community regarding the standards set by the National Council of Teachers of Mathematics?

  What science does *Math Trailblazers* include?

  How does *Math Trailblazers* integrate mathematics with other content areas?

  What kind of assessment does *Math Trailblazers* use?

  Does *Math Trailblazers* make use of collaborative learning?

  Can *Math Trailblazers* facilitate teaching children with learning styles and ability levels in a heterogeneous classroom?

Additional resources for working with parents include:

Stenmark, Jean Kerr, Virginia Thompson, and Ruth Cossey. *Family Math.* University of California, Lawrence Hall of Science, Berkeley, CA, 1986.

Funkhouser, J.E., and M.R. Gonzales. *Family Involvement in Children's Education: Successful Local Approaches: An Idea Book.* U.S. Department of Education, Washington, DC, 1997. http://www.ed.gov/pubs/FamInvolve/

Shartrand, A.M., H.B. Weiss, H.M. Kreider, and M. Lopez, *New Skills for New Schools: Preparing Teachers in Family Involvement.* Harvard Graduate School of Education, Harvard Family Research Project, Cambridge, 1997. (Available from the U. S. Department of Education http://www.ed.gov/pubs/NewSkills/index.html.)

Mira, A. *A Family's Guide: Fostering your Child's Success in School Mathematics.* National Council of Teachers of Mathematics, Reston, VA, 2005.

National Council of Teachers of Mathematics Families Web page, http://nctm.org/resources/families.aspx

Parent Information Blackline Masters

- Parent Brochure (English and Spanish versions)
- Math Facts Philosophy
- Multiplication Methods in *Math Trailblazers*
- Long Division in *Math Trailblazers*
- Internet Resources for Families of *Math Trailblazers* Students

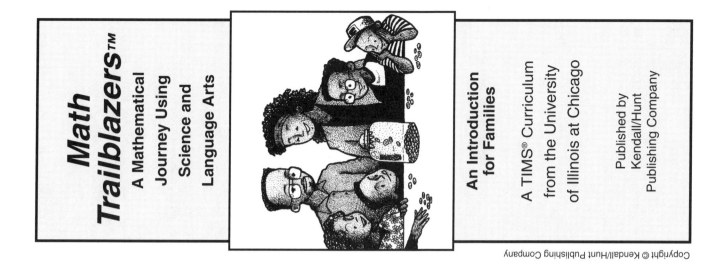

Math Trailblazers™

A Mathematical Journey Using Science and Language Arts

An Introduction for Families

A TIMS® Curriculum from the University of Illinois at Chicago

Published by Kendall/Hunt Publishing Company

How can parents talk with their children about math?

Your child will have a lot to share with you about mathematics. Here are some conversation starters to help your child communicate what he or she is doing in mathematics:

☞ What problems did you solve in math today? How did you solve the problems? Are there other ways to solve that same problem?

☞ Did you use any special materials in math today? What were they? How did you use them?

☞ Did you measure anything in school today? What did you measure?

☞ Did you collect data in math today? How did you record the data?

☞ Did you hear a math story today? Please tell me the story.

> "One of the things I've noticed … is that when he [my child] brings home an activity and he brings a measuring tape or something kind of special, he's excited about doing it. The fact that we're involved in the games—he loves that—and he's proud of what he's doing."
>
> **Parent**

You can contact the developers of *Math Trailblazers* at the following address:

UIC The University of Illinois at Chicago

TIMS Project
Institute for Mathematics and Science Education (M/C 250)
950 South Halsted Street, Room 2075 SEL
Chicago, IL 60607-7019
www.math.uic.edu/IMSE

KENDALL/HUNT PUBLISHING COMPANY
4050 Westmark Drive Dubuque, Iowa 52002
www.mathtrailblazers.com

Development of *Math Trailblazers* was supported in part by the National Science Foundation.

What connections does Math Trailblazers make with other school subjects?

> "It seems a lot of this carries over to different subject areas. It's not just isolated to math."
>
> **Teacher**

In *Math Trailblazers*, children learn mathematics, in part, by applying it in many different contexts. This makes mathematics meaningful for students and models the way mathematics is used outside of school.

Science investigations are used often in *Math Trailblazers* to provide a context for learning and applying mathematics. Children design experiments; collect, organize, and graph data; and analyze experimental results in much the same way scientists do. Measurement of length, area, volume, mass, and time is done repeatedly within the context of scientific experiments. This strong connection with science engages students in rich problem-solving activities and introduces students to the tools and methods scientists use.

Math Trailblazers also has many connections with language arts—communication of math ideas in writing and orally is an integral part of every lesson. Children write journal entries, record data, and share ideas. They also read children's books and *Math Trailblazers Adventure Books* that connect with many class lessons. As children communicate their methods for solving problems and justify their answers, they better understand important math concepts. Their writing and other communication skills also improve.

Why is my child using calculators with Math Trailblazers?

The calculator is a tool used in appropriate situations to help your child explore number ideas and relationships, solve more complex problems, and explore mathematics on his or her own. The use of calculators is supported by the National Council of Teachers of Mathematics.

A curriculum for your children

The mathematics curriculum being taught in many schools today is very similar to the curriculum that was taught when the parents, grandparents, and even great-grandparents of today's school children attended school. Many of the math skills in that curriculum remain important today. But the world has changed considerably since the time of our grandparents. Advances in technology have created many other essential math skills that your children will need when they complete their formal schooling and enter tomorrow's work force. The National Council of Teachers of Mathematics recognized these needs when, in 1989 and 2000, it made a series of recommendations for updating math instruction in U.S. schools. *Math Trailblazers* was developed to reflect these national recommendations.

Math Trailblazers will prepare students to:

★ know and apply basic math skills;

★ solve problems using many different strategies;

★ be independent thinkers;

★ reason skillfully in diverse situations;

★ effectively communicate solutions to problems and methods for solving them;

★ work alone and in groups to solve problems.

Math Trailblazers was developed and tested over a seven-year period by a team from the Teaching Integrated Mathematics and Science (TIMS) Project at the University of Illinois at Chicago. Using the results of educational research and over 15 years of previous experience in curriculum development, the TIMS Project has written an innovative program that will prepare your children with math skills needed for the 21st century.

What is in the *Math Trailblazers* curriculum?

Math Trailblazers is a comprehensive curriculum that maintains a balance between the development of math concepts and basic skills. Students apply basic math skills while working on meaningful and challenging tasks. The math content of the traditional math curriculum is studied; but other topics—estimation, geometry, measurement, patterns and relationships, algebra concepts, and statistics and probability—are investigated at an appropriate level in each grade.

The curriculum includes different types of lessons:

Activities—explorations of math concepts and skills that use a variety of tools and methods.

Labs—extended investigations that use a simplified version of the method scientists use.

Daily Practice and Problems—items that provide practice in math skills and concepts.

Games—math games that build familiarity with math skills and concepts.

Adventure Books—illustrated stories that deal with math and science ideas.

Assessments—activities that allow the teacher and student to assess progress.

"When my older daughter started out, she didn't feel confident with math. And now that she's had *Math Trailblazers*, she says that she's good at math. I feel good about that."

Parent

What is a *Math Trailblazers* classroom like?

When you walk into your child's *Math Trailblazers* class, you will probably notice that it does not look like the mathematics classroom you experienced when you were your child's age. Children might be working in groups, pulling jellybean samples from bags. As they work, children discuss different ways to solve problems. The room is filled with a feeling of excitement and discovery.

In a *Math Trailblazers* classroom, children are:

☆ learning mathematics by using it to solve many different kinds of problems;

☆ drawing on their own experiences and working with real-world problems;

☆ using concrete objects to understand abstract mathematical concepts;

☆ communicating mathematical ideas to their peers and teacher;

☆ gaining confidence in mathematics and developing an "I can do it" feeling.

"I just love walking into a classroom when you see kids all over the room doing their data gathering. Some of them are on the floor measuring this or working with that or asking questions. It is so exciting to see children engaged in this kind of math discovery."

Elementary School Principal

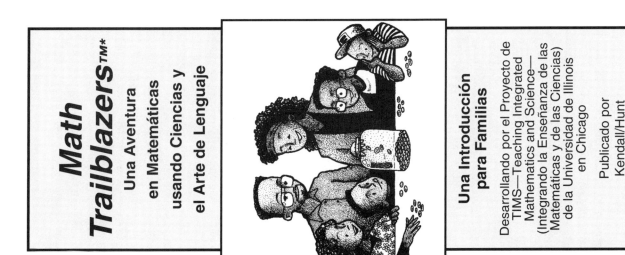

Math Trailblazers™*

Una Aventura en Matemáticas usando Ciencias y el Arte de Lenguaje

Una Introducción para Familias

Desarrollando por el Proyecto de TIMS—Teaching Integrated Mathematics and Science— (Integrando la Enseñanza de las Matemáticas y de las Ciencias) de la Universidad de Illinois en Chicago

Publicado por
Kendall/Hunt
Publishing Company

* Abriendo un camino de matemáticas

¿Qué es lo que los padres de familia pueden hacer?

Su hijo/a tendrá mucho que compartir con usted acerca de matemáticas. Aquí hay algunos temas para iniciar conversaciones que ayudarán a su hijo/a a que él o ella comunique lo que usted esté haciendo en matemáticas.

☞ ¿Qué problema resolviste el día de hoy en tu clase de matemáticas? ¿Cómo lo resolviste? ¿Hay alguna otra forma de resolver ese mismo problema?

☞ ¿Utilizaste algunos materiales especiales en tu clase de matemáticas? ¿Qué eran? ¿Cómo los usaste?

☞ ¿Mediste hoy algo en la escuela? ¿Qué fue lo que mediste?

☞ ¿Acumulaste algunos datos en matemáticas? ¿Cómo registraste esos datos?

☞ ¿Escuchaste alguna historia en matemáticas? Por favor cuéntame la historia.

> "Una de las cosas que he notado… es que cuando él [mi hijo] trae una actividad a la casa y trae una cinta métrica o algo especial, está emocionado para hacerlo. El hecho que nosotros estamos enredados en los juegos—le encanta—y está orgulloso de lo que está haciendo."
>
> **Un padre de familia**

Se puede comunicar con los diseñadores de *Math Trailblazers* a la siguiente dirección:

UIC The University of Illinois at Chicago

TIMS Project
Institute for Mathematics and Science Education (M/C 250)
950 South Halsted Street, Room 2075 SEL
Chicago, IL 60607-7019
www.math.uic.edu/IMSE

KENDALL/HUNT PUBLISHING COMPANY
4050 Westmark Drive   Dubuque, Iowa 52002
www.mathtrailblazers.com

El desarrollo de *Math Trailblazers* fue ayudado en parte por la National Science Foundation.

¿Qué conexiones hace *Math Trailblazers* con otras materias escolares?

En *Math Trailblazers*, los estudiantes aprenden matemáticas, en parte, aplicandolo a diversas situaciones. De esta manera las matemáticas se hacen interesantes y adquieren sentido.

Investigaciones científicas en *Math Trailblazers* proveen la oportunidad frecuente de la aplicación de las matemáticas. Los estudiantes diseñan experimentos; acumulan y organizan datos; hacen gráficas de datos; y analizan los resultados de los experimentos en una manera semejante a lo que hacen los científicos. Se hacen mediciónes de longitud, area, volumen, masa, y tiempo como parte de experimentos científicos. Esta fuerte conexión con la ciencia hace que los estudiantes resuelvan problemas como "científicos," usando métodos y herramientas de la ciencias.

Math Trailblazers también tiene muchas conexiones con el arte de lenguaje. La comunicación de ideas en matemáticas—a través de escribir, hablar, y dibujar—es una parte integral de cada lección. Los estudiantes escriben en sus diarios, registran datos, y comparten ideas. Ellos también leen libros infantiles y "libros de aventuras" que se conectan con muchas lecciónes. Los estudiantes mejoran en su entendimiento de conceptos matemáticos al comunicar sus métodos de resolver problemas y explicar sus respuestas. Sus habilidades en escribir y comunicar también mejoran.

¿Por qué mi hijo/a está usando calculadoras en *Math Trailblazers*?

Las calculadoras son instrumentos usados para ayudar a su hijo/a a investigar ideas con números y sus relaciones, resolver problemas complejos, y explorar la matemática. El uso de estas herramientas es recomendado por el Concejo Nacional de Maestros de Matemáticas.

Un programa para sus hijos

Los programas de matemáticas que se encuentran hoy día en muchas escuelas son muy semejantes a las classes que tenían los padres, abuelos, y aún bisabuelos de los estudiantes de hoy. Mucha del material de esos programas todavía se necesita hoy. Pero el mundo ha cambiado desde el tiempo de nuestros abuelos. Avances en tecnología han creado la necesidad de desarrollar otras técnicas especiales que sus hijos necesitarán en el mundo de trabajo del futuro. El Concejo Nacional de Maestros de Matemáticas reconoció estas necesidades cuando hizo una serie de recomendaciones para mejorar la enseñanza de matemáticas en las escuelas de los Estados Unidos. Hemos desarrollado el programa *Math Trailblazers* para incorporar esas recomendaciones nacionales.

Math Trailblazers preparará estudiantes para:

★ aprender y usar técnicas básicas en matemáticas;

★ resolver problemas usando varias estrategias diferentes;

★ pensar independientemente;

★ razonar con habilidad en diversas situaciones;

★ comunicar efectivamente tanto las soluciones como los métodos;

★ resolver problemas trabajando solos y en grupos.

El programa *Math Trailblazers* fue desarrollado y ensayado por un equipo del Proyecto de TIMS—Teaching Integrated Mathematics and Science—(Integrando la Enseñanza de las Matemáticas y de las Ciencias) de la Universidad de Illinois en Chicago. Han creado un programa innovativo que proveerá a sus hijos con las bases matemáticas necesarios para poder competir en el campo del trabajo en el Siglo XXI.

¿Qué hay en el programa *Math Trailblazers?*

El programa *Math Trailblazers* es un programa integral que mantiene un balance entre el desarrollo de los conceptos y las técnicas básicas de matemáticas. Los estudiantes usan las técnicas básicas mientras están trabajando con problemas interesantes y estimulantes. Se estudian los tópicos matemáticos de un programa tradicional; pero también se investigan otras materias—estimación, geometría, medición, patrones y relaciones, conceptos de álgebra, estadística y probabilidad—en un nivel apropriado para los niños.

El programa contiene varios tipos de lecciones:

Actividades—exploraciones de conceptos matemáticos y técnicas usando diferentes herramientas y métodos.

Laboratorios—investigaciones que usan una versión simplificada del método que los científicos usan.

Prácticas y Problemas Diarios—problemas breves que proveen práctica con técnicas y conceptos matemáticos.

Juegos—juegos matemáticos que estimulan familiaridad con técnicas y conceptos matemáticos.

Libros de Aventuras—historietas ilustradas que tratan con conceptos de las ciencias y matemáticas.

Evaluaciones—actividades que permiten al maestro y a los estudiantes evaluar el progreso.

¿Cómo es una clase de *Math Trailblazers?*

Si usted entra a un salón de clases *Math Trailblazers*, probablemente notará que no se parece al que usted asistió cuando tenía esa edad. En ese salón, los niños pueden estar trabajando en grupos, poniendo gotas de agua a toallas de papel, o analizando muestras de confites. Mientras los estudiantes trabajan, ellos discuten diferentes formas para resolver los problemas matemáticos. Se percieve en clases *Math Trailblazers* los sentimientos y la emoción de descubrimiento matemático.

En un salón de estas clases los alumnos están:

☆ aprendiendo matemáticas en la resolución de problemas;

☆ usando experiencias propias y trabajando con problemas verdaderas;

☆ usando objetos concretos para entender conceptos matemáticos abstractos;

☆ comunicando sus ideas de matemáticas a sus compañeros y maestros;

☆ adquiriendo confianza en las matemáticas y desarrollando un sentimiento de, "Yo sí lo puedo hacer."

Math Facts Philosophy

The goal of the math facts strand in *Math Trailblazers* is for students to learn basic facts efficiently, gain fluency with their use, and retain that fluency over time. A large body of research supports an approach in which students develop strategies for figuring out the facts rather than relying solely on rote memorization. This not only leads to more effective learning and better retention, but also to the development of mental math skills. Therefore, the teaching of the basic facts in *Math Trailblazers* is characterized by the following elements:

Use of Strategies. Students first approach the basic facts as problems to solve rather than as facts to memorize. We encourage the use of strategies to find facts, so students become confident that they can find answers to fact problems they do not immediately recall. In this way, students learn that math is more than memorizing facts and rules that "you either get or you don't." (For information on common math fact strategies, see the *Math Facts* Tutor on the *Just for Math Trailblazers Families* page of the Kendall Hunt website http://kendallhunt.com. Click on "K–12," then "Just For Families," then "Math Trailblazers Families." Then scroll down to the list of TIMS Tutors.)

Distributed Facts Practice. Students study small groups of facts they found using similar strategies. They review the facts as they use them to solve problems in labs, activities, and games. In Grades 2–5, students are given flash cards to study each group of facts at home.

Appropriate Assessment. Teachers assess students' knowledge of the facts through observations as they work on activities, labs, and games as well as through the appropriate use of written tests and quizzes. Quizzes follow the study of small groups of facts organized around specific strategies. In Grades 2–5, students take inventory tests of facts at the end of each semester. In grades 3–5, each student records his or her progress on *Facts I Know* charts and determines which facts he or she needs to study.

A Multiyear Approach. In Grades 1 and 2, the curriculum emphasizes strategies that enable students to develop fluency with the addition and subtraction facts. In Grade 3, students gain fluency with the multiplication facts while reviewing the addition and subtraction facts. In Grade 4, the addition and subtraction facts are checked, the multiplication facts are reviewed, and students develop fluency with the division facts. In Grade 5, the multiplication and division facts are systematically reviewed and assessed.

Facts Will Not Act as Gatekeepers. Use of strategies and calculators allows students to continue to work on interesting problems and experiments while learning the facts. Thus students are not prevented from learning more complex mathematics because they do not have quick recall of the facts.

Multiplication Methods in *Math Trailblazers*

As your child learns paper-and-pencil multiplication in *Math Trailblazers,* he or she is introduced to more than one method. The **all-partials method** is introduced first since many children find it easier to learn. Then the more efficient **compact method**—the method traditionally taught in schools in the United States—is introduced. After children work with both methods, they choose which is most comfortable for them. We present both methods below so you will be familiar with them.

Both methods are based on the same idea, but the recording is different. In the all-partials method, every step is written down. In the compact method, some steps are not recorded.

Example 1. Compute 6×73.

In both methods, we break 73 into two parts: $73 = 3 + 70$. Then we multiply each part by 6 and add:

$$6 \times 73 = 6 \times 3 + 6 \times 70.$$

All-Partials Method	Compact Method
In this method, every step is written down on separate lines. $\begin{array}{r} 73 \\ \times\ 6 \\ \hline 18 \\ 420 \\ \hline 438 \end{array}$ (This is 6×3) (This is 6×70) The partial products are recorded in the lines under the multiplication sign, then the lines are added.	In this method, some steps are combined and the answer is recorded on one line. $\begin{array}{r} \overset{1}{} \\ 73 \\ \times\ 6 \\ \hline 438 \end{array}$ (This is $6 \times 3 + 6 \times 70$) The partial products are added as they are recorded: First compute $6 \times 3 = 18$; then write the 8 in the ones' column and carry the 1 into the tens' column (some people write down the carry, others just remember it). Next, compute 6×7 tens $= 42$ tens. Add the 1 that was carried to get 43 tens. Write the 3 in the tens' column and the 4 in the hundreds' column.

Example 2: Compute 73 × 46.

Again, both methods involve breaking the numbers into two parts and multiplying. Since 46 = 6 + 40, the product is

$$73 \times 46 = 73 \times (6 + 40)$$
$$= 73 \times 6 + 73 \times 40$$
$$= (6 \times 3 + 6 \times 70) + (40 \times 3 + 40 \times 70)$$

All-Partials Method	**Compact Method**
In this method, every step is written down on separate lines.	In this method, some steps are combined and recorded on one line.

All-Partials Method

```
   73
 × 46
   18   (6 × 3)
  420   (6 × 70)
  120   (40 × 3)
 2800   (40 × 70)
 3358
```

The partial products are recorded in the rows under the multiplication sign, then the rows are added.

Compact Method

```
    73
  × 46
   438   (This is 6 × 73)
  2920   (This is 40 × 73 or 4 tens × 73)
  3358
```

For the first line, compute 6 × 73 = 438 as in Example 1.

For the second line, compute 40 × 73 = 2920. (Some people omit the 0 in the ones' column because 2920 is 292 tens and no ones. In this case, be sure nothing is written in the ones' column.)

Here are the details for the second line:

40 × 73 = 40 × 3 + 40 × 70. First compute 40 × 3 = 120; record the 20 tens by writing 2 in the tens' column and 0 in the ones' column, then carry the 1 into the hundreds' column (you can write the carry or just remember it). Next, compute 40 × 70 = 2800. That is 28 hundreds. Add the one 1 hundred that was carried to get 29 hundreds. Write the 9 in the hundreds' column and the 2 in the thousands' column.

Finally, add both lines.

Long Division in *Math Trailblazers*

In *Math Trailblazers,* your child will learn a long division method that may be different from the method you learned. We teach the **forgiving method** because many students find it easier to learn than the traditional method. Both methods make estimates about the quotient (the answer to the division problem), but the forgiving method allows underestimates, so it doesn't involve as much erasing and recalculating as the traditional method sometimes does.

As an example, let's divide 95 by 3. Think of dividing 95 objects such as marbles into groups of 3. How many groups will there be? (Or, think of putting the objects into 3 groups. How many will be in each group?)

First, estimate the answer. A good estimate would be 30, but lower numbers would work too. Suppose we choose 20. Then, since 3 × 20 = 60, we have taken care of 60 marbles. Subtract 60 from 95 and record the estimate to the right of the problem.

```
   3)95
   − 60   20
     35
```

Now divide the remaining 35 marbles by 3. Let's estimate that 35 ÷ 3 is about 10. Since 3 × 10 = 30, write

```
   3)95
   − 60   20
     35
   − 30   10
     5
```

Since 3 "goes into" 5 one time, write

```
   3)95
   − 60   20
     35
   − 30   10
     5
   − 3    1
     2
```

Since 3 does not divide 2, there are 2 marbles left over. This is the remainder. Add up the number of 3s we took away: 20 + 10 + 1 = 31. Thus, 95 divided by 3 is 31 with remainder 2. We write this on top of the problem, as in the traditional division method.

```
    31R2
   3)95
   − 60   20
     35
   − 30   10
     5
   − 3    1
     2    31
```

As students become familiar with the forgiving method, they make better estimates to keep the number of steps at a minimum. Below is another way to do this problem using the forgiving method. Note that this time, making the highest possible estimates (without overestimating) results in the same number of steps as the traditional method. If the highest estimate is made each time, the two methods are essentially the same.

```
    31R2
   3)95
   − 90   30
     5
   − 3    1
     2    31
```

The forgiving method allows students to underestimate as they develop their estimation skills. But, although this method forgives underestimates, overestimates are not forgiven. When students overestimate, they have to erase, just as with the traditional method.

This method can be extended to solve problems with multidigit divisors. However, *Math Trailblazers* students usually use calculators for such problems.

Internet Resources for Families of *Math Trailblazers* Students

Here are several websites that can help families support their children's learning of Mathematics:

Mymathtrailblazers.com Family section

The publisher of *Math Trailblazers,* Kendall/Hunt, maintains a website at http://www.mymathtrailblazers.com to help the families of children using *Math Trailblazers* understand the curriculum. It contains an introduction to the program and a discussion of its research basis, answers to frequently asked questions, glossaries, TIMS Tutors (which provide an in-depth exploration of the mathematical concepts and ideas behind *Math Trailblazers*), homework help, and recommended software and literature lists. Contact Kendall/Hunt regarding granting families access to this site.

NCTM Families Web page

http://nctm.org/resources/families.aspx

The National Council of Teachers of Mathematics (NCTM) Families Web page includes lessons and activities, resources, links to other family sites, as well as brochures that answer questions such as

> Why does my child's math look different from the math I remember?
>
> What can I do to make sure my child succeeds in math?
>
> Math homework is due tomorrow—how can I help?

NCTM Illuminations

http://illuminations.nctm.org

This site contains a library of online math activities and interactive tools for students to use to explore, learn, and apply mathematics in the classroom and at home. It also has links to hundreds of online resources that an editorial panel has reviewed and rated as exemplary.

The Math Forum

http://mathforum.org

The Math Forum is a very broad-based website maintained by Drexel University. It has such features as Ask Dr. Math, where students can ask mathematical questions, and an extensive mathematics resource library for students in elementary school through graduate school. Other features include discussion groups, a collection of good problems, teacher resources, and information on issues in mathematics education.

National Library of Virtual Manipulatives for Interactive Mathematics

http://nlvm.usu.edu

Utah State University developed and maintains this web site. It includes an extensive collection of virtual manipulatives and accompanying activities. Students can work interactively with geoboards, pattern blocks, tangrams, base-ten pieces, balance scales, and other materials. This provides the opportunity to work with materials that are perhaps not otherwise available.

Helping Your Child Learn Mathematics http://www.ed.gov/parents/academic/help/math/index.html

This is a downloadable booklet available at the website of the Department of Education that contains "fun activities that parents can use with their children from preschool age through grade 5 to strengthen their math skills and build strong positive attitudes toward math."

Figure This!

http://www.figurethis.org

The Family Corner of the Figure This! website provides math challenges for families. It has downloadable brochures on topics such as Families and School, Families and Math, Families and Homework, and Math and Literature, as well as recommended books. The focus is on families of middle-school students, but much of the advice is appropriate for families of elementary-school students as well.

Manipulatives List

The Manipulatives List outlines all manufactured manipulatives and other materials needed to implement *Math Trailblazers* successfully.

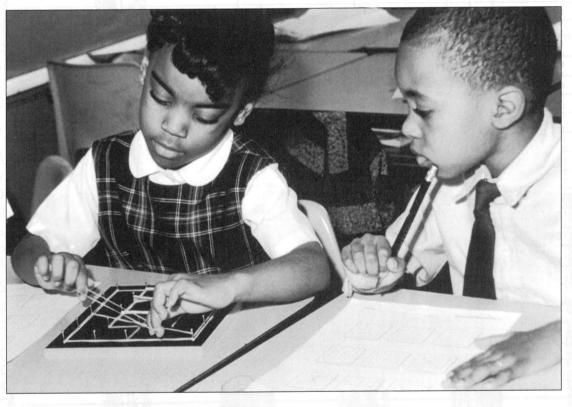

Students explore shapes using geoboards.

Manipulatives List

Following are the manipulatives for kindergarten. There are several categories of manipulatives listed here:

Manufactured Manipulatives: a list of each of the manipulatives needed to fully implement the *Math Trailblazers* curriculum. Many of these manipulatives may be available already in your classroom or school.

Manipulatives that you need can be purchased:
• in grade-level complete kits from Kendall/Hunt Publishing Company;
• as a customized kit from Kendall/Hunt;
• or individually for your specific needs.

Please contact Kendall/Hunt directly for additional information.

Other materials are needed to successfully implement the *Math Trailblazers* curriculum for the entire year. These materials are listed in three categories to aid in planning for the year:

• **Consumables** (edible or one-use items such as beans, paper cups, etc.)
• **Collectibles** (throwaway items such as magazines, egg cartons, jars, etc.)
• **School Supplies** (items usually available in classrooms such as tape, glue, markers, etc.)
• **Optional** (not essential for implementation but useful, such as graphing mat, rubber stamps, ink pads, etc.)

Manipulatives for *Math Trailblazers* Kindergarten

Manufactured Manipulative, Classroom	TOTAL per Classroom of 30 Students
cubes, small wooden	12
cubes, connecting	1 set of 600
demonstration clock	1
dominoes, colored	15 sets
geoboards	30
links, connecting	1 set of 1000
metersticks	8
Mr. Origin	30
number cubes (dot dice)	30
overhead dominoes	1 set
overhead number cubes (dot dice)	2
overhead square-inch colored tiles	1 set
pattern blocks, wooden	2 sets of 250
rubber bands (geobands)	1 package
solids, geometric set	1 set
spinners, transparent	15
tiles, square-inch colored	3 sets of 400
two-pan balances	4
videotape cases, transparent	30

Additional Materials or Equipment Needed for *Math Trailblazers* Kindergarten

Consumable Materials	Quantity per class of 30
self-adhesive dots	500
self-adhesive notes	1 dozen pads

Collectible Materials	Quantity per class of 30
bags: one-gallon size freezer	30
paper lunch	30
self-closing sandwich size	50
basin, plastic	1
beans, rice, pasta	one 1 pound bag of each
bowls, soup	4
clothespins, snap	30
cups, 2 oz. plastic	45
cups, measuring	set
empty food boxes	12
empty plastic jars and bottles	12
foam boards, 20 × 30	4
jars, clear plastic: quart size	2
baby food size	12
pint size	5
map	1
nickels	25
pairs of shoes in a variety of sizes	8
paper plates, large	60
pennies	360
shoe boxes	2
skillet, pan, or plastic plate, small	1
small objects: for patterning	
for counting	
for estimation	
toothpicks	1 box

School Supplies

brass fasteners (brads)

index cards

paper: butcher or newsprint

      chart

      construction

The following supplies are used throughout the year:

crayons

glue

markers

paints

scissors

tape (transparent)

Optional

laminated class data table

laminated class graph

graphing mat

ink pads

rectangular mirror, small

rubber stamps

Literature List

The Literature List provides suggested titles and recommended reading of commercially available trade books which are used in many *Math Trailblazers* lessons.

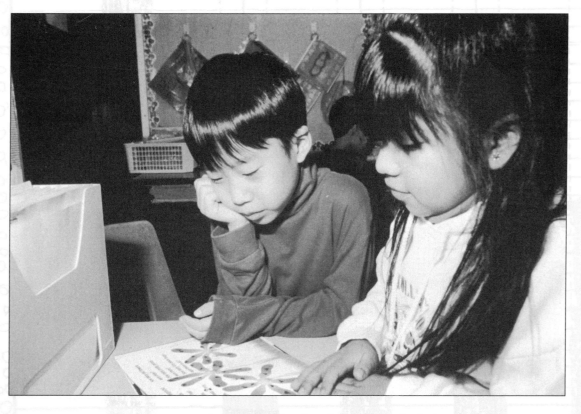

Students connect math and literature by reading a trade book.

Literature List

Math Trailblazers incorporates the use of commercially available trade books in many lessons. A listing of these trade books is provided here. These books can be used to extend or enhance a particular lesson.

Ongoing Content
Calendar Connections

Classroom Calendar

Time and Days of the Week

- Carle, Eric. *The Grouchy Ladybug.* Scott Foresman, Glenview, IL, 1996.
- Carle, Eric. *Rooster's Off to See the World.* Little Simon, New York, 2002.
- Carle, Eric. *Today Is Monday.* Philomel Books, New York, 2001.
- Carle, Eric. *The Very Hungry Caterpillar.* Scott Foresman, Glenview, IL, 1994.
- Hooper, Meredith. *Seven Eggs.* Lutterworth, Cambridge, UK, 2001.
- Shulevitz, Uri. *One Monday Morning.* Aladdin Books, New York, 1986.
- Ward, Cindy, and Tomie de Paola. *Cookie's Week.* PaperStar, New York, 1997.

Weather

- Bauer, Marion Dane. *Rain.* Simon and Schuster, New York, 2004.
- Bernard, Robin. *A Tree for All Seasons.* National Geographic Society, 1999.
- Branley, Franklin M. *Flash, Crash, Rumble, and Roll.* Harper & Row, New York, 1999.
- De Bourgoing, Pascale. *Weather.* Scholastic, New York, 1995.
- de Paola, Tomie. *The Cloud Book.* Holiday House, New York, 1975.
- Gibbons, Gail. *Weather Forecasting.* Scholastic, New York, 1995.
- Gibbons, Gail. *Weather Words and What They Mean.* Scholastic, New York, 1992.
- Koscielniak, Bruce. *Geoffrey Groundhog Predicts the Weather.* Houghton Mifflin, Boston, MA, 1995.
- McMillan, Bruce. *The Weather Sky.* Farrar Straus Giroux, New York, 1996.
- Murphy, Stuart J. *Beep Beep Vroom Vroom.* HarperCollins, New York, 2000.
- Polacco, Patricia. *Thunder Cake.* Econo-Clad Books, Topeka, KS, 1999.
- Stoeke, Janet Morgan. *A Hat for Minerva Louise.* Puffin Books, New York, 1994.
- Yashima, Taro. *Umbrella.* Puffin Books, New York, 1986.

Fifty Ideas for the 100th Day

- Braybrooks, Ann. *One Hundred and One Dalmatians.* Scholastic, New York, 1991.
- Murphy, Stuart. *100 Days of Cool.* HarperCollins Publishers, New York, 2003.
- Pinczes, Elinor. *One Hundred Hungry Ants.* Houghton Mifflin Company, Boston, 1999.

- Slate, Joseph. *Miss Bindergarten Celebrates the 100th Day of Kindergarten.* Puffin Books, New York, 2003.
- Wilder, Laura Ingalls. *Winter Days in the Big Woods.* HarperCollins, New York, 1994.

Problem Solving in the Kindergarten Day

Data Collection: How Many? How Much? How Far?

September

National Chicken Month

- Carle, Eric. *Rooster's Off to See the World.* Little Simon, New York, 2002.
- Ernst, Lisa Campbell. *Zinnia and Dot.* Viking, New York, 1992.
- Galdone, Paul. *The Little Red Hen.* Houghton Mifflin Co., Boston, 1985.
- Heller, Ruth. *Chickens Aren't the Only Ones.* Paper Star, Topeka, KS, 1990.
- Hutchins, Pat. *Rosie's Walk.* Macmillan, New York, 1968.
- Kellogg, Steven. *Chicken Little.* William Morrow, New York, 1987.
- Polacco, Patricia. *Chicken Sunday.* Paper Star, Topeka, KS, 1998.

Fall Hat Week

- Geringer, Laura. *A Three Hat Day.* Harper & Row, New York, 1987.
- Morris, Ann. *Hats, Hats, Hats.* Scholastic, New York, 1995.
- Slobodkina, Esphyr. *Caps for Sale.* HarperCollins, New York, 1987.

Farm Animals Week

- Lindbergh, Reeve. *The Day the Goose Got Loose.* Scholastic, New York, 1995.
- Martin, Bill, Jr., and John Archambault. *Barn Dance.* Henry Holt and Company, Inc., New York, 1988.
- Most, Bernard. *The Cow That Went Oink.* Harcourt Brace Jovanovich, San Diego, 1990.

Labor Day

- Rice, Melanie and Chris. *All About Things People Do.* Scholastic, New York, 1995.

Great Bathtub Race

- Wood, Audrey and Don. *King Bidgood's in the Bathtub.* Harcourt Brace Jovanovich, San Diego, 1985.

Newspaper Carrier Day

- Rey, H.A. *Curious George Rides a Bike.* Houghton Mifflin, Boston, 1973.

National Play-Doh Day

- Cohen, Miriam. *Will I Have a Friend?* Aladdin Paperbacks, New York, 1989.
- Haab, Sherri, and Laura Torres. *The Incredible Clay Book.* Klutz Press, Palo Alto, CA, 1994.

Jim Henson's Birthday

- Hautzig, Deborah. *A Visit to the Sesame Street Hospital.* Random House, New York, 1985.
- Hautzig, Deborah. *A Visit to the Sesame Street Library.* Random House, New York, 1986.
- Ross, Katherine. *Grover, Grover, Come On Over.* Econo-Clad Books, Topeka, KS, 1999.

Johnny Appleseed's Birthday

- Hogrogian, Nonny. *Apples.* Macmillan Publishing Co., New York, 1972.
- Gibbons, Gail. *The Seasons of Arnold's Apple Tree.* Harcourt Brace Jovanovich, New York, 1988.
- Kellogg, Steven. *Johnny Appleseed: A Tall Tale.* Mulberry Books, New York, 1996.
- Le Sieg, Theo. *Ten Apples Up on Top.* Beginner Books, New York, 1961.
- Wallace, Nancy Elizabeth. *Apples, Apples, Apples.* Marshall Cavendish, New York, 2004.

Native American Day

- de Paola, Tomie. *The Legend of the Bluebonnet.* Putnam Publishing Group, New York, 1986.
- de Paola, Tomie. *The Legend of the Indian Paintbrush.* Scott Foresman, Glenview, IL, 1996.
- Goble, Paul. *The Girl Who Loved Wild Horses.* Scott Foresman, Glenview, IL, 1993.
- Martin, Bill, Jr., and John Archambault. *Knots on a Counting Rope.* Owlet, New York, 1997.
- Swamp, Jake (Chief). *Giving Thanks, A Native American Good Morning Message.* Lee and Low Books, New York 1995.

October

National Clock Month

- Hutchins, Pat. *Clocks and More Clocks.* Macmillan, New York, 1970.

National Dessert Month

- Hutchins, Pat. *The Doorbell Rang.* Pearson Learning, Menlo Park, CA, 1989.
- Moncure, Jane Belk. *How Many Ways Can You Cut a Pie?* Children's Press, Chicago, 1988.
- Rylant, Cynthia. *Mr. Putter and Tabby Bake a Cake.* Harcourt Brace Jovanovich, San Diego, 1994.

National Popcorn Month

- de Paola, Tomie. *The Popcorn Book.* Scholastic, New York, 1995.
- Law, Alice. *The Popcorn Shop.* Scholastic, New York, 1994.

National Name Your Car Day

- Newton, Laura P. *William the Vehicle King.* Bradbury, New York, 1987.

World's Largest Pizza

- Barbour, Karen. *Little Nino's Pizzeria.* Harcourt Brace Jovanovich, San Diego, 1990.
- Rey, Margaret. *Curious George and the Pizza.* Houghton Mifflin, Boston, 1985.

Columbus Day

- Krensky, Stephen. *Christopher Columbus.* Random House, New York, 1991.
- Marzollo, Jean. *In 1492.* Scholastic, New York, 1993.

National Plush Animal Lovers' Day

- Freeman, Don. *Corduroy.* Scott Foresman, Glenview, IL, 1976.
- Waber, Bernard. *Ira Sleeps Over.* Scott Foresman, Glenview, IL, 1975.

National Magic Day

- de Paola, Tomie. *Strega Nona.* Simon & Schuster, New York, 1989.
- de Paola, Tomie. *Strega Nona's Magic Lessons.* Harcourt, San Diego, 1988.
- Steig, William. *Sylvester and the Magic Pebble.* Aladdin Paperbacks, New York, 1987.

Halloween

- Brown, Marc. *Arthur's Halloween.* Little, Brown & Co., Boston, 1982.
- Rockwell, Anne. *Apples and Pumpkins.* Macmillan, New York, 1989.
- Williams, Linda. *The Little Old Lady Who Was Not Afraid of Anything.* Harper & Row Junior Books, New York, 1986.

November

Children's Book Week

- Aliki. *How a Book Is Made.* Harper Trophy, New York, 1988.
- Brown, Marc. *Arthur's Reading Race.* Random House, New York, 1996.

National Sandwich Day

- Fleming, Denise. *Lunch.* Scholastic, New York, 1994.
- Hoban, Russell. *Bread and Jam for Frances.* Harper & Row, New York, 1993.
- Lord, John Vernon. *The Giant Jam Sandwich.* Houghton Mifflin Company, Boston, 1987.

Mother Goose Parade

- de Paola, Tomie. *Tomie de Paola's Mother Goose.* Grosset & Dunlap, New York, 2000.

Special Note about Estimation

- Brown, Marc. *Arthur's Thanksgiving.* Little Brown & Co., Boston, 1983.
- Kroll, Steven. *The Biggest Pumpkin Ever.* Cartwheel Books, New York, 1993.

December

Man Will Never Fly Society Meeting

- Gelman, Rita Golden. *Why Can't I Fly?* Scholastic, New York, 1986.

Kwanzaa

- Chocolate, Deborah M. Newton. *My First Kwanzaa Book.* Cartwheel Books, New York, 1999.

January

National Soup Month

- Brown, Marcia. *Stone Soup.* Scott Foresman, Glenview, IL, 1987.
- Ehlert, Lois. *Growing Vegetable Soup.* Harcourt Brace Jovanovich, San Diego, 1990.
- Sendak, Maurice. *Chicken Soup with Rice.* Scott Foresman, Glenview, IL, 1991.

Anniversary of the 55 MPH Speed Limit

- Newton, Laura P. *William the Vehicle King.* Bradbury, New York, 1987.

Jacob Grimm's Birthday (January 4, 1785)
None

George Washington Carver Day

- Aliki. *A Weed Is a Flower: The Life of George Washington Carver.* Aladdin Paperbacks, New York, 1988.
- Carter, Andy, and Carol Saller. *George Washington Carver.* Carolrhoda Books, Inc., Minneapolis, MN, 2001.
- Moore, Eva. *The Story of George Washington Carver.* Scholastic, New York, 1994.

Anniversary of the First Balloon Flight Across the English Channel

- Calhoun, Mary. *Hot-Air Henry.* Morrow, New York, 1984.
- Coerr, Eleanor. *The Big Balloon Race.* Harper & Row, New York, 1986.

National Pie Day

- Moncure, Jane Belk. *How Many Ways Can You Cut a Pie?* Children's Press, Chicago, 1988.

Chinese New Year

- Sing, Rachel. *Chinese New Year's Dragon.* Half Moon Books, New York, 1994.
- Waters, Kate, and Madeline Slovenz. *Lion Dancer: Ernie Wan's Chinese New Year.* Scholastic, New York, 1990.

February

National Snack Food Month

- Hopkins, Lee Bennett. *Munching Poems about Eating.* Little, Brown & Co., Boston, 1985.

Groundhog Day

- Kroll, Steven. *It's Groundhog Day.* Scholastic, New York, 1995.

Weatherman's Day

- Barrett, Judi. *Cloudy with a Chance of Meatballs.* Scott Foresman, Glenview, IL, 1982.
- de Paola, Tomie. *The Cloud Book.* Holiday House, New York, 1975.
- Gibbons, Gail. *Weather Forecasting.* Scholastic, New York, 1995.
- Gibbons, Gail. *Weather Words and What They Mean.* Scholastic, New York, 1992.

Babe Ruth's Birthday

- Isadora, Rachel. *Max*. Aladdin Paperbacks, New York, 1984.
- Thayer, Ernest Lawrence. *Casey at the Bat*. Raintree Children's Books, Milwaukee, WI, 1985.

Get a Different Name Day

- Lester, Helen. *A Porcupine Named Fluffy*. Houghton Mifflin, Boston, 1986.
- Mosel, Arlene. *Tikki Tikki Tembo*. Holt, Rinehart and Winston, Inc., New York, 1988.

Valentine's Day

- Bunting, Eve. *The Valentine Bears*. Houghton Mifflin, New York, 1983.
- Hoban, Lillian. *Arthur's Great Big Valentine*. Harper & Row, New York, 1991.

March

National Noodle Month

- de Paola, Tomie. *Big Anthony and the Magic Ring*. Harcourt Brace Jovanovich, San Diego, 1979.
- de Paola, Tomie. *Strega Nona*. Simon & Schuster, New York, 1989.

Physical Education and Sports Week

- Fox, Mem. *Koala Lou*. Harcourt Brace Jovanovich, San Diego, 1994.

National Wildlife Week

- Guarino, Deborah. *Is Your Mama a Llama?* Scholastic, New York, 1997.
- Waber, Bernard. *You Look Ridiculous*. Houghton Mifflin, New York, 1979.

National Pig Day

- Galdone, Paul. *The Three Little Pigs*. Houghton Mifflin, Boston, 1984.
- Scieszka, Jon, and Lane Smith. *The True Story of the 3 Little Pigs!* Viking, New York, 1989.

Dr. Seuss's Birthday

- Seuss, Dr. *The Cat in the Hat*. Random House, New York, 1966.
- Seuss, Dr. *Horton Hears a Who!* Random House, New York, 1954.
- Seuss, Dr. *One Fish, Two Fish, Red Fish, Blue Fish*. Random House, New York, 1981.
- Seuss, Dr. *Yertle the Turtle and Other Stories*. Random House, New York, 1988.

Doctor's Day

- Rey, Margaret. *Curious George Goes to the Hospital*. Houghton Mifflin Co., Boston, 1966.

First Pencil with Attached Eraser Patented

- Monchure, Jane Belk. *Word Bird's Magic Wand*. Child's World, Elgin, IL, 1990.
- Stanley, Diane. *The Good-Luck Pencil*. Four Winds Press, New York, 1986.

April

Tomato Month

- Ehlert, Lois. *Growing Vegetable Soup.* Harcourt Brace Jovanovich, San Diego, 1990.
- Ehlert, Lois. *Planting a Rainbow.* Harcourt Brace Jovanovich, San Diego, 1992.
- Kraus, Ruth. *The Carrot Seed.* Harper & Row, New York, 1988.

April Showers

- Aardema, Verna. *Bringing the Rain to Kapiti Plain.* Scott Foresman, Glenview, IL, 1992.
- Branley, Franklyn. *Flash, Crash, Rumble and Roll.* Harper & Row, New York, 1999.
- Freeman, Don. *A Rainbow of My Own.* Viking, New York, 1978.
- Polacco, Patricia. *Thunder Cake.* PaperStar, Topeka, KS, 1997.

April Fool's Day

- Brown, Marc. *Arthur's April Fool.* Little, Brown & Co., Boston, 1993.

Earth Day

- Peet, Bill. *The Wump World.* Houghton Mifflin, Boston, 1981.
- Seuss, Dr. *The Lorax.* Random House, New York, 1971.
- Van Allburg, Chris. *Just a Dream.* Houghton Mifflin, Boston, 1990.

Arbor Day

- Cherry, Lynne. *The Great Kapok Tree.* Voyager Picture Book, San Diego, 2000.
- McCord, David. *Every Time I Climb a Tree.* Little, Brown & Co., Boston, 1999.
- Rockwell, Robert E. *Hug a Tree.* Gryphon House, Mt. Rainier, MD, 1990.
- Udry, Janice. *A Tree Is Nice.* Harper & Row, New York, 1987.

May

Be Kind to Animals Week—Pet Week

- Brown, Marc. *Arthur's Pet Business.* Joy Street Books, Boston, 1995.
- Keats, Ezra Jack. *Pet Show.* Scott Foresman, Glenview, IL, 1987.
- Noble, Trinka. *The Day Jimmy's Boa Ate the Wash.* Scott Foresman, Glenview, IL, 1992.
- Smyth, Gwenda. *A Pet for Mrs. Arbuckle.* Random House, New York, 1984.

Cinco de Mayo

- Brown, Tricia. *Hello, Amigos!* Henry Holt & Company, New York, 1986.

Japan Children's Day

- Friedman, Ina. *How My Parents Learned to Eat.* Houghton Mifflin, Boston, 1987.

Calaveras County Fair

- Langstaff, John. *Frog Went A-Courtin'.* Harcourt Brace Jovanovich, New York, 1983.
- Lobel, Arnold. *Frog and Toad Are Friends.* Harper Junior Books, New York, 1983.

June
Ice Cream Sold for the First Time

- Lobel, Arnold. "Ice Cream" in *Frog and Toad All Year*. Harper & Row, New York, 1976.

Baseball Hall of Fame Opened

- Thayer, Ernest Lawrence. *Casey at the Bat*. PaperStar, Topeka, KS, 1997.

July
Anti-Boredom Month

- Seuss, Dr. *And to Think That I Saw It on Mulberry Street*. Random House, New York, 1989.

National Blueberry Month

- Degan, Bruce. *Jamberry*. Harper & Row, New York, 1995.
- McCloskey, Robert. *Blueberries for Sal*. Penguin Books (Puffin Books), New York, 1976.

United States Stamp Anniversary

- Ahlberg, Janet and Allan. *The Jolly Postman*. Little, Brown & Co., Boston, 2001.
- Keats, Ezra Jack. *A Letter to Amy*. Viking Childrens Books, New York, 1988.

United States First Zoo Established

- Campbell, Rod. *Dear Zoo*. Little Simon, New York, 1986.
- Ehlert, Lois. *Color Zoo*. HarperCollins, New York, 1997.
- Hoban, Tana. *A Children's Zoo*. Greenwillow Books, New York, 1985.

August
National Clown Week

- Wiseman, Bernard. *Morris and Boris at the Circus*. Harper Collins Publishers, New York, 1988.

Counting Connections

Kindergarten Month-by-Month
Month 1

- Anno, Mitsumasa. *Anno's Counting Book*. Harper Trophy, New York, 1986.
- Aylesworth, Jim. *Old Black Fly*. Henry Holt and Company, New York, 1992.
- Bang, Molly. *Ten, Nine, Eight*. Tupelo Books, New York, 1998.
- Butler, M. Christina. *Too Many Eggs*. Godine Publisher, Inc., New York, 1988.
- Carle, Eric. *Rooster's Off to See the World*. Little Simon, New York, 2002.
- Child, Lauren. *I Will Never Not Ever Eat a Tomato*. Candlewick, Cambridge, MA, 2003.
- Chorao, Kay. *Number One, Number Fun*. Holiday House, New York, 1995.

- Christelow, Eileen. *Five Little Monkeys Jumping on the Bed.* Houghton Mifflin Audio, Boston, MA, 1993.
- Christelow, Eileen. *Five Little Monkeys Sitting in a Tree.* Clarion Books, New York, 1993.
- Crews, Donald. *Ten Black Dots.* Scott Foresman, Glenview, IL, 1995.
- Dodds, Dayle Ann. *The Shape of Things.* Candlewick Press, Cambridge, MA, 1994.
- Dunbar, Joyce. *Ten Little Mice.* Econo-Clad Books, Topeka, KS, 1999.
- Ehlert, Lois. *Fish Eyes: A Book You Can Count On.* Harcourt Brace Jovanovich, San Diego, CA, 2001.
- Falwell, Cathryn. *Feast for 10.* Clarion Books, New York, 1996.
- Feelings, Muriel. *Moja Means One: Swahili Counting Book.* Scott Foresman, Glenview, IL, 1992.
- Fox, Mem. *Zoo-Looking.* Mondo Greevale, New York, 1996.
- Giganti, Paul, Jr. *How Many Snails?* Mulberry Books, New York, 1988.
- Haskins, Jim. *Count Your Way Through Korea.* Carolrhoda Books, Minneapolis, MN, 1990.
- Hoban, Tana. *Over, Under, and Through and Other Spatial Concepts.* Macmillan Publishing Company, New York, 1973.
- Keats, Ezra Jack. *Over in the Meadow.* Puffin, New York, 1999.
- Kitamura, Satoshi. *When Sheep Cannot Sleep.* Farrar, Straus & Giroux, New York, 1988.
- Lobel, Anita. *Alison's Zinnia.* Mulberry Books, New York, 1990.
- Lottridge, Celia. *One Watermelon Seed.* Stoddart Pub., Toronto, 1997.
- Martin, Bill. *Brown Bear, Brown Bear, What Do you See?* Holt, New York, 1996.
- Martin, Bill. *Polar Bear, Polar Bear, What Do you Hear?* Holt, New York, 1997.
- Morozumi, Atsuko. *One Gorilla.* Farrar, Straus & Giroux, New York, 1990.
- Pallotta, Jerry. *The Icky Bug Counting Book.* Charlesbridge Publishing, Watertown, MA, 1992.
- Pinczes, Elinor. *A Remainder of One.* Houghton Mifflin Co., Boston, MA, 1995.
- Pluckrose, Henry. *Counting.* Children's Press, Chicago, IL, 1995.
- Pluckrose, Henry. *Pattern.* Children's Press, Chicago, IL, 1995.
- Snyder, Inez. *Tomatotes.* Scholastic, Inc., New York, 2004.
- Stoeke, Janet Morgan. *A Hat for Minerva Louise.* Puffin Books, New York, 1994.
- Tildes, Phyllis. *Counting on Calico.* Charlesbridge Publishing, Watertown, MA, 1995.
- Van Fleet, Matthew. *One Yellow Lion.* Penguin Books, New York, 1992.
- Wallace, Nancy Elizabeth. *Apples, Apples, Apples.* Marshall Cavendish, New York, 2004.
- Walton, Rick. *How Many, How Many, How Many.* Candlewick Press, Cambridge, MA, 1996.
- Williams, Rozanne Lanczak. *Mr. Noisy's Book of Patterns.* Creative Teaching Press, Cyprus, CA, 1995.

Month 2

- Crews, Donald. *Ten Black Dots.* Scott Foresman, Glenview, IL, 1995.

Month 3

- Brisson, Pat. *Benny's Pennies.* Scott Foresman, Glenview, IL, 1995.
- Carle, Eric. *The Very Busy Spider.* Philomel Books, New York, 1995.
- Hill, Sandi. *Barnyard Math with Farmer Fred.* Creative Teaching Press, Inc., Cypress, CA, 1998.
- Hoban, Tana. *Is It Larger? Is It Smaller?* Scott Foresman, Glenview, IL, 1997.
- Kellogg, Steven. *Much Bigger Than Martin.* NALDutton, New York, 1992.
- Murphy, Stuart. *Bug Dance.* HarperCollins Publishers, New York, 2002.
- Swamp, Jake (Chief). *Giving Thanks, A Native American Good Morning Message.* Lee and Low Books, New York, 1995.
- Titherington, Jeanne. *Pumpkin Pumpkin.* Mulberry Books, New York, 1990.
- Wallace, Nancy Elizabeth. *Apples, Apples, Apples.* Marshall Cavendish, New York, 2004.

Month 4

- Christelow, Eileen. *Five Little Monkeys Jumping on the Bed.* Houghton Mifflin Audio, Boston, MA, 1993.
- Christelow, Eileen. *Five Little Monkeys Sitting in a Tree.* Clarion Books, New York, 1993.
- Fanelli, Sara. *My Map Book.* HarperCollins, New York, 2001.
- Howard, Arthur. *Mr. Putter and Tabby Walk the Dog.* Harcourt Brace, New York, 1994.
- Hutchins, Pat. *Rosie's Walk.* Aladdin Paperbacks, New York, 1968.
- Lindbergh, Reeve. *The Midnight Farm.* Puffin Books, New York, 1995.
- McMillan, Bruce. *Mouse Views.* Holiday House, New York, 1993.
- Myllar, Rolf. *How Big Is a Foot?* Econo-Clad Books, Topeka, KS, 1999.
- Yolen, Jane. *Owl Moon.* Putnam, New York, 1987.

Month 5

- Hoban, Tana. *26 Letters and 99 Cents.* Mulberry Books, New York, 1995.

Month 6

- Ferguson, Don. *The Disney Classics' Aladdin.* Penguin Books, New York, 1990.
- Koscielniak, Bruce. *Geoffrey Groundhog Predicts the Weather.* Houghton Mifflin Company, Boston, 1995.

Month 7

- Adams, Pam. *There Were Ten in the Bed.* Child's Play (International) Ltd., Singapore, 1989.
- Barrett, Peter, and Susan Barrett. *The Circle Sarah Drew.* Scroll Press, New York, 1973.

- Barrett, Peter, and Susan Barrett. *The Square Ben Drew.* Scroll Press, New York, 1973.
- Fernandes, Eugenie & Kim. *Big Week for Little Mouse.* Kids Can Press, Ltd., Tonawanda, NY, 2004.
- Geddes, Anne. *10 in the Bed.* Cedco Publishing Co., San Rafael, CA, 2000.
- Giganti, Paul, Jr. *How Many Snails?* Greenwillow Books, New York, 1988.
- Hamm, Diane. *How Many Feet in the Bed?* Aladdin Paperbacks, New York, 1994.
- Hoban, Tana. *Shapes, Shapes, Shapes.* Greenwillow Books, New York, 1986.
- Johnson, Stephen. *Alphabet City.* Viking, New York, 1995.
- Matthias, Catherine. *Too Many Balloons.* Children's Press, Chicago, 1982.
- McKee, David. *Elmer.* Lothrop, Lee & Shepard Books, New York, 1989.
- Murphy, Stuart J. *Circus Shapes.* Harper Collins Publishers, New York, 1998.
- Murphy, Stuart J. *Double the Ducks.* Harper Collins Publishers, New York, 2003.
- Peek, Merle. *Roll Over! A Counting Song.* Clarion Books, New York, 1981.
- Pluckrose, Henry. *Shape.* Children's Press, Chicago, 1995.

Month 8

- Bernard, Robin. *A Tree for All Seasons.* National Geographic Society, 1999.
- Child, Lauren. *I Will Never Not Ever Eat a Tomato.* Candlewick, Cambridge, MA, 2003.
- Graham, Joan Bransfield. *Splish Splash.* Houghton Mifflin Company, Boston, MA, 1994.
- Jonas, Ann. *Splash!* Mulberry Books, New York, 1997.
- Murphy, Stuart. *100 Days of Cool.* Harper Collins Publishers, New York, 2003.
- Nelson, Robin. *Earth Day.* Lerner Publications Co., Minneapolis, MN, 2003.
- Rockwell, Anne. *One Bean.* Walker Books for Young Readers, New York, 1999.
- Roth, Carol. *Ten Dirty Pigs/Ten Clean Pigs.* North-South Books, New York, 1999.
- Schiller, Melissa. *April Fool's Day.* Scholastic, Inc., New York, 2003.
- Slate, Joseph. *Miss Bindergarten Celebrates 100th Day of Kindergarten.* Puffin Books, New York, 2003.
- Tang, Greg. *Mind-Stretching Math Riddles: Math for All Seasons.* Scholastic, Inc., New York, 2002.
- Walsh, Ellen Stoll. *Mouse Count.* Voyager Picture Book, San Diego, CA, 1995.

Month 9

- Murphy, Stuart J. *Give Me Half!* HarperCollins Publishers, New York, 1996.
- Pluckrose, Henry. *Shape.* Children's Press, Chicago, IL, 1995.
- Tompert, Ann. *Just a Little Bit.* Houghton Mifflin, Boston, 1993.
- Whitehouse, Patricia. *Zoo Time.* Heinemann Library, Chicago, IL, 2002.

Month 10

- Adams, Pam. *There Were Ten in the Bed.* Child's Play (International) Ltd., Singapore, 1989.
- Ehlert, Lois. *Fish Eyes: A Book You Can Count On.* Harcourt, Brace Jovanovich, San Diego, CA, 2001.
- McMillan, Bruce. *Time to . . . .* Lothrop, Lee & Shepard Books, New York, 1989.
- Peek, Merle. *Roll Over! A Counting Song.* Clarion Books, New York, 1991.
- Pienkowski, Jan. *Time.* Little Simon, New York, 1991.
- Regier, Demar. *What Time Is It?* Scholastic, Inc., New York, 2005.
- Whitehouse, Patricia. *Zoo Time.* Heinemann Library, Chicago, IL, 2002.

Thematic Units
Buildings

- Barton, Byron. *Building a House.* Scott Foresman, Glenview, IL, 1999.
- Dorros, Arthur. *This Is My House.* Scholastic, New York, 1998.
- Gibbons, Gail. *How a House Is Built.* Holiday House, New York, 1996.
- Gibbons, Gail. *Up Goes the Skyscraper!* MacMillan Publishers, New York, 1981.
- Hoberman, Mary Ann. *A House Is a House for Me.* Puffin Books, New York, 1982.
- Jackson, Thomas Campbell. *Hammers, Nails, Planks and Paint.* Cartwheel Books, New York, 1994.
- Liebman, Dan. *I Want to be a Builder.* Firefly Books, Inc., Buffalo, NY, 2003.
- McLerran, Alice. *Roxaboxen.* Lothrop, Lee & Shepard, New York, 1991.
- Morris, Ann. *Houses and Homes.* Harper Collins Publishers, New York, 1992.
- Ringgold, Faith. *Tar Beach.* Random House, New York, 1991.
- Seltzer, Isadore. *The House I Live In.* Scholastic, New York, 1992.
- Smith, Mary Lou. "Grandmother's Adobe Doll House." *New Mexico Magazine.* Santa Fe, NM, 1984.
- Wilcox, Charlotte. *A Skyscraper Story.* Carolrhoda Books, Inc., Minneapolis, MN, 1990.
- Zelinsky, Paul O. *The Maid and the Mouse and the Odd-Shaped House.* Puffin Unicorn Books, New York, 1981.

On the Go

- Amato, William. *Math in the Car.* Scholastic, Inc., New York, 2002.
- Baer, Edith. *This Is the Way We Go to School: A Book about Children around the World.* Econo-clad Books, Topeka, KS, 1999.
- Bailey, Donna. *Planes.* Steck-Vaughn Company, Austin, TX, 1992.
- Crews, Donald. *Freight Train.* Beech Tree Books, New York, 1996.
- Crews, Donald. *School Bus.* Mulberry Books, New York, 1993.
- Crews, Donald. *Truck.* Tupelo Books, New York, 1997.
- Gibbons, Gail. *Trains.* Holiday House, New York, 1987.
- Peet, Bill. *The Caboose Who Got Loose.* Houghton Mifflin Co., Boston, MA, 1971.

Literature List

- Piper, Watty. *The Little Engine That Could.* 1930. Reprint, Platt and Munk, New York, 1996.
- Roberts, Sheena. *We All Go Traveling By.* Barefoot Books, Cambridge, MA, 2003.
- Rockwell, Anne. *Cars.* Econo-clad Books, Topeka, KS, 1999.
- Rockwell, Anne. *Trains.* Penguin Books, New York, 1993.
- Rockwell, Anne. *Trucks.* E. P. Dutton, Inc., New York, 1992.
- Van Allsburg, Chris. *The Polar Express.* Houghton Mifflin, Co., Boston, MA, 1985.
- Zelinsky, Paul. *The Wheels on the Bus.* Dutton Children's Books, New York, 1990.

Crawly Creatures

- *The Audubon Society Pocket Guide to Butterflies.* Alfred A. Knopf, Inc., New York, 1990.
- Bernhard, Emery. *Ladybug.* Holiday House, New York, 1992.
- Brenner, Barbara, and Bernice Chardiet. *Where's That Insect?* Scholastic, Jefferson City, MO, 1993.
- Brown, Ruth. *Ladybug, Ladybug.* Puffin, New York, 1992.
- Carle, Eric. *The Grouchy Ladybug.* Scott Foresman, Glenview, IL, 1996.
- Carle, Eric. *The Very Busy Spider.* Philomel Books, New York, 1995.
- Carle, Eric. *The Very Hungry Caterpillar.* Putnam Publishing Group, New York, 1984.
- Carle, Eric. *The Very Quiet Cricket.* Putnam Publishing Group, New York, 1997.
- Carter, David A. *How Many Bugs in a Box?* Simon and Schuster Books for Young Readers, New York, 1988.
- Dorros, Arthur. *Ant Cities.* HarperCollins Children's Books, New York, 1987.
- Heller, Ruth. *How to Hide a Butterfly and Other Insects.* Econo-clad Books, Topeka, KS, 1999.
- Kalman, Bobbie, and Tammy Everts. *Bugs and Other Insects.* Crabtree Publishing, New York, 1994.
- McDermott, Gerald. *Anansi the Spider: A Tale from the Ashanti.* Henry Holt and Company, New York, 1988.
- Pallotta, Jerry. *The Icky Bug Alphabet Book.* Charlesbridge Publishing, Watertown, MA, 1990.
- Parker, Nancy Winslow, and Joan Richards Wright. *Bugs.* Mulberry Books, New York, 1987.
- Philpot, Lorna and Graham. *Anthony's Ant's Creepy Crawly Party.* Random House, New York, 1995.
- Rockwell, Anne. *Bugs Are Insects.* HarperCollins Publishers, Inc., New York, 2001.
- Suzuki, David, with Barbara Hehner. *Looking at Insects.* John Wiley & Sons, New York, 1992.
- Whalley, Paul. *Butterfly and Moth.* Dorling Kindersley, Inc., Boston, MA, 1988.
- Yoshi. *The Butterfly Hunt.* Simon & Schuster, New York, 1993.

Games List

The Games List includes descriptions of games used in *Math Trailblazers*.

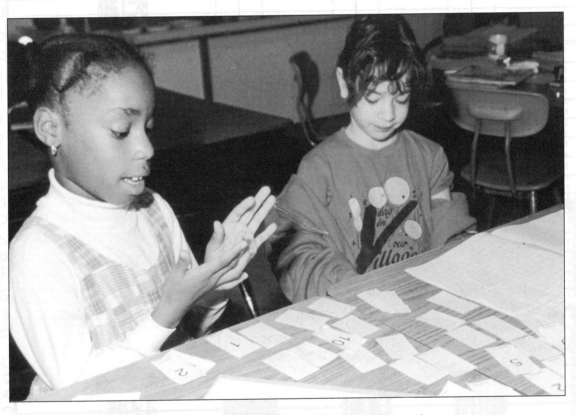

A student uses counting strategies while playing a math game.

Games List

Games are often used in *Math Trailblazers* to engage students in practicing basic arithmetic and other math concepts. A complete listing of the games for your grade and a description of the games are provided below.

Once introduced, you can use these games throughout the year for ongoing practice. We suggest that after introducing and playing the games in class, add them to a "Games Menu." Place necessary materials in a math center somewhere in the classroom so students can replay the games during indoor recess after completing other assignments, or other times during the day. TIMS Tips in the lesson guides will remind you to add each game to the Games Menu.

Kindergarten Month-by-Month
Month 1

Simon Says, Teacher Resource Book, Lesson 3, Activity 1, Page 195
Children play a version of *Simon Says* using words to describe their location in the classroom.

Month 2

Oral Counting—Buzz!, Teacher Resource Book, Lesson 2, Activity 2, Pages 212–213
In this circle game students practice their listening and oral counting skills. New variations of the game are introduced weekly.

Month 3

No Ones! Game, Teacher Resource Book, Lesson 2, Activity 3, Pages 241, 247
Students use a number cube to generate the number of spaces to move on a path. It can be played by partners at school or at home with family members.

Apple Baskets Game, Teacher Resource Book, Lesson 2, Activity 4, Pages 242, 248–249
Students work individually to match baskets of apples to a corresponding number dot pattern on a fruit stand.

Cereal Boxes Game, Teacher Resource Book, Lesson 2, Activity 5, Pages 242, 250–251
Students work individually to match numbered cereal boxes to a corresponding number dot pattern on cereal shelves.

Number Race 1, Teacher Resource Book, Lesson 3, Activity 2, Pages 253–254, 259
Students work individually using a number cube to generate numbers to practice writing the numbers 1 to 6.

Simon Says, Teacher Resource Book, Lesson 4, Activity 1, Page 260
Children play a version of *Simon Says* using words to describe their location in the classroom.

Month 4

Month 5

Collect Six Game, Teacher Resource Book, Lesson 1, Activity 6, Pages 309–312
Partners use number cubes to generate numbers and a More/Less/Same Spinner to determine which player's number qualifies to collect a point for each round.

Month 6

Domino Path Game, Teacher Resource Book, Lesson 1, Activity 2, Pages 340, 347–351
Partners draw dominoes to determine how many spaces to move along a path on a game board.

Dot Wars Game, Teacher Resource Book, Lesson 1, Activity 4, Page 341
This game is a domino version of the card game War. Partners draw dominoes and compare the number of dots to determine who has the smallest number.

Number Race 2, Teacher Resource Book, Lesson 1, Activity 5, Pages 342, 353
Students, using two number cubes, generate numbers to practice writing numbers 7 to 12.

Month 7

Month 8

Month 9

Too Big or Too Small, Teacher Resource Book, Calendar Update 17, Page 429
In a whole group game children use problem-solving strategies to locate a number on the calendar.

Secret Number, Teacher Resource Book, Calendar Update 17, Page 429
In a whole group game students use clues and elimination to identify a number on the calendar.

Month 10

One More, One Less Game, Teacher Resource Book, Lesson 1, Activity 1, Pages 191, 449–450
In this whole class game, children pull dominoes to show either one more, one less, two more, or two less than a target number drawn by the teacher.

Thematic Units

Buildings

Build Sasha's House, Teacher Resource Book, Lesson 5, Pages 485–486

In this game each child draws house parts as he or she rolls specific numbers on a number cube. The first person to complete a house is the winner.

On the Go

Crawly Creatures

Bug Race Game, Teacher Resource Book, Lesson 9, Pages 562–563

Students move "bugs" along a race course, using one or two number cubes to generate the numbers.

Software List

Software List

The Software List outlines recommended computer software used to enhance *Math Trailblazers* lessons.

Students use software to practice math facts and solve problems.

Software List

Software Titles by Topic

Patterns/Logical Thinking/Problem Solving
Math Concepts One . . . Two . . . Three . . .
Mighty Math Carnival Countdown
Mighty Math Zoo Zillions
Sunbuddy Math Playhouse
Tabletop Jr.
Thinkin' Things Collection 1

Number Concepts and Counting
Math Concepts One . . . Two . . . Three . . .
Mighty Math Carnival Countdown
Mighty Math Zoo Zillions
Millie's Math House
Sunbuddy Math Playhouse
Tenth Network: Grouping and Place Value

Data Collection/Reading and Interpreting Graphs/Probability
Graphers
Math Concepts One . . . Two . . . Three . . .
Tabletop Jr.

Geometry
Math Concepts One . . . Two . . . Three . . .
Mighty Math Carnival Countdown
Mighty Math Zoo Zillions
Millie's Math House
Shape Up!

Measurement
Math Concepts One . . . Two . . . Three . . .
Mighty Math Carnival Countdown
Mighty Math Zoo Zillions
Shape Up!
Sunbuddy Math Playhouse
Trudy's Time & Place House

Understanding of Basic Operations
Math Concepts One . . . Two . . . Three . . .
Mighty Math Carnival Countdown
Mighty Math Zoo Zillions
Millie's Math House
Tenth Network: Grouping and Place Value

Programs for Illustrating
Kid Pix

Time and Money
Math Concepts One . . . Two . . . Three . . .
Mighty Math Zoo Zillions
Sunbuddy Math Playhouse
Trudy's Time & Place House

Websites
One resource for mathematics links and sites:
    http://illuminations.nctm.org/swr/index.asp

Recommended Software List–
Brief Descriptions of the Programs

Graphers by Sunburst

This program provides a data graphing tool for young students. It allows even very young students to create pictographs, bar graphs, circle graphs, and data tables from data they collect. They can also use it to provide practice in reading and interpreting different types of graphs. Students can write their interpretation of the graphs directly into an on-screen notebook to be printed out with the graph. The program is recommended for grades K–4.

Kid Pix by Riverdeep—The Learning Company

This program allows students to create their own illustrations for many different applications throughout the curriculum. In mathematics, students can use this program to illustrate problems they have to solve or they can create and illustrate their own patterns or problems. The program is recommended for grades K–4.

Math Concepts One...Two...Three... by Gamco

This program is a collection of activities covering numeration, number sense, geometry, measurement, data management and probability, and patterning and algebra. Grade levels further divide each section and there are numerous activities within each grade level. Many activities focus on developing conceptual understanding and connecting symbols with actions with the manipulatives. Teachers can keep track of student progress and choose grade levels for individual students. There are also supplemental noncomputer activities available. The program is recommended for grades K–3.

Mighty Math Carnival Countdown by Riverdeep—The Learning Company

The program provides students with logic activities, basic operations, work with two-dimensional objects, and place value. Each of the five activities is further divided into 13 to 26 different types of problems. Carnival Cars focuses on sets and sorting by attributes, using > and < symbols and distinguishing even and odd numbers. Snap Clowns practices the basic operations and helps students gain conceptual understanding of the operations they are performing. Bubble Band focuses attention on place value. The beginning activities work in the ones place but later students work in the hundreds and see how groups of 10 are traded. Giggle Factory focuses on number sense and the concept of equivalence. Students can work up to 1000 in these activities. Pattern Block Round Up uses the manipulatives to pose questions about shapes, symmetry, area, perimeter, and basic fraction ideas. The program is recommended for grades K–2.

Mighty Math Zoo Zillions by Riverdeep—The Learning Company

In this fun program based on a zoo theme, students visit five activities that promote problem solving and skill acquisition. Each activity has about 20 different types of problems. In Fish Stories, students connect word problems with mathematical symbols as they manipulate fish in and out of tanks. Stories range in what parts are missing, the size of the numbers, and the basic operation that is practiced. In Gnu Ewe Boutique, students practice working with money. These activities range from identifying coins to adding and subtracting money and giving back change. In 3D Gallery students identify various three-dimensional shapes. Annie's Jungle Trail provides practice in adding, subtracting, mental math, rounding, and identifying odd and even numbers. The last activity is Number Line Express. In this activity students locate numbers on the number line and then later move backwards and forwards and find missing addends. This program is recommended for grades K–2.

Millie's Math House by Riverdeep—The Learning Company
This program develops early number concepts using seven activities. One activity focuses on size—big, little, and small. Two activities help students recognize shapes and patterns. The names of geometric shapes are heard as students drag them to matching pictures. The remaining activities focus on numbers, building one-to-one correspondence, recognition of number symbols, number words, and amounts. Students can also do simple addition and subtraction problems with manipulatives and count objects into the thirties. The teacher's manual provides blackline masters and activities to enrich the computer experiences. The program is recommended for grades pre-K–2.

Shape Up! by Sunburst
Shape Up! is a versatile geometry program consisting of five sets of shapes. The user can choose to work with pattern blocks or tangrams designed to correspond to the manipulatives. Another set of shapes involves regular triangles, pentagons, hexagons, octagons, squares, and circles. These shapes can be dissected and put back together in any desired fashion. In addition, the user can choose from two sets of three-dimensional shapes. One set is the platonic solids and the other a variety of shapes. Students can explore area, symmetry, tessellations, similarity, and congruence. It allows users to view inside 3-dimensional shapes using the Transparent function. Any of the shapes can be moved and rotated. The teacher's guide includes an extensive implementation guide to use the program to its fullest capacity and an in-depth reference section. This program develops student van Hiele levels with opportunities to explore shapes more easily than working with concrete materials. The program is recommended for grades K–8.

Sunbuddy Math Playhouse by Sunburst
The program setting is a musical production. Backstage, students can explore four mathematical activities. Test your memory with Tiny is a three-level memory game. The first two levels involve counting while the third level involves matching digital and analog clock faces. Figure it out with Hopkins provides practice with addition and subtraction facts with increasing levels of difficulty. Sort it out with Cassie is an excellent attribute game in which students place musical instruments into boxes. At the third level there are several attributes and the boxes overlap. Go to town with Shelby helps students understand how a coordinate grid system is labeled and also works on compass directions. The program is recommended for grades K–3.

Tabletop Jr. by Sunburst
This program focuses on developing logical thinking and working with data as an age-appropriate introduction to statistics. Students make objects from as many as 13 different kits. The objects have a variety of attributes. Students can then use these objects as data to manipulate. They can arrange the data, for example, on axes, as pictographs and Venn diagrams. Students sharpen

their discrimination skills as they look for like and unlike objects and patterns in the data. There are many excellent classroom activities in the teacher's manual. The program is recommended for grades K–5.

Tenth Network: Grouping and Place Value by Sunburst
This program develops the concept of groups by students using the computer mouse to easily move muffin pans and other containers and group objects on the screen into 2s, 5s, and 10s. The program helps students count a large number of objects by skip counting. In one activity students find a target number by grouping, in another they package table tennis balls. In still another activity, students receive coins in denominations of 1s, 10s, and 100s and they must buy items with exact change. Students exchange larger denominations for the next smaller by breaking up a 10. The program has many extension activities and although it is recommended for grades 1–3, it can be used by younger students.

Thinkin' Things Collection 1 by Riverdeep—The Learning Company
This program is meant to develop general thinking skills rather than numerical skills. The program is divided into six activities; three having very strong mathematical connections. In Fripple Shop, students must find the characters with specified attributes. At the more advanced levels, students must match up to four attributes using "and," "or," and "not." Similarly, in the activity Feathered Friends, students must build a bird with specified attributes that increase in difficulty and require pattern discrimination. Problems can be heard (by clicking the telephone), seen (by clicking the fax machine), or both by clicking on the door. The activity Blox-Flying Shapes develops spatial sense as students move shapes and change color, motion, and sound. The program is recommended for grades K–3.

Trudy's Time & Place House by Riverdeep—The Learning Company
This program allows students to explore clock and calendar time, map symbols, relative and compass directions, and geography. In the calendar activity students explore seasons and elapsed time as they develop an understanding of time units. In many of the activities the program uses a split screen. For example students manipulate a digital clock, and the analog clock moves as well. In another activity students place map symbols on a map and a picture of the representation appears. In each activity students can choose from several difficulty levels and from explore or question and answer modes. The program provides a wealth of supplemental activities and is recommended for grades K–2.

Software Companies Addresses and Telephone Numbers

Gamco
The Siboney Learning Group
325 N. Kirkwood Road, Suite 200
Saint Louis, MO 63122
1-888-726-8100
www.gamco.com
www.siboneylearninggroup.com

Riverdeep—The Learning Company
100 Pine Street, Suite 1900
San Francisco, CA 94111
1-888-242-6747
www.riverdeep.net

Sunburst Technology
1550 Executive Drive
Elgin, IL 60123
1-888-492-8817
www.sunburst.com